Disturbing Calculations

THE NEW SOUTHERN STUDIES

SERIES EDITORS
Jon Smith
  The University of Montevallo
Riché Richardson
  University of California, Davis

ADVISORY BOARD
Houston A. Baker Jr.
  Vanderbilt University
Jennifer Greeson
  Princeton University
Trudier Harris
  The University of North Carolina, Chapel Hill
John T. Matthews
  Boston University
Tara McPherson
  The University of Southern California
Scott Romine
  The University of North Carolina, Greensboro

Disturbing Calculations

The Economics of Identity in Postcolonial Southern Literature, 1912–2002

Melanie R. Benson

The University of Georgia Press
Athens and London

© 2008 by the University of Georgia Press
Athens, Georgia 30602
All rights reserved
Set in Ehrhardt MT
by Graphic Composition, Inc. Bogart, Georgia
Printed and bound by Thomson-Shore
The paper in this book meets the guidelines for permanence
and durability of the Committee on Production Guidelines for
Book Longevity of the Council on Library Resources.
Printed in the United States of America
12 11 10 09 08 C 5 4 3 2 1
12 11 10 09 08 P 5 4 3 2 1
Library of Congress Cataloging-in-Publication Data
Benson, Melanie R., 1976–
Disturbing calculations : the economics of identity in
postcolonial Southern literature, 1912–2002 / Melanie R. Benson.
        p. cm. — (The new Southern studies)
Includes bibliographical references and index.
ISBN-13: 978-0-8203-2972-7 (alk. paper)
ISBN-10: 0-8203-2972-X (alk. paper)
ISBN-13: 978-0-8203-3112-6 (pbk. : alk. paper)
ISBN-10: 0-8203-3112-0 (pbk. : alk. paper)
1. American literature—Southern States—History and criticism.
2. American literature—20th century—History and criticism.
3. Value in literature. 4. Value—Psychological aspects.
5. Numbers in literature. 6. Fetishism in literature.
7. Narcissism in literature.
8. Ego (Psychology) in literature.
9. Identity (Psychology) in literature.
10. Southern States—In literature. I. Title.
PS261.B48 2008
813'.5093553—dc22   2007045060
British Library Cataloging-in-Publication Data available

For Mum, Pa, Hiya, and Alan

Contents

ix   Acknowledgments

1   INTRODUCTION
    The Fetish of Number
    Narcissism, Economics, and the Twentieth-Century Southern Ego

27   CHAPTER ONE
    The Fetish of Surplus Value
    Reconstructing the White Elite in Allen Tate, William Alexander Percy, William Faulkner, and Thomas Wolfe

59   CHAPTER TWO
    Stealing Themselves Out of Slavery
    African American Southerners in Richard Wright, William Attaway, James Weldon Johnson, and Zora Neale Hurston

94   CHAPTER THREE
    The Measures of Love
    Southern Belles and Working Girls in Frances Newman, Anita Loos, and Katherine Anne Porter

129   CHAPTER FOUR
    Contemporary Crises of Value
    White Trash, Black Paralysis, and Elite Amnesia in Dorothy Allison, Alice Walker, and Walker Percy

164   CHAPTER FIVE
    Re-membering the Missing
    Native Americans, Immigrants, and Atlanta's Murdered Children in Louis Owens, Marilou Awiakta, Lan Cao, James Baldwin, Toni Cade Bambara, and Tayari Jones

202 CONCLUSION
    Disturbing the Calculation
207 Notes
233 Bibliography
253 Index

Acknowledgments

This book has been an absolute joy from start to finish, and for that I thank the many individuals who have directly or indirectly contributed to that experience. Since this project began as a dissertation at Boston University, my first and deepest gratitude goes to Jack Matthews, my incomparable dissertation advisor. People never seem to tire of saying that Jack has a nearly supernatural capacity to know with stunning clarity what you are trying to say (but had no idea you were), and then to help you to say it in words you never imagined you had. My long-winded drafts and addiction to adjectives and adverbs may have been the greatest challenge yet to his magic, but he never complained or discouraged in any way. For that alone, and for every ounce of wisdom and insight along the way, the insecure, fish-out-of-water graduate student in me is eternally grateful; neither this book nor my career would have happened without him. My second reader, Anita Patterson, was an unwavering model of confidence, encouragement, and good advice; and Bill Carroll, who directed the Graduate Studies Program during my time at Boston University, was a fairy godfather who somehow provided me with intellectual and financial support at critical moments. He even gave me my very first computer, without which I would probably still be typing footnotes on a dusty electric typewriter.

The editors and staff at the University of Georgia Press (who I am sure are grateful that I at least have a computer, even if I haven't learned to use it very well) have been extraordinarily kind, patient, and generous with their time and advice, especially to a naive first-timer. I was fortunate to have the help of outstanding copyeditors, Courtney Denney and Deborah Oliver, who improved this manuscript with great precision (and had infinite patience with my own occasional lack thereof). In particular, Nancy Grayson has been an exemplar of kindness and encouragement ever since we first met at the Society for the Study of Southern Literature conference in 2004; I can't thank her enough for showing enthusiasm for what this book would eventually become, and then for waiting so patiently and confidently for it to happen. Portions of this work have been previously published elsewhere; I am grateful to the editors of *Mississippi Quarterly* for permission to reprint selections from chapters 1, 2, 3, and 5, which appeared in their Fall 2003 (56.4) and Winter 2007 (60.1) issues.

Several colleagues have managed at one time or another to hear or read selections from this manuscript despite my general reluctance to impose upon them, and their masterful fingerprints are all over *Disturbing Calculations*. For several years Jon Smith has been an abiding figure of support, collegiality, and friendship. He read the manuscript in full, and in more than one incarnation, and I hope the finished product does justice to his extraordinary faith in it, and especially to his faith in me. George Handley also reviewed an initial draft and astounded me with his ability to see with exceptional clarity and generosity exactly why this work is so important to me—as a human being first, and a scholar second—and then helped me immeasurably to articulate it. If there is any message of hope at all in this book, it is because he showed it to me. Another superlative editor and friend over the years has been Martyn Bone; both my scholarship and my music collection are dramatically better for his influence. Eric Gary Anderson remains one of the rare kindred souls I have encountered in academia, and one of the few colleagues with whom I can commune on the joys of both Native American literature and good, strong coffee on an autumn morning. My colleagues at Regis College, Penn State Worthington Scranton, and the University of Hartford have all enriched my work and made my daily life a continuous pleasure; I am most grateful for a job in academia because it means being able to talk about good books with good friends nearly every day, and then to get paid for that joy.

This awe and appreciation brings me to my family. My life now is far removed from the world I grew up in; but I know with certainty that I wouldn't be here at all without the strength, courage, and tireless support of my family. My sister and best friend, Hiya, is one of the wisest, wittiest people I know; she makes me know the world and myself better, and she makes me laugh when I take any of it too seriously. Wherever I go, I will always remain most grounded by my parents, Kim and Terry Enos, who worked harder and sacrificed more than I would have liked them to. There was never any doubt in their minds that I was "going places," even if it meant that they were staying behind; I hope they know that I carry them and their lessons with me every day. In writing a book about economics and identity, I bore in mind my mother's maxim that "money is just green paper" and that it did not define who I was or what I was worth. She couldn't always be right about this, but her faith in me and protection of me have been unfailing.

One of the best parts about family is that you get more as you grow older. So finally, I am grateful to Polly the Cat, who from her perch on my shoulder oversaw the writing of this book with unflagging attention and unconditional approval. For Alan Taylor's companionship, I am not sure I have words to express my gratitude. With superhuman patience and care, he has taken on the thankless task of teaching me that in my writing, "less is more"; and in every other way, he has shown me just the opposite.

Disturbing Calculations

Introduction

The Fetish of Number: Narcissism, Economics, and the Twentieth-Century Southern Ego

> *Oh I know. I know. You give me two and two and you tell me it makes five and it does make five.*
> WILLIAM FAULKNER, *ABSALOM, ABSALOM!*

> *Never mind about algebra here. That's for poor folks. There's no need for algebra where two and two make five.*
> THOMAS WOLFE, *LOOK HOMEWARD, ANGEL*

> *The boss wants to break a colored boy into the optical trade. You know algebra and you're just cut out for the work. . . . But remember to keep your head. Remember you're black.*
> RICHARD WRIGHT, *BLACK BOY*

> *Count, count. They came to her straight from math and waited for the logarithms of poetry. Measure me, Miz Walsh. Am I sufficient?*
> DORIS BETTS, "BEASTS OF THE SOUTHERN WILD"

Moments of mathematical reckoning like these are ubiquitous in the literature of the twentieth-century South. In works by white and black, male and female, rich and poor, and native and immigrant southerners, these calculating fixations impart critical lessons about southerners' tendencies to measure, divide, and value themselves and the Others against whom they find balance. While many of these writers have little to connect them by race, class, gender, or even geography, they consistently—if variously—fetishize the numbers, figures, and calculations that come to signify their most personal equations of self-worth. As we see throughout *Disturbing Calculations*, this phenomenon is rooted in the history of the South, of capitalism, colonialism, and the language and technologies of Western rationality. Delivered from slavery, Reconstruction, and segregation, the twentieth-century South finds itself at least nominally integrated into an American capitalist economy of limitless opportunity, but increasingly attached to slavery's prescriptive calculations of worth, value, certainty, and hierarchy. Yet between these seemingly inimical economies, an unexpected affinity emerges; confronted by the tools and promises of a new order, modern southerners find themselves uncannily revisiting the discourse and calculations of the old.

That is, the calculations of twentieth-century southerners are so "disturbing" precisely because they evoke not slavery's cold calculus but that of American capitalism in its most basic and enduring forms. Southern exceptionalism has long been asserted and perpetuated by both citizens and critics of the South for a variety of motives. However, I suggest instead that southerners' anxiety over maintaining an exceptional status in fact uncovers surprising correlatives between the antebellum southern and the modern American capitalist psychology. When abjected southerners apprehensively calculate their sense of self-worth and status in the new order, they respond to the liberties and limitations of modern American capitalism generally—imperatives that echo plantation codes in both comforting and alarming repetition. In the twentieth century's agonized spaces of wage labor and free-market capitalism, industrialization and modernization, economic expansion and social progressivism, New Southerners find themselves haunted by slavery's methods yet both tantalized and curtailed by capitalism's uncannily analogous promises and priorities.

In various readings that span the earliest works of the twentieth century to the most recent productions in the twenty-first, I propose a new way of viewing U.S. southern literature that draws variously on neo-Marxist, psychoanalytic, and postcolonial theories in order to account for the apparent transformation of a material reality into a calculation-obsessed discourse. While the origins of this phenomenon plainly include slavery and its principles of human quantification and commodification, it is not just former slaves but white women, elite men, Native Americans, and immigrants who have precise economic value in this system and betray anxious fiscal attachments and desires lasting long beyond emancipation. At the same time that elite southerners distance themselves from capitalism's dehumanizing mechanisms, the marginalized yearn to realize the uniquely American narrative of accumulation and ascent. For both, the fetish of number emerges to signify the futility and danger of overidentification with the figures and measures of their fragile value.

As a concept, the fetish originally denoted a man-made object perceived to have supernatural or religious significance and transformative power, particularly for the so-called primitive cultures of Egypt and Africa in collision with European Christianity in the sixteenth and seventeenth centuries.[1] Already saddled with latent implications of material value, the trope found ready applicability in Marx's notion of commodity fetishism, central to his critique of capitalism, as well as in Freud's theories of sexual fetishism; for both Marx and Freud, fetish objects reify material or physical desire while concealing an essential lack of materiality or substance.[2] For Marx, commodities are abstractions with talismanic power but no inherent value beyond their manufactured worth in a capitalist economy that replaces social relations with empty, alien objects; likewise for Freud, the fetish is both an expression of and a denial of a lack or a loss (specifically of the penis), which the individual attempts to both repress and compensate for through the mediation of an object charged with the transference of meaning and significance.[3] Lacan's later reworkings of the fetish introduce a wider field of applicability, extending it beyond the physical male-female, mother-child model and into the realm of the symbolic and the literary.[4] In both Marxist and psychoanalytic understandings of the fetish, what is most striking is this elemental sense of a felt or present absence, the material representation of endlessly deferred longing and desire. In different ways throughout this book I rely on these foundational concepts to explain the economic and psychological desires both portended and denied by the southern fetish of number. Works by southern writers insistently circulate numerical figures and calculations as textual fetishes that reveal and repress various degrees of economic foreclosure, entitlement, and desire, but which are often disguised as more humane or spiritual wants. As Henry Krips explains in his pivotal work on fetish as a "psychocultural" phenomenon, "the function of fetish is as much that of a screen as a memorial," taking the place of "that which cannot be remembered directly" or that must for some reason remain repressed (7). Put another way, as Laura Mulvey explains, the fetish can conceal its own process of value making and historical specificity, leaving it "up to the critic or analyst to reveal its significance" (524). In this book I aim to uncoil the tangled desires and denials of the southern fetish of number, seeking to understand the significance and stakes of such screens for the various individuals differently bereft in the twentieth-century New South.

In doing so, my understanding of the fetish in southern literary discourse exceeds these psychoanalytic and economic contexts. As Anne McClintock describes and demonstrates in her pivotal *Imperial Leather*, the fetish, saddled with multiple and complex confrontations with race, sexuality, and nationalism, has a vital function within colonial cultures, standing "at the cross-roads of psychoanalysis and social history, inhabiting the threshold of both personal and historical memory" (184). McClintock thus endeavors to "open fetishism to a more complex and variable history in which racial and class hierarchies would play as formative a role as sexuality" (184). Enabling such an investigation are developments within postcolonial theory that add to the Marxist-Freudian concept of fetish the manifold desires and denials involved in confronting racial difference. In particular, Homi Bhabha suggests that the fetish, like the stereotype, operates in colonial discourse as a way to signify "*negative difference*," denoting a structure of both deficiency and desire, which the subject tries desperately to mask through fetishized tropes of mimicry and substitution (75).[5] While critics have taken issue with what Bhabha himself admits is a "reckless" application of racial fetishism to colonial situations ranging widely from the antebellum South to British India, we can learn much from his expansive focus on the "temporality of repetition that constitutes those signs by which marginalized or insurgent subjects create a collective agency" (199). This inclusive and comprehensive project in some sense inspires my own: while my study remains situated in the U.S. South, I explore broad expanses of time, geography, and subject position within the field of twentieth-century southern literature in order to diagnose a collective and persistent colonial trauma through the recurrent signs of number and calculation. In doing so, I find that elite southerners fetishize their own racial primacy (as "original," whole, and superior) by engaging mathematical fictions of increase, multiplication, and accumulation—tropes that have a bona fide correlative in the inequitable world of free-market capitalism, and that often betray a sense of compensatory entitlement incited by the loss of automatic privilege and prosperity in a postslavery economy. Likewise, marginalized southerners register their difference as a lack or "minusness," a sense of perpetual absence or depreciation that they are ceaselessly attempting to factor away in order to achieve the fullness and prosperity associated with white mastery.

For both groups, the fetish of number collides with the enabling condition of narcissism, which lends to the desire for reconstitution and increase a distinctly personal, psychological character. Regardless of their position on the social spectrum, southerners are not necessarily interested in inflating their wallets (and often actively reject currency as a signifier of wealth) as much as their egos. Put another way, the tangled operations of fetish and narcissism indicate precisely how synonymous economic affluence and self-worth become within systems of postslavery, capitalist competition. Such an analysis requires that we understand narcissism not as a pathology but as a widespread symptom of postcolonial trauma. According to Freud in his 1914 essay "On Narcissism," self-love is a relatively normal human drive that actually motivates and preserves the survival instinct; at the stage of primary narcissism, the individual's normal libidinous impulses may be directed both inward (to the self) and outward (to objects associated with the self), with the ultimate psychoanalytic goal of replacing self-love with object-love.[6] Certainly, this concept echoes the operation of what I am calling the fetish of number, by which the southern self both desires and identifies with objects that signify economic and personal value. The precise coincidence of narcissism with economic desire is what occupies Christopher Lasch in his influential critique of late twentieth-century American consumer society, *The Culture of Narcissism*. Acquisitive, hedonistic, and self-obsessed, the culture of Lasch's America has been replaced by fetishistic, narcissistic overidentification with the signs and symbols of consumer capitalism.[7] Lasch does not dwell specifically on the southern narcissist belatedly navigating integration into an inimical national economy, as other critics have done;[8] but postcolonial theory has more recently revised the concept of narcissism in ways that facilitate its application to a southern postslavery context.[9] According to Frantz Fanon and Homi Bhabha, elite whites and males in colonial situations classically display a kind of "narcissism of mastery," which aptly characterizes the manufacturing of superiority and power on the basis of racial, ethnic, or sexual difference. For both Fanon and Bhabha, however, narcissism is dual: while it primarily defines the elite's attempt to derive status and value by exploiting and debasing inferior "others," it also captures the marginalized's desire to achieve the wholeness and integrity of the oppressor.[10] In this way, the narcissistic desire is transferred onto numerical and monetary proxies that serve as fetish objects for the increase of both economic and psychological welfare.[11] What postcolonialism strikingly reminds us is that narcissism is a condition not of grandeur but of contingency and desperation, an expression not of solipsism but of "dependency on others," a state not of strength but "weakness," not inherently whole but desperately seeking an alliance that will "firm up a self prone to fragmentation" (Williams and Adams 20).

For both privileged and debased southerners, these desires thus emerge as fetishes that simultaneously expose and obscure their attachment to the figures and calculations of wealth and self-worth. Under Reconstruction and modern American capitalism, formerly elite white southerners paradoxically share with their marginalized others a sense of loss and foreclosure, which is answered by a narcissistic desire to own the colonizer's (that is, the northern capitalist's) world.[12] In doing so, the primacy of monetary wealth as an index of self-worth needs to be repressed in order to perpetuate myths of an anticommercial, feudal South; the fetish of number emerges with uncanny force in such contexts to neutralize these fictions. What is perhaps most "disturbing" about these fetishistic calculations of authority and accumulation are the uncanny ways in which minority figures can become narcissists as well—watching, desiring, and mimicking the strategies of the master.[13] As Mahatma Gandhi famously described the conundrum of colonial domination: "we want the English rule without the Englishman. You want the tiger's nature but not the tiger" (qtd. in L. Gandhi, 21). In the South of the twentieth century, however, the tiger's nature—that is, the tantalizing state of not just economic prosperity but simple self-ownership and human value—never ceased to be both desirable and dangerous. Because modern southerners find the new world of market capitalism often an uncanny repetition of plantation principles, the factors being measured, exploited, and debited remain those of darker skin or the "gentler" sex. It is the multiple, vexed iterations of both desiring and repudiating material wealth and psychological solvency, for southerners from all positions and conditions, that I explore in the following chapters.

From Slavery to Capitalism and Back

In the opening pages of *What Made the South Different?*, Kees Gispen puzzles: "in light of Max Weber's *The Protestant Ethic and the Spirit of Capitalism* I have often wondered why the culture of this overwhelmingly protestant region resembles so little the European or Yankee capitalism with which I am familiar. Or does it?" (ix). Moreover, he asks, "why should slavery and capitalism be considered mutually exclusive in southern history when few if any historians in my field [European history] dispute the reality of their combination"? (x). An outsider to southern studies, Gispen's perspective illuminates what has been so distinctive and puzzling about much of the region's history: a labored but ultimately untenable distinction between plantation paternalism and market capitalism. As Bertram Wyatt-Brown suggests, the South's regional identity has always been "and in some ways still is founded on its claim to being anti-capitalist" (183). Yet this assertion became most fervent only in the South's reluctant integration into a postslavery American economy and its deepening struggles to adapt and flourish in the twentieth century. In 1930, a full sixty-five years after the surrender at Appomattox, the Nashville Agrarians (writing as "Twelve Southerners") famously—or infamously—collaborated to produce *I'll Take My Stand: The South and the Agrarian Tradition* in defense of "a Southern way of life against what may be called the American or prevailing way . . . Agrarian *versus* Industrial" (xxxvii). "Eager to claim for themselves a tradition hostile to northern capitalism," Persky explains, the Agrarians' explicit hope was to return to a system of subsistence farming closely modeled on the plantation precedents of the antebellum idyll, which they saw as a container for the highest ideals of leisure, culture, art, and humanism (117).[14] Yet it is precisely in the fissures between an anticommercial myth and a capitalist machine that catastrophic revelations about history, slavery, and the persistence of human calculation emerge to trouble the South's modern inhabitants. That is, the South's agonized confrontation with American capitalism was not a violent and unnatural collision so much as a fateful homecoming.[15]

The financial incentive of slavery has not been simply a private debate between southern conservatives and their opponents but among economists and historians as well. As Mark M. Smith notes, "questions concerning the economic and social character of antebellum southern slavery still inform modern historical debates which have raged with increasing volume and occasional acrimony in the twentieth century" (1). Eugene Genovese, one of the most prolific Marxist historians of the South, himself famously vacillated on this matter, moving from the position that slaveholders were anticapitalist figures with an "aversion to profit" to a partial admission that planters desired a return on their investments but were neither fully integrated into the market economy nor very successful at negotiating it (M. Smith 13). In *Time on the Cross*, their groundbreaking statistical analysis of slavery's profitability, Robert Fogel and Stanley Engerman exhaustively argued that the plantation was categorically a business enterprise, organized and geared for revenue and participation in both local and national economies.[16] After presenting arguments from both sides of this debate, Mark M. Smith concludes that the Old South may well have constituted "a society where plantation capitalism and conventional capitalism articulated" cohesively (94).[17] Indeed, most analysts are now willing to acknowledge that the South's plantation system clearly embodied the characteristics of a protocapitalist economy even without pure market relations.[18] To be sure, the South's conversion to a system of capitalist agricultural production was swifter than occurs in most postslavery societies, indicating that it had been poised on the brink of such a transition for some time.[19]

This revelation indeed contradicts assumptions about the South's "protracted route" to capitalist relations, as Stephen Hahn acknowledges (74); despite protests to the contrary, there is evidence that by the end of Reconstruction in the 1870s, southerners generally began to adopt and support northern-style industrial development and modernization, with an eye toward reestablishing economic prosperity. As Mark Twain observed of the New Southern farmer in the 1880s, "the dollar [is] their god, how to get it [is] their religion" (qtd. in Woodward, *Origins* 153). Yet this drive for progress and profit was hampered by the South's quasi-colonial economic condition, as it remained under the loose financial control of the industrial-capitalist North long into the twentieth century.[20] As Woodward reports, "the control exercised by the British merchant over the [southern] tobacco colonies was extensive, but it never equaled that of the Northeastern banker" (*Origins* 318). By 1889, a sense that the South's resources and labor were being exploited had become pervasive. Henry Grady, after attending the funeral of a Georgia man, remarked bitterly that "the South didn't furnish a thing on earth for that funeral but the corpse and the hole in the ground": the coffin, gravestone, and burial attire were all purchased ready-made from northern manufacturers, even though their original materials may well have been extracted from southern soil and factories (qtd. in McLaughlin and Robock 3). As Woodward hypothesizes, the South "seems to have had a fatal attraction for such [low wage, low-value creating industries]" (*Origins* 309). Long hampered by a rural, agricultural, labor-intensive system, many southerners quite simply lacked the preparation and skills necessary to propel them into higher-wage, more technologically advanced fields (G. Wright 158).

U.S. involvement in the Spanish-American War of 1898 and then World War I provided an opportunity and a necessity for the South to ally with the North on something more like equal terms, and many seized upon this prospect greedily.[21] An economic upturn associated with World War I also meant that the South's surplus labor would be for a time more fully utilized. Following the war, however, the South plunged again into isolation and economic despair; and Barbara Ladd has suggested that southern writers during this period intensified their appeals to the past partly as an idyllic refuge from the nation's increasingly imperialistic international entanglements (*Nationalism* xii).[22] A regional sense of foreclosure and entitlement deepened as well; by the 1920s and 1930s, the South's colonial economy seemed to reach its nadir even before the sinking national economy. As Thomas Daniel Young reports in *The History of Southern Literature*, the early decades of the century found the South "at the bottom of the list in almost everything: ownership of automobiles, radios, residence telephones; income per capita, bank deposits; homes with electricity, running water, and indoor plumbing. Its residents subscribed to the fewest magazines and newspapers, read the fewest books; they also provided the least support for education, public libraries, and art museums" (262).

In 1935, Rupert Vance was among the first to identify the system of interregional dependency as a colonial economy.[23] Similar observations followed, culminating in the preparation of the federal *Report on Economic Conditions of the South* incited by President Roosevelt's infamous and belated lament that "the South presents right now the Nation's No. 1 economic problem.... For we have an economic unbalance in the Nation as a whole, due to this very condition of the South" (1).[24] New Deal programs, particularly the Agricultural Adjustment Act of 1933, were instituted federally in an attempt to excite the region's stagnant economy and crop prices; finally, the government was responding to the straitened conditions that southern farmers had been facing for decades. Yet even the introduction of aid programs, crop diversification, and industrial progress seemed paradoxically to deepen the region's dependency: mining and processing metals, fabrics, grains, timber, and other raw materials simply allowed the South to continue exporting its cheaply-prepared products to factories and companies in northern cities for finishing and distributing. As the production of export staples grew dramatically, so too did the areas of the South that had previously been independent of this system; as a result, the extractive economy came to envelop more and more of the South: rural areas and urban locales formed a virtual assembly line of production and export, but the main centers of finance and profit were still based above the Mason-Dixon Line (Kirby 26). Bruce Schulman reports that in 1937, southern per capita income amounted to "barely half the standard of the rest of the nation"—a statistical reality, he asserts, that surely "translated into concrete human suffering" (*From Cotton Belt* 3).

Crippled by protracted dependency and stagnation, the literature of this period begins to manifest textual preoccupations with the figures and calculations of slavery, capitalism, and ascent as vexed and ambivalent desires for compensation, accumulation, and a renewed sense of value and integrity. Along with these preoccupations often come nostalgic retreats to antebellum idylls, where anticapitalist humanism fueled the social economy and presumably supplied a richness of virtue and luxury that could not be quantified; but the persistence of quantifying tropes in such back-looking reveries troubles the claim that capitalist priorities were not always integral to the South's storied past. As I discuss in greater detail in chapter 1, texts by elite white southerners betray a lurking lust to have it all: a return to economic prosperity and racial hierarchy under slavery, an ambivalent collision of modern financial opportunity and a mystified protocapitalist plantation order. Such desires were actually coterminous with the deepening racial stratification of the Jim Crow South; as Dewey Grantham notes in *The History of Southern Literature*, "while urging economic innovation, [New Southerners] accepted the prevailing racial attitudes" and failed to denounce the injustices of the past (241). C. Vann Woodward notes similarly that "the deeper the involvements in commitments to the New Order, the louder the protests of loyalty to the Old" (*Origins* 155).[25]

Not in dispute about the plantation economy is the fact that the profit of the system was prioritized over the value and humanity of its exploited laborers. Many historians have argued that racial subjugation developed as an ex post facto justification for slavery's palatability rather than an a priori assertion of blacks' natural inferiority. As Eric Williams notes in *Capitalism and Slavery*, "the features of the man, his hair, color and dentrifice, his 'subhuman' characteristics so widely pleaded, were only the later rationalizations to justify a simple economic fact: that the colonies needed labor and resorted to Negro labor because it was cheapest and best" (20). The intensification of racist ideologies in the Jim Crow South can be seen as, in part, an elaborate attempt to justify the apparently natural and advantageous system that predated the cheap, inefficient, dehumanizing world of capital relations. Not everyone agrees with this position: as George Frederickson protests, "no readily perceptible class interest can account for this kind of racial hysteria... sustained over such a long period and in the face of massive economic and social changes" (157).[26] Yet the point I seek to make here is that such racial attitudes and antagonisms, whatever their origins, intensified well into the twentieth century as a telling symptom of a largely narcissistic, self-serving project and crisis of individual value. As Cheryl Harris argues in "Whiteness as Property," simply being white has historically come with the privilege of ownership, even (if to a lesser extent) for poor whites.[27] Having lost a system in which ownership correlates so rigidly with racial identity, many twentieth-century white southerners naturally yearned for the return of the plantation's simpler, more reliable mathematics at all costs. Conservative historians of the South like Ulrich Bonnell Phillips began even more energetically to recast the fundamental morality of the plantation system, seeking to redress what he felt were unfair stereotypes of cruelty and avarice.[28] "To get into the records is to get away from the stereotypes," Phillips avers. "It is from the records and with a sense of the personal equation that I have sought to speak" (vii–viii).[29] Yet nothing in those "records" could alter the fact that they harbored on their pages the details of a system that tallied together cotton and human chattel. These records themselves become a key fetish in works by modern southerners ambivalently recalling the serenity and shame of the Old South. As Walter Johnson describes, to the typical southern slave trader, "slavery looked like this: a list of names, numbers, and outcomes double-entered in the meticulous *Slave Record*... he could and did turn thousands of people into prices" (45–46). Account books patently commodify human chattel and spectralize the plantation's capital flow in a way that makes the system's cash-driven imperatives difficult to suppress. Yet, as we see in chapter 1, writers such as Faulkner and Allen Tate employ the device in order to dramatize the collision between seemingly incongruous social orders: slavery and capitalism. Indeed, these books appear frequently in the fiction of the depressed elite as fetish objects wherein the mercantilism that supplanted this humanistic order is both demonized and made potently seductive.

Textual appearances of the ledger trope naturally occupy a portion of my attention in the chapters that follow, as the account book is the mathematical instrument most obviously tied to the protocapitalist economy of slavery. But my argument rests more broadly on the assumption that "number" and calculations in general become a textual fetish arising directly from these southerners' participation in and repression of their roles in a capitalist economy. I arrive at this extrapolation in several ways, each of which I expand on in the pages that follow: first, I acknowledge the obvious, which is that mathematics is the primary language of economics and that a calculation-obsessed discourse may on some level be a response to conditioning within a capitalist environment, something southerners are for radically divergent reasons both eager and reluctant to demonstrate.

Second, I recognize that mathematics as a discipline has a genealogy apart from and preceding its function within economics, but that this history has traditionally been a Western-imperialist one, endowing its applications with disturbing significance when adopted wholesale by members of suppressed classes anxious to compute and thus appreciate their own human value and identity. Finally, I draw on the sociohistorical uses of number as a tool in colonial contexts, where mathematics and calculations serve as elite technologies to quantify, define, categorize, and control the "other." The implications of number arising in this book differ depending on the context and stakes of the author and his or her creations; but taken together, the manifold significance of mathematical discourse captures the complexity and urgency of the South's fetishized imbrications in capitalism, imperialism, and colonialism.

Origins of a Calculating Discourse

The role of mathematics as a primary function in the order and maintenance of a market capitalist system is indisputable. Marx himself acknowledged that mathematics developed partly in order to help negotiate the needs of society, showing its most remarkable advances particularly as it engaged with the abstract calculations of market capitalism.[30] In a study of the developments in algorithmic function in the fifteenth century, Frank Swetz explains that such advances radically changed and facilitated the training of European merchants and money changers, in a sense helping capitalism itself to develop and flourish.[31] As capitalism progressed, innovations in mathematical analysis often developed alongside it, providing a language and a methodology for calculating and computing its functions. A prominent example is general equilibrium theory, the mathematical analysis of an entire market economy, which emerged from the attempts of nineteenth-century mathematicians Leon Walras and Vilfredo Pareto to legitimize Adam Smith's notion of the "invisible hand" through math (C. Young 164). Interestingly, while the equilibrium theory was largely ignored at the time, it was revived (and known as the GE/Welfare economists project) by mathematical economists working in the United States during the Great Depression and attempting to regulate the flow of the market through a series of elaborate mathematical prescriptives. While perfectly and even amazingly rational, this "mathematical torturing" generated only what Cristobal Young calls "a grand narrative on the fragility and implausibility of perfect market equilibrium" (166). The American economy was "rescued" from such regulation by free-market champions like Milton Friedman, for whom even the most precise mathematical elegance could not capture or dictate the glories of the market. In this brief sketch of mathematics' long investment in market capitalism, what I mean to demonstrate above all is the diverse and fervent use to which mathematics has been put in the service of alternately demystifying, revolutionizing, and glorifying the institution of capitalism. Whether engineered in the service of promoting social welfare, public demystification, or corporate profiteering, mathematics emerges above all as an initially neutral instrument that becomes laden with the values and desires attached to it by those invested in understanding, improving, or dismantling capitalism as a governing social structure. As Cristobal Young comments in a review of Robert Nelson's *Economics as Religion*, if "economists are a priestly class.... The bishops of this class are mathematicians" (161). Nelson's book itself provides a kind of "theology of economics" in which he ultimately argues for an understanding of the free market as a solid foundation for values endorsed by God (C. Young 162, 170). As such, mathematics rises to the level of talisman or fetish, much like its original iteration as a sacred object endowed with transformative potential.

What interests and troubles me most in such formulations is the function of mathematics as a fetishized discourse through which the capitalist marketplace is raised to the level of social salvation or religious pulpit. If mathematics is the bishop of the capitalist religion, what scripture does it preach? What fundamental emptiness and unrequited lack must the fetish of number disguise when yoked to a system of alienation and abstraction? Part of what I argue in *Disturbing Calculations* is that capitalism generally, particularly in its peculiarly advanced, modern American forms, engenders in its subjects a crippling sense of narcissistic delirium (as Lasch argues) as well as the illusion of a desire or a lack that must be filled or gratified. The first part of this characterization has roots in liberal-democratic theory hearkening back to the seventeenth century where, as C. B. MacPherson has famously outlined, a new individualism came into being that characterized a "possessive quality . . . in its conception of the individual as essentially the proprietor of his own person or capacities" (3). MacPherson's theory of "possessive individualism" sees freedom itself as a "function of possession" and thus a cornerstone of liberal democracy (3); such freedom in twentieth-century market societies in fact comes to define and delimit one's very humanity (271–72). This fact haunts U.S. southerners in their transition from a neoaristocratic order of privilege to one of apparent equal opportunity and competition, where former slaves are accorded humanity and freedom at the same time that they enter into a game in which property ownership signifies not just wealth but individual human value. What Lasch identifies as a pervasive, pathological narcissism has its origins in the amplification of a system encouraging the democratic individual to overidentify with his or her pocketbook. For southerners, the transition to this system excited an exacerbated sense of narcissistic yearning, paranoia, and rivalry, as individuals from across the social spectrum seemed to perceive themselves (with varying degrees of accuracy) as both depreciated and deserving of prosperity.

As narcissism betrays a desire for fulfillment by an Other that will both reflect and complete (and presumably empower and enrich) the self, the world of object consumption promises to satisfy an ingrained human hunger for possession. Yet the simple, well-documented fact that the marketplace abstracts rather than fulfills desire, along with a wayward notion that the human self can be validated and amplified by engaging in such an exchange, insures that these dislocated southerners simply replace one lost cause (the plantation) with another (the marketplace). In this way, my approach to these texts draws on critiques of Marxist thought that seek to replace its overemphasis on production and labor as concrete (if mystified) categories with the bleaker recognition that such "realities" are traps, indeed mirrors (according to Jean Baudrillard) further imprisoning us within the marketplace, disguising what is fundamentally an abstract environment of signs without referents.[32] Even the sense of lack itself is an illusion, as Eugene Holland summarizes Deleuze and Guattari's sweeping critique of capitalism (which topples psychoanalysis as a capitalist institution along the way): "there is no real lack, except as engineered retroactively by social systems of representation" (293). For southerners, the numerical fetish emerges to signify a sense of loss and desire at the same time that it dooms them to the essential emptiness of this modern narcissism, a material and psychological yearning and a loss that can never be compensated.

My interest throughout this book lies in the moments when mathematics emerges as a discourse patently attached to a market that gives its numbers substance and value. The title page of *Foundations of Economic Analysis*, Paul Samuelson's pioneering work in Keynesian economics, states simply that "mathematics is a language."[33] The work that follows (and Samuelson's massive body of writing in general) demonstrates how deeply he believes that this language could and should be used to appreciate the mechanics of market capitalism; but I am interested in exploring the literal and literary implications of his pronouncement. As a language, mathematics is a collection of empty signifiers waiting to be accorded situational significance; as Eugene W. Holland explains in a review of Deleuze and Guattari's *Anti-Oedipus*, "The basis of capitalist society is . . . the abstract calculus of capital itself" (296). Deleuze and Guattari go on to imagine a radical decoding (and eventually a re-coding) of this environment, but my attention remains on the way that this "abstract calculus" becomes an inexorable feature of discourse in capitalist societies, and in a more sweeping sense, a substanceless code attached to a world of substanceless signs. When asked to measure and compute individual human worth and hierarchy, such calculations become, as my title avers, truly disturbing. Yet, as Erik Dussere notes in *Balancing the*

Books, the language of finance suffuses our contemporary discourse from the mundane to the sublime, and there has been no shortage of critical attention to the intersections of economics and literature from various stages and locations in the global progress of capitalism. Dussere reminds us of the peculiar implications this discourse has in the South, where slavery engendered "a particular economic configuration, a crucible in which economic analysis takes on special urgency" (11). Dussere examines the terms and significance of accounting as a textual feature of Faulkner and Toni Morrison's fictional engagements with slavery. Ultimately, he finds both authors able to manage this discursive haunting in some way, either by rejecting its insuperable vicissitudes (as Faulkner does) or by harnessing its language and an entry into modern capitalism as the only available means to self-ownership (as in Morrison's efforts). Dussere's readings are rigorously and passionately rendered but cannot ultimately overcome the adhesive context of a postslavery capitalist society, wherein such victories amount to little more than continued imprisonment within a discourse of painful and intimate abstractions. What the following chapters demonstrate is that the progress from slavery to capitalism indeed endows southerners' mathematical language with a peculiar complexity, ambivalence, and tenacity.

Just as free-market capitalism cannot be analyzed apart from the Enlightenment-driven Western values driving its growth and profusion, neither can mathematics as a discipline be divorced from the same intellectual conditions of rationality and progress that fostered its most revolutionary period of growth in the seventeenth and eighteenth centuries. While early forms of math were known to have existed in the earliest Egyptian and Babylonian societies (largely in response to business, agricultural, and surveying needs), it was not until the Enlightenment's seismic shifts in philosophy and politics that mathematics rose to widespread prominence as a mode capable of producing scientific certainty in accordance with new ways of approaching and understanding the world and human society.[34] Mathematical methods such as Gottfried Leibniz's avowed to advance positive, unerring knowledge about the universe.[35] Championed by Hegel as a science of quantity that could endow individuals with concrete information about the material world, mathematics represented the primary, exemplary mode by which one could measure and produce knowledge. Following this rather naturally were theories about ethical and moral positivism; as Kant would later contend, since morality is consistent among rational beings, the guidelines for moral reasoning must be considered as prescribed and reliable as the rules of arithmetic. In philosophy, the "calculus of reasoning" describes the methods employed to rationalize nebulous ethical problems; mathematically, the word *calculus* itself refers to "the system of rules for manipulating symbols, which extends the possibility of thought in solving problems and proving statements" (*Dictionary of Philosophy*); already encoded in this definition are the possibility for manipulation and the intervention of the thinking consciousness, elements saddled with subjectivity and self-interest.

Indeed, the fundamental problem with all such systems of positive knowledge is that knowledge itself is, according to Descartes and myriad subsequent thinkers, inherently narcissistic. As Max Weber observes about mathematics in particular, calculating operations fundamentally violate the universe's mysteries with the narcissistic presumption that one may "master all things by calculation" (139).[36] Enlightenment thinking helps accomplish the conversion of narcissistic desires and needs into calculable categories; and often, the desire to mathematically apprehend the world is also to codify or control it for one's own purpose or gain. Foucault once observed with some alarm that the forces of Western rationality itself could be used to justify and sustain colonialism's "economic domination and political hegemony" (54). And as Derrida had already noted quite simply in 1974, the "very structure of Western rationality is racist and imperialist" (qtd. in L. Gandhi 26). Enlightenment ideals, which championed the virtues of scientific and mathematical thinking as paths to true cultural maturity, sophistication, and advancement, were often the very same values invoked to justify the expansion of European power (i.e., colonialism) over the savage, uncivilized masses of India and Africa; even Marx absolved the costs implicated in the conquest of India because colonization had a seemingly beneficent civilizing effect on its apparently primitive peoples (Said, *Orientalism* 153).

Of course, modernity brings with it the sober realization that morality is neither certain nor impartial; in imperial societies in particular, it can be and has long been distorted to suit the ends of the dominant culture. In *After Virtue*, his investigation of modernity's disintegrating moral code, Alasdair MacIntyre suggests that "reason is calculative; it can assess truths of fact and mathematical relations but nothing more" (54). But when "truth," "fact," and "mathematics" are already corruptible categories, reason itself is vulnerable to the definitions and revisions of those whose ends may be self-serving and exploitative. As Alan J. Bishop has argued in his studies of Western mathematics and Mary Poovey in her investigation of modern accounting, numbers and calculations can be perverted to serve the moral, political, economic, or narcissistic needs of the master calculator—and when the calculations affect either one's economic or ethical accounts, they may accomplish a theft of existential proportions.[37] This is the calculus of reason confronted by modern southerners poised between worlds—a network of rational forces employed to render an unethical, exploitative system natural, scientific, and unerring in its logic. As an imperial tool, mathematical determinacy is broadly powerful. Cartography, for example—the practice of dividing land into quadrants easy to parcel, command, and possess—imposes mathematical and geometric grids onto an unruly landscape and thus converts it into property to be appropriated and exchanged.[38] Such projects could be rationalized morally, as in Thomas Jefferson's grand democratic plan to divide U.S. land equally among its industrious farmer-citizens. Jefferson's democratic aspirations did not extend, of course, either to his own numerous chattel or to the region's Indians, whom he considered an expensive nuisance that needed to be expelled in order to stage his spectacles of democratic and agricultural efficiency.[39]

The attachment of numbers to such imperial projects and philosophies matters because their authority came to solidify mathematics as a discipline of truth and fact, ends that are not inviolable but rather catastrophically vulnerable to self-serving manipulation. But such long-held and classically mandated presumptions have helped to perpetuate our confidence in mathematics, logic, rationality, and the supreme clarity of numbers. When the fundamental artificiality and manipulability of mathematics and Western knowledge generally slips behind the curtain of faith and hope—particularly in the economic systems whose simple arithmetic (more work + more money = more happiness) would seem to offer unerring promise and salvation—we find modern Americans, and particularly modern southerners, most crippled by their indoctrination into a beguiling system of abstractions and dreams.

The applicability of postcolonial theory and analysis to the culture and literature of the United States has been vigorously debated for nearly two decades. Foremost in the hesitancy to accord America "postcolonial" status is the country's apparently exceptional status as a monumentally "successful" nation, which distinguishes it from other former British and European colonies; moreover, opponents of U.S. postcolonial studies (and often of postcolonial studies in general) have sharply critiqued the irony that studies of non-Western cultures proceed audaciously from the ivory tower of Western academic remoteness and privilege whose campuses are located mainly on U.S. soil. Beyond these political objections exist additional concerns about the simple accuracy of a label to describe a nation that inaugurated its own independence by in turn colonizing and exploiting others, first at home and later abroad. As Anne McClintock was quick to argue in "The Angel of Progress," the hasty addition of a "post" prefix to America's own colonial projects is optimistic at best, and at worst dangerously myopic. Indeed, as subsequent critics have gone on to show, America's colonial and postcolonial character is much too complex, evolving, and disturbing to be easily dismissed or defined.[40] Particularly in the recent, post–September 11 resuscitation of xenophobic nationalism and imperial invasions of Afghanistan and Iraq has the relevance of a colonial critique to U.S. studies become decidedly more credible and urgent. Moreover, the continued dependent status of American Indians corralled on federal reservations, along with glaring domestic policy disasters such as Hurricane Katrina, demands that we look closely at internal structures of both colonial and postcolonial inequity.[41] Such views have striking contemporary relevance, but the awareness of intellectual categories and historical contexts within which we might situate them are not new: as Peter Schmidt and Amritjit Singh outline in *Postcolonial Theory and the United States*, concepts of postcoloniality inspired by the pioneering works of Edward Said, Frantz Fanon, and W. E. B. DuBois found an earlier, natural convergence with U.S. ethnic studies and its issues of immigration, exile, diaspora, and assimilation. And there is a real-world imperative to make such issues viable and visible, as current events like Hurricane Katrina remind us: indeed, in her introduction to a new anthology of American literature and postcolonial theory, Deborah L. Madsen claims that such critical approaches have the potential to raise "important questions about the complicity and potential for resistance offered by the practice of literary study, and specifically the study of American literature" (10).[42] More particularly, I hope this book incites such questions and possibilities in the long-segregated field of U.S. southern literature.

The delusions of exceptionalism that hampered early efforts to view the U.S. as a postcolonial entity are precisely the forces that have discouraged attempts to situate the American South as anything but distinctive, peculiar, and backward. Jon Smith argues as much in "Postcolonial, Black, and Nobody's Margin: The U.S. South in New World Studies," which promotes emergent recognitions of the U.S. South as "simultaneously center and margin, colonizer and colonized, global north and global south, essentialist and hybrid," orientations that represent "a crucial locus for the development of such [postcolonial] theory" (144). Most broad theoretical considerations of American postcoloniality, while they routinely treat African American confrontations with slavery and apartheid rooted clearly in southern spaces, tend ultimately to overlook a specific analysis of the South's particular role in promulgating the ideologies of suppression begun by American exploration and settlement (narratives that prominently include and traverse southern territories), continued in the region's plantation economy and segregation policies, and enduring even now in regional politics.[43] Yet, as a May 2007 *New York Times* article acknowledged, citing new scholarly works by Matthew Lassiter and Kevin Kruse, "what is most distinctive about the latest research on the South is its claim that the South is no longer distinctive" but rather that the region's perceived backwardness is actually a small symptom of a much broader national trend toward reactionary conservatism (Cohen).[44] The comparative tide is turning not just North but abroad as well, with a distinct transnational shift in the field of southern studies giving rise to numerous symposia, special issues of academic journals, critical anthologies, and full-length studies. Most notably, works like Deborah Cohn's *History and Memory in the Two Souths* and (coedited with Jon Smith) *Look Away!*, George Handley's *Postslavery Literatures in the Americas*, and Jose Limon's *American Encounters*, no doubt among many others soon to appear, represent sustained comparisons of the U.S. South to other New World, postcolonial regions. The titles alone of much recent scholarship on southern studies and southern literature broadcast nothing if not the notion that the U.S. South is no longer where or what we assumed it to be: Suzanne Jones and Sharon Monteith's (eds.) *South to a New Place*, Fred Hobson's *South to the Future*, Martyn Bone's *The Postsouthern Sense of Place*, and, again, Smith and Cohn's *Look Away!* This wealth of critical activity has reconceptualized the South, often postcolonially, as a particularly diverse container of settlement and racial histories, stretching its purview to the global, Latin American, and Caribbean "Souths" with which it shares histories, cultures, and legacies of economic and racial domination.[45] Two excellent collections of essays on the global South include *The American South in a Global World* (edited by Peacock, Watson, and Matthews) and *Globalization and the American South* (edited by Cobb and Stueck).[46] Both works advocate viewing the South as inherently and historically transnational, born of early global forces and continuing in critical ways to reflect and interact with other nations' economies, histories, cultures, and citizens. Long assumed to be an aberration inside U.S. borders, the South is more recently and judiciously being appraised as a region among other colonial and postcolonial sites globally, "taking its place in a world of regions, not simply of nation-states" (Peacock, Watson, and Matthews 2–3). While my own approach is not in practice comparative or global, it is indebted to these studies for broadening the purview of southern studies to include new and unsettling narratives of economic exploitation and psychological catastrophe, and for lobbying aggressively in argument and example for the adoption of postcolonial theory and methodology as a lens for better understanding and contextualizing the perceived peculiarities of southern literature.

Edward Said's monumental work of postcolonial analysis, *Orientalism*, advanced the notion that textual discourse might reveal the colonial practice of fashioning, governing, desiring, and disciplining the image of the other; more recently, theorists like Homi Bhabha, Gayatri Spivak, Bill Ashcroft, Sara Suleri, and Salman Rushdie have explored the myriad ways in which colonized subjects engage in anticolonial self-representations, attempting to disrupt the totalizing authority of an imperial center by speaking back, often in the colonizer's own tongue. What is so intriguing about southern discourse is the infinitude of ruptures within its voices: neither colonizer nor colonized in a strict sense, whites, blacks, males, females, and ethnic others apprehend one another and themselves in a complicated web of narcissistic desire and expression. All, regardless of subject position, are imbued with a primary drive issued by the logic of global capitalism and its earliest, perverse iterations under slavery: accumulate, dominate, exploit, and increase at all costs.[47]

Under such intense conditions of expropriation, suppression, and desire, the language of economics and mathematics dogs southerners well into the twentieth century. As I have already argued, the fetish of number is motivated by the logic of both economics and rationality; what the postcolonial context adds to this drive is the use of number as a tool to measure, subdue, and control. In societies bred out of colonial contact, hybridity and syncretism threaten the clarity of social order and hierarchy; these slippery, in-between figures—whom Bhabha terms "incalculable"—need to be calculated, identified, categorized, and thereby mastered (62). In this project of reckoning subjectivity, as Arjun Appadurai has argued, number itself becomes a "pedagogical and disciplinary" tool of the colonial regime, a way to "tame . . . diversities" and deny the disruption of hybridity (125, 123). Such leveling methods are applicable to African Americans during slavery and even upon emancipation, when, as we have already seen, their racial calculability and classification were perceived as vital to maintaining an economic and social order. These operations had lasting provenance not just for blacks but for whites and women involved in the system as well; as Nell Irvin Painter asserts in *Southern History across the Color Line*, "the calculus of slavery configured society as a whole," wreaking its effects not just on slaves but masters, "their white families, and, ultimately, on their whole society" (20, 30).

More explicit gestures of control employed scientific and mathematical principles to "prove" that African Americans were inferior biologically, or that they in fact constituted a subspecies of the human race. The height of this scholarship emerged in the 1840s and 1850s, leading up to and helping to ignite the Civil War, and included northern scientists such as John H. Van Evrie as well as southerners like the Louisiana physician Samuel A. Cartwright (Stanton vii). "Proofs" of racial inferiority were used to justify slavery, but they did not disappear after emancipation; in fact, attempts to measure race biologically saw various developments and extensions well into the twentieth century: in *Deviant Bodies* Jennifer Terry and Jacqueline Urla explore various "medical and scientific studies" used to determine racial and moral character precisely at moments "of heated debate about who would enjoy the privileges of legal and economic enfranchisement" and to "police" those found unworthy (1). The worst of these impulses have materialized in the "science" of eugenics; practiced not just in Nazi Germany but indeed (and first) on U.S. southern soil in government-sponsored operations like the Tuskegee Syphilis Experiment, which allowed 399 poor black sharecroppers to languish in the late stages of syphilis in the name of medical science.[48]

Such outrages were possible because, in the eyes of authority, the humanity of slaves and their descendants was dubious at best. Perhaps the most famous evidence of this comes in the Three-fifths Compromise of 1787, where it was determined that the Constitution would designate African American slaves "three-fifths of a person."[49] Ironically, it was the South's delegates who lobbied for slaves to be counted at all, since doing so would insure white southerners additional seats in the U.S. House of Representatives.[50] The fractional compromise did not point up the attenuated humanity of the black who could be thus diminished so much as it highlighted his significance as a pawn in a larger game of regional politics. That the slave's existence as a person was up for such protracted debate emphasizes the cruel fact that exploitable others could be quantified to benefit those who control them, and not just in the pages of a plantation ledger. The compromise was effectively nullified when the Thirteenth Amendment abolished slavery in 1865, but its impact was much longer lived.

Such language of apportionment is not mere rhetoric but has a profound effect on one's sense of integrity, agency, and value. Censuses function similarly, particularly in a capitalist economy where there is nearly always a cost-benefit consideration accorded to how (and how many) citizens are counted. Census counts have long been attributing whole number status to African Americans, but only in the year 2000 did census-takers begin allowing respondents to choose more than one category designating race, ending a long-standing procedure that has helped to perpetuate essentialist notions of racial difference.[51] As Bhabha notes of colonial calculability, Benedict Anderson agrees that "the fiction of the census is that everyone is in it, and that everyone has one—and only one—extremely clear place. No fractions" (166). The implications of this totalizing imperative can be profound; as a recent study suggests, "the census does more than simply reflect social reality; rather, it plays a key role in the *construction* of that reality" (Kertzer and Arel 2, italics added).[52] Such methods carry over into the needs of slavery and Jim Crow, when determining racial difference with certainty was critical to the maintenance of an entire economy and social hierarchy; elaborate mathematical equations helped to determine just who qualified as black (and, indeed, helped *to* qualify as black anyone with a drop of African blood, as the "one-drop rule" famously accomplished) in order to classify and contain them properly.[53] Not surprisingly, the methods for determining racial makeup thus became nearly hysterical. Werner Sollors describes the complex equations used as early as 1815 to gauge degrees of racial mixing; he comments that

> the premise of such a text would seem to be that "race" was foremost a mathematical problem, and that "algebraic notations" could resolve some of the political issues of mankind.... The fractions, especially the more intricate ones that serve to draw out

the nuances of the only boundary that matters, are likely to intimidate the non-expert. The text embodies the dialectic of Enlightenment, though . . . the mathematical approach moves into the realm of "science" what amounts to little more than . . . a complex legitimation of racial hierarchy. (115)

As Sollors notes, such equations and proofs carried the assurance of Enlightenment positivism, merging mathematics with scientific fact in an effort to "resolve some of the political issues of mankind"; plantation society relied on these equations to reflect the fetish of racial identity, and indeed such mathematics wielded a powerful ability to determine one's lawful status as chattel, and with it the capacity to strip not only material and psychological wellbeing but basic humanity. Such power lends chilling resonance to the students' voices in Doris Betts's fictional classroom in "Beasts of the Southern Wild": "Count, count. . . . Measure me, Miz Walsh. Am I sufficient?"

Haunted by the oppressive discourses and practices of antebellum slavery, patriarchy, and segregation, twentieth-century southerners enter a capitalist world ruled and contaminated by the politics of ascendance and the fetish of garnering surplus personal value at all costs. The anxiety of integration and modernization is not so much a reaction to change, I argue, but a dawning realization that the world of numbers, figures, and disturbing calculations is hauntingly coterminous with the mechanisms of the Lost Cause—"lost" in practice, but not in its uncanny power to return, demean, and systematically efface all those implicated in the contemporary logic of modern capitalism. By looking briefly in chapter 1 at works by white southerners as seemingly diverse as Allen Tate, William Alexander Percy, Thomas Wolfe, and William Faulkner, we begin to see how pervasively economic dispossession and social flux unsettled white male subjects in the modern South. I explore the following questions: what do these elite southerners both know and repress about the plantation order that conditioned their families' and their own perspectives on class, segregation, hierarchy, and personal value? How do they register an awareness that market capitalism not only propels them rudely into a modern, imperial nation, but in fact returns them uncannily to the operations of chattel slavery and its dehumanizing mechanisms? Within these panoramic narratives of defeat and decline, I suggest, members of déclassé white dynasties tend to subordinate money to status, recognizing currency as a mere proxy for a "true" value located in morality, character, and a challenged belief in natural aristocracy. By returning irresistibly to finances and figures as textual means to appreciate and bolster the self, however, these writers reveal their continued attachment to systems of commodification and elevation descending from the practice of chattel slavery and continuing to shape the character of market relations in the modern South. By disavowing pecuniary interests at the same time that they reveal their paradoxical reliance upon such measures and methods, southern elites imperfectly repress the economic order that both created and unseated them.

Richard H. King's *A Southern Renaissance* is memorable for claiming that the sudden effusion of literary productivity lasting from about 1930 to 1955 and known commonly as the Southern Renaissance could be explained and characterized mainly by white male southerners' preoccupation with "'the Southern family romance'" (7).[54] King's controversial decision to leave black and female southerners out of his study confirms their marginality to the elite, quasi-aristocratic world of bloodlines and postwar cultural bankruptcy; but one must labor intensely to prolong the illusion that these discrete social realms are not deeply entangled, that in fact the white patriarchy's perceived health and prosperity rests specifically on the steadying presence of its devoted wives, mothers, and slaves who could not help but develop opinions and perspectives on their subjection.[55] In chapters 2 and 3 I return to explore the material and psychic costs to African American and female southerners, respectively, of their rigidly prescribed and enduringly codified roles in support of a slave economy, a patriarchal society, and an elaborate illusion of paternalism and virtue.

Struggling to adapt to an order that touted free wage labor and opportunities for cultural and material advancement, the modern African American southerners discussed in chapter 2 find themselves detained instead within a system still orchestrated to insure segregation, disenfranchisement, exploitation, and sacrifice. With little choice but to participate in an inimical economy, I argue, black southerners resort either to theft (Richard Wright), migration (R. Wright and William Attaway), mimicry of white mastery (Attaway and James Weldon Johnson), or suicidal retreats (R. Wright, Attaway, and Johnson). All of these fates constitute acts of narcissistic desperation and repetition; that is, in their attempts to own and value themselves in the twentieth century, African American southerners find themselves staring into mirrors that reflect back to them the methods and priorities of the white master. Put another way, the structures of modern capitalism seem orchestrated to benefit and enrich the same old characters all over again; as James Weldon Johnson's narrator in *The Autobiography of an Ex-Coloured Man* observes, "'Have a white skin, and all else may be added unto you'" (155). Claudia Tate explains that there is a long African American tradition of avoiding such psychoanalytic theorizing as "anathema" because of its tendency to pathologize the black family and underestimate social (i.e., racist) contributions to individual psyche formation (16).[56] Hortense J. Spillers agrees that "little or nothing in the intellectual history of African-Americans within the social and political context of the United States would suggest the effectiveness of a psychoanalytic discourse" (376); but she softens this stance by suggesting that such an approach, if properly contextualized, could aid in the pursuit of "ethical self-knowledge" (427). Postcolonial theory has done much to draw out the potential for a socially responsible psychoanalytic approach; indeed, in such contexts "ethical self-knowledge" often points disturbingly (and narcissistically) back to the self's desires, constructs, and calculations as conditioned by the master. Accordingly, my chapter 2 ends with a brief reading of Zora Neale Hurston's deceptively sweet short story, "The Gilded Six-Bits," and a caution that romantic notions of subordinating the evils of money to more fulfilling resources of love and community are shortsighted at best; neither Hurston nor any of the other writers in that chapter envisions a viable way to surmount the structures of privilege, exploitation, and dependency that delimit their worlds and restrict their opportunities and voices. The fetish of number emerges in the pages of these works repeatedly to taunt modern African American southerners with a world of prosperity offered to them with one hand and foreclosed by the other. Such prospects never stop being reifications of a void in the black southern experience, an invitation to use corrupt mechanisms in order to mediate a deep sense of loss that American postslavery market culture cannot yet compensate.

In a similar way, chapter 3 invites rereadings of three southern women writers traditionally considered to be—however modestly for their time and location—feminists: Frances Newman, Anita Loos, and Katherine Anne Porter. While these authors promote the principles of women's liberation, autonomy, and self-expression, none manages to harness an uncontaminated or effective means of self-possession divorced from their traditional roles and priorities in a hierarchical, sexist community. As Anne McClintock argues in *Imperial Leather*, "controlling women's sexuality, exalting maternity and breeding a virile race of empire-builders was widely perceived as the paramount means for controlling the health and wealth of the male imperial body" (47). While such imperatives are not always explicit directives in southern women's writing of the twentieth century, they nonetheless haunt even bold attempts to locate "health and wealth" in the female body and mind rather than those of her male oppressors. In their most fervent, savvy, and at times light-hearted quests to flout authority in favor of autonomy and self-fulfillment, these women calculate their way into a net loss of emotional destitution and sometimes literal physical wasting.

Despite the unprecedented and largely unpredicted prosperity of the contemporary Sun Belt South, the prospects and psychologies of its inhabitants deteriorated further in the post–World War II, post–civil rights era. Chapter 4 surveys the radical proliferation of narcissistic calculations in the midst of rapid industrial and economic growth, a paradox that highlights the failed promise of capitalism and the compensatory fetish of number and accumulation. By juxtaposing white and black, female and male, rich and poor southerners, I suggest that the rhetoric of loss, accumulation, and narcissistic isolation has become not just pervasive but increasingly disabling and pathological. In novels by Walker Percy, Alice Walker, and Dorothy Allison, characters wander without volition, memory, or companionship through the wasted, "bombed-out" landscapes of southern "progress," foreclosed from the apparent richness of that world in a way that suggests a totalizing lack of reality, substance, and fulfillment for southerners—indeed, for all Americans—regardless of class, race, or status. Following Baudrillard, I suggest that it is the structure of capitalism itself that has finally impoverished the contemporary southerner, who subsequently retreats in masochistic ways to false historical idylls and, in the failure of the fetish to persist and fulfill, to terms of personal, psychological depreciation. For the female characters in these novels, the vacancy of contemporary reality is symbolized in repeated references to self-mutilation, abuse, and physical emaciation. For Walker Percy's displaced neoaristocracy, the future holds a sense of permanent elite amnesia, an inability to connect emotionally with other human beings or the self, and a pathological desire to return to the safety and order of a mathematical world that is "as elegant as algebra."

At the end of chapter 4 I turn briefly to an issue that receives more sustained consideration in chapter 5: the lurking Native American presences in all three works that deepen and complicate the plights of the South's traditionally biracial subjects. These reminders of a precolonial culture underlie and disturb the mythology of autocthony and innocence upon which not just southern but American exceptionalism rests and depends. In the introduction to *Look Away!* Smith and Cohn describe southern studies itself as historically narcissistic, and encourage instead a turning outward of our critical gaze, "away from . . . nativist navel-gazing" (13). But what about looking within? In moving beyond the South's borders, I argue, the New Southern studies' transnational gaze obscures the Native American displacement and genocide at the very origins of this transcontinental New World narrative, avoiding altogether the Indians who predated its discourse and survive to testify in the contemporary South.[57] We need to begin to account for the parade of apparently extinct Indians resurfacing in the writings of present-day southerners like Walker Percy, Alice Walker, and Allison, among others. I read the Native influences emerging in these writers' works as reminders that the past as they know it, and particularly the democratic grandeur and economic prosperity upon which the region and the nation has been constructed, has been an elaborate artifice marked by glaring absences and omissions; by resurrecting the Indians at the occluded heart of not just the South's but of the nation's foundation, these subjects elicit an awareness of counternarratives and histories beneath both the plantation and capitalism's master chronicle, and they draw power from the dispossessed indigenous figures with whom they find an uncanny alliance.

Ultimately, however, these contemporary southerners are too preoccupied with their own crises of value for this historical awakening and cross-cultural association to do much good, and I argue that their ruminations revert again to narcissism as they subsume the Native experience in order to restore the self. In chapter 5, then, I turn attention to southeastern Indians themselves, acknowledging their vibrant survival in the present-day South, along with other ethnic and racial voices who have been silenced, erased, or made "zero" in the ruthless mathematics of the region's biracial economy. I explore works by the Choctaw Cherokee writer and critic Louis Owens and the Cherokee Appalachian poet and essayist Marilou Awiakta in the larger context of framing the voices of those occluded or exempt from the biracial economy of the South. In an effort to intervene in this persistently black-white monolith, I introduce these indigenous voices alongside the testimony of the Vietnamese American Lan Cao, whose novel *Monkey Bridge* reveals uncanny convergences between feudal and postwar U.S. South and Saigon. Examining the South from comparative and marginal Indian and immigrant perspectives helps us to see more accurately how the South's material and discursive legacy, in its insistence on distinctiveness and naturalness, obscures the "others" who trouble this narrative and the disturbing expanse of colonial histories that it resembles. At the end of chapter 5, I find it critical to return to the writing of African American southerners who, like these outsiders, attempt to rearticulate and reverse the terms of their depletion. In a devastatingly literal way, black writers confront the Atlanta child murder cases of the late 1970s and early 1980s, figuring the events as parables of the culture's existentially lost and missing, the exploited and the slain, and the elaborate political machinery invested in keeping the bodies quiet and making a black man publicly and dubiously bear the blame for crimes committed upon his own people. All of these writers endeavor to re-member not just the bodies of their cultures' victims but their own histories and communities as well, piecing back together the lives and narratives fragmented or effaced by the elaborate and exclusive mathematics of a violent order.

My title is drawn from a moment in Homi Bhabha's *Location of Culture*, a field-shaping work of postcolonial criticism that explores the crisis of subalternity and modernity broadly.[58] About subaltern narratives generally, he states hopefully:

> The aim of cultural difference is to rearticulate the sum of knowledge from the perspective of the signifying position of the minority that resists totalization—the repetition that will not return as the same, the minus-in-origin that results in political and discursive strategies where adding *to* does not add up but serves to disturb the calculation of power and knowledge, producing other spaces of subaltern signification. (162)

Impoverished literally and spiritually by their participation in an exploitative colonial economy, the southern writers I examine in this book all struggle to compensate for their "minus-in-origin" by either embracing old hegemonies or testing new iterations of selfhood. While these endeavors often result in more "repetition" than disruption, I, like Bhabha, leave open the possibility that the prevailing calculations of a master narrative might be resisted, disturbed, or re-written. Number can totalize, Bhabha cautions, but it can also subvert. As the duality of this project's title suggests, calculation has "disturbing" significance in imperial societies, but we need to begin searching for moments when subaltern writers themselves do the disturbing, finding new solutions to the calculations that divide and destroy them.

Chapter One

The Fetish of Surplus Value: Reconstructing the White Elite in Allen Tate, William Alexander Percy, William Faulkner, and Thomas Wolfe

> *A family owning one hundred slaves of varying ages, sex and skills easily had an investment of one hundred thousand dollars in a readily marketable product. On the day the Civil War ended, this value became zero.*
> E. GREY DIMOND AND HERMAN M. HATTAWAY,
> LETTERS FROM FOREST PLACE

Images of the modern South have long featured conservative white gentlemen in Sunday best whose genteel breeding and humane values starkly oppose the crass materialism of northern industrialism and finance capitalism. Such fictions tend to attach themselves to antebellum idylls and the cataclysm of Civil War; when they do engage the twentieth-century context, it is often to dramatize how the Old South's befuddled descendants navigate a coldly calculating, inimical modern economy that operates on the principles of competition and ascent rather than natural aristocracy and automatic privilege.[1] As a counterpoint to the unscrupulous mechanics of market capitalism, the antebellum myth, complete with its racial hierarchies, needed to be refigured as benevolent, refined, and anticommercial; novels (and subsequently films) with the broadest appeal included Civil War epics like Margaret Mitchell's *Gone with the Wind*, which "depicted a cohesive nineteenth-century South that, in its hierarchical but mutually binding interracial culture, provided precisely the sustaining anticapitalist values often called for in contemporary discourse" (52). While many of the South's modern writers harbored Agrarian

27

sympathies, their works often betray material anxieties of a much more ambivalent order; that is, for the white elite and those ambivalent in-between classes, capitalism offers an opportunity for accumulation and restoration that is, in fact, compatible with the plantation's obsolete, antebellum priorities. In direct response to this crisis, an abundance of numerical metaphors and quantifying pathologies for human identity and worth emerges in the psyches and vocabularies of the white elite. Such revelations seem at times conscious and reflective, and are often bitter and hungry; at other moments, however, these writers evince only a dawning recognition that the modern systems of capital suppressing them are precisely the technologies that have always already colonized the elite southern experience.

After the Civil War and the subsequent dismantling of chattel slavery, slaveholders lost their primary source of "self-amplification." As one historian puts it, the emancipated slave's market value suddenly became "zero" (Dimond and Hattaway xvii); with the plantation ledgers thus cleared, the master's literal worth and figurative sense of position and authority would (theoretically) diminish as well. Yet a new ledger of value making soon emerged to take its place. In "The Hind Tit," Andrew Nelson Lytle argues that the introduction of capitalist methodologies into the South's agrarian arcadia will have disastrous consequences: "It is the numbering of a farm's resources . . . and as the only reason to number them is to turn them into cash . . . the agrarian South is bound to go when the first page is turned and the first mark crosses the ledger" (*I'll Take My Stand* 234). Yet it takes a significant amount of repression to presume that ledgers were not commonplace in the practice of recording the array of a plantation's "resources," the most vital of which was its chattel. Still, it behooves white southerners to imagine that the cruelties of numbering and converting goods into cash supplanted a kinder, more humane system; Lytle's thesis can be explained partly by a sense of regional foreclosure, captured in the image of the "hind tit": he and his fellow Agrarians are simply tired of being relegated to the back of the litter, suckling last and least at the hind tit of American capitalism's fat, nurturing sow.

As a largely rural, agrarian periphery of production and labor within a dominant national economy, the South of the early twentieth century was still attempting to emerge from the crippling dependency of Reconstruction, in which the South was regarded as a domestic colony: "Lacking capital, Southerners became foremen and workers for Northern masters, and farmers were even further removed from the lines of power and wealth" (Daniel, *Standing at the Crossroads* 3). This condition of dependency was not new to modern southerners but had, as Joseph J. Persky explains, long characterized the national system of "'unequal exchange' between metropolis and periphery" (2). In this sense, and perhaps only in this sense, we may see the South's former slaveholders as "colonized" individuals suffering the psychological effects of servility and exploitation.[2] As

Jack Temple Kirby argues in *Rural Worlds Lost*, even by 1920 much of the South remained exactly as (or, in some ways, worse than) it had been in 1870, plagued by neoplantation sharecropping, exhausted soil, boll weevil infestations, and debilitating price gouging (xiv–xv). Bereft and subjugated by a national economy, southerners seem anxious to disavow capitalism's inequities while cashing in on its profits—material and otherwise. Thus, this chapter is not simply about the South's traditional elite such as Allen Tate and William Alexander Percy, but also its ambivalent, in-between figures like William Faulkner and Thomas Wolfe, who find themselves poised ambiguously amid a lost order of white privilege and a new world of economic opportunity. Indeed, such figures often dramatize in their own works and consciousness the dialectic between the Old South and the New, and between northern progress and southern struggle. When numbers and figures emerge in the texts of these reluctant modern southerners, then, they are heavy with ambivalence: foremost is a cultivated fear of converting the South's goods—and presumably also its people—into cash, a process that relegates even the region's white elite to positions of dependency and subjection. Yet increasingly, these modern writers thus betray their fear that such vulnerability would destroy the ledger's neoaristocratic logic, whereby landowners had long achieved virtually automatic solvency and integrity at the terrible cost of the others over whom they measured, enriched, and elevated themselves. As Walter Johnson points out, "the buyers imagine the slave market as a vehicle of self-amplification . . . they strip, question, and discipline the enslaved people through whom their imagined identities become literal" (15). When white southerners were placed in the outrageous position of subservience, their methods for recuperation and recompense naturally returned to the priorities of slavery and the principles of automatic ascendancy on the basis of race and gender. The Jim Crow laws of the 1880s and 1890s, which overtook the South in the form of widespread segregation well into the twentieth century, offered a mechanism for reinstituting racial and economic order in a region that struggled to get back on its feet.[3] In this chapter's readings, white male writers from various positions on the social spectrum converge in their recourse to racial hierarchy as a means to secure not just social but economic mastery; and in their hunger for the fetish of number, they evince a desire for the mechanisms of capitalist ascent that reveal more about the cruel calculus of plantation math than they can perhaps imagine or intend.

"The World Where People Counted and Added Things": From Slavery to Capitalism

One of the most prominent Agrarians to emerge from the group responsible for *I'll Take My Stand* was the young Kentucky native and Vanderbilt graduate

Allen Tate. Widely recognized for his culturally conservative essays, biographies of Confederate heroes Stonewall Jackson and Jefferson Davis, and modernist poetry (in particular, his 1928 "Ode to the Confederate Dead"), he also published one novel, *The Fathers*, in 1938. Neither the poems nor the novel has received significant critical attention in recent years; indeed, many of his works are now out of print, and as David Yezzi notes, Tate is "simply not part of the contemporary discussion." The reason for this neglect seems in part a negative judgment on his artistry, and in larger part a perception that his work rather uncritically and unfashionably attaches itself to a "bygone South" that academics have labored to leave behind (Yezzi). Yet Tate's alliance with Agrarianism and its literary critical offshoot, the New Criticism, is not the end of the story, nor are his sympathies without ambiguity and ambivalence: *The Fathers* in particular seems to indicate not so much a rejection of modern America's market culture as much as a fearful fascination with its tantalizing energy and promises; moreover, like other writers of the period, Tate's reluctant engagement with capitalism's perversions reveals just how familiar and appealing its operations are to these neoaristocrats.

Set in 1860 Virginia, in an embattled society on the brink of Civil War and social ruin, Tate's novel is narrated from the distance of half a century by sixty-five-year-old Lacy Buchan. In both authorial and narratorial remove, the novel is a retrospective, regretful look at the world of squandered gentility and aristocracy, an exercise in ironic mourning for a lost way of life. The aging Buchan articulates as much in an opening apologia:

> Is it not something to tell, when a score of people whom I knew and loved . . . either out of violence in themselves or the times, or out of some misery or shame, scattered into the new life of the modern age where they cannot even find themselves? Why cannot life change without tangling the lives of innocent persons? Why do innocent persons cease their innocence and become violent and evil in themselves that such great changes may take place? (5)

Throughout *The Fathers*, Tate seeks to explore the demise of an aristocratic family whose "innocent" lives become fragmented and tainted by the intrusion of an alienating "modern age." Buchan's lament echoes Tate's own agrarian nostalgia, so much so that biographer Thomas Underwood deems Tate's novel a thinly veiled effort to vindicate his own Virginia ancestors and their fall from economic prominence: "Haunted by the ghost of his own mother and her family, Tate worked on the novel like a man possessed" (269).

The major rift in the novel occurs between two families—the aristocratic Buchans and the modern capitalist Poseys—and is emblematic of the collision of antagonistic social orders. Significantly, as Richard King points out, it is not just the Buchans but the Posey family that is also steeped in tradition, "an old

Maryland family, one which is 'more refined . . . but less civilized' than Lacy's. We learn significantly that George's father died early and that George was a 'mother's boy'; and thus he lacked anyone to master his energies and give them form. He is always 'elsewhere' and 'without people or place.' The result is that George inadvertently destroys whatever he touches" (*Southern Renaissance* 108). While economics are hardly mentioned, it is the shift in the family fortunes that precipitates a loss of patriarchal order; concomitantly, what fades is geographical and ancestral rootedness—he is "elsewhere" and "without people or place." George's corruption, as we will soon see, is in his sacrilegious conflation of capitalism and paternalism, the two realms that aristocratic southerners labored most to polarize; yet for all this, he is also a dangerously seductive figure. His ambivalence perfectly mirrors the perilous desires of the modern South's elite in crisis: while unseated aristocrats might desire the wealth of the new order, they want none of the disgrace of participating in its corrupt operations.

A scene early in the novel establishes fifteen-year-old Lacy's dawning recognition that his father's genteel, paternalistic ways are on the verge of being replaced by this inimical economy. From a window high above the yard, he watches one of the family's many slaves heading brazenly toward the front of the house with an armload of firewood; while Lacy objects to this untoward behavior—"'He's carrying it to the front door,' I said"—his older brother Semmes simply replies, "'It don't make any difference where he totes it. . . . Twenty negroes are too many for this place'" (19). What Semmes acknowledges here is an utterly foreign concept to Lacy, who believes that "some people had negroes as naturally as others did not, that it was all chance" (19). Semmes, however, equates the work of these black bodies with the family's production and profit, exposing to Lacy the glaring imbalance in the books: "Good God, boy, look around you—there hasn't been any tobacco in the barns for nearly ten years. And how much corn do you think papa makes? Fifteen bushels to the acre!" (20). In one swift calculation, Lacy's universe utterly changes, and he transitions abruptly from a space of paternalism and natural aristocracy to "the world where people counted and added things, the first intrusion of change into my consciousness, and I only dimly knew what it meant" (19). As the grammar here makes clear, it is not simply Lacy's consciousness that has "changed," matured, or awakened to a knowledge of slavery's economic character; rather it is the "change" taking place in the world beyond that has intruded upon his consciousness and his family's affairs, altering the value of his father's possessions and rendering them something to be counted and calculated. Encoded also in this scene is the fear that the negroes themselves may now be counting, too: Semmes uses the word "tote" to refer to the black man carrying wood—not the first nor the most natural descriptor for this action—which has a secondary meaning of "total" or "sum"; used as a verb, it also connotes the related "tot," meaning to add or total up a sum, and in accounting terminology means "to make a note against a name in a list or a sum or item in an account" (OED). Given that slaves themselves constituted the items in a plantation's accounts, powerless over the figures of their own reckoning, the reversal of agency here—the negro "toting" in the wrong place—clearly portends the dangerous freedom heralded by the new capitalist order.

Tate seems to want us to believe that individuals who never had to worry about reckoning accounts must suddenly do so now, while the human quantities once comprising a slaveholder's worth have also won entry into the same calculus of advancement. The shock of conversion jars Lacy so harshly because he has until now professed to be ignorant of slaves as owned "things"; instead, they are mere presences in his world who serve the family by "chance" and by nature rather than by compulsion or hegemony. Interestingly, the impending Civil War is what shatters his innocence: for what seems to be the first time, the family's looming misfortunes alert him to the surplus value around him. In effect, by giving us Lacy's untainted gaze, Tate attempts to show a compassionate order made cold and calculating by emancipation rather than slavery itself. Mr. Buchan refuses to sell his surplus slaves, even though he has "too many" for his estate's needs, out of a sense of paternalistic duty on the one hand and, on the other, a suppressed desire to preserve an illusion of material comfort. This is precisely what Max Weber would describe as an "irrational" feature of slave economies: "the master cannot adjust the size of his labor force in accordance with business fluctuations. In particular, efficiency cannot readily be attained through the manipulation of the labor force if sentiment, custom, or community pressure makes separation of families difficult" (paraphrased by Genovese in *Political Economy of Slavery* 16).

In stark contrast, George Posey, the renegade capitalist and Mr. Buchan's foil in *The Fathers*, readily sells his own half-black brother in order to reap a needed profit, informing his mulatto sibling that he represents "'liquid capital'" (54). Where the Buchans embody an embattled gentility and aristocracy, Posey heralds the intrusion of disastrous commercial priorities. Yet it cannot escape us that Posey plays the part of slavedealer perfectly, suggesting that his market instincts derive specifically from plantation principles. Nonetheless, Tate's dichotomous view clearly encourages us to believe that Posey has been perverted into such behavior by a cold entrepreneurial calculus utterly inimical to the Buchan brand of paternalism, as Mr. Buchan would never deign to sell his own slaves. As Radcliffe Squires suggests, Posey "is good at 'business' but does not know the 'value' of anything"; presumably more respectable is Mr. Buchan, whom we might say is terrible at "business" but at least knows the worth of things—that is, people and family, white, black, or mulatto. Dangerously deluded though this appraisal may be, it highlights the perforated notions of "value" as they mark the gulf between mercantilism and aristocracy (138).

Dazzled and, like so many around him, seduced by the new order that George Posey represents, Lacy's naive detachment from historical knowledge is figured as the problem of the New South: as Tate himself explained to his friend and fellow poet John Peal Bishop, Lacy embodies "'the Virginian lack of historical perspective—a lack that permits him to see in George Posey mystery and excitement; whereas you and I know that Posey is only the American dream, which you've often called the American nightmare. I hope my moral is clear—that the Dream is not naïve and vital, but disorderly, coming out of a background of decadence'" (Underwood 267). The Buchans could just as easily become Poseys, Tate's moral suggests, if young men like Lacy do not use the lessons of history and gentility to expunge calculating desires and dangerous "decadence" from true nobility. Caught between Posey's new world of counting and adding and his own heritage of humanism and decorum, Lacy is left to find a path into the New South that the Civil War would usher in. In the novel's closing scene, he vows dramatically to finish the work of the man he loves "more than I love any man" (306); but just who that man is, ultimately, remains ambiguous. The person he professes such great devotion to is identified only as "he," a man who could be George as he gallops off into the sunset at that very moment; or it may instead be Lacy's father, recently killed but invoked in Lacy's memory at this key moment. Indeed, of the many attempts to interpret the novel's title, critics most commonly conjecture that Lacy's central crisis lies in choosing which of his two "father" figures—his actual paternal figure or George Posey—he will follow into his and the South's future.

But just a few pages earlier, after a visitation from his dead grandfather, Lacy reflects on a broader ancestry and tradition: "The house, the big sugar tree, the back gallery, papa's affectionate glance were all that I was; under the chestnut tree was all that I would be" (281). This revelation, paired with Tate's commitment to historical perspective, indicates that Lacy does ultimately find his first allegiance to his father and the family honor that he represents. In choosing thus, he rejects not only capitalism but all labor-centered notions of value, adopting instead an attitude of natural aristocracy: "The individual quality of a man was bound up with his kin and the 'places' where they lived.... 'Class' consisted solely of a certain code of behavior. Even years later, I am always a little amazed to hear a man described as the coal man or the steel man or the plate-glass man, descriptions of people after the way they make their money, not after their manner of life" (135). Even a half century removed from emancipation, Lacy still goes reluctantly and perplexedly into that new world of counting and adding, of capitalist relations and identities rooted in work and profit margins. The older Lacy's studied resistance perhaps brings us closer to Tate's own modern ambivalence, wherein "money" is embraced only inasmuch as it restores the true "value" of aristocratic tradition; encumbered by the calculating priorities of this system, Tate's prose uncannily reveals how money-driven these elite values always were.

In order to conceal this complicity, the true character of slavery's perverse accounting needed to be mystified and subsumed by assertions of humanism and "true" value. Déclassé aristocrats often claim proudly that their prosperity had and still has little to do with cash. William Alexander Percy, for example, writes economics out of the equation for nobility in his autobiography *Lanterns on the Levee*, which is generally dismissed for its patronizing racism but is, as Scott Romine contests, "interesting precisely for that reason; perhaps more than any other single text, Percy's work registers and attempts to resolve the contradictions of southern paternalism" (113–14). Despite the fact that true racial custodianship is by now "a distant memory" even in the lingering neoplantation structure of Percy's Deep South (Romine 112), Percy works vigorously to reinject the terms of this arcadian social order into his text. First, compatible with Tate's rejection of labor in his definition of "class," Percy proposes a completely nonmaterial coordinate for assessing social worth: "No class or individual with us has ever known riches," he claims (24); but Percy's "us" is, it turns out, an elite and exclusive group of neoaristocrats who thrive on blaspheming the new modern commercialism and constructing a vision of the plantation past curiously absent of financial prosperity.[4] Like Tate, Percy recoils from the notion of being equated with the value of his own or anyone else's labor: "maybe in time someone will pay us more for our cotton than we spend making it," he fantasizes (24). Yet at the same time that he disavows both money and work, he evinces a bitter antagonism toward those who seem to be getting more than they deserve and a tacit desire to divorce earned wages from inherent capital—the latter being naturally greater than the former. His dreams of recompense exceed mere exchange, replaced by a myth of surplus value.

This anticapitalist fantasy is more than mere acquisitive wistfulness: indeed, it reaches deliberately beyond the South's condition of economic subjugation and returns to the practice of antebellum slavery wherein slaveholders' profits inherently exceeded their own labor and also outpaced their rate of investment. That is, while a requisite number of field slaves needed to be purchased, a slaveholder could and did easily encourage the multiplication of his possessions as they mingled and reproduced among themselves (and, not infrequently, with male members of the white master's family). The blacks who used to labor in the fields and enrich a thriving leisure class Percy now appraises as idle, teeming, and dangerous. During the devastating flood of 1927 (when Percy serves as chairman of the Red Cross), he viciously censures the local Negroes with the claim that "we served you with our money and our brains and our strength and, for all that we did, no one of us received one penny. . . . During all this time you Negroes did nothing, nothing for yourselves or for us" (267). The rhetoric of slavery here is clear, and so is the uncomfortable reversal of positions from Percy's perspective; his moral, intellectual, and physical superiority is dangled as a method of suggesting inherent supremacy, but with unsatisfying returns on his investment. He stubbornly clings to the notion that he deserves more, demanding a material return from the blacks whom the white townspeople have supported financially. But the blacks did "nothing, nothing" for themselves or for the whites, he claims. At least by establishing the profound dependence of the inferior black on the hierarchically superior white, Percy restores to his class a sense of purpose and position. In this moment of paternalism, he openly congratulates himself for his generous service to these shiftless hordes; yet the desire for recompense—in excess of, in fact utterly divorced from, market value—haunts these moments. The intimate union of white and black capital lingers in the modern world of market relations, perilously leading, as Richard Godden suggests, "to the disabling insight that a white master's body is little more than a receptacle for appropriated black property" (4).

The desire for compensation as expressed in these terms harkens suggestively back to a precapitalist, plantation idyll that laboriously concealed its relationship to commercial interests. In their efforts to dissociate class and character from the tawdry materialism of the New South, white southerners inevitably find themselves tangled up in it—and not simply because the forces of modern, northern capitalism offer restitution of a satisfying sort, but also because (as many of these writers come slowly to realize) capitalism's logic is a mathematics they can understand. As much as Tate's young southerner resists immersion in the world of "counting and adding" and Percy denies the primacy of bottom lines over genealogical ones, these other dislocated aristocrats find themselves in a seemingly new calculus of orientation and hierarchy, anxiously quantifying and measuring the worth of their own persons and seeking to engineer a quotient of surplus value that will restore them.

More and more, though, what throws these equations off kilter is the loss of enforced racial organization after emancipation, and the dramatic mobility that characterizes American capitalism and offers the illusion that anyone who works hard might ascend the class scale. The discomfort William Alexander Percy experiences at this particular historical moment derives from the increasing realization that "for the aristocrats, history assumes the form of devolution; for the poor whites, ascendancy" (Romine 116). Indeed, increasingly blacks are being outnumbered in the South, Percy claims, by the poor whites who "so throve and increased" in certain Delta counties that they changed the entire landscape and culture of those regions; Percy's royal "we" as it refers to a homogeneous white community strains under the unpalatable ascension of these hordes. His tacit desire to have more—which is distinguished viscerally from any desire to pull any other pairs of dirty bootstraps up with him—is palpable as he "rhetorically obliterates the role played by capital within the community, which he is eager to portray as an organic social order rather than one based on economic hierarchy" (Romine 117). The cracks in Percy's paternalistic facade come precisely at those moments when his economic fears overtake his racial anxieties. The solution to this problem for Percy and others like him is to reinstate automatic white privilege and accumulation, racial subordination, and the easy mathematics of plantation efficiency.

There are really three sorts of people in the Delta as Percy sees it: "aristocrats gone to seed, poor whites on the make, [and] Negroes convinced mere living is good" (23). In order to revive the decaying elite, the "poor white on the make" must be relegated to a position of categorical subjection; that is, he must be in a sense lumped in with the black proletariat. Percy states unequivocally that elite whites and the working class (black and white) are inherently dissimilar, "aliens of all sorts that blend or curdle" (23). Of the three groups he identifies, Percy dismisses out of hand the "poor whites" whose existence he desires neither to fathom nor acknowledge; only Negroes are "worth talking about" because they are certain, calculable, and they insure a ready balance against which the white can steady himself. Whites of lesser stations simply cannot commune on the racial problem, Percy theorizes, because they "through poverty, lack of inheritance, and ignorance misunderstand and dislike the Negro," while the elite "by training and opportunity feel themselves his friend and protector" (227). Paternalism renders this simple racial dichotomy not only natural but beneficial; the racial antagonism that remains between whites and blacks laboring under similar conditions of poverty and exploitation is something Percy exorcises thoroughly from his anachronistic vision. Yet powerful enmity boiled between white and black tenant farmers, as we will witness more vividly in the following chapter. Even into the 1950s and 1960s, the working-class white writer Rick Bragg remembers, it remained a "time when a young man in a baggy suit and slicked down hair stood spraddle-legged in the crossroads of history and talked hot and mean about the colored, giving my poor and desperate people a reason to feel superior to somebody, to anybody" (xvii). Caught within the dynamics of a system where racial privilege is not awarded on the basis of color but rather on nebulous and hostile notions of "class," poor whites throughout the twentieth century struggled in often racist ways to work themselves out of the demotion inflicted upon them by elite white anxieties.[5]

Yet the problem of the poor white becomes very simply, under capitalism, the barely concealed, irrepressible problem of the devolving aristocrat. To poor whites, capitalism signaled opportunity but also fierce rivalry and intense racial antagonism against the blacks whom they struggled alongside and with whom they now shared a simple class affiliation. In 1938, a U.S. Emergency Council Report documents, "Approximately half of the sharecroppers are white, living under economic conditions almost identical with those of Negro sharecroppers" (46). Indeed, the economic mobility of these whites was impeded because they were competing with a continued system of "black slavery" that limited the need for white farmhands (M. Smith 39). As Arthur Raper put it bluntly, "'Cropper farming . . . is a Negro institution'" (qtd. in Kirby 232). In "The Briar Patch" Robert Penn Warren confirms the commonly held belief that "the fates of the 'poor white' and the negro are linked in a single tether. The well-being and adjustment of one depends on that of the other" (*I'll Take My Stand* 259). By forcing these two struggling and antagonistic groups into the same position of denigration, elite whites could secure their own position above both.

The Fetish of Surplus Value; or, What the Ledgers Say

In her influential study of Faulkner's class anxieties, Myra Jehlen agrees that both the neoaristocracy and the striving white poor "rightly viewed the other as a threat to its survival" and suggests that William Faulkner "was heir to both of these viewpoints and unable fully to approve either one" (21).[6] He certainly seems more intrigued by the suffering of the latter: families like the Compsons, who have fallen from histories of leisure and wealth, are less common in Faulkner's corpus than common folks trying desperately to work their way up. He was simply, he maintained, more fascinated by the colorful hill folk who "'made their own whiskey from their own corn and . . . fought over elections and settled their own disputes'" (393). Such figures arguably receive the most sustained attention in Faulkner's work, populating the sidelines and backdrops of all of his major novels and preoccupying him completely in the trilogy of the upwardly mobile redneck clan, the Snopeses (*The Hamlet*, *The Town*, and *The Mansion*). As Theresa Towner has argued, these later novels receive scant critical attention but in fact expose some of his most mature and complicated reflections on not just class but race.[7] The Snopeses' saga is primarily about social ascent, which Jehlen suggests is the underlying focus of Faulkner's entire career; as Don H. Doyle explains in *Faulkner's County*,

> These poor white country people were the first subjects he explored when he began writing about Yoknapatawpha County, and he returned to them again and again. He explored their inner psychology of class and racial resentment and the social and

historical context that gave rise to their "impotent rage." Faulkner seemed most interested in the alternative responses to poor white resentment, some choosing violent acts of revenge, others a dogged ambition to escape the plight of their class, to rise and emulate their social superiors. (293)

Part of a wholly "imperialized people," as Joel Williamson notes, southern whites face one another across a chasm of cultural and economic difference that approximates that of a racial divide. In the attempt to "emulate" aristocratic others, poor whites enact Bhabha's concept of "mimicry," the self's appropriation of otherness "as it visualizes power," meanwhile destroying "narcissistic authority through the repetitious slippage of difference and desire" (90).[8] In other words, in Faulkner's attention to the ambitions of poor whites, he exposes the tenuousness of white narcissistic mastery generally and deepens our notions of how race and oppression are figured in his work—a protracted "story of the collective politicization of class resentment and racial anger" simultaneously (D. Doyle 296).

Late in William Faulkner's *The Sound and the Fury*, Jason Compson's boss accuses him of embezzling money from his own family: "'A man never gets anywhere,'" Earl warns him, "'if fact and his ledgers dont square'" (229). Jason's bitter defensiveness and sense of entitlement produce a skewed sense of moral rectitude that allows him to condone his dishonest bookkeeping; but elsewhere in Faulkner's works, instances of fatally botched accounts signify more encompassing crises of value in the scrupulous New South. Richard Godden and Noel Polk have demonstrated brilliantly—by way of a fifty-nine-page explication of the ledger entries in *Go Down, Moses*—that the ledgers in Faulkner do, indeed, matter. The McCaslin family's "facts" become, under Godden and Polk's scrutiny, "cryptic" recordings filled with "abbreviation and aporia," proffering meanings that are not absolute but "necessarily provisional" and perhaps "uninterpretable" (339, 359). But for Isaac McCaslin as well as Jason, such hindrances do not preclude the desire for definitive, self-enriching products—ones that might exalt Ike's sense of personal honor as surely as they swell Jason's tightly guarded pockets. In the postplantation South, the ledgers are no longer operative mechanisms of a fiscal order, but residues of what their obsolescence signifies: the certainty of hierarchy under slavery, the moral satisfaction of balance, and the allure of profit by engineering surplus value. At the same time, the ledgers announce the succession of a mercantile order associated with northern industrial interests and exclusions that incites Jason's representative sense of divestment and distrust. Faulkner's southerners respond to this historical double bind in compromised attempts to balance the books: while Jason might doctor his ledgers to produce a compensatory excess, Ike overreads the account-book "facts" that will inflate his moral superiority.[9]

Between these familiar yet obverse objectives stands a single textual stratagem: the ledger. Rather than unearthing all of the suppressed histories and traumas that the ledgers themselves might disclose, as Godden and Polk's reading encourages, it seems crucial instead to determine what the instrument of the ledger itself signifies in Faulkner's New South. That is, we should dwell not so much on what the ledgers say, but on what Faulkner's characters ask them to accomplish. In an age of expanding market relations on a global scale, the modern South famously retreated into its own sense of Agrarian nobility and exceptionalism. Yet the ledger, a relic dating from the earliest iterations of British and European mercantilism, registers its relevance to both modern commercial practice and its anomalous perversions under chattel slavery.[10] An encumbered symbol, it holds in purposeful collision the two social orders disgruntled New Southerners labored most to polarize. Throughout Faulkner's novels, the ledger emerges irrepressibly to negotiate these antagonisms, disclosing its persistent entanglement with the twin objects of race and economics.[11] Kevin Railey locates Faulkner's compromise in a notion of "natural aristocracy" wherein individuals are judged by their ethical rather than material superiority, a quality conveniently innate to the social elite. Yet Faulkner's class loyalties seem complicated by a growing awareness of America's persistently colonial culture. One of the most circulated clichés in Faulkner studies is his admission that "the past is never past," and his work tacitly unveils a South still very much shackled to an archipelago of occluded histories. In keeping with the transnational cues of both American and southern studies, Faulkner's best critics—John T. Matthews, George Handley, Deborah Cohn, and others—are beginning to excavate Faulkner and the South's connection to other New World terrains and histories.[12] The ubiquitous ledger trope suggests another conduit by which Faulkner registers not only an awareness of a traumatic colonial legacy but also, because of the capital culture the ledger signifies, a chilling recognition that the plantation's priorities carry over into the New South's global economic exchanges, that the principles of exclusion, privilege, and contrivance encumber the national "free" market system as trenchantly as mercantilist savvy dominated the "humanist" order of chattel slavery. Burdened by a regional sense of expropriation and foreclosure, Faulkner's novels witness again and again the doom of recognition that not only is the past never past, but the postcolonial is far from postcolonial.[13] More than anachronism, more than encrypted historical "accounts," the revenants of the ledger in fact mark a neo-imperial order unable to dispense with the imperatives of a perverse, racially exploitative economic precedent. In their troubling returns, the ledgers constitute a fetish of compensation and restoration, an irrepressible enunciation of the return—*with interest*—of the indomitable master class.

Beyond the actual commissary records that are the centerpiece of *Go Down,*

Moses or the diurnal, double-columned fixations of Jason Compson, the ledgers become unmoored from their historical and textual origins to function like free radicals in the southern body: the language of quantification infects the racially interpellated body of Joe Christmas, paralyzes the vulnerable ascendancy of Thomas Sutpen, and haunts the tormented, romantic Quentin. The instantiation of what I call a calculating discourse infiltrates not just Faulkner's writing but southern discourse more generally, as the recourse to precise numbers and figures in the wake of accounting signify a way to validate social facts as well as gentlemanly honor and "credit." When Jason's boss insists that a good man's "fact and his ledgers" must "square," he echoes a widespread conviction in genteel society that "moral rectitude . . . was signified by the balance and harmony so prominent in the double-entry ledger" and so cherished by God (Poovey 11). In a more literal and opprobrious migration, the ledgers also speak from the haunted soil of other New World terrains, testifying to the vestiges of colonial trauma in a continuous line from Haiti to Yoknapatawpha and back.[14] These are the moments, we shall see, when the calculations break down, when the evasions and exclusions of the ledger become clear, and when the despair of modernity's global, imperial entanglements fatally unsettles Faulkner's most ambitious characters.

Perhaps the most prominent of these strivers is *Absalom, Absalom!*'s protagonist Thomas Sutpen, known to many critics as the antebellum Flem Snopes (D. Doyle 294).[15] Sutpen is a poor Appalachian white "on the make" certain to strike a hostile chord in the beleaguered New South.[16] As the young son of an indigent tenant farmer, Sutpen's inspiration to ascend occurs in a moment of racial sublimation at the front door of the wealthy white planter's house, where he is rebuffed by a Negro servant who orders him to the slave entrance around back (184–88). Sutpen's shock of racial degradation forces him to confront his debased position within the South's social hierarchy as a white whose landless status renders him someone a slave might look down upon with impunity. He combats this debasement with an ambitious "design" to erect his own plantation and dynasty, and to elevate himself to mastery by careful economic and mathematical reckoning.[17] These calculations typify Sutpen's ledgerlike mentality: he manufactures a marriage, a house, children, and a social reputation out of carefully planned sums and equations. But the uninitiated Sutpen must first be schooled in what are to him, by birth, unnatural methods: his first arithmetic lessons are baffling, incompatible with his very nature. While he remembers that his "blood . . . forbade him to condescend to memorize dry sums," noticeably, his blood *does* "permit him to listen when the teacher read aloud [about the West Indies]" (195). As John Matthews has persuasively argued, Haiti represents a periphery of colonial trauma that white southerners avoid assimilating as an adjunct to the plantation South ("Recalling the West Indies"). Part of this process of fetishization, I would add, is Sutpen's eagerness to veil any interest in numbers—and, by extension, economic figures—with these more romantic, exotic narratives. He listens innocently but intently to his teacher's stories about the West Indies, not yet knowing that "I was equipping myself better for what I should later *design* to do than if I had learned all the addition and subtraction in the book" (195, emphasis added). While his desire to segregate these sites of imperial pedagogy signifies a commitment to protecting American exceptionalism and innocence, Sutpen soon learns that dry calculations are in fact the very language of these ominous Caribbean lessons. He adds to his design a wife, the daughter of a Haitian sugar planter, but learns too late of her occluded racial heritage; outraged, he registers her in his accounts as a flaw who must be subtracted: at first an "unknown quantity," and then a dark "factor" not "adjunctive or incremental to the design" he has set out to accomplish (312, 194).

Such a miscalculation will haunt and in fact duplicate itself over the remainder of Sutpen's attempts to achieve white mastery. As he admits uncannily from the start, it is his own tainted "blood" that prevents him from absorbing the arithmetic lessons in school and presumably from accomplishing his presumptuous design—he literally cannot master the ledger.[18] His first attempt a miserable failure, he returns from Haiti and sets to building his plantation anyway; accordingly, he converts his own body into a kind of ledger of exacting accounts: he spends thriftily and consumes food and drink frugally, "with a sort of sparing calculation as though keeping mentally . . . a sort of balance of spiritual solvency" (40). Yet such solvency connotes not just equilibrium but also a "dissolving" and "disintegrating" effect.[19] He clings to "his code of logic and morality, his formula and recipe of fact and deduction" but the "balanced sum and product declined, refused to swim or even float" (275). His wife is not, as he believes, a negation of his design as much as a reification of his own innate deficiency. That the mixed-blood Bon is the yield of this disastrous union only heightens the sense that his shortfall cannot be fractioned away but will go on reproducing itself. Bon is, quite literally, a product of Sutpen's botched books.

And yet Bon is his father's son; in a stunning textual moment, he embodies the catastrophic delusion of compensatory bookkeeping. Sutpen takes a proper white wife, who produces an unblemished son, Henry; this correction negates the error that was Bon. We know that this brotherly sum does not "swim or float" either, but instead engages in a murderous duel. Before the clash, however, and even prior to learning that Bon is his half-brother, Henry is enchanted by the mysterious Bon. Spellbound, he confesses, "you give me two and two and you tell me it makes five and it does make five" (94). Read in the context of Sutpen's ledgers, the calculation is telling: the miscegenated son inflates the product of a simple arithmetic problem, effortlessly convincing his white rival that his math is indeed correct, that "five" might conceivably replace "four." As Bhabha hopes, the "supplementary strategy suggests that adding 'to' need not 'add up' but may disturb the calculation" (155). By such rules, surplus value can be added to the simple product, a return with interest for what has been debited through racial or class accounting; he can make the product of two plus two something more than mandated without having to "show the work"—a veritable aristocrat's dream, much like the one William Alexander Percy harbors.[20]

But is this Bon's math or Sutpen's? Is it the calculation of the decadent black son or that of the aspirant white master who controls the books and covets their increase? Either way, Faulkner drives home the point: such fabrications are as ineffectual from a black man's lips as a poor white impostor's pen. The extravagant, dangerous Bon is the one who is eventually silenced in the text, not the innocently and temporarily duped Henry. The white heir—vessel and hope of Sutpen's continuing order—seems to welcome the solution to Bon's innovative arithmetic; but by the end of the book, he lies wasted on a deathbed, replacing Bon's "five" with the same "*four years*" repeated over and over again in a mantra of futility (298). Henry expires knowing that "revenge could not compensate him" (274); neither can Sutpen's "payback" for his original outrage at the planter's door balance out the minus-in-origin that marks his birth.[21] He is excluded from the ledger entirely, an expulsion mirrored by Sutpen's unexpected correlative: the ever-diminishing Rosa Coldfield who knows she will never be a wealthy planter's wife because she is not, by birth, a wealthy planter's daughter. This lament fuels her own sentimental, poetic laments scribbled on "the *backsides* of the pages within an old account book" from her father's store (137, emphasis added). The substitution of a merchant's commissary book for a planter's ledger indicates powerfully that the South's new, commercial accounting simply subsumes the tenacious plantation code belatedly excluding the likes of the Coldfields and the Sutpens.[22] The account book Rosa inscribes harbors these conflicted calculations, but Rosa rejects both the order that precludes her and the one that stymies her by recording her unspent desires only on the "backsides" of the ledger pages.

Back in Haiti, Sutpen crucially overlooked his opportunity to learn what Rosa seems to know. On the plantation that he oversees, he initially observes

> a soil manured with black blood from two hundred years of oppression and exploitation until it sprang with an incredible paradox of peaceful greenery and crimson flowers and sugar cane sapling . . . valuable pound for pound almost with silver ore, as if nature held a balance and kept a book and offered a recompense for the torn limbs and outraged hearts even if man did not. . . . And he overseeing it, riding peacefully about on his horse while he learned the language. (202)

As Matthews has suggested, Sutpen oversees the workings of this New World plantation yet manages not to see its unsettling reality at all; but the text discloses in plain view the sobering recognitions that these peripheral scenes should arouse. Sutpen does recognize the black blood that "manures" the rich plantation crops, and sees the sugar cane burgeoning with the weight of its own value—nature's own reparations. Sutpen knows that these gifts will be usurped by the white master who continues to appropriate and exploit them; yet his portentous response to this is simply to "oversee" it "peacefully" and "learn the language"—the calculating discourse of not just the overseer but the master himself. He fails to see that nature itself foretells his doom, fails to see the personal augury in this scene: those born to toil on the earth in colonial societies will not reap its rewards.

While Haiti's colonial lesson finds uncanny resonance in Sutpen's antebellum South, it also reflects the anachronistic anxieties of the New South's reluctant evolution. More deeply imbedded in the Haitian example is the imperial fiction that "nature" chooses its elite; in the New South, a sharpening commitment to the idea of "natural aristocracy" attempted to authenticate the exploitative rights of the master class. Neither Sutpen nor his sons can finally circumvent their social estrangement. His dream is brutally undone when Wash Jones, symbol of the white underclass Sutpen has fled, cuts down the ambitious impostor who pretends to master him: as Ramón Saldívar suggests, Sutpen "dies at the hands of a representative of the class he has forsaken" (119). Ultimately, the mobility made possible by American capital culture finds its fatal deadlock in the ledger's neo-imperial logic.

My reading of *Absalom, Absalom!* considers the ledger at least partially an anachronism, a narrative device to epitomize Faulkner's struggle to reconcile modern economic opportunism with the more occluded material order of plantation slavery. This crisis sharpens in *Go Down, Moses* with Ike's updated quest to reject both the racial outrage and the fiscal boon that the faded, indomitable ledgers proffer.[23] Ike's repudiation of his legacy comes with an ancillary profit: the notion that men do not need shamefully inflated dividends in order to be fantastically wealthy in gentle graces and honor. But Ike soon discovers that his birthright means not necessarily being able to separate currency from nobility.

Imagining a scene similar to the field of bloody outraged limbs Sutpen "oversees," Ike's more penetrating gaze surveys an analogous, ravaged Mississippi wilderness:

> The tamed land which was to have been his heritage, the land which old Carothers McCaslin his grandfather had bought with white man's money from the wild men whose grandfathers without guns hunted it . . . and in their sweat scratched the surface

of it to a depth of perhaps fourteen inches in order to grow something out of it which had not been there before and which could be translated back into the money he who believed he had bought it had had to pay to get it and hold it and a reasonable profit too. (244)

Here Haiti's blood-stained fields become a site of pure, American financial exchange, a transactional fiction to camouflage the brutal Amerindian genocide and removal that evacuated the Deep South's once-wild land for the agricultural baptism Ike describes. As he notes bitterly, the white man only "believed he had bought it" and now looks for a lucrative return on that investment. The transition from Sutpen's Caribbean parable to Ike's Mississippi iteration underscores the fetishized distance between these two Souths: the blood of Haiti's vanquished is replaced by the noble "sweat" and toil of American settlers; the Indians simply evaporate with "white man's money" in hand and suffer no ostensible trauma. In America, neither the weak nor nature has a claim over the agency of the lusty pioneer poised to bleed the lands wrested from Indians and tilled by Africans. The two scenes present a purposeful intertextual slippage that has the effect of distancing New World colonialism from southern Agrarian enterprise, but both Ike and Faulkner seem aware that the South's brutal origins are only thinly concealed by these sanitized fiscal transactions and the artifice of birthrights. The connections and substitutions Sutpen fails to make in the West Indies are implicitly supplied in this passage. Ike in fact mentions Sutpen in an immediately subsequent moment: "knowing better," he recalls, "old Thomas Sutpen" nonetheless indulges in this immoral colonial practice. Ike is right: Sutpen knows better, or at least he should know better, but his desperation compels him to spurn the evidence he refuses to assimilate.

Presumably, Ike believes he knows better too. In order to set the books right, he endeavors to reverse the usurious practice of agricultural profit-extraction. He scours the family accounts for evidence of sexual and racial transgressions, decoding feverishly the books' irregular combinations of economic figures and journalistic jottings, which often evolve into cryptic, shorthand conversations between different bookkeepers.[24] He has read these ledgers before and knows already, either by force of memory or will, just what chronicles of perversion they harbor. Richard H. King echoes many of Faulkner's critics in suggesting that Ike's moral outrage over these offenses compels him to "transcend" his genealogical burden entirely, renouncing the land and property that is his birthright.[25] What Sutpen works so scrupulously to attain Ike casts off in a quest for ethical rather than monetary deliverance; but Ike is as duped as Sutpen in his subscription to a "characteristically American" belief that he might escape his heritage

(Early 55), a desire that cannot ultimately combat the ledgers' fatal insistence on genealogical priority.[26]

One of Ike's signal mistakes comes in his assumption that "what the old books contained would be after all these years fixed immutably, finished, unalterable, harmless" (256). What, then, of the wreckage of postplantation disorder surrounding Ike, the disastrous living legacies of that incest and miscegenation and exploitation, and the novel's repeated instances of suicidal withdrawals from modern commerce and human relations? The ledgers' disclosures are neither "harmless" nor "fixed" and "finished" chronicles at all; indeed, Faulkner tells us that Ike "would never need to look at the ledgers again nor did he; the yellowed pages in their fading implacable succession were as much a part of his consciousness and would remain so forever, as the fact of his own nativity" (259). Despite his "never" looking again, the next passage immediately features another ledger excerpt that Ike presumably mimeographs autonomically, the account of his family's sins already transcribed in his "consciousness." Or perhaps he is still reading but is engaged in the act of "not seeing" that Matthews would characterize as fetishized knowledge. Such disciplined evasion would correspond exactly with Sutpen's own failure to reconcile the traces of global colonial trauma in Haiti, and indeed, the McCaslin ledgers burst geographic bounds as well, comprising the master register of the entire South—"that record . . . that chronicle which was a whole land in miniature, which multiplied and compounded was the entire South" (280). In not just Ike's consciousness but in a collective New World landscape of sweating planters and violations of blood, the ledger testifies and persists. In the corners of *Go Down, Moses*, it lingers to haunt Ike of his empty, self-beguiling sacrifice. The discursive logic of the ledger is the sinister "birthright" that, despite its harrowing disclosures, neither Ike nor his peers can repudiate as long as they live.

Tellingly, Ike is possessed by the language of plantation math even as a boy: he refers to his age in "ciphers," a term originally designated to signify "zero" and only in modern usage applied to all numbers or figures.[27] As a neutral term of reckoning, it applies the bookkeeper's computational activity to Ike's very person, while its association with a null set foreshadows both his errant desire to nullify his birthright and the suicidal mechanisms that are the only plausible means to accomplish it.[28] Ike's crisis is incited early as he registers an incomplete shift from the notion of native entitlement to ascendance through work: in "The Bear," he interprets the role of hunter as something to "earn," even though he believes he has "inherited" the allegorical and elusive bear (184–85). If the Bear in its most prosaic interpretation represents nature, this tells us volumes about the birthright Isaac believes has been given him, supported and mentored by the mystical black Indian Sam Fathers. Ike means for his desire to appear exculpatory: with a convenient Indian ally resurrected from the obsolescence of his earlier vision, he seeks to emancipate nature from man's proprietary claims; but the endeavor is deeply compromised by his tacit assumption that he has "inherited" the moral graces and the prey necessary to carry out the noble task. A more mature Ike is known by the next generation of hunters for his self-promoting quip: "man is a little better than the net result of his and his neighbor's doings" (330). He posits value not in bank statements but in evidence of neighborly and communal goodwill—respectable southern traits by the most standard definitions. Yet his version of neighborly benevolence and moral decency does not extend to the light-skinned black female who lives near the hunting camp and has a sexual tryst with her own white cousin, Carothers ("Roth") Edmonds, producing yet another mixed-race heir. Ike berates and dismisses her with a parcel of money, bemoaning inwardly, "*Maybe in a thousand or two thousand years in America. . . . But not now! Not now!*" (344). For all his attempts to bury the past, Ike refuses to move forward. It is not the bereft, lovelorn young woman he pities, and neither is his lament for the revivified dishonor in the family line; rather, he evinces an almost classically supremacist disgust that "*Chinese and African and Aryan and Jew, all breed and spawn together until no man has time to say which one is which nor cares*" (347). The collision of races—*not* the system that drove them bitterly apart to begin with—is what he ultimately scorns. Indeed, Ike's next generation of entries in the commissary accounts actually serves to codify another line of modern slaves in the form of emancipated sharecroppers: in his merchant's log, he "ration[s] the tenants and the wage-hands for the coming week" (241). While he is distributing commissary goods on credit, the grammar here makes the tenants and wage-hands *themselves* the rations, converted into figures and entered into the columns that permanently subdivide the South's social classes, communities, and souls.

In the end, the novel's mixed-race offspring suffer most for their detention within the governing priorities of the ledger. Roth's black mistress tries to spurn the money Ike hands her, wanting only an uncompromised love that Ike ensures she will never receive. Lucas Beauchamp, part-black heir in the Edmonds line of the family, is more preoccupied with his own accounts, perhaps because he knows he is still not their primary custodian. After searching for a buried treasure night after sleepless night, Lucas finally capitulates. His surrender completes what seems to be a perverse trilogy: a third version of the Haiti-Mississippi plantation parables. He reflects:

> A heap of what [man] can want is due to come to him, if he just starts in soon enough. I done waited too late to start. That money's there. Them two white men that slipped

in here that night three years ago and dug up twenty-two thousand dollars and got clean away with it before anybody saw them. I know. I saw the hole where they filled it up again, and the churn it was buried in. But . . . I reckon that money aint for me. (126–27)

The hardy sweat, toil, and ruthless profiteering Ike envisions become pure subterfuge in Lucas's estimation: instead of digging and raising crops, as both Sutpen and Ike variously witness, these white men simply remove a massive amount of money from the earth, and then attempt literally to cover their tracks. And as in Sutpen's and Ike's chronicles, somehow no one sees it happen. In a distinctly postplantation perversion of gathering coins rather than crops, former slaves and disenfranchised whites continue to fixate on what is "due to come" to them at last until they are forced to admit defeat by white artifice, relinquishing their just rewards as money that "aint for" them.

Debits to Credits: The Southern Empire Writes Back

Another of Faulkner's tortured protagonists, the mysteriously mixed-race Joe Christmas of *Light in August*, may not actually be black but hopes bitterly that he is or else, he says, "damned if I haven't wasted a lot of time" (254). To fit neatly into the South's social order, then, even in a position of (quite literal) denigration, invests one's life with purpose and meaning; those shiftless, incalculable and uncalculating others like Quentin and potentially Joe Christmas are simply, as Dilsey characterizes Quentin's suicide, "a sinful waste." Dilsey's commentary reminds us, moreover, that the frugal instincts of the region's impoverished African Americans are now relevant to the suddenly cash-conscious elite; these former members of the plantocracy must find new ways to cope with the fact that the South now effectively serves as the "white trash" segment of the nation.[29] Christmas's impoverishment begins to evoke that of the entire South when he engages in a relationship with a white northern woman named, conspicuously, Joanna *Burden*. His masculine agency is challenged by the Yankee Joanna's fiscal superiority, a relationship that mirrors the South's reliance on northern capital; accordingly, his ambiguous racial identity apparently reflects what we have just seen as the tendency to "race" poor white others to cement their inferiority by race as well as economics. Joanna tries philanthropically to seduce him with her funds—as she does with the lavish spread that she leaves for him in the kitchen—in order to send him to "a nigger college" (276). But he furiously rejects the education that her prestige would buy ("We wont even have to pay. . . . On my account," she says), and the money he could then earn: "I will turn over all the business to you, all the money. All of it," she promises. Christmas spurns her aid because both the initial investment and the ensuing profit require him to acknowledge and embrace his racial debasement: "'Tell niggers that I am a nigger too?'" he cries in outrage (276–77). In the first place, he is "a nigger" only on the barest rumor of tainted blood, which may not be black at all but rather Mexican; importantly, however, economic subservience—if he gives in to it—will articulate what could otherwise remain unspoken and unacknowledged indefinitely. When he brutally kills Joanna, then, the murder constitutes a measure of self-preservation; moreover, he decapitates her, suggestively removing the controlling, thinking, superior "head" of this antagonistic North/South dyad. Locally, his branding as "nigger rapist and murderer" and punitive slaying at the hands of an angry town mob signifies the paranoid refusal of the small white southern town to submit themselves to the politics of indeterminacy. Yet, as Romine has argued perceptively, the numerous critics who attempt to explain the cultural dynamics of Christmas's sacrifice all tend to overlook Faulkner's ultimate "displacement of guilt onto poor whites, Yankees, and quasi-southerners"—in short, "onto *disreputable* social groups—that is, those other than 'true southerners'" (172). Certainly this transference raises difficult questions about both Faulkner's and his narrator's allegiance; more pertinent to my purposes, however, is the suggestion that poor whites and Yankees would also have motivations for sustaining the Negro criminal myth as powerful as those compelling the fanatical white supremacist Percy Grimm.

The imaginative return to an order that inherently privileged whiteness could help mitigate the power of class over the poor white by replacing it with an illusion of "natural" value. For poor whites, money per se is often denied importance in favor of the commodities of education and culture that often provided the only distinction between indigent whites and blacks.[30] Thomas Wolfe's world, depicted at feverish length in *Look Homeward, Angel*, turns a mirror on just such an aspirant white underclass. The novel is set in the rural Appalachian locale Thomas Sutpen tries so desperately to leave behind; positioned near the natural attraction of the Great Smoky Mountains and with the railroad running through it, however, Wolfe's hometown of Asheville developed into a substantially more cosmopolitan place where Wolfe could see both the progress and the decadence associated with the spread of capitalism. Heir of a financially struggling lineage, Wolfe's perspective on this issue would seem to bear little resemblance to that of the elite ex-slaveholders of the Deep South. Indeed, while he shared with the Agrarians a fervent belief in the dangers of industrialism, he rejected their practice of "resurrecting antebellum myths of paradisiacal plantations and natural aristocracies" in the service of promoting agrarian ideologies (38).[31] For his part, Wolfe considered himself staunchly working class, as he indicated emphatically in a 1936 interview: "My people were all working people, had to work for their livings, and my natural instinctive feeling is on the side of the working class" (Magi and Walser 62). Even his art had a vocabulary of toil attached to it: "I can't swallow things whole," he averred; "I've got to sweat and labor" (Magi and Walser 63). Yet it is also clear that Wolfe's resistance to the Agrarians and the elite world of privilege they memorialized was, at least in part, defensive and prideful; he wanted the prosperity and fame that would signify his talent, and even when he claimed to have outgrown the desire for quantifiable success, he nonetheless conceded, "I would be untruthful if I said I did not still like the kind of success I have mentioned" (Magi and Walser 62). In an earlier interview, he had invited a journalist to his Fifth Avenue apartment, where he apologized for the absence of his housekeeper, who came "only" three times a week; *Look Homeward, Angel* had only recently been published and accorded attention, and already Wolfe was working to distance himself from the small "sweat shop . . . a real sweat shop" on Eighth Street where he had written the entire book in longhand (Magi and Walser 2–3). For the remainder of his brief life (he died in 1938 at the age of thirty-seven), he labored to cultivate an innate intellectual superiority that he figured in terms of economic prosperity. As much as he tried to repress it, this struggle was at least as much about money as it was about art; indeed, the fetish of number emerges yet again to signify his futile attempt to evacuate money of exchange value and replace it with a different kind of lived, experiential worth. "I have a mania for figures," he confesses, "though I can't keep track of how much money I spend" (Magi and Walser 61). Instead, he says he makes "lists" of places he has visited and those he still wants to see; he transmutes his "mania for figures" into quantities that broaden his experience, his knowledge, and his cosmopolitanism. Like a true aristocrat, his automatic counter stops when he opens his wallet.

While Wolfe asserts the familiar aristocratic technique of replacing monetary value with less-quantifiable worth, his project is never fully persuasive. The pervasive emphases in his work on matters of wealth, education, and elitism indicate an enduring anxiety about the Appalachian upstart's laborious path to the Agrarians' cosseted world of tradition and gentility: by harnessing intellect as a proxy for wealth and inheritance. This is precisely the birthright Wolfe imaginatively fabricates for himself in his most well-known novel, *Look Homeward, Angel*, which is essentially autobiographical.[32] Much like the fictional Gants, the author's own family was of modest means, and his mother was preoccupied with increasing their wealth and standing by operating a boarding house (as does the fictional Mrs. Gant) while his father engraved tombstones—an occupation that would seem heavily symbolical if it did not happen to be true. In the novel, the class-obsessed Eugene Gant is further conditioned by his humble teachers, the Leonards. Proud of the intellectual capital they help to cultivate, the pedagogues maintain passionately that "there are lots of things money can't buy . . . and one of them is the society of cult-shered men and women" (258). In Mr. Leonard's estimation, culture and wealth are two entirely different realms, the former occupied by antimaterialist intellectuals and the latter by acquisitive dolts: "What do these little whippersnappers [lawyers and millionaires] know about the things of the mind?" he complains. "'They may be Big Men on the tax collector's books, but when they try to associate with educated men and women . . . they just ain't nothin'" (258). Education offers a substitute for value measured in books that would not appear on the "tax collector"'s shelf but rather in the library stacks; such a refiguration of intellectual capital offers a strategy for making the poor academic "something," but only by diametrically rendering the elite "nothing." Interestingly, the reversal that sees the Big Men as "'nothin'" also imagines them as black: "'You might as well expect some ignorant darky out in the field to construe a passage in Homer,'" Mr. Leonard spits (258). His comment betrays again an anxiety over his own class and their potential elision with black laborers.

What is also compelling here is the way the "tax collector's book" merges with the hierarchical and racial priorities of the plantation ledger in order to redeem the poor white. The ledger, though dismissed rhetorically as of no account, remains a haunting presence in the Leonards' school, looming over the identity of Wolfe's fictional proxy Eugene. The boy is sent to boarding school in hopes he will be a "credit" to the family name (262). To evaluate his performance, the teacher keeps a meticulous "book," a "record" in which all failures or moments of disorder are entered "by careful markings." The description almost exactly connotes the activity of bookkeeping; but in this ledger, Eugene is more often than not rendered a debit rather than the expected "credit," gifted intellectually but "lazy." That is, like so many of the elite we have seen so far, he simply does not like to work and cannot grasp how the efforts of his labor might translate into tangible profit. Moreover, the mathematics of engineering such a fate escape him entirely. In another closely autobiographical twist, Eugene's greatest struggle is with "algebra"; and in defense of this failing, his teacher assures him: "Never mind about algebra here. That's for poor folks. There's no need for algebra where two and two make five" (267).[33]

In what terms can "algebra" be only for "poor folks"? Given the intensity of Wolfe's own struggle with complex mathematics and the collective class aversion to the tax collector's unscrupulous calculations, this equation seems to suggest that struggle and "work" are reserved for the poor and needy and acquisitive. The elite, on the other hand, need not labor to see the fruits of their efforts—and this is the condition to which these workaday intellectuals aspire. As Tate's young protagonist acknowledges, only those who deign to engage in tawdry capitalism need to "add and count things," while the privileged may instead wantonly assert a new answer to a familiar equation as naturally as birth. The poor schoolmaster behaves here like Charles Bon, who oversteps his racial position in order to claim a surplus value for himself—not coincidentally, perhaps, in the inflation of an addition exercise so basic it has entered our vocabulary as a cliché. The real education here is emphatically not about learning algebraic methods, we discover, but the principles underlying the need for math at all—and the uplifting of those who are elevated by their mathematical license. By such rules, surplus value can be added to the simple product, a return with interest for what "poor folks" have lost; like their privileged white compeers, they too can make the product of two plus two something more than expected without having to "show the work."

For the privileged, these narcissistic overcalculations are geared toward compensation and amplification, a kind of profit and "receipt" for all they believe they have given to society and deserve in return. When Wolfe himself does the math on his own meager identity, he factors in intellect and ability and thus generates his own surplus value. In a narcissistic reverie on his artistic gifts, he employs a flood of monetary, mathematical imagery: he writes to his editor, "'I feel packed to the lips with rich ore. . . . I want to tear myself open and show my friends all that I think I have. I am so anxious to lay all my wares on the table . . . , to say, 'You have not seen one tenth or one twentieth of what is in me. Just wait.'" He admits that this is "'colossal egotism'" but continues, "'I feel that no one else has a quarter of my power and richness'" (Donald 209–10). In the higher realm of aesthetic creation, Wolfe finds an abundance of "rich ore" and costly "wares" that exceed what is visible; there is no way of even calculating the enormity of it, he insists. No algebra here, but pure mathematics bent upon inflating the final product—simply more "power and richness" in "a quarter" of his body than in anyone else in the world.

In William Alexander Percy's writings as well as in Wolfe's, an insidious kind of personal accounting commences to help measure and solidify this narcissism. Percy begins with an elaborate exercise in the humility topos: "One by one I count [my] failures," Percy says at the close of the autobiography, "and I acknowledge the deficit" (348). In another moment, Percy attaches to this nebulous self-flagellation an ironically redeeming material motivation; the formula of production that leaves him lacking lies in the New South's insidious new math: "The necessity of earning a living plus a desire to live plus the failure to discover in myself any quality convertible into cash—here was a combination sufficient to fling one tailspinning into the deepest inferiority complex" (113). The "failures" mentioned earlier are subtly configured to reveal no shortcomings at all; that is, to find in himself some "quality convertible into cash" would signify his own entry into the plantation ledger as a deficit, as a denigrated slave who does not simply submit to the "necessity" of labor but equates himself with the value of it. The cruel logic of capitalism, Percy insinuates, inspires even a neoaristocrat to revert alarmingly to the calculations of a plantation order that produces "the deepest inferiority complex." As a stay against this devolution, Percy voices something oddly revealing: "I've got your number and people's numbers don't change" (241). Even in "failure," it seems, the aristocrat remains staunchly himself: in the energetic equations of personal value being computed obsessively in the New South, plantation calculations do not have the power to reassemble the status quo. The math might change, and so may the products, but not (he hopes) the man who always disavowed the tawdriness of calculations and exchanges to begin with; while poor folks engage in labor and algebra to find profit in the answers, the elite white simply sits back in the security of inherent superiority and stability. Indeed, the acknowledged "deficit" in his personal accounts merely paves the way for, in the next moment, a compensatory narcissism much like Wolfe's: "Of all the people I have loved . . . I have loved no one so much as myself" (348). Rather than believe in the ascendancy of others, Percy commits to the inflation of himself.

Despite the realities revealed and feared by bookkeeping, elite whites preferred to obscure the operations of the system that placed them on the same lines as poorer whites and potentially at a disadvantage in relation to them. Numbers simply can not change for men like Will Percy, who clings to the principle of patently mathematical, harmonious lines in art as well: in a moment resonant of a New Critical appreciation, he admires the "axes and balances, geometric design, formal arrangements" of creations like the Luxembourg gardens. Such regularity and precision may constitute oriental complaints about man-made art, as the fundamental "problem in mathematics" is its appropriation into the antithetical realm of accident, flux, and creativity; but Percy reacts against this assumption, declaring that mathematical wonders like the gardens should be tended and cherished, for they exist "in peace, a peace full of sadness and without regret" (109)—language suggestive of a somber but resolute and still-methodical South, one both indisputably natural and yet meticulously ordered. Indeed, these organizing principles conjure the mandates of the Agrarians and their influential New Criticism, whose practitioners believed, as Thomas Underwood puts it, that "the ideal South, like a well-wrought poem, required no complex theories to explain the simple geometry and aesthetically pleasing hierarchy of its internal relationships" (*Allen Tate* 32). The theories of unity and aesthetic enjoyment that characterize a New Critical approach to art are rooted in principles of social order, ones associated with the "ideal" South—presumably, for Agrarians, the plantation South and its racial and class hierarchies. No complex theories or calculations or algebra are needed in this "ideal" place, where "hierarchy" is as simple and stable as geometry, and just as pleasant in its result; its relationship to art, however, indicates subtly that this order may be created as efficiently as a "well-wrought poem," and that its appearance will seem natural rather than labored. There would be the illusion that "numbers don't change" covering over the sweat of production, much as the plantation ledger slyly conceals the violence of its calculations and the perceived innocence of its social order. In the loss and apparent desirability of such precedents, the neoaristocrat's impulse is to return to the "simple geometry" of the ideal South and its hierarchies, positing others in the gutter of inferiority in order to return to one's former altitude.

The following chapters explore in greater depth the enormous cost incurred by those upon whose backs and figures this elevation depends: African Americans, women, and uncategorizable others. On the surface, these elite white attempts at recompense and penance are ultimately aimed at themselves and not necessarily (or more than nominally) at blacks or poor whites; as Erik Dussere notes similarly about Faulkner's work, the "engagement with economic figures, the attempt to disrupt or negate the narrative provided by the ledger, is a problem posed for his white characters as a means to deal with *their* suffering, the crushing weight of their inherited sin and debt" (339). Yet while Dussere implies that somehow these white characters will be able to assuage both their guilt and debt in these maneuvers, by finding an equation between modern capitalism and chattel slavery their confrontations with the ledger are not exculpatory so much as repetitive and exploitative. In these equations, the ambitious southern white necessarily collapses into a narcissism that protects and inflates him while fixing and demeaning the inherently less privileged. Returning briefly to *Go Down, Moses*, we can see that Faulkner recognizes clearly the injurious arithmetic of the South's racial relationships, which repeatedly reveal that the inequitable logic of plantation slavery collides viciously with the calculations of capitalism, and that African American others—even when they are kin—must necessarily be debited from in order for the elite to recover personal integrity and profit.

Faulkner allows such an acknowledgment in Roth Edmonds's evolution into the cruel racist who rejects and devastates the part-black cousin with whom he has a sexual affair (one that happens to produce another miscegenated child). As a.young boy, Roth saw Lucas Beauchamp as a mere "adjunct" to his wife Mollie "as simply as he accepted his father as an adjunct to his existence" (106). Significantly, people beyond the self are conceived of as separate and additional, a family member comprising an "adjunct" to the narcissistic reality and fullness of the primary self; the word *adjunct* literally connotes a quantity that is "added to another thing but not essential to it" and "joined or associated" not as an equal but in "an auxiliary or subordinate relationship" (Dictionary.com). Significantly, Faulkner uses this word in *Absalom, Absalom!* as well to signify Sutpen's octoroon wife as a failed "adjunct" in his carefully designed accounts (124). In time, Roth learns how to enter those "adjuncts," those bare "extra" figures, on his social register—that is, he learns "the old curse of the fathers, the old haughty ancestral pride based not on any value but on an accident of geography" (107). The logic that should keep the races separate, entered in different books of value (Lucas + Mollie; Roth + his father), is bequeathed by the South's "old curse," the "accident of geography" that made slavery dictate its social calculations. "Pride" (narcissism) intuitively stems from "value" (economics) in this society, where adjuncts collide to support the white self but must be made statistically and hierarchically "subordinate" to it.

Again, the motivation for this arithmetic stems from a new and discomposing sense of inferiority. Ike says to Roth that "'every man and woman, at the instant when it don't even matter whether they marry or not . . . the two of them together were God'" (332). Clearly Ike is referring to the "instant" of sexual union, and the idea of such an apotheosis strikes a sensitive chord in Roth, as by now he has committed the ultimate sin of practical marriage with his black cousin, a corrupt math that violates his earlier lesson in adjuncts and segregation. "'Then there are some Gods in this world I wouldn't want to touch, and with a damn long stick. . . . And that includes myself, if you want to know'" (332). Perturbed, he moves off to bed—and the next day deals with his black paramour by sending her the simple and unequivocal message "no" (339). That's when Ike visits the unnamed girl in outrage, telling her to "'marry: a man in your own race. . . . Marry a black man'" (346). It's unclear whether Roth develops his own self-hatred before or after he went "coon-hunting" and touched a black woman, so to speak, with his long stick; but it is certain that Ike labors to return the situation to what he sees as an order God would approve. Ike views the opprobrious mixing of races as the repulsive issue of a modern order where "*white men can own plantations and commute every night to Memphis and black men own plantations and ride in jim crow cars to Chicago to live in millionaires' mansions on Lakeshore Drive, where white men rent farms and live like niggers and niggers crop on shares and live like animals . . . and usury and mortgage and bankruptcy and measureless wealth, Chinese and African and Aryan and Jew, all breed and spawn together*" (347). This brings us back to the scene examined earlier, but with more context now: the miscegenation Ike violently disavows represents, to him, the world of capitalist corruption where whites and blacks no longer occupy their proper roles and places. This, then, is what Ike's elegy for the ruined arcadia of the southern landscape constitutes: a paranoid displacement of plantation legacies onto industrialism's ravages.

Not a split second after this trembling reverie, Will Legate bursts into Ike's tent to announce that Roth has just killed a deer—"'Just a deer. . . . Nothing extra'" (348). Knowing that a "doe" is Roth's euphemism for a woman, Ike "crossed hands once more weightless on his breast" in an image heavy with religious symbology and declares meaningfully "'It was a doe'" (348). The line ends "Delta Autumn" and thus perversely sets the world right, the innocent black female "doe" exterminated by Roth's violence and his rejection, no longer "extra" or adjunctive to anything or anyone at all. For men like Roth, the last of the Edmonds line, such an other can offer him nothing "extra" unless she is eliminated from the position of wife and mother to the next (and the novel's final) mixed-race Edmonds heir. What cannot be undone historically, it seems, must be accomplished symbolically, textually, and mathematically. The gravity of literature's obliterations comes through chillingly in moments like this one.

But to again paraphrase Spivak: in the literature of the white South, can the adjunct speak? In Faulkner's novels, mixed-race figures like Lucas are frequently preoccupied with money and status, exhibiting what Matthews has described as a "ledger mentality" ("Touching Race" 32). But these figures have no real access to the ledger—just as their ancestors had "absolutely no way under the sun . . . [to verify] how the account stood" (255)—and barely have agency in the bank where their money is held ("'too much to keep hidden under a brick in the hearth,'" the white banker tells Lucas. "Let me keep it for you. Let me keep it," 106). Still, it is "the white man at the desk [who] added and multiplied and subtracted" (279). Roth, who grows up viewing Lucas as an adjunct, has assimilated him finally into a specific kind of accounting: "Lucas said, 'Wait a minute.' 'Wait a minute?' Edmonds said. 'Hah!' he said. 'You've bankrupted your waiting. You've already spent—' But Lucas had gone on" (125). Edmonds's lexicon draws together the language of value and experience, assessing with managerial efficiency the slow deliberations that characterize Lucas's plotted behavior. Yet uncannily, while Edmonds tries to force the books to an inauspicious close, Lucas simply "goes on" (much, it seems, as Dilsey "endures"), speaking over Roth's pronouncement of bankruptcy.

However, as with Joe Christmas's racial indeterminacy, Lucas's also requires him finally to be placed in a position of impoverishment. He is calculating and estimating like a white man, but his hybridity and his dangerous liminality strictly prevent him from coming out on top. At the end of *Intruder in the Dust*, Lucas Beauchamp makes a central reappearance. Content to find his self authorized in the mirror of his financial possessions, he stares into his coin purse "exactly as you would look down at your reflection in a well" (240). The moment acknowledges with stunning pathos that Lucas himself is the debt, and that he is the only figure in Yoknapatawpha who can erase that deficit from the register—by extracting still more money from his own metaphorical pocket. Gavin Stevens makes him count out the coins one by one, after which Lucas waits for proof that he has calculated and satisfied his debt correctly. His entire existence seems to hang in the balance, as the narrative ends with the evocative question, "'what are you *waiting* for now?'" followed by Lucas's answer: "'My receipt'" (241, italics added). The personal pronoun confirms the narcissistic importance of this financial verification of a balanced and closed account; but the novel simply ends here, and we have no idea whether or not he receives such closure.

Faulkner's apparent sympathies for defeated men like Lucas—which we explore further in chapter 2—are undercut by his more pronounced investment in the futility of the noble sacrifices of white men like Ike. What he and other southern writers seem ultimately to register throughout their works is an ambivalent desire to both recuperate and renounce the contaminated social codes of plantation slavery, while bitterly critiquing the advent of a capitalist order that offers little better or different. What these unsettling, global purviews announce is the degree to which moral choice itself has been hijacked by a colonial machine that expands and replicates ceaselessly. In Quentin we find, as many critics have argued, perhaps the voice closest to Faulkner's own on such matters. In *The Sound and the Fury* Quentin is at Harvard but his mind is elsewhere, thinking

> of home, of . . . the niggers and country folks . . . and my insides would move like they used to do in school when the bell rang. I wouldn't begin counting until the clock struck three. Then I would begin, counting to sixty and folding down one finger and thinking of the other fourteen fingers waiting to be folded down, or thirteen or twelve or eight or seven, until all of a sudden I'd realise silence and the unwinking minds, and I'd say "Ma'am?" "Your name is Quentin, isn't it?" Miss Laura would say . . . "Tell Quentin who discovered the Mississippi River, Henry." "DeSoto." Then . . . I'd be afraid I had gotten behind and I'd count fast and fold down another finger, then I'd be afraid I was going too fast and I'd slow up, then I'd get afraid and count fast again. So I could never come out even with the bell. (88)

Quentin evades the southern schoolboy's imperial lessons; while he botches a simple internal counting exercise, another student effortlessly places the Spanish conquistador De Soto at the "discovery" of the Mississippi River, taking Ike's vision of Indian eviction one step further by implying that the Natives were never there at all. Significantly, it is a memory of "niggers and country folk" that prompts Quentin's classroom memory, continuing the comparative sweep with which Faulkner brings together the poor white, the former slave, and the Indian similarly divested by white imperialism. But Quentin resists this knowledge: he miscalculates his own digits absurdly ("fourteen" fingers?), literal somatic facts subsumed by the priorities of an imposed order he cannot master; but the ticking clock and tolling bell signify that he must move forward and learn how to keep up. His compulsion is to come out as "even" with the bell as his older brother Jason believes he might square with his own ledgers.

But Quentin is apparently not as good as Jason at faking it. His desire for escape is as futile as Ike's attempt to disqualify himself from his birthright, and as unrequited as Sutpen's yearning to see his own ledger generate a surplus value. Alive, neither Ike nor Sutpen seems able—or willing—to move forward. Perhaps Faulkner answers their plight with Quentin, creative reteller of Sutpen's tale and witness to its coda—Henry's dying body, the haunted house consumed by flames—and now unable to move forward or backward or even to count himself accurately into the present. Significantly, the only math Quentin gets right is the calculation of how much weight it will take to sink his body to the bottom of the Charles River: "The displacement of water is equal to the something of something. Reducto absurdum of all human experience, and two six-pound flat-irons weigh more than one tailor's goose. What a sinful waste Dilsey would say" (90).[34] His equations are pointedly imprecise, exemplifying the unliveable, "reducto absurdum," the colossal waste of American capital culture. In order to assimilate such absurdity as knowledge, Quentin remembers, "the minds would go away"—allowing for the rest of the students' automatic participation in an established but not always intuitive order of things. This is ideological experience as Slavoj Žižek, revising Karl Marx, defines it: a reality that depends upon the ignorance of its participants for its perpetuation (316); according to this theory, the ideological being "can reproduce itself only in so far as it is misrecognized and overlooked" (318). This formula also describes the southern narcissist, engaged in a process of fetishistic representation of self and community *fundamentally* through learned "misrecognition" and oversight of what that vision entails. As Jean Baudrillard extends this notion, the entire modern world is inherently a simulation of the real, an illusion and a fabrication, a dazzling world of "simple geometry" and order that belies the violence of its coherence. Quentin's body resists participation in a world whose rules have made him a math problem that he cannot figure out; the "simple" math is not so clear after all.

Quentin's narcissistic and mathematical failures here reveal a larger cultural detachment from his own reality and production, and the alienation produced in a people who have been doomed to quantify themselves and their relationships to one another. Here an obsessive focus on the fetishized parts of his own body as elements in a counting exercise stand in for (and explicitly subsume) the classroom lessons, while clearly evincing an attempt at projecting order and control gone astray upon his very body. Quentin's participation in this troubled order is made obvious in the image of "niggers and country folks" carrying "toy monkeys"—a moment that successfully conflates "niggers" and poor white "country folks" in their pseudomirrors, as "monkeys" inherently suggest aping and mimicry as well as stereotypical suggestions of animalistic blackness. Here, blacks and poor whites alike tote these self-identifying objects, which give back to them images that the privileged need them to reflect. By figuring the doubling mirror as a "toy," Faulkner suggests that this phenomenon marks a child's acculturation into the ideology of this society—a perverse kind of regional and psychological coming-of-age explored at greater length by writers like Lillian Smith in *Killers of the Dream*. As a plaything, the toy functions as an object of "repressive desublimation," an item that Baudrillard identifies as an attempt to disguise by the opposite quantity that makes its existence possible and necessary; that is, the element of play here obscures in plain view the presence of labor underwriting the scene and yoking together the blacks and whites victimized by the South's exploitative capital culture.

It is no accident, then, that Quentin submerges much of his own precocious knowledge about himself and this social order; he simply has no other choice. A kind of panic over the dissolution of his world and identity invigorates his attempt to grasp these illogical models of self-computation; but the disruption has been too violent, and Quentin cannot get the math to come out right. His numbers have, despite Percy's arrogant assurance to the contrary, changed fundamentally. "Niggers say a drowned man's shadow was watching for him in the water all the time," Quentin remembers (90); ultimately, it is this absorption of "nigger" superstition that explicitly prefigures his own soon-to-be "shadow" waiting for him in the water of the Charles River. The image is, again, classically and catastrophically narcissistic; and again, Faulkner sketches the mathematical character of this disabling narcissism when Quentin ponders that "the displacement of water is equal to the something of something. . . . What a sinful waste Dilsey would say" (90). The attempt to measure the self against this cold calculus of the "ideal South" is, ultimately, the "reducto absurdum of all human experience"; success simply results in the loss of humanity in the most literal terms, by calculating the weight necessary to sink one's body to fatal and irreversible depths. Quentin's self-immolating calculations are disastrously revealing: not of honor or recompense or restoration, not of anything that the ledgers might utter, but rather of what only the practical, labor-centered, exploited Dilsey could say: "what a sinful waste."

Chapter Two

Stealing Themselves Out of Slavery: African American Southerners in Richard Wright, William Attaway, James Weldon Johnson, and Zora Neale Hurston

> *Eventually, the masters left, in a kind of way; eventually, the slaves were freed, in a kind of way.*
> JAMAICA KINCAID, *A SMALL PLACE*

In his "Economy of Manichean Allegory," Abdul JanMohamed describes the perverse, exploitative energies that keep colonial subjects locked in a narcissistic struggle with their oppressors:

> By allowing the European to denigrate the native in a variety of ways, by permitting an obsessive, fetishistic representation of the native's moral inferiority, the [Manichean] allegory also enables the European to increase, by contrast, the store of his own moral superiority; it allows him to accumulate "surplus morality," which is further invested in the denigration of the native, in a self-sustaining cycle. (23)

While it is not his primary concern in this passage, the economic language suffusing JanMohamed's description of the colonial dyad is by no means unremarkable. In JanMohamed's view, the elite white may "increase" and "accumulate" his own "'surplus morality'" in contrast to, and at the expense of, the fetishized inferiority of the native. As we have seen, this process depends fundamentally on the "denigration" of the regional other upon whose bodies and labor the colonial master historically acquires and "invests" his extravagant superiority. As Baker observes in *Turning South Again*, the fact that blacks were "tallied as three-fifths persons in matters of 'representation'" accomplishes a "fracture of the black body [that] enables a sustainable southern mind" (23). The fetish of surplus value entertained by the southern white can be maintained only by deriving some of that worth over and against the darker, lesser "other."

For postslavery southerners, this metaphorical debiting retained real economic impact well into the twentieth century. In *The Fire in the Flint* Walter White's black protagonist asks a local white why he won't stand up against the practice of lynching: "'Who? Me? Never!' Mr. Ewing looked his amazement at the suggestion. 'Why, it would ruin my business'" (70). Ewing cites other reasons for his hesitation, but the health of his "business" is his instant, primary rationale for condoning the radical torture and extermination of black bodies in his midst; and he names several other local businessmen who would be "out for the same reason" (70). Such moments are disturbing because they expose the deeply material basis for the continued suppression and often the extermination of African American southerners whose denigration—if not their outright extermination—remains vital to the prosperity, order, and coherence of southern society and particularly for its grasping white aristocracy and proletariat.

In his thousand-plus-page sociological study, *An American Dilemma*, Gunnar Myrdal suggests that the American white psychology might eventually exorcise its racist preoccupations by force of morality and religion; while he considers economics and employment patterns as part of his analysis, these factors are not nearly as critical to the formation of racism as are psychological ones. Yet colonial societies routinely display that materiality and psychology cannot be easily disentangled: Aimé Césaire writes in *Discourse on Colonialism* that the native Bantu of the Congo desire "not the improvement of their economic and material situation, but the white man's recognition of and respect for their dignity as men, their full human value" (58). In the modern South, these twin desires cannot be separated (and I suspect they could not for the Bantu either). In this chapter I explore the manner in which African American southerners retain a disturbingly literal sense of "human values" and thus endeavor to improve both their economic and their psychological health simultaneously; yet in their conditioned responses to the South's own Manichean allegory, we find not liberation but ineluctable participation in the "self-sustaining cycle" that infects, interpellates, and fractures their minds and bodies.

Indeed, as Walter Johnson shows, the paternalism used to make slavery appear more caring than calculating was nonetheless "sometimes best measured in cash" (26); that is, the prosperity of a plantation directly influenced how kindly owners appraised their human investments:

Slaveholders . . . could track their fortunes in *Affleck's Planter's Annual Record*, which provided a convenient table by which slaves' annual increase in value could be tracked in the same set of tables as their daily cotton production, and a page at the back where the "planter" could fill in the value of his slave force, and calculate the "interest on the same at ten percent." Indeed, slaves' market value—"advantage, worth, quality"— was often cited as the best guarantee that their owners would treat them well. (26)

"It should be remembered," Mark M. Smith notes, "that it was precisely on plantations that masters employed the most rigorous, capitalist management techniques" (43). Given the importance of the slave's value to the owner's fiscal and social status, the appraisal of the black body's worth had a direct impact on that slave's existence. That a special kind of ledger was published in order to satisfy the particular needs of the agricultural business is revealing: *Affleck's* was one of the most popular record book brands because it facilitated calculations of property and material production, and because, importantly, it included an instructional section on the "Duties of an Overseer" and, in some editions, advertisements from New Orleans' slave markets. Affleck, a Mississippi planter, was gratified by the results of his first edition in 1847: "'Business habits were induced, and everything moved along more smoothly'" (Stephenson 356); over time, keeping an *Affleck's* record book became an indication of managerial efficiency and respectability. Fittingly, in letters he wrote soon after emancipation, Affleck promptly evaluated what he perceived to be the value of these newly freed chattel: "'The bulk of them, including almost all of the young and able-bodied, [are] already worthless'" and predicted that landowners would have "'no hope of working our plantations by free negro labour'" (qtd. in Rozek 6).

Yet Affleck and other white landowners had no choice but to adapt to this new economy, and in doing so they found ways to make the new wage labor system as profitable as it had been under slavery. Former slaves continued to toil as they always had, often on the same land; even under the dazzling new opportunities nominally promised by the free labor system, in practice the promise of capitalist ascent seemed radically limited. Reconstruction and the decades leading into the twentieth century saw antebellum peonage reconfigured in a similar form, that of wage-labor-based sharecropping.[1] As J. A. Bryant Jr. puts it succinctly, "for all practical purposes the Old South was recognizable as the Old South through the years of World War II. Slave or free, black was black, and white was white" (4). Though slightly reductive, Bryant's assessment nonetheless has force. While large numbers of blacks had fled north in the Great Migration, many remained to make their way in the only home they had ever known; little had changed in their ability to resist white authority and become self-sufficient. Jack Temple Kirby describes "the system's class and racial resemblance to slavery" wherein white landlords used financial, juridical, and fear tactics to keep their black laborers in permanent peonage; by controlling their access to cash and goods, these bosses effectively detained their black workers in an economy of abject dependency. Kirby describes a black man named Ned Cobb who in the 1930s compares his treatment as a prison inmate to his prior existence as a sharecropper on white land: "'I safely could say, them white people at Wetumpka [prison] treated me better than any of their color have treated me on the outside.' Inside, he was unavailable for commercial exploitation [Kirby interjects], but 'outside they raised figures against me in place of wire'" (241).[2] Indeed, the new mode of sharecropping uses the exploitative potential of capitalism to the fullest, and in the process resurrects the calculating fictions of the plantation ledger. Throughout the literature of the modern South, African American authors begin to articulate the crisis of having "figures" raised against them like prison wire, as they attempt in their own books of value and liberation to conjure figures and freedom of their own.

Ultimately, however, these writers generally fail to revise the terms of their subjection; they tend instead to adopt the methods and tropes associated historically with the machinations of the white master. Carla L. Peterson describes the haunting dilemma of antebellum black writers who "repeatedly pondered such questions as: How can I escape being a commodity? How can I own myself? How can I possess property? and, more abstractly, How can I achieve and maintain self-possession?" (176–77). At a central moment in *Huck Finn*, Jim resolves to purchase his wife and children out of slavery; if the masters refuse to sell, he plans to "get an Ab'litionist to go and steal them" (123). Throughout the book Huck also contemplates "stealing" Jim out of slavery as well, strengthening the notion that African Americans are cultural property who may be bought, sold, traded, or filched—and who must literally steal themselves in order to be self-possessed. The economy of chattel slavery normalized such crises of personal value for the humans whose bodies and souls were identified fundamentally with price tags and production. In the literature of the modern South, we discover again how closely the structures of market capitalism thus replicate and foster the priorities and exclusions of chattel slavery. In their inability to jettison the tropes and techniques of white mastery, former slaves reveal that the new capitalist economy offers them little more or different in the path to self-possession.

It was not uncommon for plantation slaves, particularly house servants, to mimic their white masters. Genovese demonstrates that slaves' mimicry could be subversive, "narrowing the distance between white and black" until "identification with the masters . . . gave them a device for asserting superiority over many whites" (*Roll, Jordan, Roll* 330); further, "when house servants could, they risked pressing their masters and mistresses into a reversal of roles" (346). In postslavery society the impulse to continue emulating such figures could have subversive potential, producing what Bhabha describes as a "slippage" or "excess" in the repetition of authority (86). Yet such emulations tend to be unpalatable for former chattel: as Frantz Fanon suggests, "the first impulse of the black man is to say *no* to those who attempt to build a definition of him"; nonetheless, he often finds himself reluctantly assimilating elite expectations and behaviors and being accused by his people of "self-aggrandizement" (36–38). Fanon calls this kind of mimicry the "narcissistic cry" (*Black Skin* 45) and warns that it generally leads paradoxically to the subject's "devaluation of self" (75); similarly, texts by southern African Americans may approximate white methods and personas subversively in ways that betray a self-effacing, narcissistic desire to embody whichever identity will garner the greatest success and "self-aggrandizement" in the twentieth-century South. The choices are painfully limited and equally destructive: act "like a nigger," as Richard Wright finds he must do, or "have a white skin," as James Weldon Johnson finally decides. Repeatedly, the African American southerner must gauge his or her own identity and worth as property before attempting to declare ownership of this commodity—the self as fetish.

Of Mules and (Almost) Men: Lessons in Sharecropping and Stealing

In his stories and autobiographical sketches of the 1930s and 1940s, Richard Wright portrays a South still organized to insure black dependency and desperation. In his lesser-known 1938 short story "Fire and Cloud" collected in *Uncle Tom's Children*, Wright depicts an African American community stricken by poverty and hunger and seeking intervention from their black preacher, Dan Taylor. The good reverend shares their deprivation acutely; it inhabits his body in the form of a bitterly sardonic counting exercise, which Wright uses pointedly in the opening paragraphs of the story:

> *"A naughts a naught . . ."*
> As he walked his eyes looked vacantly on the dusty road, and the words rolled up without movement from his lips, each syllable floating softly up out of the depths of his body.
> *"N five a figger . . ."*
> He pulled out his pocket handkerchief and mopped his brow without lessening his pace.
> *"All fer the white man . . ."*
> He reached the top of the slope and paused, head down.
> *"N none fer the nigger . . ."*
> His shoulders shook in half-laugh and half-shudder. He finished mopping his brow and spat, as though to rid himself of some bitter thing. He thought. Thas the

way its awways been! . . . Seems like the white folks jus erbout owns this whole worl! (129–30)

Significantly, we meet Rev. Taylor first through his intonation of this well-known old rhyme, which is so deeply immersed in his identity as an African American that it emanates from the very "depths of his body."[3] He tries to spit the "bitter thing" out of his being but knows it has "awways" been his lot and probably always will be. The lines of the song punctuate his progress on the dusty road, his tireless climb up the hill, his perspiration and fatigue. Weaving this bitter rhyme into the man's motions, Wright reminds us vividly that the labor and the faith of the black man in the American South are impotent against the white man's self-serving arithmetic, which continues to put the profit in his own wallet while the African American community struggles along in poverty and hunger.

The story's opening thus sets an inauspicious stage for the dilemma facing Taylor. While his community desperately needs him to serve as a liaison to the local white government, Taylor is being pressured from yet another side: local, biracial Communist activists want him to inspire his flock to demonstrate. Meanwhile, the town's white mayor and officials appeal to his influence as a "responsible man in the community" capable of squelching the uprising of "bad niggers" swayed by the "Goddamn sonofabitching lousy bastard rats trying to wreck our country" (148–49)—that is, the Communists. Taylor is torn between moral probity and cautious circumspection in the turbulent racial climate of the 1930s, when many blacks (Wright included) turned to interracial Socialist movements promising to improve their economic and social conditions; so he tries tentatively to convince the mayor that his people "wouldnt be marchin ef they wuznt hongry" (152). While the white elite repeatedly try to convince Taylor that his people are no hungrier than anyone else's, the reverend looks out across the hills and knows acutely that the earth's bounty is being foreclosed from his community, that "the white folks" keep them from owning and using the rich green land that surrounds them and "wont let em eat" what it produces (131). Taylor's penalty for trying even feebly to draw attention to this starvation is a "nigger-lesson" (160): taken out to the woods, he is beaten and whipped nearly to death and left to crawl home as a bleeding warning to his people.

Published just a year after *Uncle Tom's Children*, William Attaway's brutal novel *Blood on the Forge* delves more deeply into the arithmetic of black subjection in the New South. Set in 1919 in the clay hills of Kentucky, Attaway portrays the three Moss brothers who know as deeply as Rev. Taylor that "share-cropping and being hungry went together" (1). Just as Wright's story opens with a historically resonant rhyme, Attaway's novel begins with Melody Moss slicking his ever-present guitar and singing a blues song about plantation math and hunger:

> "*Done scratched at the hills,*
>   *But the 'taters refuse to grow. . . .*
> *Done scratched at the hills,*
>   *But the 'taters refuse to grow. . . .*
> *Mister Bossman, Mister Bossman,*
>   *Lemme mark in the book once mo'. . . ."*

There were more verses like that than any one man knew. And after each verse the refrain:

> "*Hungry blues done got me listenin' to my love one cry. . . .*
> *Put some vittles in my belly, or yo' honey gonna lay down and die. . . .*" (3)

Just as Taylor knows he'll never have the profits the white man calculates for himself, so too these black sharecroppers have learned that the meager bounty of the earth belongs to the white "bossman" while they remain locked in debt peonage, every additional mark in "the book" tying them inescapably to the landowner. Not precisely a plantation ledger, the account book nevertheless records the fact that their very bodies and souls remain dependent on their employer, a widespread communal experience more vast and various "than any one man knew" yet bound by the simple language and sensation of hunger. Melody's leisure- and gold-loving brother Chinatown characterizes the situation bitterly: "We jest niggers, makin' the white man crop for him. Leave him make his own crop, then we don't end up owing him money every season" (5). Chinatown knows as well as his brothers, though, that being "jest niggers" disallows such detachment, that their social subjection keeps them indebted to the "white man" year after year. As the subsequent verse of the rhyme Rev. Taylor intones reminds us,

> Ten's a ten
> But it's mighty funny;
> When you cain't count good,
> You hain't got no money.
> (*Negro Folk Rhymes* 207)

The inaccessibility of education for rural blacks was a constant concern even into the twentieth century.[4] In a larger sense, however, the verse quoted above suggests that knowledge is irrelevant when whites control the laws, the books, and the social mathematics that keep black farmers in permanent debt and dependency. While the Moss family harvests a good crop, one that would draw "'a couple hundred dollars or so,'" Melody knows that they'll never see that money because "'Mr Johnston keeps the book. He don't let us see what's writ in it . . . he say what we made, and what's writ leaves us owin' him'" (31).[5] Melody's phrasing

Stealing Themselves Out of Slavery   65 here is delicate—he is speaking to a white "jackleg" recruiting millworkers to migrate North—but nonetheless clearly indicates that "what's writ" is fundamentally a different figure from what the Mosses actually "made." Such power was common: as Pete Daniel recounts, the landlord "dictated the rations the family received, the acreage planted, the mix of crops, and the ledger books" (7)—in short, their entire equation of subsistence. The arithmetic may have been fuzzy to many uneducated blacks, but the powers of white manipulation were no secret; as one former slave interviewed by a New Deal WPA worker commented shrewdly:

> It's like dat sum dem scholars couldn't git; standing alone dat naught ain't worth nothing, but set it up against dat which is of value and it takes on value. Set a naught ag'inst dat which is one and you has ten; set up another naught dar and you has a hundred. Now if somebody was to give me a note worth $10, and I found room to add another naught along side of de first; den dem two naughts what ain't worth nothing by deirselves gives de note de value of $99 if dey is sot along wid de one. Ed'icated folks calls dat raising de note. I is ig'nant and I calls dat robbery.[6]

The products differ depending on who is doing the math, but it is clear that as long as white men like Mr. Johnston could keep such calculating fictions alive, black workers like the Mosses would always be "owin'" their lives and livelihoods to them.

Repeated references to entrenched mathematical paradigms in these moments remind us of the persistent power and relevance of plantation codes and calculations. Under such spurious mathematics, African American southerners find themselves in nearly the same positions as their ancestors who had to steal in order to obtain what was rightfully theirs. The opening pages of *Blood on the Forge* are consumed with hunger and the hungry blues, the family's playful banter suggesting that the only strategies for combating the pangs are in "'sleepin'" or "'thievin'" (2). But by participating in this economy, even (presumably) subversively, these individuals are unwittingly helping to perpetuate it; attempts to steal, own, or increase their value end up reinscribing the terms of their subjection and eventually effecting their own suicidal erasure.

Amplifying the somber cadences of the opening scenes of *Blood on the Forge* is the revelation, six pages in, that just four weeks earlier the Moss boys' mother "had dropped dead between the gaping handles of the plow" while Chinatown and Melody were fooling around in the dust. "The lines had been double looped under her arms," Melody remembers, "so she was dragged through the damp, rocky clay by a mule trained never to balk in the middle of a row. The mule dragged her in. The rocks in the red hills are sharp. She didn't look like their maw any more" (7). Wild with grief, the eldest and freakishly large brother Big Mat "took a piece of flint rock and tore the life out of that mule, so that even the hide wasn't fit to sell" (7). It's clear that the mule is a proxy for the boys' mother, and that a tireless dedication to labor killed them both; more than that, both are violently disfigured after death, suggesting the grotesque extent to which their laboring bodies have betrayed them. Like the mule, "you couldn't stop [their mother] from working . . . she probably started in right away to plow for God" (7). But Big Mat's attempt to destroy the symbol of fruitless toil that ruins his mother—making the hide itself unfit to sell—only backfires. Mr. Johnston takes away their food credit and "claimed their share of the crop for the next two years in payment for his mule. He didn't say where the crop was coming from when there was no animal to plow with. He didn't say how they were going to eat without food credit. All they could do was wait for him to change his mind" (7). Raging desperately against the forces that stymie and starve them only places these workers at a more acute disadvantage, fatally bound to their condition of peonage and to Mr. Johnston's whims; resistance proves their plight to be just as adhesive and lethal as their mother's plow lines double-looped under her arms. Killing the mule ultimately constitutes a futile and suicidal display of exhaustion and grief.

It is not surprising that another mule, symbol of tireless toil, is slaughtered for similar purposes in Richard Wright's "The Man Who Was Almost a Man," first published in 1940 (the same year he released both *Uncle Tom's Children* and *Native Son*) and later revised for the collection *Eight Men*. The setting of this incident is also a plantation in the rural South, and the protagonist another black sharecropper, this time a seventeen-year-old boy named Dave. At the end of a long day working in the field, Dave fantasizes about having a gun that will make him feel powerful and like "a man." He manages to use his pay to buy the coveted gun and quickly becomes drunk on the possibility that he could "kill anybody, black or white" now, and that "holding his gun in his hand, nobody could run over him; they would have to respect him" (14). Dave's sympathetic desire to feel strong, powerful, and respected rises directly out of his condition of servitude and racial inferiority. But the conditions that drive him to such rebellion also insure that he will not surmount them; Dave's folly of self-possession and pride backfire, quite literally, when he accidentally shoots and kills Jenny, his boss's mule. Not only has he "bought a dead mule" that, like Big Mat, he will have to work off of the boss's books, but in a sense he has also delivered himself into the position of "dead mule" in the debit column of the ledger. He compares himself explicitly to Jenny: "Nobody ever gave him anything. All he did was work. They treat me like a mule, and then they beat me. He gritted his teeth. . . . Fifty dollars for a dead mule" (20). In his position of servitude, "they"—a broad, inclusive term for all white landowning society—work him into the ground and beat him like a mule; in his ill-fated gesture of power and reversal, he repeats these offenses upon himself, displaced onto the body of Jenny, whose value now becomes his own. He is supposed to sell back the gun to begin paying his debt to the boss, but instead he takes it—effectively pilfering the symbol of his own misbegotten power and inevitable self-destruction—and jumps aboard a passing train heading somewhere out of the South, "away, away to somewhere, somewhere where he could be a man" (21). The story ends here, with a clear and sober indication that he will remain a mere laboring animal in the field if he stays where he is; and secondly, that "a man" of power and violence is not necessarily a condition to aspire to, but simply a fulfillment of the white models he has grown up and suffered under. Yet fleeing is his only option in the end; and this escape echoes Wright's own when, as Margaret Walker recounts in her biography *Richard Wright: Daemonic Genius*, "almost a man . . . he resolved to run away, to take flight and run, to leave, to go far from the South that thought it knew and understood him, but never could know and understand him because it denied him his black humanity" (39). Wright did not leave because, as his mother feared, he "had gotten into trouble with 'white folks'" but because he suspected he eventually would if he stayed (39); Dave's plight is a symbolic version, it seems, of that apparently ineluctable end.[7]

Blood on the Forge also features a train escape on the heels of another near-murder. Mr. Johnston agrees finally to give the Mosses a replacement mule in an attempt to pacify and prevent his tenants from being cajoled by "jacklegs" to work in the northern mills. When he approaches the riding boss about taking home their new animal, Big Mat is viciously upbraided: "'If Mr Johnston got good sense you won't never get another mule,' said the riding boss. 'You'd be run off the land if I had my say. Killin' a animal worth forty dollars, 'cause a nigger woman got dragged over the rocks'" (28). This final equation, which suggests that the life of a "nigger woman" is not worth anything near "forty dollars," simply undoes the grieving son. In a blur of transcendent rage, Big Mat quickly and decisively knocks the riding boss to the ground and bludgeons him. In a chilling moment of reversal, the boss's disrespect for Mat's mother's life is countered by Mat's dehumanization of the fallen man: "'A dead one,' was his first frightened thought" as he surveys the body, now a collection of parts rather than a whole person: "the uneven movement of *the* red throat, *the* fluttering blood bubbles at *the* nose" (28, italics added). Identified by definite articles rather than possessive pronouns, the pieces of the riding boss's body are no longer things he owns, which is the most appropriate and personal kind of revenge that Mat could possibly bestow. Sensing that the man will survive the attack, though, Mat knows that both his reprisal and his life are short-lived; thus, it suddenly does make sense for the Moss boys to take the jackleg's tip and board a cargo train headed for the northern steel mills. Like Wright's young protagonist, the Mosses sneak onto a boxcar; unlike Wright's boy, however, the Mosses join a large group of fellow escapees bound for a massive migration. Their collective tale continues on to show us exactly where the mythical refuge of "somewhere" away from the South might be, and what kind of "men" they might hope to become there.

Northern Migrations and Southern Repetitions

As James Beeby and Donald G. Nieman report, during the height of Jim Crow southern blacks began to migrate in substantial numbers away from "the poverty and violence of the South to the burgeoning industrial cities of the North, where they found problems both old and new" (344). "New" to the Moss brothers are the dank factories and the gray industrial towns filled with strange immigrants from a number of European and Slavic nations; but the newness of the industrial North quickly pales in comparison to the haunting reappearance of the Old South. Before they even reach their Pennsylvania destination, it is clear that the Moss brothers are not traveling forward in history but backward: the conditions of their migration vividly evoke the Middle Passage itself. Like African slaves crammed into the hold of a schooner, these men "squatted on the straw-spread floor of a boxcar, bunched up like hogs headed for market, riding in the dark for what might have been years, knowing time only as dippers of warm water gulped whenever they were awake, helpless and drooping because they were headed into the unknown and there was no sun" (38). The brothers become separated, delirious, and miserable among pools of urine and the growing stench; for all of the men in the railcar, the "misery . . . was a mass experience" (39). In an episode evocative of the Great Migration, which peaked at the time the masses fled, the boys join the exodus north in hopes of finding improved labor conditions, pay, and treatment. But the Mosses' abject journey constitutes a harbinger of what they will find in the North: like slaves crossing the Atlantic, they arrive at their destination still bound by the shackles of an exploitative economy and social order.

For men conditioned to expect so little, life in the northern mill at first seems luxurious: "Big Mat was not thinking about the labor trouble. . . . For a man who had so lately worked from dawn to dark in the fields twelve hours and the long shift were not killing. For a man who had ended each year in debt any wage at all was a wonderful thing. For a man who had known no personal liberties even the iron hand of the mill was an advantage" (176). Exploited, overworked, and belittled by their bosses, the workers grow restless; but the displaced southerners, long enslaved to a mentality of bare survival, are held safely by the "iron hand" of a system that will keep them from recognizing and exploring the need and opportunities for real "advantage." Attaway makes it clear that the experience of the South and its fatal economy permanently disables African Americans from recognizing their true interests and potential even above the Mason-Dixon Line; put another way, their conditioning within the southern sharecropping institution prepares them to endure conditions up north. When Big Mat is deputized as a union-bashing thug, he feels drunk with newfound power and sees his new status in a very limited way, as a vindication of his former subjection: "Maybe in the South he had been just a peon. There had been a riding boss to count the drops of sweat from his body. But here there was no riding boss" (227). Yet his folly is in his inability to exorcise the riding boss from this scene or from his imagination; he merely effects a substitution: "exalted" by his authority, he decides "There was a riding boss—Big Mat. Big Mat Moss from the red hills was the riding boss" (231). The man who "counts" the drops of sweat from his body, quantifying his labor and his person simultaneously, is now himself. For the man who has never been able to see what's "writ" in the books or to account accurately for his own labor, this reversal of power is profound; but it comes attended by profound violence as well. When Big Mat kills a man—significantly, an innocent Ukrainian man who "had never been in the South" (231) and is a stranger to Mat's historical vengeance—he perversely acts out the riding boss's revenge on himself; accordingly, the sweep of retribution swings full circle, and Big Mat himself is soon slain, too. As his eyes close on death, he thinks "he had been through all of this once before. Only at that far time he had been the arm strong with hate. . . . Maybe somewhere in these mills a new Mr Johnston was creating riding bosses, making a difference where none existed" (233). Attaway wants us to see clearly that the enforced, unnatural social divisions in the South are being cyclically recreated in post-Reconstruction America's industrial wastelands and battlefields, wreaking their baleful influence on men who have never even experienced or known such disaster. The systemic repression of people like Big Mat ensures the endless recycling of violence and the fatal lust for power fueled by dispossession and hate, transmitted in such novels by way of the symbolic Great Migration but, as Attaway demonstrates vividly enough, encoded already in the systems of capitalism they both flee and run toward. The labor bosses know, uncannily, that their perpetuation of capital enslavement depends on exploiting the buried trauma of such men: "as long as they come from the South," these workers will insure that the "union ain't gonna win. They didn't figure on the South when they started this here." (234).

Indeed, too desperate to see beyond their present condition, the southerners become unwitting allies of the labor lords. On their arrival in the Pennsylvania mill town the brothers are greeted with suspicion and hatred by the immigrant workers who know that the African American southerners have been shipped in to take their places in times of labor strife and in the threat of a strike. When union activity breaks full force into this world late in the novel, the blacks and immigrants are played against each other by the bosses to disastrous effect; the owners exploit the African Americans' conditioned poverty, tempting them with positions of authority and power both within the mill and in the community.[8] Long foreclosed from the workings of the books that control their lives and their humanity, under the capitalist practices of modern America these southerners are twisted into beings able to justify their acts of desperation on the grounds of both existential and literal hunger and rage. While Big Mat is manipulated into a situation in which he commits murder, these desperate measures reveal themselves as visceral attempts to inhabit the position of the master, the "riding boss," the one who wields the power and totes the gun and counts drops of sweat. At bottom, such acts disclose a simple desire to live and be legitimated in the holy text of southern society: the plantation account book. When the mill owners make Big Mat a deputy, he renders his satisfaction in the cruel and absolute language of the ledger: "he was a deputy. It was all down on the books. It could not be changed" (193). The entry validates his existence in a comfortingly yet disturbingly permanent way, as a credit this time rather than a "debt slave" (217). Locked into an economy of brutality, the event effectively and decisively signals his end: "It could not be changed." Not surprisingly, neither of Mat's brothers survives the year intact either. Chinatown is blinded in an explosion on the job, while a hand injury leaves Melody unable to play his beloved guitar. Both men effectively lose the capacities that not only bring them great pleasure but that evoke their very identities: Chinatown his ability to admire his own image and Melody the musical genius that gives him his name. Attaway's transformations of his characters often include literal fragmentation and mutilation to underscore the profound psychological and physical damage wrought by this cyclical, self-sustaining narrative of debasement.

Compulsive, environmentally induced, and often suicidal violence among African Americans in or in flight from the Jim Crow South is a constant presence in Wright's work as well. The most vicious and well-known of these portraits, *Native Son*, appeared in 1940, just one year before Attaway's novel. Bigger Thomas's acts of rape and murder are figured as inevitable—if extreme—byproducts of the pestilential world that constrains and distorts his humanity. After an immediate round of effusive and polite praise for Wright's obvious artistic achievement, readers, especially those from the black community, despaired over its bleak vision and potent stereotypes. Letters to editors of African American newspapers expressed anxiety that "'[white readers] will believe [Bigger] typical of all of us,'" as one woman worried. "'Our record of criminality is . . . usually against ourselves. How often does a colored man go out and kill some white person brooding over wrongs?'" (qtd. in Rowley 193). However, this letter writer fails to consider that killings like Bigger's when rendered in literature are ultimately representative of the community's crimes "against ourselves" that she plainly laments; that is, by learning to inhabit the position of their oppressors, their behavior in turn becomes criminal and finally suicidal. In effect, Wright's characters, like the African Americans in his own world, must symbolically inhabit the white man's position in order to escape the black man's lot, but in doing so necessarily become alienated from themselves and driven by self-serving capitalist priorities.

The process is simple at first: a southern black circumscribed by regional apartheid attempts to impersonate the master's methods in order to effect mere survival. To garner such authority under the stringent codes of Jim Crow, however, would involve outright theft. In his early autobiography, *Black Boy*, Wright observes that

> all about me, Negroes were stealing. More than once I had been called a "dumb nigger" by black boys who discovered that I had not availed myself of a chance to snatch some petty piece of white property that had carelessly been left in my reach. . . . I knew that the very nature of black and white relations bred this constant thievery.
>
> No Negroes in my environment had ever thought of organizing . . . and petitioning their white employers for higher wages. The very thought would have been terrifying to them. . . . So, pretending to conform to the laws of the whites, grinning, bowing, they let their fingers stick to what they could touch. And the whites seemed to like it. (218–19)

Again we see the possibility of unionization by class vetoed as "terrifying" to blacks intimidated, killed, or simply sidelined in their efforts; moreover, organizing and petitioning simply had not emerged as viable palliatives for either blacks or poor whites in the stricken South. The reality, Wright explains, is surreptitious thievery bred specifically and reciprocally within the unscrupulous world of "black and white relations"—that is, learned well by the example of whites who often engaged in such sinister practices to acquire their own property. The pilfered objects themselves—and not the act of filching them—are described as "petty," which allows Wright to transfer the word's usual association with "larceny" or "theft" to the goods themselves: *these are stolen things even before the blacks deign to take them*, he avers.[9] African American southerners are driven not only by desperation to steal, but by vengeance as well; they are, quite plainly, taking back what is rightfully theirs.

Yet Wright's objections to stealing are "not moral" but practical: "I knew that, in the long run, it was futile, that it was not an effective way to alter one's relationship to one's environment" (219). He knows that his subterfuge serves white expectations and needs, keeping him firmly rooted not specifically in a region, perhaps, but in a more abstract "environment" of desperation and subjection. Wright knows only too well that whites count on this despair and "would rather have had Negroes who stole, work for them than Negroes who knew, however dimly, the worth of their own humanity. Hence, whites placed a premium upon black deceit . . . and their rewards were bestowed upon us in the degree that we could make them feel safe and superior" (219). By stealing to get ahead, they simply insure that southern race relations stay "safe" in the old familiar patterns. Ultimately, the subterfuge proves neither subversive nor redemptive; instead, it is downright suicidal: "To go to jail in the South would mean the end," Wright knows; "there was the possibility that if I were ever caught I would never reach jail" (218).

Desperation nonetheless compels him to begin embezzling money at the cinema ticket counter where he works, in hopes of saving enough to flee North. Like the whites around him, he learns to "master" his anxiety and "calculate coldly," and he gathers enough capital to leave in a radical gesture of self-possession (222). In essence, he slyly appropriates his own identity: "it's my life," he asserts at the close of the chapter. "I'll see now what I can make of it" (227). Beyond equating his life with the funds necessary to purchase its autonomy, his language bears the ineradicable weight of production: in seizing his own life, he now needs not just to "make" his own person but also to "make" good on it. Headed north to Chicago, Wright's opportunity to work and produce in an honest fashion seems to lie only beyond the borders of the South and the limitations of Jim Crow. Literary history tells us, of course, that Wright capitalized tremendously on the investment of stolen funds, a measure that paid off in righteousness but reminds us that the methods are dangerously reproductive of the social order he was committed to leave behind. These machinations yield a flawed kind of redemption because they belong to a dissolute economy from which there is as yet no escape.

And indeed, by resorting to unethical measures to attempt escape from one (southern) iteration of capital slavery to another (northern) version, the potential for permanent psychological self-debasement is profound. One of Wright's most overlooked and generally misunderstood short stories, collected in *Eight Men* but often considered a novella in its own right, "The Man Who Lived Underground" offers a dark, surrealist vision of the underbelly of an anonymous, industrial American city as glimpsed by a modern black house servant wrongly accused and forced to confess to the murder of a white female neighbor.[10] Desperate to escape further torture by a crew of police thugs, he escapes into a sewer and thus sets into motion a nightmarish underground odyssey through the bowels of deceit, corruption, and death. While many critics have read this tale as an allusive chronicle reminiscent of Dostoevsky or classical mythology, it seems also to have a peculiarly modern American character: by descending south/ South of the city, the narrator gains a privileged vantage on the corruption above. Indeed, the reverse flight of this neoslave takes him symbolically south in order to highlight vividly and horribly the northern iniquity he is now able to witness while safely under cover. What he sees, then, both reflects and repeats typically southern patterns of usury and abjection.

We simply cannot ignore the symbology of the "underground" flight for an American black protagonist, wrongfully imprisoned and fleeing for his life. Through sewer grates and trapdoors, like Harriet Jacobs he peers in on white underhandedness in all its naked awfulness, realizing slowly and surely that there is no true escape from the shackles of racial subjection; nonetheless, in his state of terrific want he cannot help but be seduced by the world of luxurious depravity. In one particularly stunning moment, he digs his way into a basement containing a view of a safe and watches "an eerie white hand, seemingly detached from its arm" moving "in and out of the safe, taking wads of bills and cylinders of coins" (35). The hand is clearly a metonym for white society, but instead of being repulsed by its (quite literal) underhandedness, he instantly wants to watch and figure out the "combination" to the safe. Significantly, the key to gaining what the white world takes and enjoys is to learn how to spin the numbers just as the white man does. So he waits patiently for the white hand to return, and then he transcribes exactly the figures that the dial turns to: "With quivering fingers, he etched 1-R-6 upon the brick wall with the tip of the screwdriver. The hand twirled the dial twice to the left and stopped at two, and he engraved 2-L-2 upon the wall . . . [then] he wrote 4-R-6. . . . [and] 3-L-0. The door swung open and again he saw the piles of green money and the rows of wrapped coins. I got it, he said grimly" (42). But he doesn't yet have "it": he is simply watching the white hand perform the treacherous arithmetic of accumulation; he has the figures recorded in his own hand, engraved upon the very wall that separates him from the world he desires, but it remains to be seen if the secret code will yield a result for him as well. His belief and desire here overreach his reality with extraordinary pathos. As so many of these protagonists hope, simply learning the correct combination of numbers should afford them access to the riches long locked away from their communities. But even in possession of the numbers, Wright's protagonist does not, as he believes, have the magical code. He watches those two white hands go in and take out the money, and he is "astonished": "He's stealing, he said to himself. He grew indignant, as if the money belonged to him. . . . He felt that his stealing the money and the man's stealing were two entirely different things" (42). His own impulse is about "getting it," while the white man's is, he assumes, about spending it, "perhaps for pleasure" (42). What separates the two impulses seem to be deeply ingrained differences in attitudes toward consumption: for the black man, it is the personal "sensation" of acquisition he is after, while the white man treats and uses the cash itself frivolously (42). Wright's underground man desires this money viscerally, but without "possessiveness" or greed (44); something in his being simply needs and hungers for it. As Leigh Anne Duck argues about poor whites in Caldwell's grotesque, proletarian novels, these physical economic drives are not materially productive but "they do suggest a form of labor driven by the body rather than the corporation, and this configuration of intimacy with one's own labor offers a form of authenticity often longed for in Depression-era discourse" (90). For a black character associated at least symbolically with southern experience—he is, effectively, a house slave who escapes a lynching—the visceral attraction not to labor but to recompense seems to be the soul's manner of crying out for reparations.

While the protagonist waits for the man to return so he can, unseen, watch him work the combination that will unlock those funds, he witnesses what should be a glaring warning that history will not repeat itself any differently. In an attempt to determine just which room the safe is in, he begins digging new holes and ends up, not coincidentally, staring into a meat market instead. Clearly abutting and nearly mistaken for the area where the safe is located, the market presents a crucial parable and parallel to the world of money and coins: as if turning the dial to a safe, "He twisted the knob and swung the door in; a frigid blast made him shiver. In the shadows before him were halves and quarters of hogs and lambs and steers hanging from metal hooks on the low ceiling, red meat encased in folds of cold white fat. . . . The odor of fresh raw meat sickened him and he backed away. A meat market, he whispered" (37). In fact, it is "NICK'S FRUITS AND MEATS"; lest we miss what Nick is neatly and mathematically dividing, quartering, and selling here, a white woman soon enters the empty store to make a purchase from the fruit section, considers the grapes, and requests "'a pound of dark ones'" (39). To further drive home the point, it is the protagonist himself who is forced to sell these "dark" objects to her—the woman spots him lurking and assumes he is a clerk. She pays him a dime that he flings away after her exit "with a gesture of contempt"; but he does take from the market a meat cleaver, "for what purpose he did not know"—it simply adheres to his hand (40). In this swift series of events, he finds himself unwittingly attached to the objects—coins and a cleaver—that signify the selling and mutilating of his own symbolic proxies. The next moment finds him uncontrollably returning to thoughts of finding the safe and trying to decode the combination. He eventually finds and uses the magical combination to open the safe, stunned to see the money left there waiting for him. This spree of theft (he soon ends up taking a horde of diamonds and watches from a jewelry store as well) seems to constitute a compulsive act of revenge rather than a hungry desire to get rich. Despite all of the dissolution he witnesses and the portent of danger he holds in his hands, he can't resist wanting narcissistically to be part of what the aboveground men possess and experience: "'Mister,' he later explains to the police, 'when I looked through all of those holes and saw how people were living, I loved 'em'" (69).

But having what they have takes him fundamentally away from who he is; he very literally enters a foreign landscape where his prior identity is erased from knowledge. In explicit detail, Wright shows us how unfamiliar the stolen currency is to the protagonist; he inspects it curiously, "expecting it to reveal hidden qualities," but discovers finally that it is "just like any other paper" (44). At first he doesn't even realize that he has taken "wads of one-dollar bills" rather than "the big ones" (44); the money itself has only symbolic rather than actual value. He is simply enacting "what he had seen others do" and in so doing tries momentarily to live their lives and loses his own identity completely. After taking the money from the safe he thinks, "Oh yes! He had forgotten. He would now write his name on the typewriter. . . . But what was his name? He stared, trying to remember. . . . But it would not come to him" (49). Having just inspected the cash and read the standard inscription on the bills as if he were "reading of the doings of people who lived on some far-off planet" (49), it becomes clear that the protagonist now inhabits an alien space, language, and body; he even pretends to be an accountant or lawyer, delighted by his playful approximation of their lingo: "He laughed. That's just the way they talk, he said" (49). The vocabulary and laws of this world give him momentary delight and power, but at a terrible and dislocating expense. Not only does his name escape him, but he finds himself suddenly falling unconscious: "he was still standing when the thought came to him that he had been asleep. Yes. . . . But he was not yet fully awake; he was still queerly blind and deaf. How long had he slept? Where was he?" (54). This disorientation powerfully asserts his exile from his own humanity, thrust into an unfamiliar and inimical world of dollars and cents and contracts and codes. He simply is no longer himself in this realm, and an intense kind of repression and amnesia—and ultimately, utter hilarity and insanity—takes over to make this stunningly clear.

Making emphatic the notion that slavery is the "haunting" historical precondition for his current anxiety, the protagonist compulsively wallpapers his hideout with the stolen money, pasting the green bills over the dirt walls and then decorating them with "the bloody cleaver," "a fistful of ticking gold watches," and a slew of bejeweled rings (50). The decked-out hideout becomes a "mocking symbol" to "the world that had branded him guilty," and suddenly inspires him to declare, "he was free!" (50). "Free" in a nominal sense from the world of slavery, he nonetheless bears the somatic traces of the system's cruelty and desperation; even in this calculated gesture of emancipation, he is still shackled to and menaced by the world above where dollar bills, watches, and bloody cleavers can hang together in a chilling equation of value. These things are "all on the same level of value" for him: "They were the serious toys of the men who lived in . . . the world that had condemned him, branded him guilty" (45). The pointedly anonymous narrator becomes, in effect, and with all intended irony, "the Man" of the story's title. We know, of course, that under such conditions he will never be "free."

The rules and codes of this world are so deeply engraved and powerfully discomposing that they throw the tenets of logic and morality perilously off-kilter. Similar to Wright's own autobiographical reflections in *Black Boy*, the man ponders a shift in morality associated with his desperate actions: "if the world as men had made it was right, then anything else was right, any act a man took to satisfy himself, murder, theft, torture" (52). The problem is that the "men" who made the world and its laws are white, and their interpretations have the power to fatally undermine the black man's existence. Assumed "guilty" of a crime he did not commit even before the story begins, he will remain perpetually culpable no matter what he does, especially when he is driven to unlawful measures to "satisfy himself" and, more simply, to preserve his innocence and integrity. Under these skewed laws of rationality, he begins to doubt the reality of his innocence: "They know I didn't do anything, he muttered. But how could he prove it? He had signed a confession. Though innocent, he felt guilty, condemned" (40). Juxtaposed with his search for the safe, his adventure in the meat market, and the string of petty and major thefts—all of which employ the same language of condemnation—this meditation on his culpability is crucial: his imposed, inexorable guilt is inextricable from his observation of white subterfuge and theft. Tellingly, he resorts to the same crimes whites themselves commit in order to get ahead; the logically implausible but socially impervious difference is that "guilt" applies only to the black man and not the white. Once in possession of the money, the man loses his senses and his identity entirely; the white man, on the other hand, writes his own blank slip. Ultimately what the man desires is not cash so much as a reprieve from the pressure of ambient guilt and suspicion; he is, from the start of the story, running away from a wrongful accusation. "It is not the money that was luring him, but the mere fact that," like the white men around him, now "he could get it with impunity" (41). While being black means always being "condemned" without evidence, the white life offers the possibility for true artifice "with impunity." Yet he discovers harshly that such substitutions are impossible: the black man will always be guilty under the perversions of law "as men had made it."

Wright renders this sentence still more ineluctable when a worker at the radio store is accused of taking the machine that the protagonist actually stole, to which the narrator reacts in bizarre approval: "Perhaps it was a good thing that they were beating the boy; perhaps the beating would bring to the boy's attention, for the first time in his life, the secret of his existence, the guilt that he could never get rid of" (56). Next, he watches impassively as the police wrongly accuse the jewelry store's night watchman of the protagonist's theft as well, "trying to make the watchman confess, just as they had made him confess to a crime he had not done" (56). These black proxies are all interchangeable, it seems, repeatedly swapping and sharing a communal experience of shame and guilt according to the persistent inequities of their world and their chance encounters with justice-hungry, racist white law enforcers. When the watchman is brutally killed behind closed doors, the narrator processes the event through a warped lens of ambient doom: "The watchman was guilty; although he was not guilty of the crime of which he had been accused, he was guilty, he had always been guilty" (57). The shared condition fatally binding the protagonist to these clerks—mere workers and pawns in a consumer economy—is an adherent history of racial subjection, one that has worked its way into their very bodies:

> Why was this sense of guilt so seemingly innate, so easy to come by, to think, to feel, so verily physical? It seemed that when one felt this guilt one was retracted in one's feelings a faint pattern designed long before; it seemed that one was always trying to remember a gigantic shock that had left a haunting impression upon one's body which one could not forget or shake off, but which had been forgotten by the conscious mind, creating in one's life a state of constant anxiety. (55)

Like the physical sensation for money that has no practical value but only spiritual significance, guilt too haunts the body bereft of its inherent value and integrity under slavery. The "gigantic shock" of indentured servitude, subjection, and now segregation has induced the somatic hauntings that these characters simply cannot "shake off" or escape.

To drive this point fully home, Wright brings his protagonist to a fateful end. The man admits defeat when he turns himself in to the same police who had earlier tortured a confession out of him, utterly confused now about his own actual and existential guilt: he knows he didn't kill Mrs. Peabody but feels certain he is "guilty" anyway (64). He becomes desperate to show the officers his underground bunker with its symbolic decorations:

> "Mister," he said . . . "you ought to see how funny the rings look on the wall." He giggled. "I fired a pistol, too. Just once, to see how it felt."
> "What do you suppose he's suffering from?" Johnson asked.
> "Delusions of grandeur, maybe," Murphy said.
> "Maybe it's because he lives in a white man's world," Lawson said. (72)

The policemen's diagnosis is more accurate than they or the readers may realize: in the "white man's world" that the protagonist finally enters from the underground, the symbolic route from South to North that gives African Americans a distinctive perspective on American race relations, the man is fatally deluded and undone by his attempts to inhabit this space. When he leads the police to the manhole, hoping they will descend into the sewer after him, they simply shoot him from above and then close the manhole cover to hide his expiring body, submerged now forever in the buried cellar of the corrupt white consciousness. Symbolically, he dies in the quasi-southern space that has given him both terrible knowledge of and a bitter taste of white American life; in his final moments, he sees "the glittering cave, the shouting walls, and the laughing floor. . . . Then his mouth was full of thick, bitter water" (74). His own attempt to taste, mock, and deride the world that has foreclosed him only fills his gasping mouth with foul waste. He becomes once again "a whirling object rushing alone in the darkness, veering, tossing, lost in the heart of the earth" (74).

Debits to Credits: The Arithmetic of Narcissism and the Price of Ascent

While Wright's protagonist was merely peering into the white world from below, unable to access its spaces or goods without fundamentally surrendering his identity, other African Americans were making valiant attempts to enter it on level ground. The fact of white privilege in matters economic, political, and social has been well rehearsed by critics David Roediger, George Lipsitz, Grace Elizabeth Hale, and Linda Faye Williams, among many others. But while having a white skin to insure such prestige was a preposterous option for men like Wright's protagonist, other light-skinned African Americans could and did choose to better their situations by "passing" for white. The scholarship on this phenomenon, both in its historical and literary iterations, is voluminous, and generally tends to emphasize the dangers of socially constructed notions of racial essentialism. In James Weldon Johnson's *Autobiography of an Ex-Coloured Man* the protagonist is a part-black man whose ability to pass for white dramatizes both the fanatical artificiality of race categories and the opportunities accorded those fortunate enough to have a visibly white skin. His fantasy of acquiring cultural capital and material success, opportunities reserved largely for white men in the early twentieth-century South, leads him to conclude that he must reject his race altogether in order to get ahead.

New in my reading of the novel is the suggestion that Johnson presents us with not just a tragedy of racial abrogation but in fact a nightmarish postcolonial vision: by more or less becoming white in order to get ahead, the ex-coloured man devolves into a fatal kind of narcissism; but the fact that this calculating obsession plagues him even as a child suggests that the dynamics of self-valuing are bred into him as a cultural birthright, making inevitable his tortured decision to pass. The ex-coloured man's own interference in the biased arithmetic of mastery reveals much about both the profitability of race categories and the laborious, skewed equations necessary to keep them intact. Ultimately Johnson's narrator learns a simple and fateful lesson in negation and accumulation: he must be not-black in order to purchase his autonomy, yet the spiritual impoverishment he suffers is a disastrous return on his investment.

Johnson's *Autobiography* centers on a nameless, mixed-race man's struggle to define and support himself. The plights are simultaneous: he wrestles with his ambiguous racial identity at the same time that he must find a way to survive financially, having lost his (part-black) mother and been abandoned by his (rich white) father. In the end, he must choose one heritage over the other, less for psychological consistency than for material wealth. He chooses whiteness primarily because economic success is incompatible with being black in the Jim Crow South—and because, having a fair skin in a system based on the ocularity of race, he can pass with little fear of discovery. In Johnson's text, narcissism and hybridity emerge to dramatize the artificiality of postcolonial race relations by revealing the ex-coloured man's suppressed yearning for his own Otherness, a subtle reminder that his body literally contains biological traces of a socially autonomous self he must suppress. He can be either black or white, but not both in the same body; yet he is always yearning for the submerged part of his racial heritage. As Homi Bhabha asserts, the Other constitutes a "bizarre figure of desire" and that "the very place of identification, caught in the tension of demand and desire, is a space of splitting" because "the question of identification is never the affirmation of a pre-given identity, never a *self*-fulfilling prophecy" (44–45). Before he learns that he is part-black, the ex-coloured man finds himself attracted to deep colors and darkness: he has a "particular fondness for the black keys" on the piano, a sentiment articulated just after describing the "strange harmonies" he produces "on either the high keys of the treble or the low keys of the bass" (462). A sense of harmonic fusion attends the moment, which "interrupts" and "annoys" his mother presumably because she harbors the secret and knows the threat and despair of these "strange harmonies." But the narrator fixes on the contrasts: he prefers the "black" keys, and the "harmonies" emerge from either the "high keys" or the "low keys"—not both together.[11] This seems to disqualify his tune from the status of musical harmony, disturbing also the dubious logic that essential difference must be maintained in order to achieve racial euphony. His secret preference for the black keys, however, reminds us that desire and instinct naturally subvert such radical and artificial polarization. For his attraction swings both ways, but always toward the forbidden self: after he resigns himself to living as "black," he expresses increasingly sympathetic "white" characteristics, as we see later.

The ex-coloured man is nameless because, as a figure whose very identity is based primarily on race, his ambiguity begets anonymity. It is significant that the only way we may identify him is as the titular "Ex-Coloured Man." As such, he is divorced from his status as a black man; however, that identity is never erased from his name but simply negated and rendered a present absence: a chiastic X ("Ex"), evocative of racial crossing and the mirroring of opposites, becomes a marker of his existence. As a figure of the cross, the chiasmus also implies crossing racial divides or passing; but the narrator does not "pass" fluidly from the black world into white society and stay there. As Samira Kawash suggests, "passing is the *continual* motion of crossing the color line" (64, italics added); the ex-coloured man, on the other hand, passes back and forth ambivalently and is never simply content with whom he has chosen to be. A figure perpetually in transition, he is always responding to and yearning narcissistically for his "other" self left on the far side of the line of racial demarcation.

It is clear that some choice needs to be made in order to steady the narrator's fickle whims; narcissism develops early as a sign that this evolution is in process. In a classic scene of narcissistic contemplation, the young narrator, having just been made by his schoolteacher to stand up with the other black children and realizing in sudden horror that he is one of them, rushes home to inspect his new dark self in the mirror. He notices not a repulsive, bestial, dark creature but rather gentle, lustrous features and skin that appears "whiter than it really was" (17). He focuses on the "ivory whiteness" of this skin, the pale forehead, the "soft" and "glossy" hair (17). The reflection is clearly his own, as was Narcissus'; but he interprets his self as an exaggerated version of an ideal and fetching whiteness, the self he wants society to appreciate. Or does he? In fact, he *is* white by appearance—though perhaps not as white as he sees himself—and his narcissism steps in to assert the full richness of this knowledge; but he does notice black elements, too: his dark, wavy hair and the "liquid darkness" of his eyes. He will be haunted by this irrepressible duality throughout the novel, forced to deny it and choose one identity categorically over the other. While Henry Louis Gates Jr. argues that "the narrator is 'white *and* black, at his whim and by his will'" (qtd. in Kawash 70), in fact, any agency or "will" has been predetermined by the rewards available to him for making one choice over the other. He *sees* himself as white and cherishes that image, a foretelling of the active, calculating narcissism that will rule his racial and material choices.

For a time he struggles mightily to realize his black identity; but this endeavor is complicated by the fact that he also aspires to be an artist. Historically, the ability to engage in artistic endeavors has held revolutionary potential for African Americans, as the earliest slave narratives testify.[12] As Henry Louis Gates Jr. attests, however, we must always also acknowledge "the commodity function of black writing" in the rare cases in which his slave could actually write, the master owned and profited from his slave's words (*Figures* 25). More often, of course, blacks were prevented from learning to read and write at all; in turn, as Gates claims, "Race and reason, ethnocentrism and logocentrism, together were used by the enlightened to deprive the black of his or her humanity" (25). Thus, blacks were either foreclosed from the realm of literature, what philosophers like "Hume, Kant, Jefferson, and Hegel, seemed to decide was the signal measure of the potential, innate humanity of a race" (25), or else that literature was stolen from them when they did create it. Even during the Harlem Renaissance, the greatest concentrated outpouring of African American art within a single period and location, a system of white patronage often facilitated and influenced the works produced.[13] Nonetheless, for Houston A. Baker Jr. in *Turning South Again*, black creativity signals an "economic solvency" that heralds a more general "life-enhancing and empowering" condition, but that also preserves categorical race identity—either "*black modernism*" or "mulatto modernism" (33).[14] As Walter Johnson powerfully reasserts, the cultural legitimacy of the African American writer is tied intimately not just to race pride and uplift but to reversing a history of economic insolvency that equated the black body with labor and currency.[15] Yet for blacks more than perhaps any other individuals, the very act of producing art is indelibly encoded with the threat of exploitation.

The ex-coloured man experiences this peril in his desire to be a musician, which seems at first a vehicle for expression and liberation but ultimately reinscribes the precise arithmetic of his marginalization. As Johnson indicates subtly (and not so subtly) in numerous textual moments, his narrator's identity as an artist or a creator is inextricable from the fact of his blackness—and, what is more, from the haunting politics of chattel slavery. As a child just learning to play the piano, he avoids the "incremental," "one-two-three," and "counting out" styles in favor of simply "reproducing" the songs of others (26–27);[16] such a preference signifies his musical genius, certainly, but at the same time it cannot be divorced from the precedence of numbers and counting that lingers in the black cultural memory as a reminder of being measured and priced on the block and in the planter's record. Instinctually, he chooses the slave's role of mimicry rather than autonomy, ventriloquizing the scores of white masters rather than inventing sequences of his own. Playing the piano, the narrator becomes overwhelmed with emotion and often begins sobbing, or else he falls asleep in exhaustion after his "whole body" has been engaged in the production of music; the emphasis on exertion and depletion suggests that the activity mirrors a kind of physical toil, much like the ingrained somatic connection to labor that Duck identifies and Wright's work reveals. Also like Wright's underground man, Johnson's narrator becomes dimly aware in these moments of a kind of haunting impressed on not just his body but his soul, as these moments of work produce the deepest, sobbing sorrow.

Yet the ex-coloured man represses much of the reality that these moments conjure, first because music is something that brings him enormous pride, and also because it brings him considerable profit. He is discovered by a very rich white man who brings him home to play the piano for him, and for whom he soon begins working regularly as a veritable musical slave. The millionaire reserves his services exclusively; the protagonist begins playing privately for his new employer or as the entertainment at his grand dinner parties, taking his own plate of food back in the kitchen with the other help during his brief breaks. The narrator remembers that "occasionally he 'loaned' me to some of his friends," with the emphasis on "loaned" indicating that he represents a prized possession rather than simply an employee (120). And he is worked apparently to the bone, commanded to play for interminable stints: "He seemed to be some grim, mute, but relentless tyrant, possessing over me a supernatural power which he used to drive me on mercilessly to exhaustion" (121). This tyrant clearly approximates an overseer or plantation boss whose hegemony over the slave is so potent that it appears mystical, operating wordlessly like a kind of "possession"—a word whose double meaning is felt heavily in this context. "But these feelings came very rarely," the ex-coloured man reasons. Why?—"he paid me so liberally I could forget much" (121). "Payment" is the apparent arbiter for blacks whose status as postslavery wage laborers prioritizes the necessity to earn an honest living, yet even lavish compensation cannot undo the persistent reminders of systemic exploitation. Rather than laboring in the fields or as a house servant, though, as do Attaway's and Wright's protagonists, the ex-coloured man enters the realm of artistic production in order that Johnson may show how pervasive this crisis is even—and especially—for the black intellectuals and elite that DuBois championed as the "Talented Tenth," the great hope of the race. As talented as he is, the narrator will rarely be paid or treated as well as his white peers; instead, his expansive skill and ambitions are purchased and controlled by one wealthy man. In postcolonial terms, Johnson's narrator finds himself governed by a kind of cultural neoslavery.[17]

As a correlative to his ambiguous racial identity, the musical forms he innovates do not just mimic white forms but rather promote a version of cultural hybridity. He begins with mainly white templates upon which he builds his own artistic dreams, blending African American folk and white European elements in order to produce new forms that exceed and disrupt the originals. While the ex-coloured man rejects the idea of the musical "duet" (29), he does, importantly, enjoy playing with beautiful and beloved white women twice in the text—first, a girl on whom he has a desperate boyish crush, and later, a white woman who ultimately becomes his wife and inspires him to pass permanently as white. He thus safely preserves his essential "black" charade as a segregated figure, while allowing his music as proxy to extend outward and mingle erotically with these distinctly white others. As he matures, the ex-coloured man learns to blend his classical, white European training with a more indigenous ragtime sound, attempting to forge something of mixed and therefore "universal" appeal to the music scene (100). With masterful skill and success, he fulfills Baker's notion of "mulatto modernism" and Bhabha's belief in the seditious capacity of mimicry and hybridity.

Americans are well aware that such hybridity is the foundation of modern rock and jazz music, that the iconic Elvis owes his mass appeal to the African American roots of his soulful sound and gyrating hips. Yet in Johnson's text, black art is still classified and commodified simply for what it offers the white race, as something to consume as entertainment or to appropriate for its cultural cachet and profit potential.[18] Resonant again of slavery, African Americans provide the work and the material while whites earn the credit and reap the fiscal harvest. In an early description of the New York "Club" the narrator frequents, there is an impressive photo gallery "of every coloured man in America who had ever 'done anything.' . . . The most of these photographs were autographed and, in a sense, made a really valuable collection" (104). We cannot fail to notice, though, that the pictures of "every" successful black fit somehow on the walls of this small club, or that they comprise a "collection"—only valuable "in a sense," by being framed, hung, stylized, and owned by a white arbiter. "Authentic" African American art held primitivist appeal for the fashionable white Americans like the ones who would have visited such a club, and who often served as patrons for aspiring black artists (much like the millionaire who hires Johnson's narrator, or the rich white woman shot by the black lover she financially supports) or simply imitated or outright stole their work and royalties—again, a system of unacknowledged production and profit resonant of slavery. As Ross Posnock asserts, "without white plundering of black talent, American popular art, especially music and dance, would be radically impoverished. Yet . . . the scandal of white plagiarism resides not in the violation of black ownership but in the refusal to acknowledge indebtedness" (20). Much like the false sense of inflation granted by slavery's exploitation, "white plagiarism" of artistic material usurps black production as personal property and attempts to obfuscate the origins of its wealth; in a remarkable reversal, however, the white is "indebted" to the black for its most public acts of expression, one that mass culture circulates and makes visible much more readily than stores of private wealth.[19] Moreover, "plagiarism" itself constitutes a kind of mimicry; such a turnabout bears out Toni Morrison's thesis that white American culture is, in fact, fundamentally underwritten by its African-American influences, as not just narcissistic "ego-enforcer[s]" but ego-fabricators (*Playing in the Dark* 8). Nonetheless, the inequities of capitalism combined with the politics of racism disguise the true nature of this indebtedness. By the end of the narrative, the narrator has given up music altogether in favor of a more lucrative occupation. When he abandons his artistry, Johnson's narrator also jettisons his African American heritage.

It thus becomes clear that entrenched economic inequities preempt not just the narrator's career but his very racial identity. The indissolubility of race and economics materializes in his frequent use of mathematical expressions, which tend to appear irrepressibly in moments of racial ambivalence or self-doubt. When for example the ex-coloured man tries to insert himself into the psyche of racism, he finds it explicable as a mathematical problem:

> The main difficulty of the race question does not lie so much in the actual condition of the blacks as it does in the mental attitude of the whites. . . . By a complex, confusing, and almost contradictory mathematical process, by the use of zigzags instead of straight lines, the earth can be proved to be the centre of things celestial; but by an operation so simple it can be comprehended by a schoolboy, its position can be verified among the other worlds which revolve about the sun, and its movements harmonized with the laws of the universe. So, when the white race assumes as a hypothesis that it is the main object of creation and that all things else are merely subsidiary to its well-being . . . all are required to maintain the position. (166–67)

The ex-coloured man astutely realizes that mathematical and scientific "laws" can be laboriously manipulated by the white race for personal gain. So facile that even a "schoolboy" can understand it, the rules of racial interaction are rendered as transparent and veridical as science. Underlying this analogy is a sardonic awareness that he himself, living as a black, is compelled to serve as "subsidiary" to the "well-being" and advancement of the whites around him. His metaphor matches exactly the etymological definition of a "solipsist," who narcissistically apprehends oneself as a primary object around which others revolve as mere satellites or planets.

As patently distasteful and malevolent as this position can be, knowing the rules and abuses of his world will not necessarily save him from being governed by them—and, indeed, falling prey to their apotheosis of "well-being." Appearing white gives him a ready advantage; beyond that, it is simply a matter of comprehending the rules of logic that the white man manipulates at will. And if a mere "schoolboy" can achieve such knowledge, certainly, the exceedingly self-confident ex-coloured man seems to imply, he can too. Indeed, many of my students openly recoil from the narrator's haughty, vaunting tone.[20] While this reaction is certainly warranted, we eventually come around together to appreciate the more complex import and peril of that proud voice; it signifies the ex-coloured man's desire not just to lay forth his neglected wares (as Thomas Wolfe tries so desperately to do) nor even to overstate the case for his fundamental humanity (all that Césaire's Bantu natives seem ascetically to want), but rather to inhabit fully, authentically, and redemptively the position of white authority.

Of course, his "well-being" in both monetary and psychological terms is at stake in his eventual decision to pass for white—or, more accurately, to simply let the world "take him for what he is." Since he does not *appear* to be black, he tacitly affirms his deep-seeded belief in the ontological value of his own whiteness through and through. He attempts to enact what his wealthy patron encourages him to realize: that he is "by blood, by appearance, by education, and by tastes a white man" and ought to enjoy the privileges that go along with it (144). The beautiful white boy he sees in the mirror is, indeed, "what he is" and not merely what he hopes to be. A horrific incident in the South transports him fully into this mindset: while traveling through Georgia, he witnesses a lynching and feels irreparably ashamed to be "identified with a people that could with impunity be treated worse than animals" (191). While critics have struggled to understand the self-hatred that would allow a black man to absorb with such disgust his community's abjection, the truth here seems deceptively lucid: because he is free to elect white privilege, he can simply choose not to suffer. Thus, he moves north and leaves both race and shame behind.

This choice can easily be seen as a betrayal, a literal enactment of the black bourgeois desire to "sell out" and live a life of apparent comfort, that is, whiteness.[21] By giving his protagonist the dubious gift of hybridity, Johnson allows him the power of choice—but that choice, he ultimately suggests, is an illusion: he must select his white part and not his black heritage in order to succeed. By forcing the ambitious ex-coloured man into the realm of whiteness, Johnson dramatizes the fact that the fortuitous road to what looks like cultural and economic success is strictly unavailable to lower-class and darker-skinned blacks. In New York, where Johnson himself famously claimed to be reborn (he was actually raised in Florida), the narrator has heard of "several coloured men worth a hundred or so thousand dollars each, and some families who proudly dated their free ancestry back a half-dozen generations"; these neoaristocrats own "a large colony" of posh homes. The parody of southern (white) aristocracy is clear here, suggesting that its rules, however abstract and fetishized, are being imitated by ambitious blacks—whether they can pass for white or not. "But," he concludes, "at no point did my life come in contact with theirs" (114). Instead, he remains a bitter impostor in the world of bloodlines and privilege.

Yet it is not just his person but his entire "life" that is straining for identification with this world, made real and accessible only by generations of freedom from slavery or, more easily, by a white key. He has "the best blood of the South" in his veins, but what that means is ominous; his white father gives him a gold piece to hang around his neck, an object that the boy fixates on and treasures reverently. Jennifer Lea Schulz perceptively reads this gift as a symbol of the "wholly economic relationship in which the father claims the son simply as property" (43), but it seems more sinister even than this: the white man passes along to his nearly white child a potent symbol of the aristocratic South, hanging it around his neck to signify that the boy both owns and can identify with it, too. The father's lesson is profoundly affecting, as the narrator learns to covet what that superior blood confers. Most troubling, again, is the pointed proliferation of this desire: no matter where Johnson's narrator travels in the United States, this acquisitive, white character haunts him. His only path to self-possession is by choosing the "best blood" but his "lesser half"—and thus living in relative material comfort as a white man.

Gates has noted that Johnson associates "his protagonist's desire to be white with an almost erotic investment in the project of money-making" (intro. *Autobiography* xx). Indeed, he succumbs to a virtual pathology of "money fever" and possession, the prose overwhelmed with possessive personal pronouns attached to objects of finance capitalism: "*my* capital," "*my* money," "*my* equity," "*my* place of employment" (194, 196). He lives by the maxim, "'Have a white skin, and all else may be added unto you'" (155); like his young self in the mirror seeing surplus whiteness ("whiter than he really is"), he continues to seek the part of himself that promises the most material gain—the complete compensation for his original minus-ness. Piano has become a mere pastime, relegated to recreation in a life filled with the more serious business of money-making. In this substitution, financial accumulation becomes a metaphorical proxy for narcissistic delirium. He learns to revere his tyrannical employer, until he in fact "looked upon him at that time as about all a man could wish to be" (121); indeed, he becomes startlingly like the fanatical white master who desires the extinction of the unruly racial element—that is, of *himself.*

The fullness of identity and self-worth that the protagonist has been striving for is at bottom a problem of social mathematics; only by mastering the equations that relegate him to a position of denigration can he maneuver his way into a position of wholeness and integrity. So he sets to work on the calculations. In his repeated expressions of revulsion for the "desperate," violent, resentful black underclass, his prose is cluttered with numerical references to their "proportion," "numbers," "increase" and "moral deduction"—until finally, he calls for "decreasing their number by shooting and burning them off" (76–77). The precise, mathematical nature of his disgust implies a suppressed awareness of his own quantification and depreciation, himself as part of the categorical "poverty and ignorance" that immure blacks. The association is made deeper through the shame-inducing lynching he witnesses in the South, wherein the victim uncannily substitutes for the narrator: he had recently watched a rich white patroness murdered in (and, in part, because of) his presence. The idea of "shooting" or "burning" the black insurgent resonates chillingly in both the lynching and the murder of the white patroness; his mathematical measures of extinction and decrease have effectively been turned on himself in this narrative displacement, and his only method of salvation comes perversely through obliterating his perilous racial heritage.

Such constraints and prejudices work against his half-hearted, closing regret that he has "sold [his] birthright for a mess of pottage" (121). Can there be latent empowerment in the notion that the authority to "sell" his black heritage makes him the owner and master of himself? Dussere suggests something similar when he finds Toni Morrison revising the language of accounting, and its attachment to economic slavery, to herald instead the promise of black self-ownership (125–27). Jim's fantasy of purchasing his family and himself echoes poignantly here as well. But the messages throughout Johnson's novel, and the stunning lack of choices in the postplantation psychological economy, indicate that this is far from an emancipatory feat. The ex-coloured man accomplishes what many white masters did by achieving the social death—to borrow Orlando Patterson's term—of his own black self. As Walter Johnson recounts, slaves would often mutilate their bodies or kill themselves in order to destroy their market value (33–34); in a sense, the ex-coloured man commits nothing less than psychological suicide specifically to *increase* his "market value" as a white man. Thus, he also distinctly embodies the role of slavedealer and "sells" himself all over again for profit, albeit passive (he simply lets himself be "taken" as white) and diminished ("a mess of pottage").[22] A small plate of food, bare subsistence—he is not worth much even to himself.

No matter how rich he becomes or how beautiful the ethereally beautiful white woman he marries, the erotics of acquisition and racial extinction leave him fundamentally at a loss, as when he returns to Connecticut a newly baptized white man and finds himself "completely lost," a virtual "stranger" to all he has been conditioned to know (192). Yet he is white, and to claim this is indeed "an economic necessity" (154), though the stringent politics of this vertiginous fate leave him bereft of an uncontaminated sense of self. What he "is" is always already overdetermined by racial forces and economic need. Johnson's narrator defensively casts his ultimate choice as "natural": why shouldn't a black man "give to his children every advantage he can which complexion of the skin carries [just as] the new or vulgar rich should purchase for their children the advantages which ancestry, aristocracy, and social position carry" (155)? Put this way, no reader can disagree with his fatherly sacrifice. But the sacrifice is considerable:

in a clear critique of southern social politics and their expansive, proliferating effects, Johnson's narrator nonetheless tries to buy his way into a corrupt system and ideology that will win him and his children great material advantages but will leave his soul ultimately empty, meager, unsatisfied—a mess of pottage indeed.

Gold-Tooth Smiles and Candy Kisses

It is significant that so many of these tales begin and end on the bare facts and images of hunger and the symbology of sustenance. In this final section I want to return to a few of these mouths left open in anticipation. Some, like Wright's protagonist at the close of "The Man Who Lived Underground," have their expiring mouths filled with bitter, foul sewer water, the waste of the white world above; others, like Johnson's ex-coloured man, grow fat off the pottage of this otherworld but find it an awful exchange: a pulpy mush for what should be a fulfilling life. The hole drilled through the gold piece hung around the ex-coloured man's neck signifies not just the coin's importance but also its uselessness—it is no longer currency but an object of extravagant display and a psychological sedative. In Attaway's *Blood on the Forge* and Zora Neale Hurston's "The Gilded Six-Bits," more gold appears—in the form of gold teeth—as symbols of the material prosperity associated with the white world, coveted by African American southerners particularly during the Great Depression and located strategically and defiantly in the very orifice of hunger and consumption. But as imports from the world of white exploitation and foreclosure, these gold teeth in the mouths of their hungry wearers and admirers bring more suffering and the mere illusion of satiety.

In the opening scenes of Attaway's novel, the ambient presence of hunger among the Moss family is mocked by Chinatown Moss's extravagant gold tooth: "His back was flattened against a tin patent-medicine sign that covered the chinks in the cabin. Because the tin held the heat of the last sun he rubbed his back up and down and grinned. His gold tooth flashed. There had never been anything wrong with his teeth; he had just had a front one pulled to make room for the gold" (2). The juxtaposition of China's gold tooth and the tin patent-medicine sign is striking: both cover up gaps or "chinks" in these places of domicile—cabin and body, respectively. The word *chink* can signify both a crevice and a derogatory word for a Chinaman, the latter being in current usage as early as 1901.[23] While there is no overt discussion of Chinatown's parentage, his name and his "slant eyes" make it clear that his father was probably an Asian immigrant; the latent notion of hybridity, coupled with his more obvious plight as an African American sharecropper, creates fissures in Chinatown's being like the cracks in the family's flimsy cabin. While a consumer advertisement for medicine suggestively patches and "cures" the building's structural ills, Chinatown inserts another commercial object into his own mouth as a palliative. His original teeth are functional, we learn, leaving China to actually mutilate his own body in an effort to display and remedy what he feels is psychologically missing: "'When I jest little Chinatown,' he muses, 'I seen the way things is an' I know I got to have somethin' to make me feel like I somebody. So all the time I dream 'bout a gold tooth, shinin' and makin' everybody look when Chinatown smile. . . . And I jest got to have that tooth. Without it I ain't nobody'" (40–41). Even at the end of the novel, when he's been mutilated into blindness, "lost" without the "outward symbols" he lives by, he still broods nervously "'Got to keep that tooth. . . . I ain't nothin' if I loses it'" (162). Melody has to distract him from the obvious, disabling fact that he can no longer stare at it in the mirror: "'I got to see my tooth. Only it's too dark. What good a good tooth in the dark?'" (164). The vanity of the tooth is what sustains him, making his blindness in the end a calculated death sentence: having given over his identity to the symbol of gold, Chinatown really does become "nobody" without it.

A mouthful of gold teeth also plays a central role in Zora Neale Hurston's highly regarded yet little-discussed 1933 story "The Gilded Six-Bits," a tale of young newlyweds Missie May and Joe, whose blissful marriage is interrupted by the arrival in their small Negro settlement town of a rich (also black) stranger, Otis D. Slemmons, a "'heavy-set man wid his mouth full of gold teethes'" and what Joe describes as "'de finest clothes Ah ever seen on a colored man's back'" (89). Joe is envious of Slemmons's trappings of finery that "'make 'm look lak a rich white man. . . . He's got a five-dollar gold piece for a stick-pin and he got a ten-dollar gold piece on his watch chain and his mouf is jes' crammed full of gold teethes. Sho wisht it wuz mine. And what make it so cool, he got money 'cumulated. And womens give it all to 'im'" (89–90). When Missie sees how much Joe desires these adornments for himself, she resolves to "find some" for him; Joe is tickled by her naïveté, but she insists "'You don't know whut been lost 'round heah. Maybe somebody way back in memorial times lost they gold money and went on off and it ain't never been found. And if we wuz to find it, you could wear some 'thout havin' no gang of womens lak Slemmons got'" (91). What seems like fanciful play is in fact a serious articulation of loss and desire; Missie's sincere longing to give Joe the riches he desires—to look "lak a rich white man" too—compels her to violate their marriage by sleeping with Slemmons. She is devastated when Joe catches them in the act, and defends herself by claiming "'he said he wuz gointer give me dat gold money and he jes' kept on after me—'" (94). Her excuse is believable precisely because her love for Joe and her desire to please him are cast so intensely and innocently, and her despair over her transgression so profound. The coveted gold coin that Joe tore from Slemmons in his moment of escape taunts her, "like a monster hiding in the pocket of [Joe's] pockets to destroy her" (95). It nearly destroys her marriage, the only thing that brings her a sense of inherent value and agency: "No need to die today," she thinks at one low moment: "Joe needed her for a few more minutes anyhow" (94).

But the marriage triumphs when Missie May gives birth to a son, the spitting image of Joe. And it turns out that Slemmons's flashy gold pieces are nothing but gilded coins, a quarter on his stick-pin and a half-dollar for the watch charm Joe nabs. The revelation further debunks Slemmons and cheapens Missie's prostitution in the name of love. On the one hand, Hurston seems determined to expose the dangers of white commercial culture, which tantalizes the deprived African American community into cheating, stealing, and lying in order to buy into its trappings; in this way, her vision is not far from Wright's, Attaway's, or Johnson's dismal depictions of moral compromise and suicidal despair when faced with the politics of racial impoverishment and the staggering obstacles to economic mobility. Many critics find optimism in Hurston's story, though; in the introduction to Hurston's *Complete Stories*, Henry Louis Gates Jr. and Sieglinde Lemke declare that the story "teaches us the importance of an emotional attachment over material wealth" by featuring a "love that seems to be stronger than money" and that ultimately proves able to be "retrieved and reactivated" (xix). Gayl Jones, John Lowe, and Valerie Boyd all read the story's ending ultimately as happy, hopeful, even (as Boyd avers) "delightful." Joe is the only gold Missie May needs, it would seem, and vice versa.

It would be lovely to end with such a triumphant counter to the collection of doomed strivers we have seen in this chapter; but I believe Hurston's story is much darker than Gates and Lemke allow, darker even than much of what we've seen elsewhere in this chapter because it introduces the category of gender and the compounded plight of being both black *and* female. For one thing, May and Joe's love is not a sacred thing apart from the corrupting influence of gold and chicanery, but is rather part and parcel of it: the story both opens and ends with the supposedly playful and touching ritual of Joe "throwing silver dollars in the door for her to pick up and pile beside her plate at dinner" (87), the proximity of coins to food—much like the gold teeth—making matters of subsistence patently material. Every Saturday, the coins hit the threshold "Nine times" and May calls out in "mock alarm": "'Who dat chunkin' money in mah do'way?'" (87). This charade is followed by play wrestling, which culminates in Missie May finding all the things he's bought and hidden in his pockets "for her to find" (88). Her innocent desire to simply "find" money on the road, then, is not very far-fetched; and her "finding" objects on Joe's body is tacitly equated with "finding" gold pieces by having sex with Slemmons. In this way, her mock questioning of "who" might be chunking money at her door is disturbingly suggestive; love in this world is ultimately a kind of prostitution, a cooptation of emotion by the more pressing and visceral demands of money and food. There is a reason, Hurston seems to suggest, why the coins get piled up next to her dinner plate and not the nightstand.

If the relationship between Missie May and Joe is supposed to signify a romantic refuge apart from the tawdry world of capitalism that makes them grasp and hunger and prostitute themselves, such a haven does not bode particularly well for women. Without either Slemmons's gold or Joe's love, Missie May is absolutely bereft and suicidal; she has no identity apart from these men or the proxies of value they harbor. When Joe finally feels compelled to resurrect the ritual at the end of the story, we should be chilled to the bone: he tosses his coins through the doorway as small symbols of his returning affection for her. In order to solidify the "reactivation" of their love, moreover, he uses Slemmons's counterfeit "gold" half dollar to buy Missie May the candy kisses he always used to bring her. The exchange is clearly meant to be symbolic: he trades in the cheap commercial illusion for the true, enduring love he has at home, in the symbolic form of "good ole lasses kisses" for his wife (98). Joe returns home with the candy and fifteen coins to chunk through the doorway, to which Missie May eagerly responds in her usual way. But Hurston obviously means for the blissful return of domestic harmony to be a sweet illusion; when the white store clerk comments upon Joe's exit "'Wisht I could be like these darkies. Laughin' all the time. Nothin' worries 'em'" (98), we recognize the deep irony in his bitter judgment, the dark subtext of pain beneath Joe's mirth. And surely we are to see that Slemmons's counterfeit gold is what buys back the couple's love, a relationship founded from the start on chunking coins and consumption.

But most troubling of all is the suggestion that this offering constitutes an even exchange and a restoration of the status quo: Slemmons's gold, Missie May's prostitution, and the price tag attached to love are constants in their world. Theirs is not a world fancifully removed from material concerns or, as Gates and Lemke assert, from the white man's control (xvii). Indeed, the opening lines of the story set them powerfully within an economy of regulation and segregation that no quotient of romantic love can subvert or escape: "It was a Negro yard around a Negro house in a Negro settlement that looked to the payroll of the G. and G. Fertilizer works for its support" (86). As Hildegard Hoeller asserts, "it is a dependent community artificially fertilized by white capital" (767). Though the houses in this settlement are neat, tidy, and seemingly full of joy, this gilded sheen—like Slemmons's gilded coins, or the blacks' mask of laughter—conceals the racial and economic politics of the world that hampers them at every turn.

As a woman, Missie May's implication in this economy of dependence and subjection is more vexed even than Joe's. While Joe obviously feels betrayed by his wife's infidelity, her alienation from any guiding sense of self-worth, morality, and personal integrity is clearly the story's greatest tragedy. The wrong she commits is the ineluctable result of her conditioning within an order that designates her the payee, the prostitute, whose sustenance and happiness both are dependent on the coins stacked next to her dinner plate. In this order, "she didn't deserve a thing" and Joe deserves everything (95). This spiritual emptying seems exactly the motivation for her adultery: Slemmons manipulates her into thinking she might actually be getting something nice for Joe in the bargain. The role of women in these ruthless scrambles for accumulation and self-possession is a marginal one; as we will see in chapter 3, southern women generally function as mere domestic commodities whose worth enhances and enriches the men to whom they belong. Clearly, the experiences of African American and white women cannot be equated; but at its simplest, for black and white southerners alike, "woman" is quite literally a quantifiable, calculable figure to be factored into a domestic, erotic, and aggressively masculine economy.

This stratification becomes clear when Joe and Slemmons converge in an early (preadultery) textual moment: Slemmons introduces a new mathematics of female appraisal, a dehumanizing calculation that Joe eagerly endorses:

> On the way home that night Joe was exultant. "Didn't Ah say ole Otis was swell? . . . Wuzn't dat funny whut he said when great big fat ole Ida Armstrong come in? He asted me, 'Who is dat broad wid de forte shake?' Dat's a new word. Us always thought forty was a set of figgers but he showed us where it means a whole heap of things. Sometimes he don't say forty, he jes' say thirty-eight and two and dat mean de same thing. Know whut he tole me when Ah wuz payin' for our ice cream? He say, 'Ah have to hand it to you, Joe. That wife of yours is jes' thirty-eight and two. Yessuh, she's forte!' Ain't he killin'?" (91)

Yet Joe's throwaway remark reveals a sober truth about the effects of not just a racist but a sexist economy based on desire and exploitation: it affects the spiritual "killin'" of those calculated, measured, and owned by men—white and black alike—desperate to master and own anything at all.

Chapter Three

The Measures of Love: Southern Belles and Working Girls in Frances Newman, Anita Loos, and Katherine Anne Porter

> *It? She. Her. Woman. Not a category, not a sex, not one of two sexes, a human female creature, but an infinity. ♀ = ∞.*
> WALKER PERCY, *LANCELOT*

In *As I Lay Dying*, Faulkner's polyvocal narrative of the death and burial of the poor white matriarch Addie Bundren, Addie ruminates on the measures of her domestic sacrifices: "The shape of my body where I used to be a virgin is in the shape of a   . . . . It was not that I could think of myself as no longer unvirgin, because I was three now. . . . I gave Anse the children. . . . That was my duty to him, and that duty I fulfilled. I would be I" (165–66).

The most illustrative moment in this passage, and perhaps in all of Addie's narrative, is the long, purposefully blank textual space to signify the shape and substance of her virgin body. The implication seems to be that purity, while culturally mandated, renders the southern woman an empty vessel; having not yet produced anything of social value, her body is of no discernible worth and is essentially invisible. She is simply nothing, a zero represented here as a textual absence. But in the years following her marriage, Addie becomes "I" in flat mathematical terms: the expectation of bearing children accomplished, she is no longer zero but "three now." Reproduction is her "duty" to her husband, but it is also figured as an inescapable obligation to herself: if her identity can be realized and made visible only by "giving" Anse children and perpetuating the family line, then she has no choice but to keep on giving.

Faulkner transmutes into a metaphor of domestic economy the profound spiritual sacrifice of the southern woman who *must* be zero, and who then must give away still more of her body in order to create and preserve an idyll of familial harmony. What happens, then, when the new woman of the twentieth century's apparently New South deigns to harness her own inclinations instead? Addie does makes a clear separation between "duty" and desire by engaging in an extramarital liaison that produces Jewel, a quantity she then labors to balance mathematically out of existence by the production of additional, legitimate children. By naming the boy after a gem, Addie indicates none too subtly that he represents something precious and beyond both the dollar economy and domestic duty evoked by his legitimate brother "Cash." In Faulkner's vision of earthy feminine desire and its brief, erotic triumph over conjugal duty, certainly, following one's heart's desire is more romantically compelling than grudgingly fulfilling social and domestic obligation. But we simply cannot forget that Addie, remote as she is from the elite realm of belles and bloodlines, is nevertheless purposefully, emphatically, and necessarily nothing, akin to a proper virgin waiting to be married, and that she "would be I" only by giving herself and her virginity away to her husband, and, further, that she can be "three" only by giving away even more in the form of babies.[1] If the children represent quotients of value reflective of participation in a cash economy, precious alternative desire yields results no better than the textual blank space—in Addie's case, death.

As Zora Neale Hurston's critique of romantic love in "The Gilded Six-Bits" makes clear, a woman's gold is her ability to win, please, and fulfill a man; without his presence and aid, both economic and emotional, she is virtually nothing, a useless waste on her way to death. This assessment is perhaps reminiscent of extreme, reactionary feminist critiques of male patriarchy; but such intensity characterizes the psychological calculations of self-worth and integrity in southern women's writing in the first half of the twentieth century—particularly in works by women who are considered, and who often considered themselves to be, early feminists. While this period witnessed unprecedented social and economic progress not just for the region but for its women, it is curious that the priorities of domestic sacrifice and subjection return with such haunting force at precisely this point. As do the African American southerners yearning to manufacture social and economic autonomy in a barely postslavery world, these women find themselves stymied in their attempts to locate value and satisfaction apart from the husbands, fathers, and lovers who complete their identities. Indeed, a haunting discourse of narcissistic self-evaluation and mathematical diminishment fatally undoes even the most openly progressive female writers of the period—Frances Newman, Anita Loos, and Katherine Anne Porter.[2] In narratives that intend to be alternately subversive, shocking, comic, and sensitive to the plight of the southern woman struggling for self-determination, these authors are finally unable to exorcise the priorities of white planter capitalism that leave them to quantify and measure themselves and their bodies into the shapes of someone else's desire, complicated by the new demands and promises of the early twentieth-century market economy.

What is surprising about attitudes like the ones in this chapter is their appearance during the heyday of women's liberation, suffragism, increased participation in the work force, and seemingly relaxed morals ushered in by the twentieth century, World War I, and the Jazz Age. My look at a few of these southern feminists begins at a revealing moment in the late 1920s and 1930s, which for women represented a critical collision of social optimism and economic despair. Indeed, as Christina Simmons reports,

> The years 1900 to 1930 were a period of dramatic and self-conscious cultural, political, and intellectual change in the United States, the beginning of a shift from a Victorian to a modern mentality in which feminism and female public roles, the emergence of a sexological science and modern psychology, and the effects of an ethnically diverse urban culture conjoined to undermine Victorian marriage and sex codes. This change occurred especially among sophisticated and educated urbanites, artists, and intellectuals and most publicly and intensively in major cities like New York and Chicago (171).

Newman, Loos, and Porter are indeed sophisticated intellectuals who create protagonists of the same ilk (albeit, in Loos's case, craftily disguised as the opposite) transported to urban locales like Atlanta, Philadelphia, and New York and abroad to London, Paris, Venice, and beyond; Loos and Newman both feature slyly ironic references to Freudian psychology (Freud himself makes a cameo appearance in *Gentlemen Prefer Blondes*); and all attempt without success to subvert the traditional, cloistering narratives of marriage and sex.

Few critics acknowledge just how deeply such ingrained cultural expectations saturate southern women's prose well into the twentieth century. Not surprisingly or without merit, the overwhelming tendency is to read southern women writers by default as feminists; daring to write at all, and often detaching themselves superficially from supporting segregation, patriarchy, aristocracy, or oppressive religious structures, certainly these women intend to embrace progressive reforms and liberal ideals as a way to look ahead, as Will Brantley contends (7–8), when so many of their male compatriots were still peering longingly into the past.[3] This is not to deny that true feminist energies existed either above or below the Mason-Dixon Line; surely, as Brantley notes, many of these new women "did openly denounce the glaring constraints placed upon women, racial minorities, and political dissidents, as well as the constraints that white men have placed upon themselves" (35–36); moreover, refined women offended by the "vulgarity, venality, and power-grabbing arrogance" of the infamous Louisiana governor Huey Long banded together to form the Independent Women's Organization (IWO) that "worked successfully to oust the Long regime from the governor's mansion" in 1940 and replaced him in 1946 with the progressive Chep Morrison (Turner 360–61). But such coups were rare and limited in their effectiveness and vision; the IWO, for instance, resisted desegregation and enjoyed political opportunity and activism because of their privileged economic backgrounds that financially supported such efforts. By and large, women in the South faced numerous and ponderable obstacles in the path to actualization, including economic and social prohibitions, intimidation at the polling places, and often outright squelching of their efforts by white male authority, as happened when control of the League of Women Voters in New Orleans was usurped by "a group devoted to the Old Regulars" (Turner 360).

My argument that this phenomenon has a particularly southern character may on the surface seem arbitrary. On the one hand, there is something pervasive and western about these female struggles; as Slavoj Žižek paraphrases Lacan: "Precisely when I seem to express my authentic innermost longing, 'what I want' has already been imposed on me by the patriarchal order that tells me what to desire, so the first condition of my liberation is that I break the vicious cycle of my alienated desire and learn to formulate my desire in an autonomous way" (*How to Read Lacan* 39).[4] The southern context merely compounds this plight by burdening the woman with her role as symbol and mirror in a fetishized economy resistant to market capitalism. What was distinctive about southern women in the nineteenth century according to Anne Goodwyn Jones was their centrality to the "region's self-definition; the identity of the South is contingent in part upon the persistence of its tradition of the lady" (4); even more dramatically in the twentieth century, it seems, the southern woman is hinged irretrievably to the region's deepest impoverishment and greatest hopes. Often, the writers themselves make reference to plantation economies amid meditations on their own modern crises, though these analogues are markedly distinct from early feminists' dubious cooptation of the slave experience.[5] Instead, the plantation trope seems a reminder that the southern woman has yet to escape the pillared vestiges of the South's storied past. As Jones finds, "the idea of southern womanhood . . . stretches across time in the southern mind with fewer variations than one might think" (17) and tends to accelerate defensively during periods of intense economic and social flux. Patricia Yaeger's investigation of "gargantuan," grotesque, and dirt-eating women is original and constructive precisely because it refuses any longer to pay attention to the fragile, petite, bellelike southern archetypes.[6] Yet these exemplars persist, and they often continue to have a disastrous effect on the women conditioned to conform to their expectations and measurements. As A. G. Jones notes at the start of *Tomorrow Is Another Day*, even in 1920 the image of the ideal southern woman was still associated fundamentally with, in Lucian Lamar Knight's words, "the Confederate woman, in her silent influence, in her eternal vigil. . . . Her gentle spirit is the priceless heritage of her daughters" (qtd. in A. G. Jones 4). As striking as the belle's "gentle" and "silent" power is the "priceless" quality of that character—neither the "heritage" nor the tradition she represents is quantifiable in a crass market economy. No longer able to recognize themselves in such images, modern southern women respond by extending radical critiques, moving away from the South, or by rejecting these cultural norms altogether (22).[7]

Yet this chapter wonders: what about the women who resolve to subvert the prototype but then lose rather than win a restored sense of self? Indeed, the New South and the myth of the New Woman offer the hope of escaping the pressures of upholding an entire social order with purity, grace, and silence. Yet these alternatives yield disturbing repetitions and fetishes for the priorities of old: in pervasive tropes of narcissistic desire, economic necessity, and mathematical precision, we find women again evacuated of desire, selfhood, and substance. Caught in a ruthless new economy of acquisition and self-preservation, these women turn to ingrained southern paradigms dictating that beauty and charm are their best chances for marital and material success.[8] In place of the feminist triumph most critics are eager to find in women's writing from this period, there are troubling signs that these women have merely adopted white male imperatives and measures in the search for their own value, and that in many cases a male (husband or lover)'s desires and methods subsume her own. Southern women and wives, seemingly regardless of social origins, find themselves belatedly implicated in an order that subordinates desire and agency to the quantifiable worth of social relationships. To have it all, the equation goes, women need to abdicate everything of themselves. In short, the continued emphasis on women's capitulation to male demands—the compulsion to "give" all of one's self in order to receive personhood in return—thinly veils a continued attachment to the social and economic order that cemented such priorities. In many cases, money per se functions as a fetish or proxy for personal worth, translating textually into the adding up, valuing, and mathematical measuring of body and soul.

Yet financial survival is not a metaphor or an abstraction so much as it is, first and foremost, a literal preoccupation. Many women, such as Katherine Anne Porter's industrious protagonists, do struggle in the workplace to support themselves and to establish autonomy. Susan Hegeman notes that sex and wifely duty become increasingly figured as the woman's occupation, "work that is not really work" but nonetheless serves a vital social function (546); whether or not the woman gets "paid" for her service seems a point of near obsession for women like Lorelei Lee in Anita Loos's comic *Gentlemen Prefer Blondes*, which I examine in greater detail later in this chapter. Like the men of the period and region, southern ladies now participate in a feminine version of a Horatio Alger, American capitalist success narrative: in this iteration, "work" and "money" become fetishes for female sexuality and domestic value, and numbers and figures morph into the language by which these women measure the size and worth of their bodies and souls. The southern woman of privileged birth was a domestic commodity whose value on the marriage market depended on maintaining a proper, carefully constructed appearance and demeanor reflective of her polished pedigree. This "value" was not necessarily exchangeable or profitable for the woman herself but was intended to enrich her potential husband and family; accordingly, efforts to assert autonomy and exercise personal, nonproductive desire were fraught with danger. Even the subversive "femme fatale" archetype, which Betina Entzminger explores and which I suggest is embodied in Loos's Lorelei Lee, shares many traits with the southern belle: that is, both are "trained from childhood in the arts of allure for the sole purpose of capturing the suitable husbands on which their futures depended. . . . And both, though at first glance they appear to give power to the woman, end by silencing her" (11). The middle-class upstart faces expectations of a different sort, but even more grittily than does the belle, she finds herself and her survival dependent on an auspicious marriage. Unable to use her newfound independence or industry to purchase autonomy or even identity, she, too, is bound by a sexual economy that demands her subjection and subordination to male desires and amplification.[9]

Such determinism necessarily changes the way we read women's defiant writing from this period. Within just a year of each other, Frances Newman and Anita Loos published groundbreaking novels about New Southern Women who rebel against the social and sexual codes of 1920s American society. In *Gentlemen Prefer Blondes* Loos fashions the savvy gold digger Lorelei Lee as an ironic subversion of the "dumb blonde" archetype, while Newman's brunette heroine Katharine Faraday in *The Hard-Boiled Virgin* elects intellectual capital and sexual emancipation over the expectation of marriage. Critics have read these novels as feminist triumphs in which Lorelei and Katharine manipulate and negotiate their way to personal enrichment both literal and figurative. Yet such readings have troubling implications for our overestimations of not just the mythologized "New Woman" but the "New South" as well. In 1928 Loos and Newman both published new, darker novels—*But Gentlemen Marry Brunettes* and *Dead Lovers Are Faithful Lovers*, respectively—featuring adultery, domestic battery, and hints of bulimia.

Together, Loos and Newman's four major novels envision the New Woman as a sexual object in a consumer society colliding with the New South's concurrent attempts to both enjoy and repudiate the consuming world of market capitalism and its promise of material and personal satisfaction. Striving to be intellectual, emancipated, and successful, these new southern women instead signify their authors' deepest anxieties about the hopelessly diminishing returns of the middlebrow, hard-boiled brunette—and of the South's darkest future. Just a decade later, Katherine Anne Porter shows us women still navigating the dangerous waters of self-possession and domestic sacrifice and, no matter which option they choose, finding themselves part of a class, gender, and region apparently doomed to be emotionally and economically bereft.

Belles' Letters, Numbers, and Figures

Atlanta librarian and author Frances Newman compensated for her lack of good looks by becoming bookish and analytical, decidedly not virtues for an aspiring southern socialite; but she simply was "an unattractive child, and she knew it. Only too often had she stood before her mother's mirror and compared the image of the pallid girl with stringy black hair and stringy black-stockinged legs with the visions of grace and beauty which were her three older sisters. . . . So, with remarkable intelligence, she decided that her only alternative was to cultivate her cleverness" (Baugh in *Letters* 3).[10] She worked as a librarian at several colleges, serving longest at Georgia Tech in Atlanta, but she viewed this occupation mainly as a means to support her primary career as a prolific writer; in her lifetime, she published "corrosive" literary critical essays (Cabell in *Letters* v), translated stories from five languages for *The Short Story's Mutations*, and published two novels, *The Hard-Boiled Virgin* and *Dead Lovers Are Faithful Lovers*. A third novel, *The Gold Fish Bowl*, never appeared in print in her lifetime but in 1985 was edited as a dissertation by Margaret M. Duggan. Nearly everyone who knew Newman or has written about her comments on her indomitable good humor, her wit and vibrancy, her sharp and fearless criticism, and her staunch independence.[11] As Barbara Anne Wade reports in her literary biography of Newman, accounts of Newman and her own letters "reveal a vibrant, independent woman who simultaneously defied and was influenced by the traditional southern society she satirized in her writing" (1). Wade remarks on the tremendous "courage" needed to defect from Atlanta's high society and "choose to be self-supporting, when that meant accepting a degree of economic hardship, and to write novels with allusions to such taboo topics as menstruation, sexual arousal, and syphilis . . . she sent that city 'almost in convulsions' [as she put it in her letters] with her first published novel" (1). Her sharp critique of southern expectations pervades her work, but her writing is not satirical, and her portraits of fatally self-absorbed, unloved ladies are neither witty nor humorous. Instead, underneath Newman's almost pathologically turgid, complex, and tortured prose is a raw, aching, almost unbearable sense of divestment and loss. These traces suggest that she never fully exorcises the hold of aristocratic society's pleasures and demands or of the straitening and self-effacing role that a woman must occupy in order to receive her diluted profits of love, marriage, and status.

Newman's first novel, *The Hard-Boiled Virgin*, is not a feminist triumph but a gorgeously rendered tragedy. Torn between society's demands and her own ambitions, Newman's protagonist Katharine Faraday is a creature transparently like Newman: smart, bookish, analytical, yet deeply sensitive, lustful, and narcissistic. Katharine's self-fixation develops not because she is particularly attractive but rather because she is, like Newman herself, the dark and unattractive duckling in a family of culturally desirable golden-haired belles. Newman creates for Katharine a similar path of alternative gratification: she chooses books and brains over beauty. Unlike Newman, though, Katharine finds it much more difficult to abandon her compulsive quest for good looks and a well-born husband. Katharine thus struggles to cultivate something attractive from her dark-haired, serious, ambitious traits; accordingly, her manipulations of her image strive to satisfy society's demands and templates. Frequently she labors in front of the mirror to achieve a look "like the Degas drawing she had seen the day before" (96), suggesting that women's attempts to style their images are akin to the creation of an artistic masterpiece, preferably one that carries as much drawing-room cachet as a piece by Degas. The choice of artists, as the well-read Newman would have known, is further evocative of the preferences in Degas's and Katharine's world: the son of a wealthy banker and a "haughty" aristocrat, Degas was best known for his portraits of ballerinas and racehorses—a combination of elements and predilections with a clear affinity to southern culture and recreation. This connection is deepened by Degas's own southern connection: relatives ran a cotton plantation in Louisiana after the Civil War, which Degas visited in 1872 and was inspired to render in the painting *Cotton Exchange at New Orleans* the following year (Pioch). But Newman seems not to emphasize a provincial or stereotypical South as much as its connections to broader, cosmopolitan tastes and priorities. Katharine's models of beauty derive from an expansive, international, neoaristocratic world of ideals, perceptions, leisure, and imaginative representations cultivated by southern high society.

Within such a world, Katharine's beauty rituals aspire to meet the standards and desires of the men who might make suitable husbands who would admire her visage. After a romantic encounter with a suitor, she tries to apprehend herself through the eyes of her would-be lover: she "was not interested in anything except getting a better light on the mirror in which she was looking at the colour of the face Edward Cabot had just seen" (146). Behind Newman's characteristically oblique prose, she suggests that Katharine is anxious but nonetheless clear in her purpose: she wants to recognize herself not from her own perspective but only through the imagined light, angle, and position of the person whose opinion matters most: her potential husband.[12] In such moments, Katharine's narcissism is marked, but it alienates rather than unites her with her own desires: rather than appreciating herself from the first-person perspective, she imagines only the perspective of the powerful male benefactor who, if she is successful, will ratify her beauty and worth in the prize of marriage. That Cabot is only one of many suitors in the novel dramatizes the discomposing effect of trying to please multiple lovers with potentially disparate preferences.

Such moments give way to an odd, nervous fixation in her prose: a seemingly uncontrollable tendency to quantify and enumerate things. This novel in particular is replete with references to mathematical calculations of the self, as if Katharine is anxiously measuring the female body's size, substance, and value on its own terms, partly in hopeful defiance and partly in capitulation to already-cemented expectations. Newman's prose is distractingly full of references to geometry, numerals, and quantities.[13] Further, Katharine's world is one of unerring mathematical precision: hats are to be worn at "the correct angle" (25); lineage is clear, direct, and evidentiary; she periodically seeks realignment and order by reading nothing but a "geometry" text (84); and both in and out of school, she engages in "mental arithmetic," "working out her problems in principal and interest, according to a rule she did not understand" (20, 25). In a virtual balance sheet of emotions, Katharine scrupulously figures her "problems" as accounting dilemmas to be worked out in a ledgerbook, even as she admits pathetically that she does not "understand" the rules of the calculations. Her soaring romantic and independent instincts at first seem like urges to rebel against the lines that delimit her, even at a young age: that is, in the schoolyard—an important scene of pedagogical indoctrination—she takes one glance at the "line of submissive children" and boldly decides to walk away from it (19).[14] But she does not get far. She has, it seems, already internalized the lines of that order, mapping them onto her body—itself another thing to be controlled and stylized for her matrimonial ambitions, as when she gazes down at the "delicate brown line" of her abdomen in the bathtub (36). In the service of fulfilling her expectations as a reluctant belle on the marriage market, Katharine quantifies and objectifies nearly everything she does and imagines: "*one* hygienic hour," a "*fourth* spoonful of charlotte russe," "*nine*" readings of a love letter (86, italics added)—the examples are simply countless.

Whether or not they are able to resist such codes and rules, much less understand them, women like Katharine discover that achieving feminine perfection and domestic success are not personal victories but social manipulations. Being part of an order poised reluctantly on the brink of national depression and already damaged by regional decline and subjugation, Katharine and her marriage quest are inextricable from the expectation that she embody the enduring, antimaterial value of southern culture and tradition—values that, as both the text and material culture reveal, are inseparable from the capitalist world they have always already exemplified. In Katharine's orbit, money becomes a vexed fetish for her unfulfilled sexual promise, the empty spaces in her self-appraisal that she hopes will be filled by a prosperous marriage. That is, her desire to be chastely beautiful, flaxen haired, and charming is a capitulation to the social world that produced her, and is synonymous with sexual longing and economic ambition. While sexuality remained perhaps the most significant taboo for the southern lady, economic desire is apotheosized as the motivation for marriage. In her meditations on marriage, the central paradigm for "finding" one's purpose and identity within this world, we encounter Katharine's most disturbing mirror reflections, attended regularly by meditations on her own objective (and objectified) worth. Appraising not just her own shortcomings but the fundamental lack or vacancy attributed to women generally, Katharine warns that a wife would still be "unworthy" in marriage; repeatedly, she balances this "unworthy wife" with an inherently "honourable husband" (27–28). Katharine is blessed with vast intellect but is aesthetically bankrupt; for this reason her brother Arthur (who dies suddenly and mysteriously) tries to offset this imbalance by bequeathing to her a small windfall, leaving her his entire inheritance because he apparently believes she will need it more than her fair sisters, as she "would never have the kind of charms which were likely to get her a satisfactory husband, or which were likely to get her any husband at all" (165). The exchange is even—coins for "charms"—and one man in her life feels compelled to make up for what it seems no other man will give her.

In the end, both an abstract and a literal sense of "worth" dictates a woman's formation so fully that it contaminates all other impulses. Katharine's sharp mind is put to use mainly to scrutinize the wealth and social standing of each marriage prospect, and ultimately this compulsory quest for money uncannily elides the possibility of garnering true affection in the exchange. After being given forty dollars by her other brother, George, Katharine turns her monetary anxiety upon her current ambivalent suitor, thinking: "even if she had not known the temporal limits of one twenty-dollar bill and two ten-dollar bills, she would not have felt able to bear the strain of watching James Fuller's increasing or decreasing interest" (117). Effortlessly, she equates James Fuller's "interest" with cash, and specifically with elusive and limited funds; she does seem vaguely more emotionally committed to the fluctuations of the man than the dollar, but it is clear that both are of similar importance. In exchange, Katharine weeps with self-conscious, calculated precision, "glad that she was able to cry, and that she was able to cry more than her father or her mother or any of Arthur Faraday's four other brothers and sisters" (164).

While Katharine clearly misinterprets the meaning of Arthur's generosity, the world's disgust for her charmless existence does slowly infiltrate her consciousness. In the bathtub, her favorite place both to read and to examine her body, she luxuriates in a romantic novel titled *Sentimental Tommy*; laying it aside, she turns instantly to notice "the convex reflections of herself in the nicely polished faucets, and the reflections were both so unsatisfactory that she looked down at as much of herself as she could see" (35). Juxtaposed with the act of reading, which earns her no aesthetic capital, she is terribly unpleased with her reflection, which appears doubled and convex to underscore her split, ambivalent participation in the world that takes her away from herself and demands that she be something she is not. This same world induces shame in her body, which she "looked down at" as something despicable, insignificant, other. Before she can continue reading she feels compelled to put on a nightgown and wrap herself "with a sheet and two pairs of blankets and an eiderdown comfort," effectively shrouding the disgraceful body that cannot exist in the same space as the mind that desires simply to indulge in a novel (36–37). Significantly, the book she is so drawn to is told from the point of view of a young boy, one "whose conduct seemed so entirely reasonable to her" (37) and thus further separates her from the femininity her body is supposed to exude, although it stubbornly preserves its flat, straight, thin lines and lack of contours.

From the start, she realizes "that any boy is born to a more honourable social situation than any girl" (30); the fact that she is a female puts her at a permanent disadvantage, which is only compounded by her additional lack of "charm" and beauty. She comes to desire something socially outrageous and unpalatable: first to become a boy, and then to enjoy herself sexually as if she were a man making love to herself. This, it seems, would be true gratification of a sort she could never know as a woman. Despite her best efforts, though, she "had not been able to make her thin lips touch one of her sharp elbows before she lost confidence in a kissed elbow's efficacy in changing a girl into a boy" (30). This contorted textual moment (which actually mirrors the contortions of Katharine's body in this ill-fated experiment) suggests that, in her repeated narcissistic attempts to kiss her own elbow, she has for some time been subconsciously seeking to keep for herself what society expects her simply to give away: the fulfillment of desire and union with her own body. In doing so, she seems determined to accomplish something subversive and liberating, to transcend her feminine constraints and "change a girl into a boy"; but her maneuver seems precisely the opposite, a failure in the prospects of a woman to achieve and preserve for herself what a man takes from her. To change a girl into a boy in the moment of kissing her own elbow is to enjoy her own body as her male lover would eventually do, just as she wanted to see her face only as her admired Edward Cabot had seen it. The act still requires her to be something other than who she actually is; her own identity finds no refuge in a space beyond that which society has critically, dichotomously, and fatefully mapped out.

The transference of her desire onto a male adjunct mirrors her tendency to satisfy or imitate the writing of male counterparts as well. Her first real literary "products" are love letters, excruciatingly crafted and "carefully punctuated" (71, 75)—descriptions that, read in light of Katharine's nervous instinct for "punctuality" and propriety, vividly evoke her angst over social directives. When she finally writes and publishes plays and essays, she is obsessed with the men who will see and be charmed by them; thus, she ponders and creates sentences that are carefully "calculated" for the greatest romantic outcomes (236). She even writes an essay of exactly "eight pages" when she is desperately in love and trying to impress a man who has written "eight novels" (238, 240). She becomes modestly successful as a writer of essays, a guilty fantasy she entertains consistently throughout the novel; but what aspires to "creation" is essentially the calculated imitation and repetition of her ruling anxieties and the men who inspire them. In Elaine Showalter's phases of female writing, Newman's protagonist is hopelessly stuck at the first troubling stage of imitation and internalization, which Louise Westling has described as the problem of persona plaguing southern women writers who struggle to subvert the region's dominant male models (*Sacred Groves*).[15] There is some irony in the fact that the woman writer has long been accepted as a supporting player within southern culture, as both A. G. Jones and Brantley report (5, 35), so long as her role was seen as trivial, innocent, supportive of the current social order, and not in the least "literary" or critical. Entzminger reminds us that, if used subversively, the activity of "writing itself violated the sexual taboos that confined the southern woman" as it was "explicitly linked to a lack of proper modesty and thereby connected to promiscuity" (14). It is only more troubling, then, when Katharine views not her creative output but her own life story as a narrative drama comprised of characters and acts; she seems utterly unable to distinguish between the orchestrations inherent in art and those of her own sad and constructed reality. She does try to claim some control over this script: she "composes" the love stories that she hopes will transpire each time she meets a new male prospect, whom she refers to as "character[s] in her *own* story of her *own* life," playing out the "scenes," "acts," and "heroes" of these "romantic traged[ies]" (86, 133, italics added).[16] But even such efforts finally capitulate to the scripts of others.

Sandra Gilbert and Susan Gubar suggest that writing has long been associated with the male, his pen a phallic substitution serving to fertilize metaphorically the female imagination; it is clear that Newman herself subscribed to such a model of creation, declaring that her books had "fathers" without whose inspiration they would never have been created.[17] The equation of writing and birth has often been drawn by women writers as diverse as Denise Levertov and Katherine Mansfield, in ways that Trinh T. Minh-ha finds "abusive" for their tendency to emphasize labor, suffering, and fears of failure (17). Newman's own unconventional, independent eroticism (these "fathers" were, it seems, lovers she never married) does not allay the troubling fact that even beyond the bounds of a conscripted union, her voice is dependent on the influence of a male companion. She admitted to becoming a writer mainly "because she was not attractive" (Brantley 36); if her career is compensation for her domestic failings, it is a terribly compromised and ominous victory. And there remains an additional obstacle that proves more adherent even than gender: of Katharine, Newman writes, "the inevitability of her literary nationality was almost as great a sorrow . . . as her unprofitable efforts to kiss her sharp elbows" (15). What "nation" does Katharine the writer belong to? On the surface it is America, whose fledgling literature was never expected to rise to the level of its British and European antecedents. As an American southerner, part of H. L. Mencken's maligned "Sahara of the Bozart," her problem is compounded.[18] But the equation with elbow-kissing also places her in the "nation" of women; taken together, these southern and feminine territories are inextricable "sorrows," impoverished geographies she cannot escape in all of her "unprofitable" attempts to engineer a different fate.

While Katharine's sorrow evokes both a regional and sexual crisis, it is also simply and deeply personal. As smart and as stubborn as she is, she is also terrifyingly vulnerable. In the self-effacing quest for material and matrimonial success, what happens to the human heart? After a night of dancing with the coveted James Fuller,

> She quivered off to sleep with her left hand pressed against the envelope in which the golden twenty-dollar bill and the golden ten-dollar bill were lying inside James Fuller's second note, and with her right hand pressed against the blue spot she was trying to keep blue and tender until she danced her second evening at West Point. (110–11)

Here the two pieces of currency given her by her brother appear suggestively folded into a note from her suitor, the West Point cadet James Fuller, underscoring again both the literal and social value of the courtship. She "quivers" off to sleep, not simply in anxiety but, more noticeably, desire—a desire that again is doubled, economic and romantic simultaneously. That is, while Katharine's left hand clutches these gold coins, her other presses against a woman's more valuable currency: the "tender" "blue spot," which is actually a coin-shaped bruise left on her flesh after she has danced against James Fuller's brass buttons, symbol of military honor and its cultural currency in the South. The scene is not tender but disconcerting: all she receives from her would-be lover is a painful reminder of his masculinity and now his absence in the shape of a coin, which she holds suggestively in her other hand. The woman's body ultimately suffers physically not just from the mannered courtship dance, but also from the reminder that such unions will leave her lying alone and in pain. She "press[es]" on the bruise repeatedly in order to keep it fresh, in an implicit and masochistic gesture of masturbation—here, her narcissism is turned self-effacingly and self-destructively on her own body. She is, in effect, kissing her own elbow "unprofitably" again, in a lonely repetition of the aching forms of courtship and love.

This process of narcissistic sublimation reaches its pathetic nadir when she virtually makes love to the precisely geometric, ordered symbols of her coquetry: she enjoys "the slow undressing" of two invitations sent by cadet James Fuller (104). Waiting for the postman to deliver these letters and invitations, she trembles with anticipation that would either "leave her whole body burning from the blazing fall of disappointment or . . . an alabaster lamp for the rise and fall of its electric spray"—the latter an obvious and repeated euphemism for masturbation (247). Again, there is no satisfaction for Katharine except the sublimated, narcissistic kind. Even when she does lose her virginity—and she does, in the most exalted act of "liberation" in the book—she discovers that the moment paradoxically makes her "hopelessly virginal" (246, 253, 284). What Addie Bundren characterizes as the identityless vacancy of virginity stays with Katharine even after her purity is gone, suggesting that a proper woman can become "unvirgin" only within the sacred bounds of marriage. Katharine's "desire" has been shaped by these expectations; yet she "dreamed dreams which she thought were giving her an insight into a nature very unlike the nature a southern lady should have" (246). She doesn't want a man to fill the blank shape of her virgin body; rather she wants to complete herself, specifically by fulfilling her artistic ambitions: "she had hoped that her small celebrity would take the place of her body" (284). Nevertheless, her desires are relegated to dreams, and in waking life her body is programmed to reject its own audacious longing. Her coveted celebrity and independence, even marked by sexual license and the rejection of virginity, does not have the desired effect: she remains "virginal" and unfulfilled. Sex gives her only a kind of "suffering because she did not know what was happening in her own body, and because she could not control her own body" (275); the act meant to defy tradition and assert control effects precisely the opposite, a terrifying loss of order and knowledge. In the aftermath of lovemaking, she fears the next inevitable moment when a man will look admiringly upon her face, her hair, her body, knowing too well now the futility of consummating her narcissistic triumph. Her bold sexual abandon is, in the end, far from the social emancipation critics have wanted to read there;[19] instead, it circumscribes the strict dictates of her existence as a woman of privileged birth. The ineluctability of her fate becomes clear at the close of the novel; at the same time, we sense that she will not stop yearning futilely for something different and better: "she knew she would go on discovering that one illusion had been left to her a minute before, and that she would discover it every time she heard another illusion shattering on the path behind her" (285).

The "Stupid" South and the Erotics of Cont(r)act

While Newman's novel depicts the plight of the neoaristocratic woman, Anita Loos's *Gentlemen Prefer Blondes* shows us that the period's savvy, working-class girl also succumbs to social demands to prove her worth by charming her way into (rather than out of, as Katharine finally decides) a lucrative marriage. Loos's protagonist, Lorelei Lee, embodies the polar opposite of Katharine Faraday: she is blonde, beautiful, uncultured, and basically uneducated. Instead of showcasing the inherent privilege that a woman of Katharine's status enjoys by birth, Lorelei instead represents "a more democratic and optimistic view of marriage and society . . . the embodiment of the notion that anyone, including a woman without position, status, or an excess of brains, can, through determination and 'hard work,' pull herself up by her bootstraps. And so, not only was Loos's working-class heroine able to mingle in high society, she actually managed to marry into it" (C. Bushnell xvi). Beyond this obvious celebration of the American capitalist ascent narrative, Candace Bushnell applauds Loos's heroine Lorelei as "a new female American archetype, one that not only survives today, but thrives" (xiv). Surely Lorelei's type—known popularly as the "gold digger"—is alive and well in contemporary society, but it is unclear and troubling why her endurance might be celebrated. Such a heroine does not say "I worked hard to earn this life" but rather, "I exploited my sexual capital in order to get ahead materially, and I lost myself somewhere along the way." Yet ultimately this *is* the grand narrative of American capitalism and its bootstrap mentality. If Lorelei's victory is measured by the acquisition of diamonds and dollar bills, then certainly, she succeeds brilliantly; however, what she sacrifices for the accumulation of status and wealth is her very identity and humanity.

In fact, the author herself seems invested in seeing this character lose. Interestingly, Loos resembles Newman and Katharine Faraday far more than her own protagonist. She was, by all accounts and photographs, a decidedly beautiful, petite woman with dark hair and eyes; she was also obviously talented and well-read, a successful stage actress and screenwriter before she turned her energies to writing essays and novels. Although she enjoyed a great deal of attention and respect in the glamorous Hollywood scene where she focused much of her life and work, something was clearly missing from Loos's life, and in a sense she seems determined to retaliate against those whom she felt responsible for taking it. She knew Lorelei's "type" well—the well-formed, charming, savvy gold digger who literally stopped men in their tracks and often sent them careening off the rails—and she resented such women for the debilitating sway they held over otherwise powerful men and their wallets. Her grudge was in part personal: according to biographer Gary Carey, Loos was apparently in love with the famous, dyspeptic, South-bashing critic H. L. Mencken, who seems to have had a weakness for "witless blonde[s]" (*Gentlemen Prefer Blondes* xix). The dark-haired Loos knew that "Menck" admired her "very much indeed," but for her mind rather than her looks—admiration that, while gratifying, didn't go far to satisfy her crush (xix). Further complicating her attraction was the fact that she was already married, and she would never admit publicly to anything but pure devotion to her husband, the director John Emerson.

Despite her obvious strength of character, intellect, and professionalism, a tragic kind of repression and lack of fulfillment seemed to haunt Loos. On the surface, she appeared fantastically happy and mirthful; Carey reports that she "liked to have fun, and she selected her playmates from the rich, the celebrated, and the notorious, with a special affection for shady ladies, con men, and charlatans of both sexes. For many years, she led a plush life, moving between New York and Hollywood, Paris and London, with stopovers at all the fashionable spas at home and abroad" (3). Yet this luxury concealed an emptiness and a charade; Carey reveals that this posh and alluring exterior simply masked "another side to Anita, one barely hinted at in the memoirs and fully revealed only in the diaries she started keeping in the mid-1920s"; as those documents reveal, Loos secretly was "extraordinarily disciplined, resilient, and morally fastidious," a woman who "prided herself on being a lady" with "a strong awareness of what was proper" (Carey 4). Running constantly through her life of luxury and pleasure was also a sad sense of foreclosure; not a typical housewife with domestic burdens, she nonetheless felt her artistic energies being sapped by her husband, who often took credit for work Loos had done and "probably sincerely believed [his wife] owed everything to him" (Carey 102). She may have been reluctant to admit it, but it seems clear that in some deeply submerged way she yearned to be more like the witless blonde whom she satirizes so viciously in her novel and whom brilliant men like Mencken fell for: "girls with lots downstairs but nothing in the attic but cobwebs" (Carey 88). Fascinated and repelled by her blonde rivals, Loos confesses, "I wanted Lorelei to be a symbol of the lowest possible mentality of our nation, and Menck had written an essay on American culture in which he branded the state of Arkansas as 'the Sahara of the Beaux Arts' (which he spelled *Bozarts*). Therefore, I chose Little Rock for my heroine's early years; Little Rock which even today lives up to Mencken's choice as the nadir in shortsighted human stupidity" (xxi).

What would eventuate in this California-bred, Hollywood-style woman turning her bitter energies on the South? Loos was raised on a prosperous farm of many thousands of acres in Siskiyou County, northern California; she was privileged, haughty, and agrarian-aristocratic in a way that allied her more closely to a position of stereotypical southern "status" than Lorelei in all her determined scrabbling could ever achieve. *Gentlemen Prefer Blondes* reveals above all else a vigorous condemnation not just of the blonde, gold-digging archetype but of the puritanical codes and ethics that would impoverish even the most physically appealing, bright, and savvy female on the market—codes that stemmed from a self-effacing plantation logic inseparable from the politics of modern American capitalism.[20] While Lorelei, a poor upstart from Arkansas, tries too hard to engineer her social and cultural uplift from her poor southern origins, Loos herself bitterly judges her protagonist's materialistic desires as if she herself were bred into a plantation manor and jealously guarding the keys to that world's propriety and prosperity. The disastrous ambivalence wrought into southern culture by the advent of capitalism, which placed women like Lorelei and Loos in competition with one another, enters Loos's imagination as a kind of metaphorical construct by which Loos the high born can classify, fix, and demean the lowest of the low, the "nadir" of idiocy, and her own greatest rival.

Of the few critics who have attempted seriously to critique Loos's novel, none pay more than glancing attention to the fact that Lorelei is southern; usually this detail is mentioned to illustrate Loos's apparent contempt for her idiot savant narrator and to appeal to Mencken's regional prejudice. In a larger sense, both Loos and Mencken participate in the northern pastime of demeaning the ignorant South; yet such scapegoating is inadvertently revealing. C. Vann Woodward observes the North and South "have occasionally used each other in the way Americans have historically used Europe—not only to define their identity and to say what they are *not*, but to escape in fantasy from what they *are*" (*American* 6–7). In Loos's novel, the "stupid" South as embodied by Lorelei in fact mirrors that which Loos herself both fears and desires about her own value in a neoplantation order that continues to privilege superficiality over substance. And ultimately Loos seems to both resent and envy the ease with which Lorelei could master the American Dream and manage to have whatever she wants.

For Lorelei is nothing if not resourceful: what she lacks in book learning she attempts to compensate for in "education" of the cosmopolitan and consumer variety. In this case, "education" functions not as an alternative to but as a euphemism for commercial culture.[21] As Lorelei professes on the eve of one of many suitor-financed trips overseas, "traveling is the highest form of education" (42)—so long as the boat drops her off in the thick of an urban commercial district, preferably near a Ritz "delightfully full of Americans" abroad (45–46), and "all the famous historical names, like Coty and Cartier" which she perceives as "something educational at last" and worthy of "reverance" (70–71). Such details are enough to establish Lorelei's ignorance of true culture and knowledge in her overriding quest for the glitzy social capital of high society and "large-size" square-cut diamonds; the crass materiality and stupidity of the lower-class upstart comes through clearly. But we quickly realize that she is indeed "learning" everything that she needs to know in order to win the hearts and wallets of the rich men who swoon in her presence. This ethos is ingrained in Lorelei's character from the start, when she gave up a week of stenographer's training in "the business college in Little Rock" to be supported instead by a string of male benefactors: first, to finish her "education" with a lawyer-paramour (whom she ends up shooting upon finding him with another woman) (31, 32), then to be saved by a judge who gives her both "a ticket to Hollywood" and her name, Lorelei. Not just her prosperity, then, but her identity is dependent on the labor and wallets of others; all she must do to earn it is "improve" her looks and her mind in utterly superficial ways. Positing a practical, material, and immoral version of education in place of actual culture and intellect is profoundly threatening to women like Loos, whose brains are their richest and yet, in this economy, their least profitable assets.

Loos condemns the cheapening of culture and education by casting Lorelei as an ignorant and implicitly racist southerner. She foists off onto a poor white with no plausible historical connection to chattel slavery the behavior associated with white mastery. One of the many men bent on "educating" Lorelei sends her some reading material; "I did not waste my time on it," she reports, "but this morning I told Lulu to let all of the house work go and spend the day reading a book entitled 'Lord Jim' and then tell me all about it, so that I would improve my mind while Gerry was away" (16). Lorelei dismisses the possibility of acquiring real intellectual advantage by transferring the task to her black maid, thus making the two impulses seem constitutionally conjoined. Moreover, in the absence of a man to "improve" her mind, Lulu must do it for her; advancement happens, it seems, either by servant labor or male intervention—the southern woman herself will not "waste time" working for what others are meant to supply for her.[22] If acquiring "education" means landing diamond rings and tiaras, then Lorelei displays the classically aristocratic desire to possess things without having to work for them. Handing off the toil to her black maid, moreover, situates this compulsion specifically in a racist hierarchy based on the dynamics of chattel slavery. Loos thus shows Lorelei actively climbing an obviously corrupt ladder to the reward of high society. The fact that Lorelei almost makes Lulu read Joseph Conrad's *The Nigger of the Narcissus* is telling: Lulu *is* the "nigger" of this "narcissus," and Lorelei decides charitably that the book "really would have hurt her feelings" (16).

Lorelei's narcissism is not exactly absolved in this brief glimmer of compromised empathy; after all, the book she gives Lulu instead is Conrad's *Lord Jim*, a narrative told by *Heart of Darkness*'s Marlow and dominated by themes of honor, heroism, slavery, and colonialism peculiarly applicable to Lorelei and Lulu's joint southern past. Again, though, Lulu does all the work of gaining such knowledge, while Lorelei's narcissism shields her from actually learning anything beyond the American consumer marketplace. Though she lauds "travel" as the highest form of education, what she really wants to find abroad is a mirror: "the most delightful thing about traveling," she discovers, "is always to be running into Americans and to always feel at home" (46). Unlike English girls, Lorelei realizes, American women favor large, expensive jewelry and not simple "bangles" that they "would really give to their maid," signifying again the fetishized class distinction between the Lulus and the Loreleis of this economy (54). Impatient with British men and their cheap gifts, Dorothy wants to "'go back to the Ritz where men are Americans,'" but Lorelei, undaunted by a material challenge, sets out to "educate" them instead (54, 55). The only time the English appeal to her vanity is when she can enfold them in remembered tales about her own, stereotypically southern lineage: "I remember papa back in Arkansas and he often used to say that his grandpa came from a place in England called Australia, so really, I mean to say, it is no wonder the English seems to come out of me sometimes" (58). Of course, it is not the English coming out of her in such moments but the American southern; and her inability to get these genealogical stories straight underscores their often fantastical nature, particularly for poor whites like Lorelei.

While British and European elements appeal to Lorelei's aristocratic ambitions, she can quantify success and status only on instinctively American terms. The "English" that comes out of this Arkansas girl is, emphatically, American English; she flatly rejects anyone who does not speak "english almost like an American" (73). If the possession of expensive objects constitutes an education, then it follows that the language of this discipline is money, and its function is mathematical. Not surprisingly, it is the only language Lorelei knows. In France, she recounts "we saw a jewelry store and we saw some jewelry in the window and it really seemed to be a very great bargain but the price marks all had francs on them and Dorothy and I do not seem to be mathematical enough to tell how much francs is in money" (71). Lorelei relates this conundrum like a foreigner in a strange land where she does not speak the language; read this way, Lorelei's "mathematical" abilities—that is, her ability to translate from one language of capital to another—come up short. Underscoring the arithmetical nature of this problem, she can't even figure out how to use the telephone in her Paris hotel: "If you think you can get a number over that thing, go to it," she tells Dorothy, "but as far as we have found out, it is a wall bracket" (81). Her confusion is humorous until we remember that numbers are a universal language and would be no different in France than in Arkansas, but Lorelei's inability to "read" them in a French context tells us that her mathematical mind is trained on a specifically American notion of use value, thus rendering the phone a useless "wall bracket" rather than a functional instrument of, importantly, communication.

While Lorelei is not "mathematical enough" to make such connections, she can do American math quite proficiently, as she demonstrates in her attempts to make the French lawyer—the "advocat"—Monsieur Broussard stop "talking in French, which means nothing to us" (81). Dorothy comes up with a plan to "'see if 25 francs will stop him, because if 5 francs will stop a taxi driver, 25 francs ought to stop an advocate.' Because he was making about 5 times as much noise as a taxi driver and 5 times 5 is 25" (81). As a lawyer presumably he is about five times as important and as rich as a taxi driver, Lorelei's class scale tells her, and she knows fully well that small gifts are for servants while "large-size" ones are for more cultivated types. In a more comic but equally illustrative moment, Lorelei reiterates that her understanding of money is a quantified system and that she expects to see its value reflected visibly in the size and shape of the objects being sold. In "the Central of Europe" she struggles to adapt to yet a new system of currency: "it seems to be kronens and it seems to take quite a lot of them because it takes 50,000 of them to even buy a small size package of cigarettes and Dorothy says if the cigarettes had tobacco in them, we couldn't lift enough kronens over a counter to pay for a package" (104). In this case, Dorothy and Lorelei confuse the price of something with the thing itself; the numbers have a direct, one-to-one correlation with the priced object. Lorelei's scale has trouble recalibrating to an alien system, which suggests that the American version, while no less fetishized, has become entirely natural to her. Moreover, it reveals her alienation from everything but her narcissistic labors: her own mathematics are strictly in the service of engineering a diamond and bridal purse large enough to signify visibly their tremendous value.

In the end, Lorelei marries the poor, duped Henry Spoffard. Although the multiple musicals and the 1953 film adaptation of the novel (early versions of which Loos herself had a hand in writing) seized upon the marriage quest as the overriding purpose of the girls' machinations, in the novel Lorelei's betrothal aspirations are simply a means to the end of acquiring both wealth and support for her artistic ego. Indeed, like Newman's Katharine Faraday, Lorelei has dreams of being a writer that can only be made possible by the financial support and companionship of a man; unlike Katharine, though, Lorelei has considerable difficulties with the English "languadge," which literalizes her dependence on male patronage. It is only when Lorelei is safely in the bonds of wedlock that she will venture to say "that money was not everything, because after all, it is only brains that count" (154). Of course, we know that for Lorelei to "count" is both to have monetary worth and, quite literally, to count and quantify that value; and it is clear that Lorelei's brains can do little else but "count" her way into auspicious relationships with men. When a literary benefactor offers her "a penny for your thoughts, [little woman]," the quantification is literal, not to mention diminutive (156). Lorelei herself is the first to admit, albeit in a calculated gesture of coquetry, that before she became engaged to Henry she was "nothing but a society girl from Little Rock, Arkansas" (135). The "nothing" stands out here, especially when Dorothy destroys the illusion of Lorelei's "society" origins by outing her "debut at the Elks annual street fair and carnival at the age of 15" (135). Truly "nothing" before her opportune marriage, Lorelei enjoys in a very literal way the fact that "Henry's credit is really my credit"; on their own, her small brains are worth little more than "a penny" (151).

Yet while her botched mathematical and language translations indicate the contrary, Lorelei is simply not the "idiot heroine" that Loos claimed her to be (xx); she is, in fact, more savvy in orchestrating her coups than her creator (perhaps intentionally) leads us to believe, a fact that allows us to see more of the author in the protagonist than she probably intended. By using her witless blonde image to manipulate the men around her, Lorelei indeed gets exactly what she wants in the form of diamonds and domestic comfort. As Hegeman argues, the novel resolves itself by developing "a fantastic economy in which women can actually parlay their (albeit male-defined) assets of sexual attractiveness into what they truly want" (545). We are left, then, to balance her brilliant feat with her representation of "the nadir of shortsighted human stupidity," a balance that seems to hinge on the notion of sexual attractiveness as a commodity. While Lorelei's victory is in one way certain, the perverse logic of this conquest remains troubling: if the New Woman's sexuality—indeed, the core of the 1920s flapper's identity—is "male-defined," then how are either we or Lorelei herself to know what she "truly want[s]"? And if what she "truly wants" is monetary rather than emotional sustenance, what does that reveal about the destructive sexual economy of the period? Finally, if exchanging material desire for interpersonal connection is the "nadir in shortsighted human stupidity," then clearly we must question how and why this cold substitution stymies the southern more than the ordinary American woman.

Hegeman believes Lorelei "manages to find happiness at the end of her narrative—in spades" (545). If "credit" is all she is after, then this reading might be plausible. But Loos makes it abundantly clear that Lorelei never manages to develop a viable ego or desires of her own, and that in a sense she simply reflects the values ingrained in her as a woman of inauspicious southern birth always yearning for a higher, more prosperous, tantalizingly American ascendance. If she cannot triumph over the world of cold capitalism and its patriarchal logic herself (Loos implies that its forces operate below the belt rather than above the necktie), she will attempt to drag its beneficiaries down with her: that is, Loos makes sure that Lorelei is as emotionally bereft as she herself is. While Lorelei hungers fanatically after the material gain opened to her by the tantalizing opportunities of American capitalist ascent, she is remarkably free of sexual and emotional wants; as Carey notes, "it is perhaps the cleanest exposé of illicit romance ever written" (99). As a vessel of such cold, calculating desires, her thoughts and mind are saturated with references to pennies, diamonds, and mathematical calculations of magnitudes of value. Her body, the seat of erotic desire, doesn't escape this sublimation either: not only are all sexual references studiously repressed throughout the narrative, but in much the same way that Katharine measures and quantifies her own image, Lorelei also converts the language of physical union into fiscal metaphors. Her terrible grammar and spelling can often be revealing of much deeper import, as in her frequent declaration that "everybody I come into *contract* with always seems to become happy" (161, italics added). Indeed, in these "contracts" of sexual and domestic gratification, Lorelei apparently plays her prescribed role and pleases men abundantly. In such a "contract," it is never, for her, about "contact," but only paper and metal rewards—and, ultimately, the awful price—for fulfilling her feminine duty.[23] Through Lorelei, Loos can give with one hand what life has taken from her—economic and emotional satisfaction—and then withdraw it in a gesture of self-righteous aristocratic morality and extreme self-pity.

Even Loos's attempt to provide an alternative to this pitiful outcome seems fraught with ambivalence. Dorothy is Lorelei's intelligent, quick-witted, and decidedly brunette sidekick who tends to "tell it like it is" and offers scathing critiques of the world that she and Lorelei navigate together, revealing a level of intellectual acuity that Lorelei misses altogether but that the reader grasps instantly; in a sense, such moments reveal the author inviting the reader to have a laugh along with her at Lorelei's expense. Critics have read Dorothy as Lorelie's foil and a proxy for Loos herself; the transference is tempting, given the personal jealousies that seemed to fuel Loos's virtuoso rendition of the Lorelei type. And Loos herself often jokingly admitted that Dorothy was "pretty much a self-portrait" (Carey 100). Filtered through Lorelei's narrow voice, however, Dorothy frequently becomes the subject of Lorelei's pity and judgment because she does not fit the shallow gold digger's version of refinement and "does nothing but waste her time" on entertaining human, erotic attractions rather than orchestrating purely material connections (29). Lorelei's work ethic comes through again with ironic force; she sees herself as laboring for a payoff, while Dorothy squanders her time on matters that promise no tangible gain. There is no question about the capitalist critique posed here or the notion that Dorothy's values are more respectable than those of her gold-digging friend. But ultimately it becomes difficult to see Dorothy as better off or even significantly different from Lorelei. To begin with, it is Dorothy who leads Lorelei through the elaborate mathematical equations already discussed, first to get the French lawyer to stop speaking, and secondly to speculate on the correlation between "kronens" and the item marked for purchase. While Lorelei's perceptions of these mathematical problems are altogether serious and sometimes befuddled, Dorothy tosses off the calculations with a subtly knowing sarcasm. She is clearly aware that money talks, acts, and has weight in their world, and she comments shrewdly on their participation in this economy by observing the absurd calculations necessary to appease a taxi driver or a lawyer, or the way that bought objects like cigarettes ought to bear the heft of the expense necessary to acquire them. Dorothy appears as astute and cynical in these moments as she does elsewhere; she seems to know all too well the stratifications of their world and the difficulties of surmounting one's social origins. Yet—perhaps like Loos herself—she bitterly and knowingly continues playing the game and counting herself into it, sticking loyally by Lorelei's side throughout all of their calculating adventures.

Lessons in Love and Longing

Dorothy's story grows distinctly more troubling in the novel's sequel, *But Gentlemen Marry Brunettes*. In this work, Lorelei has settled into the domestic roles of wife and mother, and of amateur writer. Although she joins the Lucy Stone League so she can keep her own name and "write my book without my identity being sunk by having the name of a husband to crush me," she nevertheless has to wait for Henry's permission to write at all, and then he must "read it all over, and give it a sanction before it ever reached the public" (252, 254). It is clear that Lorelei's "identity" is crushed long before this, or rather that the identity she keeps is always already associated with a name and a language given to her by some man or other. Naturally, we read with a sense of irony, then, when she decides to use her writing "to teach some lesson. . . . and the best lesson I have ever come in contract with, is the life of my girl friend Dorothy. So I decided to write about that. Only the life of Dorothy is not going to be so much for girls to resemble, as it is to give them a warning what they should stop doing" (253).

By now, of course, we have come to expect that Lorelei's words will betray the opposite of her intentions; Dorothy tends to prioritize love over money, which for Lorelei represents the height of wrongheaded idealism—and her "contract" slippage again here reveals that her mind is still very much on such issues. But these choices do not get Dorothy any further along than they do Lorelei, and in the end, the life of Dorothy does indeed constitute a warning.

For one thing, while Dorothy is not southern, she does come from a "low envirament" (253): specifically, "the 'Greater Pacific Street Fair and Carnaval Company' on the Pacific Coast" (256), a revelation that gives Dorothy's mockery of Lorelei's "street fair" debut a distinctly personal, self-deprecating valence. Moreover, and more troublingly, her California origins make her roots similar to those of Loos herself. Like Lorelei, Dorothy's desire to escape these origins tends toward the crafty rather than the hardworking: she, too, transfers her labor to someone else, in this case a "small size local boy of the town, who was always more than delighted" to work the waffle machine that Dorothy was assigned to manage at the fair (269); and later, while she is trying to navigate her way into high society, she simply racks up expenses long after her money runs out because, as Lorelei notes, her "poverty always seems to consist in not worrying about bills" (329). While it would seem that money and calculations of ascent are not on Dorothy's radar screen at all, at least not to the extent that they occupy Lorelei, it appears instead that she is constantly trying to flee the dollars and cents that shadow her existence. Instead of designing to increase her capital, Dorothy always engages herself in giving it away, much to Lorelei's disapproval: "Dorothy is the kind of girl that makes gentlemen presents," she laments (316).

Yet whether she is giving or receiving, Dorothy is nonetheless a willing participant in and victim of the gendered domestic economy of this world. She ends up functioning as a commodity to the many "brokers"—aka, talent agents—who represent the women trying to win a spot in Ziegfield's Follies; and she succeeds brilliantly, becoming a Folly and proving her worth. While the men in her life take her gifts, they punish her as well, subduing her strong spirit with physical violence. Her ill-fated first marriage to an upstart street car conductor-cum-saxophone player devolves quickly into brutality, with furniture, objects, doors, and "a small lamp" being hurled back and forth between the couple (367, 370). Later, as she is being trailed by a silent, bearded man, Dorothy finally "lost all her endurants and gave him a slap" only to be more harshly hit in the jaw and knocked down by the force of the burly stranger's "manhood" (384). Stunningly, such treatment is both normalized (a friend of Dorothy's is simply "very, very ashamed to think that an American girl would slap a French gentleman," 384) and approved. Again, while Loos's intent seems to be a critique of the values of an American society that would condone such brutality, she stops short of offering any more pleasant alternatives, even for her own fictional proxy. When Dorothy finally marries properly into "society" at the end, she does so under the most compromised circumstances: her new husband, Charlie, is a roaring drunk who eventually turns sober and cruel, and then proceeds unhappily to belittle and insult her: "Charlie took to looking over Dorothy in his sober senses, and seeing her as she really was, and making remarks like, 'Go wash your face! You've got on too much make-up!' And Dorothy fell in love" (415). Suspiciously, Lorelei does not condemn Dorothy for her romantic weakness, as she routinely does, but rather applauds the fact that her friend has become, with Charlie "ordering her around . . . more refined than I have ever seen her before, and with a trace of dignity" (419). Loos emphasizes that while Dorothy has held out for "love," she has gotten little more than emotional bankruptcy and slavery to a man's whims and desires. Only to the eyes of Lorelei could such an achievement have the look of "dignity" and "refinement," possibly because she cannot see past the final glowing reward of marital security at any costs. But it is Dorothy's acquiescence to her status as belittled, demeaned, domestic servant that is finally the most troubling.

More disturbing is the notion that Dorothy seems to engineer this final result for herself, with Loos's apparent blessing. When Charlie's aristocratic mother develops an elaborate plan to get the lowly Dorothy out of her son's life and heart, Dorothy "started in to put 2 and 2 together" to crack the plot (375–76). The math she mastered in Europe works at home as well, but it delivers a product she should not want; rather than calculating herself out of such a superficial and deceitful world, Dorothy's mathematical prowess helps her to count herself right into it. Her prize is the abusive Charlie, and along with him a ticket to "New York society." The novella closes on this putative high note, ending with Lorelei's hope that both she and Dorothy can "get into the Social Register" at last (419). Given the historical uses of the "register" or account book in the context of chattel slavery, Loos clearly evokes the folly of this woman's catastrophic desire to have herself written into a new social register as an entry rather than a scribe. The fact that the register delivers both upstart women from their southern and "low enviraments" to a New York version of commercial success is distinctly defeating, as the new and magical order of American ascent nevertheless shuttles them back to the cruel order that cemented such pitiful choices and only the illusion of happiness. And Loos, spending half of her time in New York and the other half in Hollywood, would have known this only too well. And yet, both her life and her fictional proxy endorse what must have been a seductive life of leisure after all.

Indeed women are little different from slaves, the novel suggests, in an economy that mirrors the inequities and exploitations of slavery. Such a reminder helps us to make sense of an otherwise discomposing scene when Mrs. Breene schemes to plant drugs in Dorothy's handbag, which lands Dorothy in jail along with a "*colored*" girl whose name happens to be Lulu, exactly like Lorelei's maid and slave figure in *Gentlemen Prefer Blondes*. The symbology of the scene alone is powerful—white upstart and black prostitute are imprisoned together, sharing social enslavement and punishment for those who dare to defy their place in the hierarchy. The moment has implications for Lorelei, too, as she calls herself a "professional lady" in such a way that critics have interpreted as a suggestion that she is a prostitute. Indeed, when Lulu asks Dorothy what she's in for, Dorothy tries to be polite by saying "'Same thing as you, I guess,'" which for Lulu is "s'liciting" (409). Dorothy has made a practice of giving gifts to men all her life, and now her sacrifices literally imprison her. Her life is, as Lorelei warned, a "lesson." There is no doubt that Dorothy is smart, but Loos reminds us of just how far "brains" will get a woman and of how bound she is by the same rules and conditions that shape Lorelei's world; of how much she is expected to give and how little she will receive in return; and finally, of how deeply ugly and worthless a woman can be made to feel by the men she loves.

As already noted, Newman published a sequel to her dark novel in 1928, the same year Loos's depressing chronicle of Dorothy's misadventures appeared. In *Dead Lovers Are Faithful Lovers* Newman also places another autobiographical proxy, like Dorothy, in a fateful romantic situation. But this woman, the bookish, independent librarian Isabel Ramsay—even more a reflection of Newman herself than Katharine was—is only one of the novel's protagonists. The other is Evelyn Cunningham, who is married to Mr. Charlton Cunningham—who happens to be the man with whom Isabel is deeply in love and having an affair. Just as Loos ultimately hands Dorothy and Lorelei the same sober fate, so too Newman suggests that it is no more lucrative to be an educated mistress than a long-suffering wife. Newman's cluttered, complex prose reveals no shortage of erudite vocabulary and expression; pointedly, then, she uses identical language and phrases to indicate that the two women in this novel think the same complex thoughts, feel the same emotions, and are equally emotionally indebted to the man they both love and who functions as a perverse, double-sided mirror for their equal and opposite reactions to his presence and love. What we learn from Katharine's plight—of the impossibility of feminine autonomy and value outside the bonds of marriage—is made more depressing here in the suggestion that wives and mistresses receive the same measure of personal satisfaction and self-knowledge in their relationships with the men they love.[24] Both choices, Newman demonstrates, are at last the same; the emotional costs to either's sense of self are equally profound.

Evelyn Cunningham, the wife in *Dead Lovers*, has been repeatedly reminded by her mother that marriages follow an unerring pattern resting on the woman's spiritual debt: thus, when Evelyn ponders her paralyzing reverence for her husband she is already resigned to the fact that "his inevitably lessening affection for her would finally balance her inevitably growing affection for him" (83). The advice that her mother hands down comes appropriately in the form of a domestic equation fraught with numerous disastrous implications: first, that marriages begin with the desire and attraction of the husband who approves of and chooses the wife, and with the possible apprehension and ambivalence of the woman who has little choice but to submit; later, when the woman grows attached to her human lifeline, the husband finds more appealing objects for his affections and erotic attachments. Perhaps most disquieting of all is the mother's assertion, twice in one sentence, that this domestic equation is "inevitable." Like Addie's body, the married woman's self is given meaning and worth by conjugal relations, but that worth paradoxically implies her spiritual and emotional emptiness.

More pointedly even than Katharine's narcissism, Evelyn's mirror gazing is fraught with anxiety over her worthiness of Charlton's love and her fears of losing not just his affection but, in the process, her self. The process is quantified in an almost pathological way:

> for the fifteenth time, she slipped away from him to look in the long mirrors of Car One Hundred's mahogany bath-room—to open her blue bag, and to take up combs and to unfold beautifully folded white crepe de chine and lace and ribbons, and to open little jars and little boxes and little bottles until the long mirrors could give her enough courage to slip back beside Charlton Cunningham, and to wait for his brown eyes to open into her brown eyes, and to wait for another second until his lips kissed her waiting lips and his golden body kissed her waiting body. (10–11)[25]

Evelyn rises before dawn to prepare her image carefully and ritualistically to meet her husband's satisfaction, using mirrors as a substitute for his gaze; her eyes and body merely "wait" and mirror his movements and his will. In another scene, she "looked quickly and carefully from one long mirror to its reflection in the other long mirror. And she gave the mirror the smile she would give her husband" (17). Rendered in this scene is Evelyn's sense that the mirror reflects everything—another mirror, her smile—but will not illuminate her self to herself; both the reflecting surface and the refracted image are intended for someone else's consumption. This fatal narcissism betrays its carefully quantified worth when she appraises her body in the mirror in terms of calculating detachment, recognizing its strangeness much as Wright's underground man examines the stolen dollar bills as if he is completely unacquainted with them. As an object whose carefully maintained value is not accorded to her but to her husband, this alienation divulges an uncanny truth:

> She looked at the straight line which went down to the sudden curve of her hips, and which had been something called a figure, and something to be recorded in a

dressmaker's measurements when she ordered a new frock, or in a tailor's more careful measurements when she ordered a new coat and skirt or a new habit. . . . And she looked down past the curve which had been the most carefully measured part of her figure, and which became two strangely divided legs. . . . Then her eyes followed the strange division back up to her familiar shoulders . . . and she stood still and thought of the moment when . . . he could see her and touch her, and when this strange figure had united with her familiar head and when it had become her body. (50–51)

Importantly, her erogenous zones below the waist are strange to her, measured and thus known only by her husband more "carefully" and thoroughly than even the tailor who suits her in fine clothes. This unfamiliar geometrical body is unintelligible to her until her husband returns home to "see her and touch her" and unify her head and her sexuality into a complete unit called "her body" (49–50). Years later, after a lessening of her husband's affection and measurement, Evelyn glances at her throat, hips, and breasts in the mirror to remind her of the long-ago honeymoon moment when those parts first "had become her body" (290); she turns away from the mirror quickly, its reflection no longer of value.[26]

For the mistress whose love will never be authorized in the precise equation of marriage, solitude promises a more immediate physical deterioration. For Isabel Ramsay, Charlton Cunningham's deferred affection fails to give her body meaning like Evelyn's, but his teasing presence and social inaccessibility are calculated obsessively in Isabel's own "mental arithmetic" (189)—exactly the phrase used to describe Katharine's pathological calculations—of minutes, hours, and days. She can think about little else in the agonizing, measured space between their encounters; a bright, bookish, well-employed woman, she nonetheless feels her powers of attention wane, "discovering again that her memory was only part of her body, and that it was slipping away from the clutching hold of something which was not her tired mind, and which she called herself" (201). The "something" beyond her mind that she cannot identify is similar to what Evelyn perceives strangely below her waist, the foreign territory that has meaning and measure only when Charlton surveys it; Isabel does not have even that privilege, yet disastrously her identity hinges on the need for it, that thing "which she called herself" and which it seems she will never attain. She imagines ominously that the unrequited yearning leaves "little circles cut out of her own body and her own mind" (210).

When she attempts to forget him, she suffers more—and masochistically at her own hands, just as Dorothy submits voluntarily to her own debasement and abuse. Isabel engages in further emptying her body of the significance Charlton will not give her, which entails a bulimic (and precisely quantifiable) purging of her stomach's contents: "She remembered the rushing misery her body had felt while she was pressing her longest finger down her resisting throat half a dozen times"

(211–12). Isabel's only consolation, like Katharine's, comes repeatedly in the body of a letter, of paper and words and "the sharp corner of a long white envelope" held hard against "both of her breasts"—leaving her "blazing with happiness . . . because only twenty-nine hours had passed since the minute when her two names had been written on the white envelope" (212). That Newman's women are so carefully created, controlled, and depleted by the men who desire them makes the otherwise tender treatment of the love letter here wrenching; the mere appearance on the envelope of Isabel's "two names" in Charlton's hand fills her with plenitude and inspires her orgasmic happiness. Alone, she is haunted by her insignificance.

The novel ends with both women alone: Charlton succumbs to a sudden illness and disappears from their lives forever. We do not know Isabel's fate after this shattering event, but we can infer that it is desolate: as she thinks in the moments before Charlton's death, "if a life founded on love pauses for a second, it pauses like an airplane which has nothing more dependable than air and water between itself and hell" (266). In a terrible moment of foreshadowing, we thus understand that the bottom is about to fall out of her world: without him, "she would be like the letter which she had once dropped down on that hearth, and which had become ashes without ever becoming fire" (266). The wife who became fire under Charlton's touch will fare little better: she goes on but is harnessed ineluctably to a past in which Charlton's memory is still alive. In a long closing scene twelve years later, Evelyn is slowly dressing, and as she covers each "beautifully tended" foot or hand with an article of clothing, she is swept into some memory or other of her husband. Even dead, he remains a constant presence that attends her every move and appreciation of her body; the grief momentarily cripples her: "when the heavy shell of pain broke again in her body, she dropped down on her knees with her cold cheek against the smooth cold wood" just as Isabel had once "been kneeling on the floor of her apple-green bath-room on Screven Road" trying to rid her body of its "rushing misery" (293, 282). But for both women, the kneeling subjection and breaking body signifies love, and the ultimate victory is not necessarily in winning its bounty but rather in never losing it. As the novel's title implies, in death Charlton would finally and irreversibly be faithful to his wife, the guttering equation of lessening affection no longer plummeting at her expense. This sober recognition allows the novel to end with Evelyn "walking at last on the green oasis of a memory over which she was dropping the victorious curtain of her very long black crape veil" (295). A compromised victory, indeed.

Stealing the Self and Owning Nothing

Both Loos's and Newman's stories—fictional and autobiographical—make clear that resisting the compulsion and ratification of marriage does not necessarily allow the southern woman the alternative of owning herself. In the following decade when Katherine Anne Porter was writing her passionately feminist works, little had changed. Yet Porter's characters begin desperately to toss away the notion of love and to jettison the South along with it; but as far as they throw these ideas and themselves, they cannot seem to get away from the terms that define and delimit them, and they essentially become thieves of their own chances for happiness and prosperity in this world. Darlene Harbour Unrue tells us that "Porter's earliest political activities were feminist and socialist," a natural confluence to address women's particular struggle in an increasingly capitalist world ("Katherine Anne Porter" 119). Yet Porter's life was contradictory in all sorts of troubling ways; in an attempt to write an "honest biography" of the endlessly misunderstood writer, Unrue notes that it is not just the facts of Porter's life that are contradictory (no one knows, for instance, just how many husbands she had) but the woman herself.[27] A crucial incongruity at the core of her identity and art was the disjunct between her aristocratic "white-pillar" ancestry (Unrue, *Katherine Anne Porter* xxiii) and her actual, land-poor, motherless upbringing in Indian Creek, Texas. Unrue conjectures that Porter compensates for the realities of her inauspicious start by constantly searching in her work for both "*home*" and "*love*," images grounded for her in fantasies of traditionally southern high society and the adoration of men (xxvii); living far from the South most of her life and cycling through husbands and lovers at a dizzying rate, it seems she spent her entire life searching for both.

Visible in Porter's fiction is a restless desire to leave behind those fantasies of the South and the men who would complete her. Like Newman and Loos, however, Porter's work reveals characters anchored to it body and soul. Her aptly titled short story "Theft," which appears in her collection *Flowering Judas and Other Stories*, depicts one of her many independent women who resists society's expectations, is courted by several men (some married), and lives alone. In keeping with the narrator's apparently liberated persona, the title might seem to refer to her theft of herself from the demands of men and marriage; but we soon learn differently. Her symbol of both economic freedom and sexual license is, suggestively, a purse: "That's beautiful, that purse," her friend Roger notices, and she responds, "It's a birthday present . . . and I like it" (71). Associated with her birthday, the purse becomes an obvious metonym for her identity; both she and the bag are things praised as "beautiful" by a male companion—but this prettiness itself, we learn, is a gift from another man. A secondary meaning of "purse" is, of course, "a sum of money collected as a present" or "prize," tying her identity more clearly to the material reward supplied by male benefactors. When she admits "I like it," she betrays her reluctant ties to the sexual economy that supplies and endorses her beauty—her most personal possession and yet something she does not actually own.[28]

Indeed, we soon discover that this beautiful purse is perpetually empty. Living stubbornly alone, this woman continually loses more capital; she rifles through the bag looking for enough change to pay her own taxi fare home (69). She ends up sharing a taxi with Roger instead, underscoring symbolically that her mobility still depends upon male assistance. And still she pays for it: she chips in a dime at Roger's request. Once home, she sees her neighbor Bill, who owes her money; instead of paying her, he "went on to ask her if she realized his wife was ruining him with her extravagance" (72).[29] The message in the world that Porter depicts is that women are mere commodities who dole out their beauty and themselves ceaselessly to the men in their lives, cash a mere proxy for parts of their souls that they give and take like coins. As Unrue observes, in fact "all of the other characters in this story are associated with the protagonist by money" ("KAP, Politics" 123), suggesting that these are the only ties that create and define significant social relationships. The narrator continues paying out her small reserves to variously noncommittal men who seem to demand and deserve such shares. "'Let it go then,'" she tells Bill wearily, essentially forgiving the debt to preserve the relationship and avoid being perceived as another "extravagant" woman in his life (73).

The story is clearly a critique of the economic ties that substitute for relationships, much like Hurston's "Gilded Six-Bits." But as in Hurston's story, this theme cannot be separated from the narrator's embattled quest for true companionship and love. Unrue's notion that love offers the protagonist an alternative, "the only deterrent against the spiritual vacuum of materialism" ("Katherine Anne Porter" 124), and that somehow she has simply been until this point too hampered by "apathy" to realize it might be true in an idealized sense, but what the story ultimately reveals is something much bleaker about love's contamination by the exigencies of materialism, a certainty that Porter's acute familiarity with capitalism and socialism would have given her. While the narrator spends endless amounts of emotional capital on unavailable men, none of them are free to propose to her; because she is not playing the marriage market correctly, she is not being robbed but is in fact stealing from herself. Her worth as a woman lies entirely in the metonym of her purse, the symbolic container of her value to a potential husband; yet she keeps giving it and herself away to unworthy and unavailable men, which implies, as a cool breakup letter tells her, that she is "not worth" the trouble. Upstairs in her room she worries over her "empty purse"; the suggestion that she has diminished her own worth and stolen her own chances is made clearer when the purse itself is stolen. She knows instantly that the janitress must have taken it, but her first reaction echoes the way she forgave Bill's debt.

"Then let it go," she tells herself, apparently inured to the condition of divestment. But she finds quickly that she cannot simply let go of this container for her own soul, empty though it is. She confronts the janitress and explains that the item has no value to anyone but herself: "'Will you please give me back my purse? There isn't any money in it. It was a present, and I don't want to lose it'" (74). She herself is a gift, she knows, one she is anxious to keep for herself rather than continue to give away. The cleaning woman admits the theft but justifies it according to the rules of the marriage market: she has stolen it for her niece who "'is young and needs pretty things. . . . She's got young men after her maybe will want to marry her. . . . You're a grown woman, you've had your chance.'" The narrator, obviously wounded, then replies, "'You mustn't act as if I had stolen it from you,'" to which the janitress finally responds, "'It's not from me, it's from [my niece] you're stealing it'" (75).

The purse represents the woman's young, pretty, marketable self, something that belongs only to youthful nieces and not washed-up, solitary women like the narrator. Empty or not, the purse's potential has already been wasted and stolen many times over, and now it actually belongs to someone more deserving of its worth. It doesn't matter that this woman wants to keep herself for herself rather than lose that gift to a man or even to the next round of ill-fated young bachelorettes; such liberty is simply not a viable option. Her very independence amounts to the theft of her value and integrity:

> She remembered how she had never locked a door in her life, on some principle of rejection in her that made her uncomfortable in the ownership of things, and her paradoxical boast before the warning of her friends, that she had never lost a penny by theft. . . . In this moment she felt that she had been robbed of an enormous number of valuable things, whether material or intangible: things lost or broken by her own fault, things she had forgotten and left in houses when she moved: books borrowed from her and not returned, journeys she had planned and not made, words she had waited to hear spoken to her and had not heard, and the words she had meant to answer with; bitter alternatives and intolerable substitutes worse than nothing, and yet inescapable: the long patient suffering of dying friendships and the dark inexplicable death of love—all that she had had, and all that she had missed, were lost together, and were twice lost in this landslide of remembered losses. . . . She laid the purse down on the table . . . and thought: I was right not to be afraid of any thief but myself, who will end by leaving me nothing. (74–75)

In this remarkable catalog of losses the narrator realizes that her resistance to a world of locked doors and anxious possessiveness is futile; in an attempt to find "alternatives" and "substitutes" she has encountered only bitterness, death, and loss. Worse, she can only blame herself in the end, having found no substitutes to these dictates.

The alternative for such women is to exist alone and bereft. Worse, as Fanon has described the "devaluation of self," the postcolonial subject tired of being abandoned and hurt no longer wishes to be loved; the ominous aftermath of such rejection, however, makes one more vulnerable to the renewed desire simply to please others (75). While there is little in "Theft" to tie Porter's vision to specifically southern iterations, many of her works do return to this setting as a source for the spiritual impoverishment of her female characters. One of her most frequently discussed characters, Miranda, offers another example of hopeful feminist impulses thwarted by the adherent expectations and codes of southern social logic.[30] Like the narrator of "Theft," Miranda wards off traditional notions of domesticity and marriage, partly because she has grown up listening to legends about her beautiful, doomed Aunt Amy while on visits home from a convent school in the Deep South. The straitening atmosphere of Miranda's convent education is paralleled by the stories, the picture frame, and the corsets that literally confine her willful, rebellious aunt. At the end of "Old Mortality," Miranda attempts to escape the demands that stymied her aunt by marrying young and impulsively. She soon regrets the loss of her independence and, in "ignorance" and "hopefulness" decides to "run away from marriage" too: "she was not going to stay in any place, with anyone, that threatened to forbid her making her own discoveries, that said 'No' to her" (61, 60). Importantly, her rebellion is against her aristocratic southern family—"cousins," "ties of blood," "this house" (60)—as much as her husband and his family. She wants to possess her own life and mind: "It is something of my own, she thought in a fury of jealous possessiveness, what shall I make of it?" (61). She resolves to forget the past: "her mind closed stubbornly against remembering" and she thinks, like Fanon, "I hate love. . . . I hate loving and being loved, I hate it" (61).

"Old Mortality" ends with Miranda's intent to abdicate love, leave the family, her marriage, and presumably the South; we encounter her character next in "Pale Horse, Pale Rider," writing articles for a Colorado newspaper and supporting herself. Not incidentally, this movement mirrors Porter's own escape to Denver from Texas and from her first husband (Unrue, "Katherine Anne Porter" 120). But Miranda's new independence proves fraught with anxiety and lingering reminders of the past she left behind. The few overt references to the South suggest that Miranda has moved beyond her attachment to the South, though the story begins with her dreaming about it and waking to her present moment and exile only "slowly, unwillingly" (115). We sense increasingly that she has not fully forgotten the South, nor does she necessarily want to. This dream, beginning a story that will be filled with such presage and foreshadowing, indicates that her subconscious returns to these origins will prove her undoing: the dream centers on a visage of death, drawn importantly from the lyrics of a Negro spiritual: the pale horse and pale rider of the story's title, which she and her doomed lover sing together as they remember a shared plantation past. The plot turns on this ill-fated romance: now divorced, she has fallen in love with a soldier home on leave from World War I during the height of the 1918 influenza outbreak, a dark backdrop for her struggle to create a new, autonomous life.

Again, monetary worth is intimately bound to the woman's quest for self-actualization and romantic affirmation. Paid little as an underappreciated female journalist, Miranda is pressured by a government agent to buy a war bond that she cannot afford. At first, her romance with Adam is a pleasant experience that distracts her from her financial woes; soon, though, she faces herself in a mirror and realizes how deeply her love and her finances are entangled:

> [Adam] was in her mind so much, she hardly knew when she was thinking about him directly. His image was simply always present in more or less degree . . . the pleasantest, the only really pleasant thought she had. She examined her face in the mirror between the windows and decided that her uneasiness was not all imagination. For three days at least she had felt odd and her expression was unfamiliar. She would have to raise that fifty dollars somehow, she supposed. . . . No, she did not find herself a pleasant sight. . . . I must do something about this, I can't let Adam see me like this, she told herself. . . . (122–23)

With Adam always on her mind and informing her sense of herself, she finds her own reflection "unfamiliar." As we read on, we discover that her uneasiness actually signals the early symptoms of the influenza epidemic sweeping the city; before literal sickness takes over, she finds her well-being affected first by Adam's infiltration of her psyche, and second by her desperation to accumulate enough money to purchase a war bond. Figuratively, her material worth and her impression of herself as a sexual object collide, and it becomes impossible to tell just which situation is distressing her more; improving one situation thus necessarily entails remedying the other. Ultimately, the combined struggle is too great: she can neither raise the money nor keep the man. Adam dies from influenza while Miranda eventually recovers but struggles to find the desire to return to life.

In the end Miranda has nothing: a "corpse" of herself in the mirror, the ghost of Adam "more alive than she was," and her own voice saying "I love you" to him, "the last intolerable cheat of her heart" (164–65). After "Old Mortality," she was supposed to know better; but the persistent death of the southern belle's desires (old mortality, indeed) haunts her, and it is plausible that she will repeat these acts of "bitter desire" and emotional deprivation. The closing revelation of the narrator in "Theft," that she will "end by leaving [herself] nothing" is echoed by

Miranda's hopeful resolution in "Pale Horse, Pale Rider": "Nothing. Nothing is mine, I have only nothing but it is enough, it is beautiful and it is all mine" (114). The "nothing" of this existence becomes, in the end, ironically reversed as she re-enters the world of the living: "Now there would be time for everything" (165).

How can the despair, the ashes, the nothingness, and the rushing misery of the attempts of all these women at self-realization possibly come suddenly to symbolize "everything"? There is in all of these works something profoundly moving in the failed attempts to have freedom and self-fulfillment at all costs and the determination to "own" anything at all—even a beautiful "nothing." Miranda learns on behalf of all Porter's women that, as DeMouy suggests, "being free means being alone"; perhaps this option amounts to Faulkner's famously agonized choice, "between grief and nothing, I will take grief" (6). In the "free," capitalist world that succeeded slavery, the same chains of economic inequity relegate slaves and women both to a different but equally binding calculi of identity and worth. The South's variously circumscribed women seek to establish autonomy on the fringes of a new capitalist order imbued with the same exclusionary principles, declaring, "It's my life. What shall I make of it?" But in these daring moments of self-possession, the challenge to "make" something, least of all the self, in a world of overdetermined and contaminated modes of production proves ultimately defeating. The optimistic "everything" that should greet emancipated blacks and females in the twentieth century needs somehow to be purged of its old formulas and constructions for self-appraisal and worth, yet that freshness seems nowhere on the horizon of a capitalist future. Like Faulkner's Addie Bundren, these characters thus look wistfully on the blank spaces and the nothingness of self that herald their entrance into an economy that defines, delimits, and "crushes" them, making a "nothing" that is "all mine" paradoxically and tragically the most beautiful thing of all.

Chapter Four

Contemporary Crises of Value: White Trash, Black Paralysis, and Elite Amnesia in Dorothy Allison, Alice Walker, and Walker Percy

"Something's missing in me! Something's missing!"
ALICE WALKER, *MERIDIAN*

Fractional, contingent, and impoverished spiritually, the modern southerners of the previous chapters would have found the contemporary South a dazzling scene of plenitude and possibility. Or would they? "By the mid-1960s," Pete Daniel recounts, "both the rural and urban South had changed in ways that frustrated, astounded, and often upset southerners" (*Lost Revolutions* 2). So much had changed that by midcentury "southern distinctiveness appeared to be doomed. In quick sequence the region encountered the bulldozer revolution, the urban breakthrough, the civil rights movement, and the disruption of the Solid South" (Tindall 3). Following the economic crises and Depression of the 1920s and 1930s, the New Deal, and World War II, the South gathered strength, industry, diversification, relative prosperity, and the courage to confront its longstanding internal conflicts and arrested development. The 1970s saw the South gradually absorbed into a developing Sun Belt of rapid and prosperous industrialization, making the South "more prosperous than in over a century," its economic rehabilitation "matched, or almost matched, by improved education and other government services, narrowing the statistical lag of the South in almost every index of human achievement" (Conkin 177).[1] Paul Conkin was writing in 1988 in order to show how "the acclaimed success of the modern sunbelt South mocks both the critique and the goals of Southern Agrarians," a prize won when the South realized it had no other options but to stay the industrial course (177). The results have been dramatic. By 1980, much of the recognizably rural, folk South and its rigidly organized communities had been altered by urban expansion, migration and immigration, and an increased focus on individual opportunity and progress. Today, national franchises dot an increasingly modernized landscape, and cities like Atlanta could easily be mistaken for northern, cosmopolitan metropolises.

There is, of course, a dark underside to capitalist growth and advancement. Despite marked material gains, a profound "sense of loss" still marks the rise of the contemporary South for more than just belated Agrarians (178). Indeed, the shock of such vast economic and social change "exacted a heavy toll in human suffering" felt both materially and psychologically (Bartley xi). Elite members of the New South became, in many ways, more self-interested than ever; as Numan Bartley notes, a new "autonomous individualism that elevated achievement, self-fulfillment, and material gain sustained a regional commitment to economic growth and development" (*New South* xii). Put this way, U.S. capitalist principles seem to have infiltrated and reorganized the South in such a way as to insure its lasting dedication to the national ideals of economic progress and expansion through the agency of individuals rather than communities or classes. But if the earlier chapters have demonstrated anything, it has been the perverse development of southern individualism under American capitalist priorities in the early decades of modernity and regional change. Attempts at forging autonomy within such a system are figured again and again as moments of calculating narcissism, self-searching projects associated fundamentally with the fetish of material increase, human quantification, and accumulation, often at the expense of a perceived inferior other (chapter 1), or, for those "others" themselves (chapters 2 and 3), the sacrifice and effacement of the historically and persistently marginalized self. Under the vexed terms so far understood to signify economic "progress," the psyches conditioned to measure and quantify themselves within a seemingly alien, exploitative, and divisive system only intensify in the bloom of the contemporary Sun Belt South.

Indeed, the tantalizing possibility of "having it all" belies the reality that the marketplace's "all" is a collection of fetishes for the self that promise substance but deliver emptiness and waste. In his 1975 work *The Mirror of Production*, French social theorist Jean Baudrillard states that "at the level of all political economy there is something of what Lacan describes in the mirror stage: through this scheme of production, this *mirror* of production, the human species comes to consciousness" (19). Fundamentally dependent upon location within this corrupt order, the searching self disappears into a virtual prism of fetish objects in the marketplace. Significantly, Baudrillard's assessment came at about the same cultural moment that Walker Percy and Alice Walker were writing their most revealing texts about the southern self's spiraling immateriality—*The Last Gentleman* (1966) and *Meridian* (1976). By 1994, just two years after Allison published *Bastard Out of Carolina*, Baudrillard suggests that the "rational" poles by which we measure and construct our material identities have become utter, vacant quantities, expressions of their fabrication by the mechanisms of capital culture: "abstraction is no longer that of the map, the double, the mirror, or the concept. . . . It is the generation by models of a real without origin or reality: a hyperreal" (*Simulacra* 1). Baudrillard's insights cohere with the postcolonial idea that a subjugated people, inured to a practice of identifying and fulfilling themselves by means of the dominant culture's methods and values, soon becomes emptied of "real" reference and becomes a mere container for social value and orientation prescribed from an inimical without. Arjun Appadurai adapts Baudrillard's concept to describe the global migrations and exchanges of contemporary postcolonial societies as "a global culture of the hyperreal" (29). The contemporary texts I address in this chapter illustrate the ne plus ultra of the quantifying colonial pathology for subsequent generations plagued by the "hyperreal" vacancy of the present, which incites masochistic returns to the terms and figures of historical codification and presencing.

While most contemporary writers are far from memorializing the passage of the Old South, they nonetheless embody the lasting priorities of its conflicted, inimical economy of human worth and value. An increase in the possibilities for material fulfillment fails to bring real gratification to the individuals foreclosed from such goods on the basis of their class or racial immurement; and even when accessible, the world of market relations proves tawdry and counterfeit, offering only mirrors of empty satisfaction. These vacant searchers thus appeal to old methods, looking for reflections that secure wholeness and value by opposition, a credit balanced by an authorizing debit, or an authoritative master to give the self meaning and value. Unable to count on the region's shifting, ascendant, increasingly hybrid Others, the postmodern southern self recomputes a measurable, valuable identity. Often and paradoxically, though, this entails succumbing to a reality of emptiness and worthlessness, a masochistic retreat into a quantifiable nothingness that renders the self abject, lonely, debased—but recognizable and measurable in a postcolonial world unable to shake its mathematical moorings. In short, the simple triumph of owning "nothing" heralded by the women in chapter 3 becomes in fact the only available retreat for contemporary southerners.

As the previous chapters have demonstrated, the self-seeking and credit-hungry position is occupied, with differing degrees of comfort and success, by both dispossessed white elite and their victimized subjects; whites, blacks, and women are alike dependent on precise balances of value making. In the recuperating South of the twentieth century, all too are grasping in isolation for the means of material success and personal gratification. Many contemporary southern writers seem troubled not so much by the threat of miscegenation or loss of purity embodied in these new hybrid identities; rather, they all seem increasingly aware that they simply do not know how to *be* without recourse to the equations of identity and value that have long contributed to the southern sense of self. Often without even knowing why, these dislocated and spiritually impoverished figures find themselves reacting to the guttering of regional and personal identity by grasping for the mathematics of self-presencing.[2] Inevitably, one person's rise requires another's debasement. What they often end up accepting, paradoxically, is the emptiness and estrangement associated with their perceived denigration, palatable simply because it is measurable and real. This chapter purposefully brings together a representative from each of three radically divergent subject positions—the elite white male from the Deep South (Walker Percy), the "white trash" South Carolinian lesbian (Dorothy Allison), and the cross-cultural African American woman (Alice Walker)—in an effort to show how pervasively, unsparingly, and increasingly the rhetoric of value, hierarchy, and debasement continues to saturate contemporary southern culture.

The triumph of American individualism and entrepreneurship in the contemporary South did not thoroughly dispel this region's attachment to class, race, and community-based thinking. Likewise, the apparent success of desegregation legislation and the improvement of civil rights for southern blacks did not yield an immediate abandonment of long-held attitudes toward race. Local southern governments were resistant and at times openly hostile to federal interventions, such as 1954's *Brown v. Board of Education* decision, to dismantle the region's stubborn attachment to racial apartheid (Bartley, *Rise* 187). While the expansive body of scholarly work on the civil rights movement rarely fails to comment on local white governments' resistance to these changes, only a handful of scholars have produced close, sustained studies of white segregationists' and supremacists' violent opposition to the dismantling of legislation that preserved the racial boundaries of their world.[3] Likewise, while women throughout the nation have enjoyed substantial gains in civil rights and social equality since the time when Newman, Loos, and Porter were writing, their successors have had to contend with the religious Right and organizations like STOP ERA, which resisted the "forced equality" of federal policies in the arenas of gender as well as race (E. Turner 364). In keeping with the tangle of racial and sexual codes that had always defined the Old South, the same southerners who opposed desegregation tended also to resist women's liberation. While there are a growing number of excellent studies on feminist activism, including the South's contributions, Elizabeth

Hayes Turner points out that there remains a significant dearth of attention to women in several areas and moments of southern history, particularly during the civil rights movement and in the rise of southern Republicanism that followed (365). Critical evasions like these seem compatible with a general American tendency to focus on progress and to value any and all signs of growth (particularly economic) as unequivocally positive. Surely the abandonment of racial apartheid and stifling gender inequities deserves to be celebrated; but what happens when we ignore the casualties along the way, the fault lines of personal devastation left behind by moments of earth-shattering change? Further, what happens when progress itself deepens the chasms of inequity that already exist in a society? Indeed, as individuals from different classes, races, and genders, the writers in this chapter all awake to a bleak awareness that their lives and identities remain fatefully intertwined.

For example, whiteness as a concept and race developed in America as a fiction to support the segregation and debasement of a darker other; as W. E. B. DuBois once noted, "the discovery of a personal whiteness among the world's peoples is a very modern thing—a nineteenth and twentieth century matter indeed" (qtd. in Hale 3). In *Making Whiteness* Grace Elizabeth Hale uses this observation to launch her own investigation of how the American South under Jim Crow served "to give whiteness a color" and to intensify our modern American "biracial genius" wherein we deny the ambient fact of racial mixing (3). Even in its postslavery reconfigurations, southern identity remains a recognizably, essentially black or white phenomenon. Yet the writers discussed in this chapter all seem acutely aware that the biracial paradigm anchoring them to coordinates of status and value have increasingly less reality but continued force in a contemporary South marked by a grudging awareness and repression of its hybridity, immigration, and mobility. Chapter 5 examines the voices emerging from these disruptive, occluded, non-black-or-white elements of the contemporary South; but at the end of this chapter, it is important to turn briefly to the uneasy and revealing ways in which these "other" traces have infiltrated the biracial bodies of this chapter's authors and protagonists. Specifically, in an attempt to move beyond the binary fictions of identity that constrain them, these figures revert to perhaps the deepest and most submerged traces of otherness in southern culture: those of removed Native American Indians.

While these resurrections seem partly to be attempts to revive the remnants of a radically demolished and kindred race upon whose bodies and lands the biracial plantation South could flourish, in the end these possessions by Indian ghosts serve uncanny nativist or elegiac purposes. Scholars have been slow to acknowledge the survival of the Southeast's Indians in its communities and texts. One explanation for this may be as simple as it is troubling: contemporary southeastern

Indians were largely assumed to be either exiled or extinct after the Jacksonian removal period of the 1830s. Southerners do often mourn this shameful past, but their apologies tend to have back-looking and backhanded benefits. In *I'll Take My Stand* the Agrarians ally themselves *with* Native Americans as groups similarly victimized by America's material aggressions.[4] Such gestures indicate how powerfully the modern South—itself struggling to survive the North's economic, political, and cultural dominance—had already distanced itself from complicity in Native American displacement, actions initiated primarily in the occluded economic interests of the very plantation system the Agrarians venerate. While such narratives form the backdrop of *all* American settlement, Mick and Ben Gidley suggest that "the eradication of Indian tribes in the Southeast was probably more wholesale than in any other culture area" (167). Subsequently, the idea of a southeastern Indian has become virtually obsolete, emblematic of an "entire vanished way of life" (J. Peterson 4). Memorializing Indian extinction provides a sympathetic narrative as well as an instructive parable: both black and white southerners tend to cling to Native influences as ways to deepen their own victimization and to arouse noble resistance. Ultimately, though, these useful indigenous analogues remain submerged, surfacing only briefly to serve the narcissism of "real" contemporary southerners in persistently black-and-white equations; in this elegant algebra, the Indian is placeholder and zero—the empty figure of balance upon which these equations continue to rest and thrive. White and black writers' vexed ways of both remembering and forgetting Indians uncover the uncanny nativism still haunting the New South's struggle to come to terms with its postcolonial perforations—and not yet its repressed colonial beginnings. And importantly, they leave us with yet another vision of three diverse contemporary southerners desperate but unable to see beyond their own dizzying, debasing, depleted narcissism—and reaching fruitlessly for fetishes, both material and spiritual, that might sustain them.[5]

Empty Mirrors and Blank Pages: Illusions of the New New South

Walker Percy rarely shares more than a familial classification with his neoaristocratic uncle Will. The younger Percy and his critics have been emphatic in their assertions that, despite his deep admiration for the man who virtually raised him, Walker did not inherit the planter-lawyer's antiquated racial views, which we saw in chapter 1. In his introduction to Will Percy's *Lanterns*, Walker Percy pays touching tribute to his late uncle but is careful to note that "his views on race relations . . . diverge from my own" (xi). Percy goes on to clarify that "even when I did not follow him, it was usually in *relation* to him, whether with him or against him, that I defined myself and my own direction" (xi); he closes by asserting, "I owe him a debt which cannot be paid" (xviii). Developing his own views in contradistinction to his uncle's outdated ideals, Walker Percy nonetheless feels he "owes" much of his success to the generous man who took in and raised him and his brother after their mother's apparent suicide; it is clear that Walker Percy's "debt" to his uncle is both intensely personal and also possibly corrupted.[6] My objective here is not to prove that the younger Percy in fact turned out to be racist like his uncle, as it was clear that he held progressive views. Those who knew or studied the younger Percy have been generous in lauding his apparent "commitment to civil rights," which he made material not just in his writing and personal relationships but in actual social reform measures, such as his participation in the development of a credit union in Covington, Louisiana, that helped several African American families purchase homes (Harwell 8–9). Throughout his lifetime Percy flatly refused to be considered a "southern writer," possibly to distance himself from being read too closely with the stereotypical southern views he often represents, and because writing as a neoaristocratic white man made him an easy target for accusations of racism. But as Makowsky conjectures, Percy, like Quentin, "plainly protested too much," as it is clear that his work is indeed "preoccupied with Southern themes" from start to finish. Still, critics have for the most part tended to respect Percy's self-assessment. Brannon Costello points out that "Percy's concerns with race have gone relatively unexamined" by critics anxious to fold his racial consciousness into larger concerns about his religious or philosophical orientations (3); several years after this critical call to arms and Costello's own postcolonial reading of Percy's engagement with whiteness, there remains a dearth of attention to Percy's conflicted attitudes as a southerner.[7]

Alice Walker and Dorothy Allison also attempt to situate themselves in contradistinction to distasteful histories and attitudes; unlike Percy, these women have been personally diminished within southern society. In the end, though, they emerge on a similar plane: a hopeful position of enlightened empowerment that distances them from past forms of oppression yet evinces a troubling attachment to the terms and structures of an archaic order. If Percy represents the new generation of reformed aristocratic paternalism, rich in ethical enlightenment, Walker and Allison herald the working-class, racially and economically oppressed triumph over generations of insolvency. In her largely autobiographical *In Search of Our Mothers' Gardens*, Walker contends optimistically that "there is a great deal of positive material I can draw from my 'underprivileged' background"; she emphasizes that "the richness of the black writer's experience in the South can be remarkable," and later reiterates the setting's "enormous richness and beauty to draw from" (20, 18, 21). The emphatic return to the language of decadence as compensation for her "underprivileged" reality indicates her desire to manufacture a kind of prosperity from the terms of her subjection. Allison echoes this aspiration when she declares in an interview, "The rich and the upper class have been riding on our asses for hundreds of years, and I don't want to see us made over into a story that glorifies them. Our stories are glory enough."[8] Allison and Walker both evoke a kind of redemption that would reverse the usual terms of an economy wherein poor and unpaid workers historically sustained only the wallets and psychologies of the privileged. Assertions of "richness" by Walker or "glory" by Allison reclaim the suppressed and stolen value of their existence, economic and otherwise.

But all three of these writers are ultimately locked into the narcissistic exclusion of their own radically different and personally imperative struggles. In a world long dependent on defining the self by opposition, and especially on compensating the denigrated self by trumping the oppressor, the contaminated terms of this victimization reappear uncannily even in seemingly emancipatory gestures—particularly when the region's "progress" has made such oppositions and markers increasingly difficult to find and fix. In the three main texts under examination here—Walker Percy's *The Last Gentleman*, Alice Walker's *Meridian*, and Dorothy Allison's *Bastard Out of Carolina*—the New South emerges as a space of changed commercial relationships and consequences; thus, it is not just human identification and categorization that have altered, but the terms with and by which the self identifies. As Percy's protagonist Will Barrett observes, the South now "had everything the North had and more. They had a history, they had a place redolent with memories, they had good conversation, they believed in God and defended the Constitution, and they were getting rich in the bargain" (186). Fantastically and yet alarmingly, the South has managed to bargain its way into having both success and tradition: material progress need not come at the expense of "history" and "memories," Will observes. Indeed, market capitalism is adorned naturally here by the "redolence" of slavery. The "bargain" struck allows the region both to preserve a traditional, religious, southern way of life and to profit. A belief in the South's ethical probity and entitlement underwrites this condition, as the region's apparent surplus value—"everything the North had *and more*"—redeems its long-suffering dependency to northern whims and influences.

These signs of financial and cultural survival do not automatically yield psychological health for the region's inhabitants; rather, the sheen of progress and accumulation seems to repress the hidden costs of its new order. "Nothing was wrong," the narrator puzzles over Will's dislocation, "but he got worse anyway. The happiness of the South drove him wild with despair" (187). The dazzling riches of the world Barrett enters turn out to be false things, some of them odd throwbacks to lost "heroic ages" (189), like the anachronistic and gaudy period houses that the Vaughts and their peers build on the country club golf course. Like the past these nostalgic structures imitate, the South's new constructions harbor the artifice of their presentation, the appearance of gilded surfaces cloaking the aberrance within (just as Barrett discovers in his growing intimacy with the Vaught family itself). In the manufactured purple bricks of the Vaught castle there is no convincing relation to the "real" or "natural," no way to reproduce the old world that it desires to simulate—as Baudrillard says, the "modern sign dreams of its predecessor" but can only find value in equivalents and simulacra (*Symbolic Exchange* 493). In Percy's world these containers of hyperreality confirm the continued applicability of plantation priorities and the need to ground them more tangibly in the diffuse world of global market capitalism. Sensing cultural evacuation, Will Barrett's quest for self-fulfillment finds him magnetically drawn to the counterfeit structures and values of this landscape.[9]

The Vaughts' riches are, moreover, still not exactly the status quo in the Sun Belt South. Dorothy Allison's Boatwrights are vivid examples of those southerners still enduring the meanest kind of poverty, toiling at blue-collar jobs and struggling to maintain honest lives despite their privation. Denied access to the goods and opportunities of the elite, they invest extravagantly in family and romantic relationships: "'Love is just about the best thing we've got that don't cost money,'" one of the Boatwright aunts declares (62). But while it doesn't cost money, it does ultimately impoverish these characters—particularly the women. Doubly disadvantaged by class and gender, working-class white women are released from the neoaristocratic expectations of the southern belle; but their searches for value are more gritty and imminent, actual economic struggles. For the characters represented in such conditions, poverty functions as a mechanism to deepen their unspent desires for independence and love, the best expression of self-worth they may ever encounter. Underscoring this is the perpetuation of class and racial divisions even in an increasingly mobile and mixed South: to be white "trash" in midcentury Greenville, South Carolina is, still, to be "nigger."

As we see in Alice Walker's novel, the denigrating fact of race—whether inherited by blood or transferred by class association—still disenfranchises one from the increased opportunities of the progressive South. The book's opening scene of a mummified white woman, on display for the poor whites and blacks who work at the town "guano plant," extorts dimes from the population for a (literally) empty husk of entertainment and titillation. The image is a specter of what privileged white society offers its working-class members—cheap, empty substitutes—but it is also an uncanny reflection of their own desiccated lives: "the oddest thing about her dried-up body," the fake woman's "widower" laments, "was that its exposure to salt had caused it to darken" (20). The salt is environmental but could also suggest perspiration as a result of labor—a category that "races" her simply because she exists in these segregated, exploitative surroundings. Working at a guano plant signifies the lowest possible form of labor, the most extravagant waste of life. There is a warning here to those who believe they deserve more: the pseudo-negro, white mummy-woman apparently met her death by becoming too greedy: she "had been given 'everything she *thought* she wanted.' . . . But she, 'corrupted by the honeyed tongues of evildoers that dwell in high places far away,' had gone outside the home to seek her 'pleasuring'" (20). The mummified woman thus serves as a sort of warning to blacks, and particularly women, seeking mobility and gratification apart from their already defined and constricted domestic roles, tantalized by evildoers in "high places far away"—that is, the capitalists of the North—to "thinking" they want things or experiences they have no business desiring. As one town resident spits, "'the smell of guano don't wash off'" (20). Meridian Hill appears in this scene performing the book's first dramatic episode of protest, but her own paralysis (she needs to be literally carried away from the display) and emaciation immediately trouble the message of resistance: how far will this frail husk of a woman be able to travel from that image of desiccated exploitation?

The terms of advancement in the New South conceal the system of inequity and disadvantage still operating at its heart, and a rhetoric of ambitious self-valuing haunts these figures' most personal quests for betterment. In their most intimate self-expressions, the tantalizing prospect of wealth becomes apparent to all of these characters. The priorities and contradictions of the economy have become transparent even to the neo-elite Walker Percy, who struggles to reestablish social coordinates with and for the dislocated and ascending Others who no longer offer him automatic superiority and value.[10] Adrift without easy hierarchies, the world itself seems tawdry, cheap, and simulated. Perversely, mathematical markers become recognizable, internalized symbols of meaning and value reminiscent of a more stable way.

Fittingly, all of these texts' protagonists first come to consciousness in bombed or otherwise destroyed spaces that both sharply contradict the slick new surfaces of Woolworth's commerce (in Allison) and purple country club castles (in Percy) and mirror the internal, dismantled state of the New South and these characters' individual and communal psyches. Percy's Will Barrett is an educated young man whom the narrator at times calls "the engineer"; despite his apparent intelligence, his mind functions on a purely mathematical track and slips periodically into recurrent amnesia and fugue states. While living out of the South, in New York, he often becomes disoriented and somnambulates back to Civil War battlefields in the South.[11] "Much of the time," the narrator explains, "he was like a man who has just crawled out of a bombed building" (11). While Derek Walcott famously designated amnesia the true New World condition in "The Muse of History," it is clear that part of Will's forgetting pointedly laments the loss of a deep historical sensibility rather than the repression of a painful past. The bombed-out condition of Will's amnesia correlates precisely with his assessment of northern cities or otherwise "homeless" places, suggesting that these sites of exile are absent of the structures of history and rootedness cultivated so laboriously in the South (185, 186). When he does return home, though, he is devastated to find its homeless quality intensified, "different" in all sorts of auspicious, progressive ways: "It was happy, victorious, Christian, rich, patriotic, and Republican. The happiness and serenity of the South disconcerted him" (185). He returns there, somewhat glibly, "to seek my fortune and restore the good name of my family, perhaps even recover Hampton plantation from the canebrakes and live out my days as a just man and little father to the faithful Negroes working in the fields" (151). Michael Kobre suggests that Will's language here is "too broad to be read without irony, the claim itself exaggerated to the point of caricature" (2). Certainly, Percy's irony borders even on outright sarcasm here, but the social commentary underlying Will's campy nostalgia seems distressingly serious: the canebrakes and fields he yearns for a bit too much are irretrievably lost, signaling a similar fate for his family's "good name." That is, he laments later that "backcountry everything was being torn down and built anew"; the space where he hoped to go "and discover his identity" reflects to him only a wasteland of demolished history and a gleaming new vista of unfamiliar progress (79). The newness, not the hackneyed paternalism of old, is what plummets him into the blankness of hyperreality and anonymity. He finds himself even more dislocated now in a "bombed out," "torn down" South mirroring his own ravaged consciousness, stripped of clear coordinates or directions. He is left "like a book with blank pages," the ledger apparently cleared (13).

Meridian, the young black female activist in Alice Walker's novel, ironically finds her calling in just such a bombed-out place. Like Barrett, she has already spent much of her young life "wandering," "listless," simply withdrawn from a world she cannot seem to engage with (65, 72). She becomes promiscuous in a vacant, detached way, finds herself (with neither passion nor volition) pregnant and married as a teenager. On the same day that her young husband grows frustrated with her cold isolation and suddenly leaves her, she walks by a house that serves as headquarters for a black voter registration movement. The house is located in a black neighborhood, but is filled with both whites and African American activists involved in the increasingly interracial civil rights efforts; while watching the news the next morning, she sees the same house—or, rather, the place where the house used to be, as overnight it has been "demolished by firebombs" (73). In this moment, the narrator tells us, "Meridian became aware of the past and present of the larger world" (73). Like Barrett's vision, this bombing clearly evokes the hidden catastrophe of racial as well as economic progress; the forces invested in preserving the South's status quo attempt violently to halt black progress and interracial cooperation. The event leaves Meridian similarly disoriented, in "a time of complete rest, like a faint. Her senses were stopped, while her body rested; only in her head did she feel something, and it was a sensation of lightness—a lightness like the inside of a drum. The air inside her head was pure of thought" (74)—much like Will Barrett's "blank pages." When, a month later, she volunteers to join the movement at its new headquarters, she "had no real idea" what she was getting into, only knew that "something about the bombing had attracted her, the obliteration of the house, the knowledge that had foreseen the destruction" (80). It is not the movement itself but the potential for danger and erasure that "attracts" her, the knowledge of historical progression and inevitability that promises all steps forward will ultimately lead these sleepwalkers backward into the horrors of the past. What draws her is not the bombing per se but the bitter taste of "knowledge." Eerily like Will Barrett's stunned inability to assimilate the new, ravaged features of his world, Meridian "knowingly" retreats to a past of opposition and violence that will ineluctably effect her own "obliteration." This is the world into which she plunges boldly and in hopes of imprinting a history on her vacant and meaningless existence.

Similarly, Dorothy Allison's young white protagonist Bone Boatwright is unable to tear her eyes away from the knowledge and visage of disaster associated with her own "white-nigger" aspirations. This happens first in the literal explosion of her own obverse image: her albino friend Shannon Pearl. The daughter of middle-class but morally upstanding southerners, Shannon is by no means rich, but she nonetheless wields her family's better circumstances and morality over Bone, with irrepressible "pride of family position," offering food and treats with a mixture of condescension and "contempt" (162). But the Pearls also bring Bone along to the exciting gospel shows they manage; on one such trip Bone admires the voices of some colored singers in a nearby church, suggesting aloud that Mr. Pearl should sign them up as a gospel act. Shannon indignantly replies, "'My daddy don't handle niggers.'" Tellingly, Bone becomes incensed: "The way Shannon said 'nigger' tore at me, the tone pitched exactly like the echoing sound of Aunt Madeline sneering 'trash' when she thought I wasn't close enough to hear." In rage at being implicitly "raced," Bone screams, "You bitch, you white-assed bitch," to which Shannon responds "You . . . you trash. You nothing but trash" (171). In contradistinction to this exaggeratedly white albino girl, Bone feels the racial stigma of her "white trash" status in a way that is not at all new in southern experience. When Shannon semiaccidentally lights herself on fire during a backyard barbecue, it would seem a liberating moment freeing Bone from the conscriptions of white rivalry. But Bone watches the catastrophe as if in a mirror: "she was a little monster," she thinks directly before the incident, "but she was my friend, and the kind of monster I could understand" (200). Then, in an instant, a flame licks the lighter-fluid can in Shannon's hand and ignites "with a boom. The can exploded, and fire ballooned out in a great rolling ball. . . . Her glasses went opaque, her eyes vanished. . . . Her dress was gone. I saw the smoke turn black and oily. I saw Shannon Pearl disappear from this world" (201). In the "black and oily" absence of Shannon—and, significantly, the "glasses" and "eyes" that see and judge her—Bone is "haunted" (204). "Everything in my life was . . . uncertain," she says. "I took to watching myself in mirrors to see what other people saw, to puzzle out just what showed them who I really was" (205). With the departure of Shannon "from this world," Bone's entire world explodes as well. She is left unsure just what, if anything, her own image projects and entails.

Will, Meridian, and Bone all find themselves lost within devastated worlds in which the reflective markers of their identities have been violently eclipsed. But these incidents all assert that such explosive, bombed-out scenes are not erasures so much as absent presences: all still move in these ravaged places, in fact actively seek them out, trying to find and reassemble the parts of themselves in the only ways they know. It seems no coincidence that the term "ground zero" is used often to designate the area just below the explosion of a bomb, the equivalent of which confronts these characters in crucial moments of identity formation;[12] the ruins, like the "black and oily" mess of Shannon's burned dress, reflect the new configurations of their postmodern identities. The "blank" conditions that these episodes initially trigger are quickly followed by mirror-gazing searches like Bone's, retreats into the old, combustible methods for assembling selfhood. In some ways, they even seem masochistically to seek out despair: Will in his "upside down condition" of feeling good in bad environments, Meridian in her intrepid volunteering for "obliteration" and solitude, and Bone in her sexual fantasies about fires or being publicly beaten. These images and experiences all provide perverse narcissistic surfaces in which they recognize themselves as shattered beings; there, they begin actually to derive paradoxical satisfaction from the recognition of debasement, with hopes for value and elevation compromised or obsolete. Like those of Newman's characters, Bone's frequent masturbations (and the fantasies of fire or abuse they entail) are indications of self-pleasuring, narcissistic activities that have no productive or satisfactory outcome: "I orgasmed on my hand to the dream of fire" (63), Bone tells us; "fire" signifies sexual arousal but also the specific mode of the death of her "whiter" half, her "monstrous" twin, Shannon. Later fantasies involve being publicly beaten by her stepfather. In such perversely narcissistic dreams, the conditioned certainty of being debased proves more desirable than the terrifying alternative of being erased, nothing, "zero."

For Will this utter absence of identity is what compels him constantly to seek out a historical or affiliated self in a way that neither Meridian nor Bone can dream of doing. Yet Will is hardly more successful in his quest, as he discovers that the new world he has been born into fails to insure his automatic privilege. Descended from "an honorable and violent family," he lives at the inauspicious moment of postmodernity and the troubling sense of the ending of things: as "the last of the line, he did not know what to think" (9, 10). This disaffection seems also responsible for his fits of amnesia; Kobre suggests that Will, unable to "comfortably accept or reject his legacy . . . simply forgets it" (1). Indeed, while he finds the promise of bloodlines utterly useless in the contemporary South, he locates no alternatives and simply becomes a history-less, identity-deprived blank: "The summer before, he had fallen into a fugue state and wandered around northern Virginia for three weeks, where he sat sunk in thought on old battlegrounds, hardly aware of his own name" (12). The belated son of southern aristocratic honor loses contact with his family "name" but subconsciously ends up wandering Civil War battlefields in suppressed attempts to find it there. Will's father, unable to relinquish the role his "honorable" position no longer entails, had grown exhausted by "the strain of living out an ordinary day in a perfect dance of honor" and killed himself (10). When Lewis Lawson declares *The Last Gentleman* "the most confessional" of all of Walker Percy's novels, he refers in part to the loss of Percy's father to suicide and his mother to a suspicious (perhaps also suicidal) car accident (xii). Thus, Will Barrett's energetic attempts to combat his own blankness seem particularly and sadly urgent.[13] The nullification of this Oedipal force, with the absurd mythic dances of heroism and honor that would have been Will's birthright, should absolve the belated son from the burdens of lineage and tradition; instead, it haunts and dooms him to a life of equivalent emptiness, barely more alive than his dead father.[14] As the narrator explains, "most of this young man's life was a gap" (11–12).

Significantly, it is a mathematical version of a pleasant and ordered existence that emerges to remedy Barrett's state of vacancy and despair. He has all the trappings of success—a privileged upbringing, good looks and health, a pleasant temper—yet, "though he was as engaging as could be, something was missing" (9). People expect much but hear "nothing at all" of him after he graduates high school; "He was the sort who goes away" (9). Significantly, "the high tide" of his life and potential, now faded, belong to an optimistic time when he felt life seemed "as elegant as algebra" (9).[15] No scrappy algebraic aspirations to ascend either; that's "for poor folks," as Thomas Wolfe's Eugene (*Look Homeward, Angel*) learns. While Percy's social status should automatically garner him easy, pleasant solutions, his lineage no longer has the desired effect. And so he finds that he must engineer his own fate: "I need some mathematics," he declares (163). Scientifically minded, he scores well on "problem-solving and goal-seeking" tests, but he cannot seem to translate these problems into solutions for his life; he "couldn't think what to do between tests" (9). The old, precise, mathematical rules for finding worth and assembling selfhood very literally fail to work for him.

Alice Walker's Meridian also faces a profound spiritual vacancy that seems indicative of a larger sense of historical divestment. As a black revolutionary, Meridian is asked to commit crimes and murders that she is unwilling to perform. Like Richard Wright, she resists compromising her moral fabric simply to satisfy the perverse desires of whites or the desperate revenge of her community. But the lack of volition this implies haunts her: she perceives herself devoid of the qualities she is expected to embody as an educated, African American woman engaged in racial activism. Asked to pledge that, if necessary, she will kill for the revolution, she is paralyzed: "Through her mind was running a small voice that screamed: 'Something's missing in me. Something's *missing*! . . . Something the old folks with their hymns and proverbs forgot to put in! What is it? What? *What?*'" (27). This seems at first like a historical disconnect, an inability to live up to the hopes and expectations of her ancestors who tried to prepare the next generations for the strength and solidarity they would need. But what she is "missing," like Will, is a precise connection to the present moment: "what none of them seemed to understand was that she felt herself to be, not holding on to something from the past, but *held* by something in the past, by the memory of old black men in the South . . . by the sight of young girls singing in a country choir . . . the purity that lifted their songs like a flight of doves" (28). Will's attraction to battlefields is paralleled here by Meridian's retreat into a South of rural, simple peace and faith. Seeking the stillness of roots and religion, Meridian finds instead that she is expected to start a war on those ancient battlefields. Unable to orient herself in this new world of rage and violence, Meridian too "had left the North and come back South . . . to support herself; remaining close to the people—to see them, to be with them, to understand them and herself, the people who now fed her" (31). In a suggestive metaphor of subsistence, the habitual metaphor for self-fulfillment and possession, Meridian is presumably "fed," enriched and "supported" in her proximity to the region and people who are supposed to reflect back to her an understanding of herself. But her alienation from the present and from this altruistic community remains constant: rather than growing fuller, she becomes increasingly thin and frail, "bony . . . wasted," suffering from bouts of paralysis and collapse, often carried home across men's shoulders "exactly as they would carry a coffin" (24). The retreat to the past and into the arms of her community offers her the opposite of sustenance; history and region simply render her the empty cipher she would have been under slavery. Postmodern selfhood, fixated on the past but unable to revise or avenge it, renders her "zero" all over again.

For Dorothy Allison's young Bone, this impoverishment is still more complete. Where Meridian refuses violence in favor of a quietly devouring peace, Bone is steadily emptied and hollowed by her rage. Her very name, Bone, conjures a sense of skeletal subsistence much like Meridian's. Bone's hunger is true and physical, though, as the family often eats saltines and ketchup in the absence of real meals; but when she does eat, it is clear that food is not necessarily what she needs in order to feel nourished: the meal "stuffed me but didn't satisfy . . . I could not get full" (78). This mark of her poverty is internalized psychologically, becoming "a hunger in the back of the throat, not the belly, an echoing emptiness" (98). At a new school, under the contemptuous eyes of the teacher, this "anger lifted . . . and became rage." Her fury at being so easily identified and looked down upon turns self-consuming: "It was hunger I felt then, raw and terrible, a shaking deep down inside me, as if my rage had used up everything I had ever eaten" (98). Presumably to fill herself back up with a sense of pride and self-creation, she gives the teacher a fake name "as if I'd never been called anything else" (67). But the harnessing and remaking of identity here, which she wants to seem natural and permanent, only increases her dislocation: trying to figure out why she lied, she can only say, "I didn't know. I really didn't know" (71). The hunger of her rage necessarily means more and more "emptiness," an utter inability to fill that vacancy with anything but the things society feeds her. Her birth certificate confirms this anonymity in the end—the stigma of being marked a "bastard" finally, after her mother's repeated attempts, has been removed. The designation bothers Bone's mother so much because it authorizes their family's condition as "trash." Like Will's "blank pages," though, Bone's certification of identity now has no designation at all—the paper with such power to denigrate her and her family is rendered "blank, unmarked, unstamped" (309). In some ways, this erasure proves more difficult to overcome than the previous disparaging label; a certified government document has demoted her from "illegitimate" to effectively "invisible."

In the protagonists' inescapable returns to the terms and codes of their subjection, these texts suggest paradoxically and at times masochistically that any mark of affiliation or debasement is preferable to being "blank." Unable to find nourishment in past forms of history or spiritual returns "home" to the South, they become identity-less, amnesiac, and physically wasted—more dead than alive. What all of them search for, however self-defeatingly, is affiliation of any sort to fulfill their need for acknowledgment. These narcissistic quests have become much more humble than their predecessors', geared not toward enrichment and inflation so much as simple affiliation, recognition, and, if a necessary part of the bargain, a rehumanizing pain. For Will, it doesn't seem to matter what new social group he joins, so long as they give him a code and script for reshaping himself; he decides to try out a number of radically different groups and clubs: "so thoroughly in fact did he identify with his group companions of the moment, so adept did he become at role-taking, as the social scientists call it, that he all but disappeared into the group" (19–20). His chameleonic ability to adopt alternately all the qualities of an Ohioan, or of an expatriate southerner, or of a Princeton student makes his lack of a coherent identity even more dramatic, so that he "hardly knew who he was from one day to the next" (20). His desire for community and homogeneity is palpable, but his failures to fit in somewhere consistently reveal the absurdity of such a longing by heterogeneous, postmodern southerners, and suggest incisively that such arbitrary forms of affiliation are an absurd fiction. Yet Will's reliance on such models becomes so pronounced that he cannot function without a template of behavior. What emerges finally is not a safe return to group identity or community, but rather an outrageous surplus of groups and identities into any and all of which he can fluidly integrate himself. In the coziest of situations, sitting around a fire with "the Ohioans," he realizes in horror not intimacy and fullness but rather that "people seemed to come to the point of flying apart" (21). He doesn't seem to mean that they will fly apart from one another, but from their own centers—exploding into a million incoherent pieces.

Such groupings prompt violent ruptures because they force diversity to cohere and disappear so easily, though Will seems to know the reminders of difference lurk disruptively and discomposingly beneath the surface. The description calls to mind DuBois's famous sketch of the "double consciousness" suffered by the black American who "ever feels his twoness,—an American, a Negro; two warring souls, two thoughts, two unreconciled strivings; two warring ideals in one dark body, whose dogged strength alone keeps it from being torn asunder" (364–65). What tears apart the black community in *Meridian* is precisely the plight of its double aims, desperate to rise up against white America yet drawing its violent and homogenizing tools and energies from the white world itself. As Karen Stein has noted, "the Civil Rights movement often reflected the oppressiveness of patriarchal capitalism. Activists merely turned political rhetoric to their own ends while continuing to repress spontaneous individuality" (130). This reminder makes Meridian's reluctance to promise that she will kill for the cause a subversive gesture, but as Lynn Pifer notes, her inability to speak in this moment or to speak out against injustices generally mitigates her triumph and deepens her sense of guilt and shame (77–78).

However, Meridian never seems able to resist at all; rather, she allows herself to be folded into the group's needs though they insidiously replicate white, patriarchal, and capitalist models. But like Will, she is simply eager to integrate herself within the activist community whose values she tries desperately to make fit with her own. She joins in their marches and protests, which often devolve into police brutality and imprisonment, and begins to embody painfully their communal sorrow and suffering. She is "always in a state of constant tears, so that she could do whatever she was doing—canvassing, talking at rallies, tying her sneakers, laughing—while tears rolled slowly and ceaselessly down her cheeks. . . . Or the way she would sometimes be sure she'd heard a shot and feel the impact of the bullet against her back; then she stood absolutely still, waiting to feel herself fall" (84–85). A blank, she takes on the experience and the sentiment of the entire movement; but inhabiting others' suffering does not bring her any closer to her own person. When she describes a fellow activist's "battle fatigue" as a kind of "blankness," it deepens the sense that communal affiliation and struggle have made her still more anonymous and empty. Thadious Davis has read Meridian's union with the black collective as an optimistic sign of cooperation and progress, rendering her "born anew into a pluralistic cultural self, a 'we' that is and must be selfless and without ordinary prerequisites for personal identity" (49). Desperate times call for desperate measures, surely, but given the historical sacrifices of "personal identity" in America's black community, this additional abdication seems too much to expect or to bear. And for Meridian Hill in particular, it proves ultimately catastrophic. Similar to Will's fugue states, her body also tends to absent itself periodically; she suffers frequent bouts of paralysis, finding herself "absolutely still" and unable to move forward, and in the midst of great exertion she "falls down" (26). The peculiar physical effects that afflict her may appear cryptic, but seem in fact to mirror the lack of mobility and progress embodied not just in her own person but in the entire group on whose behalf she works doggedly. She becomes a virtual mirror for a community literally unable to move forward.

Allison's Bone also fantasizes about being recognized and loved by a group whose appreciation will give her a sense of belonging, intimacy, and value. The disaster of this dream is made emphatic in the specific type of community she imagines: in disturbing sexual fantasies, she imagines being publicly beaten by her stepfather while ringed by a group "who watched me admired me and hated him . . . Those who watched me, loved me. It was as if I was being beaten for them. I was wonderful in their eyes"; the fantasies are "self-centered and they made me have shuddering orgasms" (112, 113).[16] Her near-martyrdom parallels Meridian's, but her suffering before and on behalf of an imagined group of fellow sufferers brings not pain so much as tremendous narcissistic satisfaction. Much like Katharine Faraday's bruise-pressing compulsion, Bone's masochism promises to awaken her to an appreciation of her own person; in these moments she struggles to possess a hurt that is not momentary but historical, yoking her to a community that in a large sense has been collectively beaten down. When she is repeatedly abused sexually and physically by her stepfather Daddy Glen, she feels pain that she can barely recognize as her own: "I would go look in the mirror, expecting to see blood in my mouth, but there was nothing" (118). The reflection fails to validate her extreme suffering, in fact gives "nothing" in the way of evidence that she exists. It is no surprise when she turns this fruitless violence on herself: "When I got hungry," she remembers, "my hands would not stay still. I would pick at the edges of scabs, scratch at chigger bites and old scars, and tug at loose strands of my black hair" (71). In these moments, her rage and hunger force her to self-mutilation, a further diminishing of her body; yet at the same time, the compulsion to touch her hair and scars signifies a reverent act of acknowledging her own body by touching it, much as Claudia takes pride in her scabs in Toni Morrison's *The Bluest Eye*. This compulsion attracts her sexually to other sharp and hazardous objects as well, like a trawling hook that her aunt warns the children will "pull you up in chunks . . . pull you up in pieces" if they stumble onto it while playing alongside the river (186); fearlessly, Bone searches out the dangerous object and sleeps with it nestled erotically between her legs. Such moments of affiliation, and the narcissistic gratification they offer, are in the end promises only of deeper blankness, mutilation, and loss.

Solutions: Narcissistic, Mathematical, Re-Oedipalizing Narratives

As they do for Will Barrett, mathematical modes surface at crucial moments to reorient these characters, suggesting that their plights are not simply about the loss of community or tradition, but of the adherence of economic certitudes and inequities.

Will's former elitism is not something he openly misses or embraces, but the terms of his dislocation betray an enduring need for the social codes associated with class and identity in the traditional South. As we have seen briefly, the language of proper orientation and understanding—those very things the disoriented, amnesiac young man is so often missing—comes in economic and mathematical vocabulary. The wealthy Mr. Vaught offers Will a position with the family, handing him some large bills with the query, "'Do we understand each other now?'" and Will answers, "'Yes sir'" (155). In a moment of disorientation, the rhetoric proves true; money and figures are things he can understand and use to orient himself: lost after an amnesiac episode, he "counted his money several times" and looks at an annotated Esso map, the two methods together helping him piece together his recent whereabouts. Very literally, money orients his motions and his place in this dislocating world. Necessarily, such orientation is sporadic and short-lived, as Will lapses regularly into the amnesiac states that remind him of the precarious codes of the new world he moves in, launched back into uncertainty just as quickly as money and figures jerk him out of it.

The utter chaos of the new economic landscape, and the simultaneous murkiness of racial relationships, becomes clear when Will meets a "pseudo-negro"—a photojournalist named Forney Aiken, working "undercover" as a black man—and ends up in a fistfight for his honor. In a white neighborhood, the community perceives Will to be a real estate agent trying to sell a house to a black man, the pseudo-Negro. The tension of a rather serious moment involving racial discrimination devolves into comic violence, as Will stands up in protection of his friend and receives a blow to the nose by an enraged housewife. Suddenly, true identities are revealed: Aiken discloses that he is not a black man at all but an undercover journalist, revealing an identity-confirming "white patch" left strategically on his arm, and Will relaxes in the "cordiality of misunderstandings cleared away, of debits to be balanced" (147). The language again unmistakably evokes the sense that money secures "understanding"—but only for white folks like Will and, it turns out, Aiken. An accounting metaphor offers the intelligible language that puts people in their places and alleviates fear that racial others may stray out of such positions; and, importantly, it resurrects whites from the "debit" column where they simply do not belong and restores them to a rightful place of balance. It cannot be overlooked that the violence Will endures is partly comic—not in its implications but in its narration, which is quixotic and colorful. In his analysis of Percy's dialogic style, Kobre suggests that "whenever a tension arises between the values that are ingrained in Will's consciousness and the actual circumstances of life in the United States in the early '60s, the language that he uses to express himself becomes distorted, parodic" (2). Caught in the crosscurrents of racial reorientation, Will loses himself in parodic play: he engages in a postmodern duel of sorts, upholds the honor of his black (white) comrade, and emerges victorious. Combined with the language of human accounting, however, his parody indicates not confusion or tension so much as a reactionary desire for certainty and balance. Will's own understanding thrives in such orderly, economic moments; apparently, he is none too glad to be safely among white folks in an inviolate neighborhood, no longer under attack.

Bone and Meridian win no such duels. Meridian finds her value, it seems, by refusing to commit violence but allowing herself to endure it. When the revolutionaries ask her if she is willing to kill for the cause, she cannot say yes; and this is the moment that compels her to return South to live among the people, to "support" herself by letting them feed and nourish her. As we have already seen, this choice yields a deeply compromised kind of support and value; accordingly, her lover Truman finds her with "less and less furniture, fewer and fewer pieces of clothing, less of a social position—wherever it was—where she lived" (31–32). The sizing up of her possessions here has a direct correlation to her "social position," and even more to her body's size, which grows increasingly frail with lack of nourishment and spiritual sustenance. Before this, isolated at school, she had chastised herself as "belonging to an unworthy minority" and made suicidal demands on herself—"Why don't you die? Why not kill yourself? Jump into the traffic!"—in a voice perpetually "mocking [her] about her lack of value" (91). She realizes in a kind of horror that the voice is her own, not someone else's; the "mocking" of another is something she turns on herself, serving as her own imagined other to denigrate and nearly exterminate her. She "valued her body less" all the time and even "welcomed" the confrontations with police that leave her, like Bone's aching hunger, full of "yearning, of heartsick longing" (97).

The desire suffusing the world these women inhabit becomes deeply inner, inseparable from the violence they so readily engage in. Bone, as we have seen, harbors a perverse longing for the beatings that in her imagination can aggrandize her. Thus, we pay close attention when she turns her anger outward; such externalizations are uncanny reflections of her own desire, her own masochisms, her attempts to injure herself in some reified form. Significantly, Bone's target is the commercial world that forecloses her white "trash" self. Like Wright and Porter before her, Allison figures this attack as thievery. Upon trying to steal candy from the local Woolworth's, Bone is banned from the store; this simply makes real the bars of class that keep her out of such an arena and the privation that forces her to steal in the first place. The moment fills her with her trademark rage as "hunger . . . raw and terrible. . . . After that, whenever I passed the Woolworth's windows, it would come back—that dizzy desperate hunger edged with hatred and an aching lust to hurt somebody back" (98). The store reflects much more than a desire for products she cannot have, specifically the sweetness of the candy she tried to filch; her lustful, aching hunger and rage are aimed at an entire showcase of unsatisfying objects clogging the consumer marketplace. She develops a fierce desire to use the objects of her own debasement and self-mutilation to exact revenge: she seizes upon the trawling hook she takes to bed with her and uses it in an elaborate plan to break into the Woolworth's. She crashes through the roof after the hook plunges in first, landing on and shattering the glass merchandise cases. "I was suddenly soaking wet and shaking," she says, hurt but exhilarated, "wet" and "shaking" in simultaneous eroticism and rage. From the broken notions case, "half a dozen pocket mirrors lay in an overlapping line. A shine reflected up into my eyes. I smiled and started forward" (223). The mirrors give her a momentary "shine" of selfhood and inspire satisfaction and mobility; but within minutes she realizes how very cheap that reflection is. Everything in the store seems like "junk": "What was there here that I could use? . . . All this stuff seemed tawdry and useless. I bit my lip and went back to get my hook" (225). There is no fulfillment here, no dizzy accumulation of goods and with it self-worth; clinging to her hook and biting her lip, she recalls to us her violent, masturbatory fantasies and the narcissistic aftermath of her beatings, looking in the mirror for blood in her mouth and seeing "nothing."

But such catastrophic failures to find value apart from the old equations or languages do not deter the protagonists from their quests. All three internalize certain calculations of value so deeply that they become inseparable from their most personal quests for love and companionship. Indeed, as we saw in chapter 3, the prospect of romantic or sexual love—and particularly the affirmation offered by a desiring other—promises to rectify the self's sense of impartial or damaged identity. Unable to find such relief in group or community situations, the search narrows—and, in the process, becomes a narcissistic quest for a single, reflective Other. Not only does Will express a desire to recover Hampton plantation and become a paternalistic "little father" to his Negro field hands, he also wants to fall in love "with a certain someone. Or I shall marry me a wife and live me a life in the lovely green environs of Atlanta or Memphis or Birmingham" (151). The addition of a companion to his aristocratic restoration completes the formula, a neat equation made emphatic by the rhyme of "wife" and "life." Though he identifies a "certain someone," the immediate addition of "or" indicates that the certainty may shift: there will, indeed, be one person, but it seems to matter little who she is. The current object of his affection is Kitty Vaught, daughter of a well-to-do New Southern family; he adheres to her and waits for her love to complete him. In a bout of amnesia, "he looked at her hard, groping for himself in her eyes" (67). Over time, he learns to match her moves: "'Why are you different?'" she asks him, and he answers, "'I'm different because you're different'" (165). Indeed, in his first (botched) attempt to make love to her, she becomes embarrassed and nervous and demands "'talk to me . . . [about] anything that comes into your head,'" to which he replies, "'all right . . . I was thinking about the summer of 1864'" (111). As he describes an ancestor's experiences in the Civil War, it becomes clear that the drive to merge with her merely brings him back to his desired image and location of himself, to the comfort of a bolstering history and lineage, and to the emptiness and dislocation of his current state—like waking up on a Civil War battlefield.

Kitty is important to Will mainly as a historical anchor and a narcissistic template. She embodies order of a precise and mathematical kind: pondering her age, he thinks, "twenty-one. The very number seemed hers, a lovely fine come-of-age adult number faintly perfumed by her, like the street where she lived" (74). He is first attracted to the number itself, a figure that is "perfumed by her," a construction that relegates Kitty grammatically to the position of passive subject. For a man in search of possession, precision, and orientation, Kitty's association with the number, her adultness, and the sweetness of individuality and location (right down to a specific street) offer him a pattern upon which to steady himself; and as a proper wife, she will be a known, passive quantity. However, Kitty is not special but, in a sense, mass-produced, a generic; he tries to find himself in any female he can, surprised when his body takes over instinctually and he "fell upon" a young girl he has just met, attracted by her "rapid, cataloguing voice"—another version of Kitty's "number." Falling "ever fainter with hunger . . . as much from weakness as desire," he even attempts to kiss her (135). Later, he apologizes: "'I've been, ahem, in something of a value crisis'" (136). The weakness, hunger, and desire of his state compel him irresistibly to seek order and "value" in random, mathematical others in a process as natural and inevitable as gravity. But the math of the union is somehow off: attempting to make love to Kitty a second time, he believes he knows "without calculating the exact angle at which he might lie over against her—about twenty degrees past the vertical" but "she miscalculated, misread him and moved slightly. . . . His heart sank" (167). He wants to court her "in the old style," but the coordinates of orientation, so fragile and precise, are hopelessly off; in the new order of things, others become shifting, incalculable, crashing bodies on a collision—rather than a complementary—course.

Meridian's quests for sexual companionship are not calculated so much as troublingly automatic. As a teenager she engages in sex "as often as her lover wanted it," though she seems never really to want it herself; there is no palpable erotics or narcissism of personal desire driving her actions. Yet her purpose is tangible: she waits patiently not for an orgasm, but for her hips to grow "broader" as she's heard they do after sex, waiting to increase her own image in some way, and so "she looked carefully in her mirror each morning before she caught the bus to school" (61). Indeed, while she never receives any physical or emotional satisfaction from sex, she does gain personal sanctuary and the illusion of increase: when she inevitably grows pregnant from one of her lovers and then marries him, she thinks that the relationship "did a number of things for her" and meditates on its "worth": mainly, it saves her the effort of responding to the parade of men she is "afraid" of but cannot resist, "freed of any consideration for all of the other males in the universe who might want anything of her. It was resting" (61–62). Thus, intimacy with Eddie is a means to gaining "a number of things," though it also signifies an abdication of desire, a "rest." If her interest in sex comes, as she professes, from a "curiosity about her body's power" (65), then what she learns is disconcerting: she has absolutely no power at all.

But the mirror moments, and Meridian's desire to see her hips grow broader in that reflection, prove most troubling. The inflation of her identity, the culmination of all things "gained" through sexual activity, is of course the presence of a baby that itself symbolizes the union of two opposites. Like Faulkner's Addie, Meridian knows that producing children will make her "more" as well. She looks hungrily for this increase and gets it; the act designed to reveal "her body's power" twice leaves Meridian bigger indeed, large with child. But this process merely fractures and duplicates her sense of her self rather than consolidating and amplifying it. As her mother had also complained, pregnancy "distracted her from who she was. As divided in her mind as her body was divided, between what part was herself and what part was not" (50). Rather than bringing the self home to itself, fulfilled and empowered, the danger of sexual exploitation is reified in its literal product: the baby that further estranges one from the clear borders of personhood. Thus, Meridian gives away her first child, effectively surrendering the ultimate narcissistic prize she has gained in giving her own body away through sex. Later, after joining the revolution and falling in love with Truman, the act of lovemaking only makes her "ashamed, as if she were less" (106), particularly when he begins dating white exchange students whose color produces a sense of inferiority in her. The term "exchange" here is no accident, as the white students are traded for Meridian, making her "less" in the transaction. Her diminishing value plummets further when she becomes pregnant for a second time and has a painful and invasive abortion by a corrupt white doctor. She keeps the procedure a secret from Truman; when he next sees her, he tries to undo the lessening of his rejection, to make her blackness an asset where before it was a lack: "'You're *beautiful*,' he whispered worshipfully. Then he said, urgently, '*Have* my beautiful black babies'" (116). But the directive comes too late, the abortion already completed; and both the babies and her beauty are cast by Truman as gifts only he (a True Man) can give her. So "she drew back her green book bag and began to hit him. She hit him three times before she even knew what was happening" (116). Her body, violated and bereft, takes over here in an explosion of violence she never imagined herself capable of.

In Allison's *Bastard Out of Carolina,* having a child still represents the woman's most promising path to fulfillment, but the cost of that gift undermines the woman more than it buoys her. What is more, the state of gestation in this novel encompasses much more than the growth of the child within the mother: the baby's ability to discompose and divide the woman characterizes not just maternal relations but sexual ones as well, wherein men are figured as "'just little boys climbing up on titty whenever they can'" (123). Daddy Glen, Bone's abusive stepfather, is a particularly disturbing example of this sublation; one of Bone's aunts observes that "'he's just a little boy himself, wanting more of your mama than you, wanting to be her baby more than her husband. And that an't so rare, I'll tell you'" (123). Indeed, Bone's own mother Annie thinks that Daddy Glen's violent impulses can be cured by "being patient, loving him, and making him feel strong and important" (233). The lesson for Bone is disastrous, as the collective female effort to secure his ego results in her own crippling subjection: while Glen grows "strong and important," Bone feels "the world was too big for me . . . I knew, I knew I was the most disgusting person on earth" (135–36). For Annie, though, the domestic sacrifice is, paradoxically, the only way to feel important herself; although Glen occasionally beats her, too, she rationalizes that "being pregnant was proof that some man thought you were pretty sometime, and the more babies she got, the more she knew she was worth something" (231). The proof of "worth" gained through such perverse intimacy begets the desire to be entered and exploited still more. Yet Annie and Glen never have a child of their own; perversely, her own husband becomes her substitute child, making her feel "pretty" and "worth something" in her suppression. Meanwhile, Bone suffers deeply from her own sexual exploitation by this man; in a moment of tortured narcissism, she stares into the bathroom mirror, "knowing I wasn't pretty and hating it" (231).

Annie's encompassing motherliness also pits Bone and Daddy Glen against each other as, perversely, siblings. In a choice between the two—the raped, abused Bone and her aberrant violator, Glen—Annie chooses the latter. At the novel's final, climactic moment, Bone has just been discovered by her mother in the act of being raped and brutally beaten by Glen; Annie saves her, carries her from the house, and places her in the car where she waits to be taken to the emergency room. Outside the car, Glen, himself injured in the scuffle, begs pathetically for Annie's forgiveness, which—stunningly—she finally gives him: "She was holding him, his head pressed to her belly" (291). In a figurative gesture of pressing him to her womb, it is clear which baby she chooses in this terrible moment. The decision mystifies the family and horrifies readers of the book, but the inevitability of her choice is encoded in the text from the beginning: between a man's love and a child's, the woman's self-worth forces her to choose the man's.

The reluctant, abusive mothers in both Walker's and Allison's novels emphasize above all else the acute crisis of individual worth plaguing the contemporary southerner. In a parable of the dangers of America's new individualism and narcissism, these mothers are able to forsake their children in ruthless attempts to secure their own elusive self-worth. Walker Percy reminds us that such sacrifices are not new or foreign to the southern content; they are the birthright of all the New South's children. When Will Barrett's father commits suicide in *The Last Gentleman*, he makes literal his inability to live in the New South. Will realizes that his father "was wrong and that he was looking in the wrong place. No, not he but the times. The times were wrong and he looked in the wrong place. It was the worst of times, a time of fake beauty and fake victory. *Wait*. He had missed it!" (332). Perhaps this history is what has been "missing" in Will, forming the gaps in his consciousness and his memory: a lost time of beauty and victory usurped by the horrible newness that the elder Barrett could not endure. Yet what Will "missed" was "fake"; such counterfeiture has always been a part of both Will's and his father's world. It is not clear, then, which "he"—Will or his father—"had missed it" all; likely both did. In his poignant attempts to understand his father's suicide, Will's own partially dead consciousness is bound up: his narcissistic identification with an absent, out-of-phase father makes his own self absent as well, mixed with this figure of belated and doomed honor and futility. In the expanses of Will's amnesia are memories struggling to surface, but he can never tell if they are his own: "Either I have been here before, he thought, perhaps with my father . . . or else it was he with his father and he told me about it . . ."—and later, "Why, I know this place, he thought. Either I went to school here or my father did" (295). This confusion of self with a lost, dead, father insures that he will always be "missing" something primary to his ability to live and function in the world.

What is left for men like Will are stories, narratives, and scripts; but communication and true understanding are defunct, enclosing each individual in his own private shell of despair. Will notices a black man pass in front of his ancestral home, "a young man his own age," and reflects sadly on their common dispossession:

> They looked at each other. There was nothing to say. Their fathers would have had much to say: "In the end, Sam, it comes down to a question of character." "Yes suh, Lawyer Barrett, you right about that. . . ." But the sons had nothing to say. The engineer looked at the other as the half second wore on. You may be in a fix and I know that but what you don't know and won't believe and must find out for yourself is that I am in a fix too and you got to get where I am before you even know what I'm talking about and I know that and that's why there is nothing to say now. (332–33)

Will seems to realize here the loss of a precise, hierarchical and illuminating relationship: their now-absent fathers would have been balanced in a dialogue of dependency and affirmation, in which a pedagogical quip to black Sam (aka Sambo) would have been followed by Sam's polite endorsement of Lawyer Barrett's acuity. The sons do not indulge in such false and enabling banter; instead, they share silence and a common "fix" in their marked alienation and isolation. Yet they admit to not knowing what the other one experiences at all; there is not the remotest understanding or opening for conversation. The dissolving of racial segregation does not bridge any chasms but simply preserves a silent gulf of private despair. It is purposefully ambiguous who speaks to whom in the closing assertion that "you got to get where I am before you even know what I'm talking about." But which man will volunteer to cross the divide and inhabit the other's position? What is the incentive and the payoff?

Meridian's version of this plight rests in her vexed relationship with her mother, whose inaccessibility seems the cause of her emptiness, her sense that "something is missing" and that this absence makes itself known on the outlines of her frail body. Just as Will cannot seem to distinguish between his father's time and his own—and doesn't particularly want to—Meridian punishes herself for not living up to her own mother's example of maternal devotion and sacrifice. Shortly after she meditates on her shortcomings as a revolutionary, unwilling to kill and certain that this means "something is missing" in her, her musings turn familial: she is missing something that "the old folks," her ancestors, forgot to "put in." Her body as a vessel is not equipped to be the continuation of the past into the future, is not "worthy" of being a mother like the quintessential southern matriarchs of the past. Those women could not, under slavery, "own" their children, and therefore Meridian cannot quite forgive herself for robbing herself of her own babies: "what had Meridian Hill done with *her* precious child?" she thinks. "She had given him away. She thought of her mother as being worthy of this maternal history, and of herself as belonging to an unworthy minority, for which there was no precedent and of which she was, as far as she knew, the only member" (91). Her mother was not a slave, but her attempts at independence and empowerment are hard-won and "pitiful" (123): having worked tirelessly to become a teacher, suffering pure "sacrifice" (77), she realizes that she wants "more richness" in her life, an "increase in felicity," which she believes she'll find in love and marriage. But in the increase of her body in pregnancy, she grew paradoxically "divided" in body and mind, "distracted from who she was" (51). Even as a child, Meridian feels an inexplicable guilt over this, and "when she tried to express these feelings to her mother, her mother would only ask: 'Have you stolen anything?'" (49). Upon this, "a stillness fell over Meridian and for seconds she could not move. The question literally stopped her in her tracks" (51). Meridian knows that her birth "stole" her mother's self, and she knows that women of that generation were unable to have independence and selfhood apart from domesticity and childbirth; the "stillness" she experiences here is akin to the paralysis that dogs her forward movement throughout *Meridian*. In her desire to reconcile with her mother—to achieve the "narrowing of perspective, for mother and for child" that the old "Black Motherhood" entailed—she "valued her body less, attended to it less, because she hated its obstruction" (96–97). She lets herself be beaten, grows frail, has a baby forcefully ripped from her womb without anesthesia— the doctor "tore into her body" much the way Meridian's father "broke into her [mother's] body" in the sex act that created Meridian (114, 50). She spends her life getting rid of all her possessions (31), trying to get smaller, to figuratively reconcile and roll back into her mother's body, to be worthy to identify in unity with the woman who "*was* a giant" (122). That unity depends on Meridian "growing frailer every day" and valuing her body less. In a dramatic reversal, Meridian wants to give all of herself back to her mother to repay the debt, to discredit the self in order to honor these ancestors and, in the process, find historical orientation and peace. In Meridian's metaphorical return to her mother, Richard Gray sees her accomplish not a personal but at least a "symbolic rapprochement" with her mother, wherein she is able to "make peace with her mother's past . . . and is able to move on" ("Maybe Nothing" 12). Traveling backward, it seems—becoming small enough to return to the womb and out of existence entirely, like a slave owning nothing, least of all the self or its babies—paradoxically offers the only foothold into the future.

For Bone, too, the value and identity she seeks is literally in embodying her mother, a substitute to be molested and beaten by Daddy Glen. After hearing him making love to her mother in the room next door, Bone realizes that "something had come apart" and "there was no way I could be careful enough, no way to keep Daddy Glen from exploding" (108). It is as if the sexual union between the two adults posits Bone in her mother's position as sexual partner—but then brings her to the point of "coming apart" herself, much as the false cohesion surrounding Percy's Will Barrett portends that people will soon "fly apart." Bone's solution is to invite and rationalize Daddy Glen's violations: "he did love me. He told me so over and over again, holding my body tight to his. . . . 'You're just like your mama,' he'd say, and press his stubbly cheek to mine" (109). She is stilled like Meridian, paralyzed in these moments, unable "to explain why I stood there and let him touch me," but her need to be fixed and rendered coherent in some way is clear: "when Daddy Glen held me that way, it was the only time his hands were gentle, and when he let me go, I would rock on uncertain feet" (109). Her desire to be pretty and loved like her mother warps into a narcissistic drive to be both lover and child to her mother. Daddy Glen, again, is the template for both of their identities, the brutal presence without which neither of them would have meaning. In some sense she seems to realize that Glen as a man is the powerful force defining and delimiting her mother's existence. As a boy cousin tells her early on, "'you got a man-type part of you. Rock-hard and nasty,'" and throughout the remainder of the book Bone often wishes she were a boy, mainly so she can fight back and "run faster," away from the world and those who have the power to overtake and belittle her (54, 109). She works a rubber ball in her hands, trying to strengthen her grasp so that "one day my hands would be as strong as Daddy Glen's. . . . I was working that ball so that I could grow to be more like him" (109). In the chilling final moments of the book, after

Glen has viciously raped Bone and is begging for forgiveness, he cries, "'Kill me, Annie. Go on. I can't live without you. I won't. Kill me! Kill me!' Mama jerked away from him, and the door slammed shut. 'Oh no,' she whimpered. Her face became the mirror of his" (290). Just before this, Bone had "stared at his face like it was a road map, a route to be memorized, a way to get back to who I really was" (288). At the end of the novel, Bone is left with neither a "mirror" nor a "map," and presumably no sense of who she "really was." She also is left without her parents, hungering after the nurse in the hospital "like an infant watching the nipple," and catching a glance of herself in the mirror, "a stranger with eyes sunk in shadowy caves above sharp cheekbones and a mouth so tight the lips had disappeared" (294). Sunk, hollowed, disappeared, and crying for her mother—that is the identity-less, silent, isolated figure abandoned at the end of the book, her freedom from her parent-torturers a deeply compromised emancipation.

Past and present, the doomed methods these protagonists employ for achieving and erasing selfhood reveal the dazzling counterfeiture of progress and mastery, of nostalgia and yearning; empty promises of fulfillment leave them lusting after tradition, parents, substitutes, and fakes, and unequipped with less oppositional modes of orientation and value, hungry and alone. In the end, Meridian's failure to find romantic or filial love leaves her emphatically alone, emaciated, and claiming "'but that is my value'" (220). We find Will at the end of *The Last Gentleman* pursuing the sexually depraved Doctor Sutter, refusing his offers of money with the assurance "I have plenty," but racing after the doctor's "elegant" car that promises psychological guidance and sustenance. Always in search of a life "as elegant as algebra," Will's pursuit of value here is profoundly personal; he has "plenty" of money but no cultural capital like that which Sutter's elegant car embodies. But it is a "spuriously elegant and unsound" auto, "like a Negro's car, a fake Ford"; in a novel filled with the falseness of race, of position, of solutions and theories, such an ending is both ominous and appropriate. The "fake" element here is both an icon of American culture and a Negro's possession; that, finally, is what Will decides it is his lot to embrace, his algebra of orientation in the New South. He races forward to catch it, "elegant" and elusive and fake, like Allison's Bone breaking into the tawdry environs of the Woolworth's, seeking the richness of the New Southern world, yet finding himself, too, adrift, alone, debased, and mirror haunted.

Look Inside! Nativist Navel-Gazing and Inner Indians

As we have seen, Bone never recovers from the loss of her mirror, Shannon, whose emphatically white presence had rendered Bone "nigger," and without whom she is simply "nothing." In her pathetic and moving attempts to conjure a tangible sense of self, Bone finds some comfort in the family rumor of a Cherokee ancestor. Some of the relatives mock the association, declaring that "every third family in Greenville County swears it's part of Cherokee Nation" (27). Indeed, Joel Martin and others have documented the widespread phenomenon of southerners claiming to have a Cherokee princess in their family tree; yet such genealogical stakes seem to legitimate white southern nativism rather than cross-cultural affiliation.[17] But Bone's motivation for embracing her roots derives from a more personal, pathetic version of nativist navel gazing. She counters her uncle's mockery of her professed indigenousness with silence, "keeping my Cherokee eyes level and my face blank" (27). The blankness of her face in this moment reminds us not just of stereotypical warrior stoicism but also of the emptiness she is working so hard to defeat throughout the narrative; the vacant gaze is, moreover, the only accurate way to mimic a culture she doesn't actually know.

With no real access to or understanding of Native culture, Bone nonetheless harbors common, romantic notions of Cherokee courage and resilience. She pictures herself as a heroic warrior, fighting battles and climbing trees with agility, "night's own daughter, my great-grandfather's warrior child" (207). We notice that the great-great-grandfather she cites at the start of the book has edged one generation closer, helping to corroborate the "full head of black hair" she interprets as genealogical evidence (207). The suppressed rage that torments this abused and debased child is also attributed to Indian blood: "the only thing different about me," she muses, "was my anger, that raw boiling rage in my stomach. Cherokee maybe, wild Indian anger maybe . . . bottomless and horrible" (207). The power of Indian blood ("maybe") offers her a way up and out rather than down and in, devoured by her own hungry fury and seeing herself at the "bottom" of a pit of nonbeing. Significantly, this wild Indian wrath becomes a mechanism for fighting the man who beats her fragile identity out of her; this hope comes, narcissistically, in the mirror:

> I pushed my hair up high on my head and searched my pupils for the red highlights that sparked in the depths, dark shiny red like rubies or fresh bright blood. Dangerous, I told myself. I could be dangerous, oh yes, I could be dangerous. Let Daddy Glen yell at Mama again, let him hurt her, let him hurt me, just let him. He'd better be careful. He's got no idea what I might not do. . . . All I had to do was grow a little, grow into myself. (208)

The futility of her aspirations comes through in her grammar: the potential of what she "could be" and "could be," and all the things she "might not do," are cloaked in the false bravery of negations and litotes. Ultimately, Bone cannot overpower her abuser or "grow" as she hopes to; the mirror soon forces her to admit "I was no Cherokee. I was no warrior. I was nobody special" (209). Her momentary defiance squelched, she sees herself clearly again as a "nobody," a blank.

But *Bastard Out of Carolina* suggests further that Cherokee rage fails to save Bone because it simply races her again; that is, she discovers that being Indian is not much different from being black: "one or two of the cousins had kinky hair and took some teasing for it, enough that everyone was a little tender about it . . . people didn't even want to talk about our Cherokee side. Michael Yarboro swore to me that Cherokees were niggers anyway, said Indians didn't take care who they married like white folks did" (54). While the Yarboros are stereotypical poor white supremacists protecting their tenuous social superiority by claiming to "[drown] girls and newborns" and labeling "nigger" anyone they perceive as "'born on the wrong side of the porch'" (54), for those conditioned to defend their compromised status in the rural South, being Cherokee amounts to being black or female, a simple label of otherness and weakness to denigrate in the service of elevating marginal others. Allison tacitly deepens this sense by diluting the indigenous traits with the more socially disruptive African ones, complete with "kinky hair" to underscore the substitution. In her desperation, Bone turns back to Daddy Glen, the agent of her debasement, thinking: "Love would make me beautiful; a father's love would purify my heart, turn my bitter soul sweet, and lighten my Cherokee eyes" (209).[18] Tragically, cruelty and a perverse oedipal submissiveness seem the only available means to "purify" and "lighten" her; they exorcise the last bits of "nigger" taint, and along with it any Cherokee resistance and self-sustenance the white-trash southern girl knows. The social capital of whiteness foreclosed to lower-class southerners is made further inaccessible by the young girl's inability to resist the forces of physical and emotional abuse in her world. The presence of an Indian ally in this struggle paradoxically revivifies the biracial antagonisms in the South's lower classes, while the Native—like Bone herself—is pushed silently to the margin.

In his own search for self-definition within the wreckage of tradition, Walker Percy's Will Barrett also finds hope in the Indian archetype: "what a fine thing it will be to become a man and to know what to do—like an Apache youth who at the right time goes out into the plains alone, dreams dreams, sees visions, returns and knows he is a man. But no such time had come and he still didn't know how to live" (11). The reliability and certitude of the young, mythic Apache's visions and actions are posed against Will's "nervous condition" and the bouts of amnesia that leave him "haunted" and adrift (11). The Indian archetype serves, then, as an ironic model of certain orientation, a path toward effortlessly becoming "a man." Significantly, the Indian he imagines—an Apache—is not indigenous to the South but rather the West. The substitution allows Percy to circumvent

Contemporary Crises of Value   159 entirely the problem of the white southerner's indebtedness to Indian extermination in the old world of Will's ambivalent desires. However, another (western) Indian influence emerges to deepen the sense of repression and artifice in Will's increasingly traditional desires; Will arrives at Kitty's house to find that she has been drinking hikuli tea, swaddled in a quexquemetl and Navajo blankets. Because the herbs have made her candid and unguarded, the pair nearly makes love in the park. Before they leave the house, Kitty muses from her cocoon of indigenous comforts:

> "The Huichol believe that things change forms, that one thing can become another thing. An hour ago it sounded like nonsense."
>
> "Is that right?" He had heard it before, this mythic voice of hers. One of his aunts lived in Cuernavaca.
>
> "The hikuli plant *is* the deer. The deer *is* the corn. Look at that."
>
> "What?"
>
> "That color."
>
> He looked down at the blanket between them where forked Navajo lightning clove through an old brown sky, brown as old blood.
>
> "What about it?"
>
> "Do you see the depths opening into depths?"
>
> "No." (104–5)

The scene is revealing because the strong Indian tea is clearly what inspires Kitty's shifts in consciousness and also provokes her nearly to give Will her precious virginity. But she begins babbling what seems like nonsense, a "mythic voice" detached from reality as Will knows it, and he grows itchy and irritated by her garb, wishing she would get "out of these prickly homespuns and back into decent Alabama cotton," and that rather than drinking tea that leaves her mouth tasting of "burnt corn" that she would "chew Juicy Fruit like a proper Alabama girl" (104, 106). He eschews the notion that "one thing can become another thing" and there are "depths opening into depths." On one level, Percy parodies these notions—and Kitty's ventriloquism of them—to the point of absurdity; but on a more sober level, such parables might for the southern man trigger suggestions of reconstruction and displacement and historical depth, things Will must repress in order to survive as a "proper" neoaristocratic man. He is flatly unable, and presumably unwilling, to see the "old brown sky" and the "old blood" on the Navajo blanket. Again, it is not the Indian's New Age philosophies he rejects so much as Kitty's crusading on behalf of such flimsy spiritual newness and change. Kitty's intoxicated advances short-circuit when the strange tea makes her ill, and the botched lovemaking leaves her "hugging her decent skirted knees like a Georgia coed" again while Will, partly relieved, thinks aloud about "the summer of 1864" and his "kinsman [who] took part in the siege of Richmond and later of Petersburg . . . a rats' war, as bad as Stalingrad," but who still managed to attend balls and cotillions "even at the worst" (111). The visions of past horrors and old blood inspire not sorrow or resignation, but fables of resistance and propriety in the midst of war and upheaval. The Civil War is as far back as he will reach for lessons; the past anterior of Native precedence flirts but remains as inaccessible and irrelevant as Kitty's body.

Repeatedly, these contemporary narratives hint at hidden, correlative depths in the southern past that are finally unaccountable and unrecoverable; such traces pose potential solutions to these characters' predicaments, but only as narcissistic easements for their contemporary narratives of alienation, emptiness, and rage. We remember Meridian's frustration that "Something's missing in me! Something's *missing*! Something the old folks with their hymns and proverbs forgot to put in! What is it? What? What?" (27). Neither Meridian nor the narrator explicitly answers this persistent question, but the reference to "old folks" indicates again that a deep past shapes and influences African American lives at every turn. But which old folks, and which past? The ground everywhere beneath Meridian is possessed by memories of a plantation order that continues to contaminate the present and circumvent change—even her college rests on the site of a former plantation. On campus, a famous tree offering a ritual site of peace and meditation for the female African American students is suddenly chopped down; nearby, the house used as a headquarters for civil rights activists is destroyed by a bomb. The actual landscape of progress is consistently leveled, the ghostly specter of the past the only survivor. Meridian continues to hunger for the "missing" secrets and lessons of her own history; and she receives them ultimately in Native rather than African American guise.

When Meridian sees the black activists' house bombed on TV, she remembers suddenly "that the night before she had dreamed of Indians. She had thought she had forgotten about them" (73). The juxtaposition is revealing: a structure of black advancement is leveled like Indian priority and cultural memory, their presence "forgotten" even by the blacks who can in many ways sympathize with their dispossession. This intercultural affinity is epitomized in Meridian's father's farm, allotted to *his* grandfather after emancipation. But Mr. Hill seems haunted by the memory of its original inhabitants and becomes preoccupied with collecting Indian memorabilia in a fit of empathy and guilt that finally compels him to try to return the land to the Natives. He finds a displaced proxy—an Oklahoma Indian named Mr. Longknife—who comes to camp on the land for a summer but ultimately returns the deed to Meridian's father. Meridian understands poignantly that her father's "gifts came too late and were refused, and his pleasures were stolen away" (56). The gift of land cannot restore a sense of home to those driven from its terrain more than a century before. Mr. Hill's "pleasures"—the land itself—are literally "stolen away" when the federal government arrives and, without negotiation and for a "token payment," converts the Indian mounds and vegetable gardens into "a tourist attraction, a public park" that blacks, ironically, cannot visit under segregation laws (56). In a recursive colonization, Walker underscores just who continues to inherit the earth in the contemporary South. Mr. Longknife and Mr. Hill finally share the same dispossessed condition: the surname "Hill" itself suggests that his identity resides in the old Indian mounds and rolling farmland; the eviction is as corporeal as Meridian's steady and severe weight loss throughout the novel, her own "missing" materiality. Unlike Percy's or Allison's attempts, Walker seems legitimately interested in indicting Euramerican colonization and Indian removal on the same plane as African American disenfranchisement. For the Longknifes and the Hills alike, there is no effective way to overcome the pervasive sense of homelessness and "something missing" in contemporary American culture.

This alliance functions more forcefully and authentically in Alice Walker's work perhaps because of the historical associations and often interaction and intermixture of blacks and Indians in the white-dominated South. Walker raises this possibility in *Meridian* by suggesting that the Hill family has repressed Indian ancestry that neither Meridian nor the narrative explicitly acknowledges. But Meridian remembers a story about her father's grandmother, a woman of ambiguous heritage but a suggestively native name—"Feather Mae"—who lived on the land in question and apparently experienced moments of ecstasy on the Indian mound. Despite her affinity and sympathy for Indian experience, she referred to the Natives as "other folks"; and although she shocked the family by worshiping the sun rather than God, the rest of Meridian's family tree remained markedly black, Baptist, and pure by contrast. Meridian nonetheless feels drawn to Feather Mae's mysticism and herself experiences several moments of transcendent escape from her own materiality. This spiritual out-of-body experience seems the only physical way she can embrace a deeply repressed heritage—*not in her body*. Moreover, it provides another clue to her mysterious emaciation. In a region well-versed in manufacturing and erasing nativism, the ability to claim an occluded ancestry seems key to inhabiting both the earth and one's body fully and viably, neither of which happens in the novel. The failure is most poignant when we see how close Meridian comes to accessing that heritage: when she first sees Mr. Longknife, she suddenly feels "she could begin to recognize what her father was [a wanderer, a mourner] by looking at him" (54). The difference is that Mr. Longknife "wandered physically, with his body, not walking across maps with his fingers as her father did" (54). A flat, two-dimensional, biracial past haunts the inhabitants of the postremoval and postslavery South; the map's mathematical lines and borders colonize territory and identity, while separating and subsuming difference. Mr. Longknife—and along with him, the Indian "body" he represents—has long been evicted by this system; both imprisoned by the map and foreclosed from its spaces, like the Hills' displacement from their ancestral lands, southern blacks remain essential to the biracial order and persistently abjected within it.

That Alice Walker herself is part Cherokee comes as a surprise to those who consider her first as an African American writer and less routinely as a southern one.[19] But Walker seems to use the physically wasted Meridian to exemplify what exactly her Indian ancestry amounts to: an irrecoverable absence, a something perpetually "missing," and a frail body with constantly depreciating "value." The possibility of fullness and transcendence are "too late"; for Meridian, they have been stolen away like the "forgotten" Indians, the family land, the man she loves, and her own body. Walker's novel acknowledges that the erasure of Indians from the South rends an irreparable gap in its social fabric, not just correlative to but often vitally entangled with the existence of African American kin. But she also offers a potentially disruptive use of the Indian's zero quantity to challenge black essentialism and exceptionalism. When Meridian seizes her compromised "value" in the end, it is as an erased figure, her reduced person a resolutely present absence. While she works to memorialize its absence, Walker resigns herself ultimately to the notion that the Indian past is simply and regrettably gone; she concludes her autobiographical *The Way Forward Is with a Broken Heart* with the lament, "how empty of Indians Mississippi was . . . Without their presence the landscape of America seems lonely, speechless . . . In any case, it has been destroyed now beyond knowing" (37). Meridian is a walking testimony to this wasteland, a reminder to the contemporary South of the human sacrifices upon which its biracial economy flourishes perversely.

These Indian analogues extend, even further than I already have in the cross-cultural reach of this chapter's writers, the chronicle of dispossession wrought by American imperialism, slavery, and capitalism. As Meridian's mother puts it bitterly, "the answer to everything is . . . we live in America and we're not rich" (56). Despite this totalizing social impoverishment, in most of these stories the gulf between the marginalized, and indeed between individual citizens and communities, remains intact. Black "value," as Meridian claims in the end, is solitary. The Indian is always already "forgotten" and lost, anterior to this biracial struggle. Something is "missing," indeed, in the contemporary southern narrative; and it is unclear exactly who, if anyone, can recover it.

Chapter Five

Re-membering the Missing: Native Americans, Immigrants, and Atlanta's Murdered Children in Louis Owens, Marilou Awiakta, Lan Cao, James Baldwin, Toni Cade Bambara, and Tayari Jones

> *Give me back my language and build a house*
> *Inside it.*
> *A house of madness.*
> *A house for the dead who are not dead.*
> *And the spiral of the sky above it.*
> *And the sun*
> *and the moon*
> *And the stars to guide us called promise.*
> JOY HARJO, "WE MUST CALL A MEETING"

In Edward L. Ayers's sardonic glimpse into the soon-to-be future South we meet a young narrator who cannot fathom how his ancestors could "lump people together into two big groups," even though "they could see that people they called 'black' and 'white' were in fact all different colors"; the baffled speaker himself proudly claims a "genealogy from Scotland, Ghana, Honduras, Korea, and the Cherokee nation!" ("Inevitable Future" 89). Yet the biracial, black-white narrative that has long occupied southern letters and criticism remains prevalent in both critical treatments and popular perceptions of the region. Attention to work by southern African American and women writers was itself belated, and there is undoubtedly still a great deal left to accomplish in both fields. Only recently have the South's critics begun to address its diverse immigrant populations, its surviving Native Americans, and its hybrid descendants of multiple racial and ethnic heritages. Pushed decisively and persistently to the margins of the South's biracial economy, they seem in some sense peripheral to the adherent logic and language of the plantation and the binary, exploitative codes and economies that followed. Yet the encompassing structure of American capitalism implicates all and endows even marginal southerners with an experience of postplantation anxiety and crisis; more palpably from these perspectives than any we have seen so far, the South emerges as less exceptional than symptomatic of collective national ills. Fueled by regional and institutional disregard, Native American and immigrant southerners offer intensified narratives of loss and dispossession; yet their position on the margins of both region and nation allows them to uncover transnational, global echoes of the South's darkest logic. From these "insiders with outside information," as Lan Cao repeatedly describes her protagonist in *Monkey Bridge*, we get rather alarming indications that the South is not an aberration so much as a reflection of a widespread imperial, colonial drive to condition, calculate, and control those perceived to be darker, weaker, and lesser across the globe.

Yet the human soul yearns for place, peace, and the reconstitution of community. As Laura Doyle describes, "the bodies that together form the postbellum nation's body in the United States, be they native American, immigrant, or ex-slave . . . exiled physically from home and past yet haunted by them in memory . . . literally trek north- or westward, against themselves and out of community, feeling the pull of return and reunion in the movement of departure" (339). Their geographical or psychological remove from the heart of the South's biracial economy allows these marginal and mixed southerners to "return" and portray anew the southern self with unfamiliar methods, employing the perspective of the indigenous (Louis Owens and Marilou Awiakta) or of the immigrant (Lan Cao). "Traditional" southerners may endeavor to do the same: after exploring the revisionist works of Owens, Awiakta, and Cao, this chapter returns to several African Americans (James Baldwin, Toni Cade Bambara, and Tayari Jones) who also attempt to make their identities and their communities visible and viable in new ways. By re-membering the nonfictional bodies of Atlanta's lost and murdered children, these writers—not necessarily of or from the South, but themselves the lost and scattered children of its noxious histories—seek uncontaminated ways to write themselves back into equations of integrity and agency. Put another way, these figures attempt narratively to reassemble the bodies torn and dispersed by the violent politics of southern accounting.

By situating their diasporic, multiracial and multiethnic bodies back within the communities that shaped and dismembered them both physically and psychologically, the South's most fragmented subjects attempt to re-member their exiled, broken, suppressed, and hungry spirits. As Bhabha warns, "Remembering is never a quiet act of introspection or retrospection. It is a painful re-membering, a putting together of the dismembered past to make sense of the trauma of the present" (63). In landscapes filled with ravaged, mutilated, and dismembered bodies both abstract and actual, these writers set to work at the painful, necessary, recuperative act of piecing together a traumatic panorama of colonial disaster. But one difficult question troubles this radical decolonizing maneuver, and indeed haunts this entire chapter: under the conditions of colonial capitalism and imperial erasure that persist in Euramerican and southern societies, are such reconstitutions gestures of fullness or fetish? Can the numbers and figures dictating value and viability in either a plantation or a market culture ever be more than beguiling abstractions? And without number, is there anything left?

Indian Givers: Reterritorializing the South in Contemporary Native American Literature

While early southern nativists needed Indians to be extinct, and many southern historians, ethnographers, and writers have unwittingly played into this project, the reality is that many tribes did receive federal sanction to remain; some fled to the mountains or to pieces of less desirable land where they would be unmolested; and others "passed" or married into white and black communities.[1] Today, many have assimilated into the South's vibrantly and often energetically repressed multicultural populations. Somehow, many tribes managed to retain the semblance of tribal solidarity in revitalized Catawba, Cherokee, Lumbee, Seminole, Santee, Monacan, Poarch Creek, and Choctaw communities, and some—like the Mississippi Choctaw—have become leading employers in their regions. Yet an astonishing phenomenon of invisibility surrounds these specimens of cultural survival; as Tom Mould observes of the Mississippi Choctaw, "visit Mississippi and [one may] have no idea there is a major American Indian community here. Live in Mississippi and the Choctaw could escape you as well" (xxii–xxiii). The puzzle of why Indians have been rendered so irrationally invisible in the region differs little from the disciplined denial of Indian presence and survival on a national scale: put simply, the persistence of the Native troubles American myths of innocence and exceptionalism. The South's particularly wholesale evasion of its remaining Indians, however, drives to the heart of my thesis in *Disturbing Calculations*: an inherently exploitative economy like that of plantation slavery needed another erased integer—the removed bodies and claims of its native inhabitants—to stage its spectacles of agricultural, social, and hierarchical prosperity. Denying the persistence of Indians in the South even now preserves for some the myth of a native South that is white rather than red. Inordinate emphasis on a black-white South even in the New Southern studies also indicates that we labor under the misperception that the story of the South is simply the story of slavery.[2] If the majority of this book has examined slavery's epilogue, a turn to southeastern Indian writing offers us a glimpse into its prologue.

Thus, in the closing chapter of this broad study of slavery and capitalism's obliterating effects on black and white southerners, we turn to the Choctaw Cherokee writer Louis Owens and the Cherokee Appalachian poet Marilou Awiakta, both of whom assert their survival and southernness from the "zero" of regional forgetting. Their homelands, communities, voices, and traditions expunged, these Indians suggest ways of reconstructing and negotiating manifold postcolonial identities in the twenty-first century, in gestures that include not just their own people, and not just the South, but an inclusive human community.

This project begins paradoxically by claiming and recalibrating the Indian's status as regional zero. In *Symbolic Exchange and Death*, Jean Baudrillard describes instances of urban graffiti as acts of ethnic recuperation; he declares that the wall "alone is savage, in that its message is zero" (83). Rather than mimic white culture's references, black and Puerto Rican graffiti artists reinvent the terms of cultural expression, Baudrillard argues; these minorities defend and reconstitute their communities from the "zero" of communal resistance and reclamation. Akin to Wilson Harris's notion of the phantom limb/limbo in Caribbean societies, graffiti is a performative gesture meant to reconstruct a culture that has been badly fractured or erased. Two prominent, contemporary southeastern Indian writers are engaging in such forms of cultural regeneration in the South: Marilou Awiakta, a self-described Cherokee Appalachian writer from east Tennessee, and Louis Owens, a Mississippi Choctaw and Oklahoma Cherokee writer and academic whose southern and native roots play pivotal, regenerative roles in his fiction. I might have chosen any number of excellent southeastern Indian writing to focus on; the list of artists who testify to their survival in the region is brief but growing, as is their critical visibility. Eric Anderson's outstanding essay on Linda Hogan's *Power* turns critical attention to contemporary Florida Seminoles in *South to a New Place*, a collection of New Southern literary criticism. In several anthologies the North Carolina poet and scholar MariJo Moore (Cherokee) collects a variety of indigenous voices and works, from the amateur to the virtuoso (Moore herself is a noted author and teacher). The novels and poetry of Diane Glancy (Cherokee) have received sustained critical attention in recent years, as have works by scholar-novelist Louis Owens (Choctaw Cherokee) and poet-essayist Marilou Awiakta (Cherokee Appalachian).[3] Not all of these writers speak consistently from and about their southern homes with sustained purpose or passion; indeed, most criticism does not concern itself with their regional identities or preoccupations, and frankly, the writers themselves often don't either. As Eric Anderson suggests in a special issue of *Mississippi Quarterly* devoted to the South and Indians, perhaps these writers intend and desire not to be perceived as southern at all but are rather working toward a separate space of tribal sovereignty. While this view is persuasive, mine is slightly more retrospective: the writers that I examine seem pervasively, if not always explicitly, haunted and shaped by their identities as southerners, experiences that form black holes in their later attempts to reckon identity and creatively refigure their cultural experiences. These struggles do typify American Indian dislocation and dispossession more broadly; but in their efforts to reterritorialize the South specifically (if only metaphorically and linguistically), these writers suggest subtle ways to recuperate pan-Indian endurance, rootedness, and voice much more broadly.

Louis Owens explains that the mirror gives back "no reflection," only an identity "unseen, unrecognized for himself or herself.... In order to be recognized and to thus have a voice that is heard by those in control of power, the Native must step into that mask and *be* the Indian constructed by white America" ("As If an Indian" 17). In other words, the Indian must *become* the "vanishing American" in order to recalculate the figure of his own vanishing (17). To put it in mathematical terms, "look at zero you see nothing; but look through it and you will see the world" (Kaplan 1). Southeastern Indians tend not to memorialize the past as much as they endeavor to take the remnants of culture and tradition and construct a more inclusive, hybrid future. Both Owens and Awiakta understand the loss that assimilation and hybridity entail, but they embrace mixedblood reality subversively. Owens is acutely aware that his ethnic incalculability—he is Indian, Irish, and Cajun—renders the partially assimilated Indian still more troublesome, unable even to be stereotyped: "neither 'knowable' nor 'visible' in Bhabha's terms," he asserts, "[mixedbloods] resist racial stereotyping and fixed realities as they balance within their two sites of Native and Euramerican selves" ("Syllogistic Mixedblood" 237). In the South's rigidly biracial economy, this precarious "balance" is another way of describing zero: indeed, photographs of Owens's ambiguously mixed ancestors "are records of invisibility.... They give me nothing" (237). In an auspicious reversal of other contemporary southern identity crises, however, Owens insists that "nothing" might in fact be "everything" when being incalculable also signifies a refusal to be "neutralized or encompassed or assimilated" (237).

In affirming both her southern roots and her Cherokee heritage, Awiakta also rebels against being "hemmed in by the dominant culture, which insists that everything be squared, boxed, separated" (136).[4] She disavows the Anglo tendency to impose rigid distinctions and segregation where none may exist. Awiakta's proudly multicultural identity and integrationist politics offer a powerful antidote to this hegemony. Rather than conform to a notion of separation encoded with material value, Awiakta asserts her hybridity and attaches it importantly to region as much as ethnicity; doing so makes the South less a primary, ordering, dispossessing force and merely a component of her rich heritage. For her, being Appalachian is a genetic trait: while living briefly in France with her husband, she muses: "a foreign context really brings out the power in the blood—sets the DNA to singing" (46). There, her birthright as a southerner is figured as a biological fact like her Cherokee heritage: "Living in France made me think deeply about who I was, about the value of my heritage, and about the necessity of working out harmonies with people from different cultures. By the time I returned to America, I knew that I was a Cherokee/Appalachian poet. I was determined to sing my song." (31). For these Native authors, hybridity serves to acknowledge the cultural stigma or invisibility of mixture in the South, to bear witness to its imperial iterations, and finally to revise the terms of that effacement. Indeed, most Native Americans do not subscribe to binary or dualistic systems for defining identity; but they struggle to inhabit a world that does, a world that introduced the fact of hybridity as (from a "white" perspective) ugly byproducts of imperial conquest and assimilation that needed to be repressed and forgotten.[5] For Owens, too, this defiant hybridity takes the form of literature, where he enters an established tradition with full agency and disruptive potential: "we do not have the luxury of simply opting out," Owens reminds us, because "we already function within the dominant discourse. To think otherwise is naïve at best, for the choice was made for all of us generations ago" ("Song" 57). By entering into the realm of colonial discourse rather than eschewing it, we stand the best chance of revising its assumptions and effects from the inside; borrowing Pratt's language of the contact zone, Owens suggests that "the very act of appropriating the colonizer's discourse and making it one's own is collaborative and conjunctural" ("Song" 57).

As we saw in the previous chapter, Indian ancestries are commonly claimed by white and black Americans alike to serve a variety of needs and desires, which are typically self-serving. Yet these Cherokee grandmothers are not often people at all but abstracts and types; "real" Indians tend instead to be stereotyped as savage, uncivilized, and greedy in order both to justify white guilt over their destruction and to displace latent fears about their own barbarity. The phrase *Indian giver*, for instance, has long been a part of our U.S. English vocabulary, as have its derogatory connotations. Originally, *Indian giving* referred to what struck European settlers as an odd gift-giving ritual, wherein a Native American expected his offerings to be reciprocated in a gesture of appreciation and respect.[6] After repeated experience with whites—who assumed gifts to be unidirectional grants and beyond the standard economy—Indians began to resent the affronts to their goodwill, and in disappointment appeared to want to take back their offerings. Thus, the *Indian giving* idiom has literal weight but disturbing layers of ironic implications: not only were Natives' earliest contributions of skins, husbandry, and agricultural tutelage unreturned, but their very lands formed a gift-wrapped package of lucrative opportunity for waves of European settlers who continued to take and take until virtually nothing was left for the exploited "givers." Nonetheless, in a classic twist of colonial rationalization and hypocrisy, America's own most extraordinary and reluctant givers of an entire continent earned this disparaging idiom for ungrateful and covetous behavior. The evolution of this idiom typifies strikingly the pattern of stereotype formation still operative in contemporary America, in which Indians are often figured as greedy loafers demanding unreasonable reparations from the federal government in the form of free services, economic aid, and the license to develop casino dynasties.

Misconceptions about Indian greed have been especially common in the South, where the stubborn Natives who remained after the sweeping removal efforts of the 1830s seemed to white southerners to receive "unnatural, even scandalous special treatment from the federal government" (J. Martin 144). This misleading notion increased as the South's own economic woes mounted well into the twentieth century. It makes for a revealing coincidence, then, that the term *Indian giver* appears in common usage only in 1860—centuries after the first European-Indian encounter, and coinciding instead with the eve of the Civil War and the South's decisive loss of its plantation economy. These amnesiac renditions of irrational greed and vindictiveness virtually erase Anglo America's responsibility for Indian poverty, neglect, and exploitation. Moreover, they downplay the very real and cruel circumstances that caused indigenous dispossession and need and the federal government's inept and prejudicial policies and bureaus organized to handle such matters (generally by ignoring or deferring them).[7] Southern whites' own perceived sense of victimization and loss has historically trumped all other claims to persecution in the region.

In a sense, these native southerners are not writing about or claiming the South so much as they are reterritorializing a metonym, recapturing a dark and distant location in which to begin remapping their own indigenous selves. I linger over the work of Owens and Awiakta here because of their relatively explicit treatments of the South as a primal, formative space, as well as for their divergent perspectives: Awiakta is a lifelong and celebratory resident of Tennessee and the Appalachian Mountains, while for Owens the South functions as an obscure place of origin that affects him long after his migration to the West and into the dark web of colonial history. Together, the work of Owens and Awiakta establishes a continuum along which Native writers of the South seem to move: from shadows to light, obscurity to clarity, despair to hope—and back again. These are the Indian givers I'd like to prioritize and celebrate in this chapter: the Indians who imaginatively take back their gifts of territory, community, and self in acts of creative reclamation. Their gifts and weapons in this revolution are words and voice—precisely the tools critics must also employ in efforts to make these issues heard and understood in a postcolonial, postregional world.

Beginning Where Everything Begins

In his collection of autobiographical and critical essays *Mixedblood Messages*, Louis Owens traces his ancestry and his childhood recollections back to a muddy home along the brown, slow-moving Yazoo River in Mississippi. His visions of home are fragmented but foundational, compelling the fiction writer in him to attempt to "put things together from the scraps of stories in my memory and imagination, beginning with Mississippi, where everything begins" (167). While Owens's works are generally set outside the South, he returns frequently to primal homeland settings and scenes in order to piece together the origins of self, family, and community. Often these revisitations constitute journeys of healing for Owens's troubled characters. Clearly the South occupies an elusive yet pivotal place in his own creative and personal landscape, but his mission statement is broader and more comprehensive than mere introspection: in Mississippi, Owens avers, "*everything* begins." These dark spaces of memory and origin are often irretrievable aporia, accessible only to the creative "imagination" able to manufacture bridges between the blank spaces; such lacunae constitute a primal metonym for Native dispossession and diaspora on a much broader scale.

Indeed, Owens's public and critical comments on Native American literary and cultural production rarely dwell on regional specificities. In Owens's work, the southern Indian example functions synecdochically in relation to Native erasure nationwide, their invisibility compounded by geographical isolation and loose tribal affiliation; because the removed tribes were "rewarded" with land and recognition, those who remained have struggled since to heal their fragmented nations and recuperate ancestral lands. As individuals, Indians have often been estranged from one another in the process. Owens's paternal Choctaw ancestors (who appear as recognizable characters in his fiction) hail from the literal swamps and "backwaters" of Mississippi. In *The Sharpest Sight*, his novel set most fully in the South, Owens creates an autobiographical protagonist, the mixedblood Cole McCurtain. McCurtain's father Hoey shares with Owens's father a name and a home along the Yazoo River in Mississippi. Because of their distance from the main tribal settlement, McCurtain's family suffers invisibility even among their own people: as Hoey comments sardonically, "those Choctaw down there in Mississippi don't even know I'm Indian, the ones that run the new reservation they got. . . . They started up the dances and everything again, but I don't know shit about any of that" (58). As Clara Sue Kidwell has noted, the Mississippi Choctaw have been "lost almost entirely to scholarly interest. . . . Outside the mainstream of historical developments on the western frontier, the tribe remained in the backwaters of southern history" (ix).

In the South, this marginality amounts to a kind of double erasure, a sense of being twice removed from an already occluded Native community. In spite of his Choctaw ancestry and upbringing, Hoey's part-white heritage requires that his birth certificate declare him "White"; the classification is as injurious to his sense of self as Bone's "illegitimate" stamp. Such institutional choices have specific resonance for Indians in the South, where the desire to erase the Native was diametrically opposed to the mania over isolating and separating blackness. As Hoey observes, "being Indian in Mississippi back then was almost as bad as being a nigger. But colored people can't choose, one drop of colored blood makes a white person a nigger. But the same people think it takes a hell of a lot of blood to make somebody a real Indian" (58). In the same way that isolating blackness safeguarded whiteness (psychologically more than biologically), failing to acknowledge Indianness strengthened white southerners' visions of themselves as an autochthonous, naturally elect, "native" race. Despite the certain fate of social ostracism, Hoey chooses to defy his birth certificate and embrace his Indian self (58), but he soon realizes the power of the original mandate. "'You know,' he tells Cole, 'I guess I don't understand how to be Indian anymore. . . . I've been reading books and trying to remember how it was back then and trying to figure out how to act and think'" (56). The Indian's cultural erasure and overwriting prove stronger than Hoey's desire to maintain his embattled heritage.

These literal acknowledgments of the vacancy of southern Indian identity are paired in *The Sharpest Sight* with a more symbolic instance of vanishing. For Owens, the heart of the narrative seems again autobiographical: the fictional Cole McCurtain returns to his Mississippi home in order to find and inter the bones of his brother, Attis, a Vietnam veteran who returned from the war only to go missing and then rumored to have been murdered; similarly, Owens recalls searching for his own brother, Gene, who had also disappeared after returning traumatized from Vietnam. While Gene was eventually found living in exile in the Ozarks, a saga Owens recounts in the heartrending essay "Finding Gene," the fictional brother has been killed by a mysterious murderer. While Cole and his friend Mundo search for both a killer and a body, Hoey articulates the irrelevance of the pursuit: "'My boy never really came back from that war. They killed him and gutted him over there'" (142). Cole ultimately finds his brother's body and reverently collects the bones as his elders dictate, but locating culpability is more difficult. He emerges from the swamp, using his field jacket to swathe Attis's bones as if they were in a body bag shipped home from Vietnam. Indeed, the moment is meant to elide the difference between Indians compelled, in an outrageous twist of irony, to participate in America's imperial entanglements abroad and its systematic erasure of Natives at home. "'It doesn't matter who killed your brother,'" an FBI agent tells Cole at the end of the novel. "'I saw a lot of men in bags like that, and it never mattered who did it. It was just done. Part of a very big pas de deux that's being danced out everywhere. We learned the steps more precisely over there, but we were dancing before we went and the ball goes on'" (253–54). Gene's permanently damaged psyche and Attis's literal death amount to the same fate, a symbolic slaying at the hands of American colonialism "everywhere"—another indication that the South is an incidental place of birth and burial, and that the exploited are dancing across the globe. What is perhaps most striking about this comment is the agent's near-comic glibness and utter elision of responsibility, the sense that "it never mattered who did it. It was just done." Yet Owens makes clear just who or what is responsible for Attis's and Gene's invisibility, and for the control and erasure of so many Indians like them: the federal agent is commissioned specifically by the government to "make sure [Attis] never surfaced again. They want him controlled and invisible" (254).

Within this national parable, an analogy to the South and southern literature emerges unmistakably. Just as Hoey tries to learn how to "be Indian" from books, Owens's characters understand that canonical literature offers white America's version of Indian identity in renditions that accomplish the spiritual and sometimes literal murder of the actual Native. After discussing works of racial and southern import like *Moby-Dick* and *Huck Finn*, Cole's Uncle Luther invokes the most prized and influential of all southern writers, Faulkner, to suggest that Faulkner's Indian characters epitomize white attempts "'to write all us people away . . . try to write us to death . . . [Faulkner's Chief Doom] was death, was dyin' in every word that white man wrote'" (216). Unmistakably, Owens's characters and Owens himself engage in the act of telling stories that endeavor to write their identities back into the American and the southern narrative, constructing personhood from scraps of collective indigenous memory. "'A man's got to know the stories of his own people,'" Luther reminds Cole, "'and then he's got to make his own story too'" (91). While Uncle Luther gives this advice in *The Sharpest Sight*, young Cole doesn't put the mandate into use for himself until Owens's later novel *Bone Game*, which follows Cole into adulthood and a professorship in Santa Cruz, California.

Like Owens himself, Cole leaves the South to settle on the West Coast; Owens discusses his decision to resurrect Cole there in *Bone Game* as a distinctly postcolonial gesture: "I reentered the life of Cole McCurtain," he writes, "in order to examine the imprints of evil left upon the American landscape by European invaders' destructive violence" (*Mixedblood* 182). For Owens, the power of his stories lies in such migratory habits, which "carry us from the muddy waters of the Yazoo River to a tent in California" (*Mixedblood* 183). Mississippi and California are compatible sites of colonial trauma that find connection in Owens's historical investigation and creative reimaginings as he replicates narratively the pattern of westward removal and colonial expansion. Ambitious white U.S. settlers in California encountered a landscape already stained with the blood of centuries of Spanish colonization and greed. Owens confesses that the novel emerged from his impression of Santa Cruz as a place with "a dark presence . . . a definite, haunted feel," which prompted him to begin researching the area's history; what he discovered was a staggering record of brutality, "what seemed like a pattern of almost ritualistic violence spanning almost two centuries" (Purdy 9). Owens explained in an interview the novel's attempt to convey both "the enormous sense of loss" that the Bay Area Ohlone experienced as well as the concomitant notion that "Santa Cruz is a microcosm for the U.S. There's been so much violence perpetrated in its history" (Purdy 10). My reading of *Bone Game* adds to this a sense of its story's portability from the Yazoo to the Pacific, and thus the ways in which *both* the South and Santa Cruz are microcosms for American imperial violence against Indians.

While the impetus for this novel is clearly historical, the narrative is again a contemporary one that seeks to depict the dislocation and anonymity of twentieth-century Indians—the Choctaw Cherokee Cole and his Navajo colleague Alex Yazzi. Cole is haunted by a regional history that mingles with details of a contemporary crisis, producing complex and vivid nightmares about a serial killer who has been abducting and dismembering young women from the campus where he teaches. The dreams collide with visions of the actual 1812 murder of a Spanish missionary priest, Padre Andrés Quintana, by a vengeful Ohlone Indian pupil named Venancio. "The Indians killed him when they couldn't take his cruelty anymore," Yazzi tells Cole; "he was a cruel bastard; he used a whip with wire ends to shred their backs" (52). In return for this torture, the tormented Ohlones strangled the priest and "hung him there by what the Ohlone informant called his '*conycañones*.' I think that means his balls" (52). This image of body parts chillingly evokes the serial killer's modus operandi: as Cole's teaching assistant reports grimly, "'Parts of a woman washed up on three different beaches in the last couple of days'" (17). These images additionally evoke Cole's memories of collecting and separating his brother's bones out of a different body of water and transporting them home to Mississippi in *The Sharpest Sight*. The vivid, grotesque dismemberment signifies just how much has been dismantled by American colonization, and how difficult it may be to locate and assemble the farflung "scraps" of memory (and here, body) into something resembling a coherent, functional, living whole. In his haunting nightmares and memories, Cole's own being becomes a storehouse for this long trajectory of imperial cruelty and personal tragedy across centuries and regions.

Indeed, what the serial killer comes to represent is the violence done by whites who endeavor to capture Indian "essence" and polarize it ethnographically, with the kind of innocent but bedeviled imperial authority that effectively constructs the Indian from and for a white perspective. Significantly, both of the murderers—yes, there are two—turn out to be McCurtain's students; and the primary killer is Cole's own white teaching assistant and a fervent scholar of Lakota spiritualism, Robert Malin.[8] Malin's romantic and scholarly interest in Native culture is a reminder that seemingly benign white attempts to understand and describe Indian identity have proven effectively genocidal. As Vine Deloria Jr. asserts with deadpan frankness in *Custer Died for Your Sins*, "Indians are certain that all societies of the Near East had anthropologists at one time because all those societies are now defunct" (83). In Malin, Professor McCurtain sees the epitome of all of his curious, narcissistic students: "In their own mirrors, they were the explorers, the raiding parties, horse thieves of life, and some of them were mad" (11). Alan Trachtenberg has described white fantasies of indigenousness as annihilations— "repeated rituals of symbolic sacrifice" intended to strengthen Anglo American nationalism and innocence (xxiii), a compulsion Cole sees the potential and desire for in nearly every "mad" white scholar in the lecture hall. Importantly, while his description of their narcissism captures the sense of indigenous fantasy, it also encompasses the white settlement narrative that such romantic transferences would aim to conceal: white conquerors were "explorers," "raiding parties," and "horse thieves" in their totalizing collision with the inhabitants of the new world.

Malin thus becomes a symbol of this imperfect repression of colonial violence, playing out an Indian charade and a settlement pageant simultaneously. His body crudely painted half black and half white, he similarly colors the naked body of Cole's daughter Abby as a prelude to raping and killing her. While doing so, he explains his perverse spiritualism: "Native Americans know that the world is precariously balanced between good and evil, light and dark, black and white. It is up to us to maintain that balance. Mother Earth gives us life and asks that we give something in return" (238). His murderous rampage is an ironic perversion of the Indian giver paradigm, ascribing the compulsion to "return" a gift to a generic and savage "Native American" sensibility. Yet Owens's message runs deeper: what gift would require such violent retribution? Malin's butchery seems precisely resonant of the mutilation in Cole's historical dreams, where the painted murderer appears with "hands outstretched, a severed head in each palm" while "waves rear back and hurl bodies from the sea—heads, hands, arms, and legs"

(66). Sent as a missive from a bloody colonial past, the figure merges imperceptibly with details of the current slayings. With "hate too strong for death," the vengeful Venancio is condemned to wander perpetually "between worlds," apparently resurfacing in contemporary iterations like Malin's to restore "balance" by unleashing the worst kind of revenge and retribution. It is an Indian gift only in the most perverse, corrupt sense.

The true key to cultural salvation as Owens sees it lies in creative, Native-centered spiritualism and storytelling. Cole himself is, like Owens, a writer of fiction whose dust jackets hang in frames on his office wall, making it seem that these scraps of histories and events are infiltrating his body in order to be assembled into a coherent narrative. But only Cole's Mississippi relatives have the power to authenticate Cole's words by reminding him of the locus of family, community, and the transcendent power of storytelling. "This story's so big, Cole sees only a little bit of it," Uncle Luther declares (79); when Luther arrives in California, he asks Cole "'How come you ain't wrote no more of them books? You used to write good stories'" (226). Owens makes it clear that Luther may not be interested in the content of the stories so much as their import and capacity to heal—he asks Cole this question just after affirming the value of his visit: "'Ain't you glad I made you get up from that floor now, Grandson?'" (226). Indeed, the Mississippi perspective is what completes the panorama and heals Cole's crippled soul; even before the nightmares began, he had been plagued with the idea that his novels were made up of "someone else's words" (19). In his disappointment over this idea, Cole suddenly remembers "an image of Onatima in Uncle Luther's cabin as she had been when he met her, pulling a paperback from the pocket of her apron and smiling . . . 'That's how they make the world,' she had said that day, and for twenty years he'd tried to make his own world with words, like they did, always remembering Onatima" (20). It is Onatima's wisdom that compels him to keep writing, though his faith in the authenticity of his own words is fragile at best. The events of the novel make him yearn for that aid even more strongly: "He thought of the old woman, and his father and great uncle the last time he'd been back in Mississippi. . . . The moist air of the Yazoo River had lain heavily on them all, and the old man, Uncle Luther, had looked upon him as though lost in shadow. Now Cole found himself here in this farthest point of the world where something, finally, had sought him out" (20). He is wracked by horrible images; nauseated and trying to eat something out of a can (the only food that appeals to him), Cole "levered the tab open, thinking of the girl they'd found in the sea, imagining a story that could end that way. Somewhere in that story was a moment of shrieking horror so great it struck at his soul. And again, he felt the strange sense of responsibility, a terrible weight" (20). Yet he is paralyzed, drowning his anxiety in alcohol, perpetually sick to his stomach, and unable to do anything—until his uncle, aunt, and father come from Mississippi to help him put together the pieces of the story, to change the ending—to absolve him of the terrible burden of responsibility and guilt for crimes done to his own people.

Different from the guilt imposed culturally on African Americans like Wright's protagonist, Cole's sense of disgrace seems to stem from his own ineradicable distance from his past and his community. Cole remembers being "just a visitor down there" in Mississippi (47), thinking back explicitly to the events in *The Sharpest Sight* that introduced him to the Choctaw "shadow world" that "was threatening to subsume the life he'd constructed out of books" (93). Clearly the English professor's existence has been dominated and constructed by the "whiteness of his other self," both ethnic and cultural, and his struggle now becomes the one of embracing his shadowy Indian half. California itself is not the answer, because it represents a place where Owens, like Cole, felt he "never stopped being a stranger" (*Mixedblood* 144). Indeed, the message seems to be that the fate of contemporary Indianness is a perpetual marginality, a sense of permanent homelessness in the world. Faced with the burden and (literal) nightmares of history, Cole must learn to make his own words and worlds; he must piece together "home" and family and survival across landscapes, histories, and states. His diasporic condition and his relatives' aid tell us that "home" for the contemporary southeastern Indian is fragmented, migratory, shadowy, and scattered. Given the graphic events of the novel, we might even say mutilated. Indeed, Cole first meets his Navajo friend Alex when Alex is dismembering a deer (24–25), and later in the novel Cole himself uses a chainsaw to downsize the dead dog (suggestively named Custer) that he must fit into a small backyard grave (192). Cole's world is filled gratuitously with fragmentation of all sorts of bodies, a sense that things have, as Walker Percy's Will Barrett intuited they would, come "flying apart" at the hands of meddling humans—and the only solution seems to be in reuniting families, geographies, and colonial traumas.

Postcolonial theory helps us see Cole's plight in clear and devastating terms: as Bhabha describes, the horrific violence of colonial violence must be remembered in order to be exorcised. Part of the decolonization process, then, is an active engagement with history and trauma, a purposeful "re-membering" of the past. Not surprisingly, both African Americans and Native Americans have appropriated the concept of re-membering (or, for Toni Morrison, "rememory") in order to dramatize the very physical process of piecing together a mutilated colonial body through the subversive conduit of discourse and creation. Thus Cole's weapon is not a chainsaw but a pen. Uncle Luther's mandates are clear enough; in urging Cole to write again, he complains, "'They got too many stories about us. We need to write books about them now. Get even'" (226). What Onatima adds to Cole's lessons are more subtle reminders of what the South's exclusive social order has wrought: "My father was an important man among the Choctaw. He had a big house and fields and horses and was richer than any of our neighbors, including the whites . . . but when we were with white people I saw my father grow small" (139). The young Onatima, similarly debased, remembers her own erasure reflected back to her: "I looked in a mirror and saw nothing" (139). When Onatima recounts these memories, Abby is still shaken from having just seen the murderer peeping in the window of Cole's house and frantically shooting out the glass with her father's gun; Onatima's story contextualizes the scare, relates it not just to southeastern agrarian social history but to Native diminishment under white domination generally: "Perhaps the man who frightened you today wants to make you see yourself only through his eyes, so that you can only imagine yourself from outside the window looking in. That way, every time you look in a mirror you will see only what the man sees. You will always be outside yourself, and your own reflection will be a trap. When that happens we become like ghosts who can't see our own bodies" (140). Her answer to Cole's crisis is disarmingly simple: Indians must resist the white authority that Malin's murders and window-peeping represent, and then "make others see us so we can know we exist. . . . We have to have our own stories" (140).

But telling such stories is neither simple nor easy when the content is elusive. Cole begins to heal his besieged body and mind only with the help of Luther, Hoey, and Onatima's presence and wisdom; importantly, he commences trying to put a narrative to the dreams, to begin telling the Native story. Over coffee soon after the Mississippians' arrival, Uncle Luther ponders the history behind Cole's dreams: "'Alex gave me a copy of an 1877 interview with an Indian named Lorenzo Asisara, the son of one of the men who killed the priest. His parents were Venancio and Manuela Asisara'" (227). Cole continues the story as it has been written not in books but in his psyche: "'That's the name I woke up with,'" he says, "'Venancio Asisara'" (227). Reflecting on young Lorenzo's green eyes, Cole begins to construct a version of history not yet recorded: "'How do you think the son ended up with green eyes?'" (227). Cole's question seems in part rhetorical, as his dreams have the answer already encoded in them: the priest had raped Manuela, resulting in a mixed-race child and compelling Venancio's murderous revenge. In subtle moments like these, Owens suggests that Cole is beginning to put together the pieces of not just this particular mystery, but the panorama of his own and his people's violation.

His ability to relate these historical lessons to the present crisis becomes critical when Robert Malin abducts and attempts to kill Cole's daughter Abby. As Cole rushes to help her, Abby is already saving herself with the memory of her father's words—an old Indian song that Cole repeats at several points throughout the novel: "*I had been looking far*," the lyrics go, "*sending my spirit north, south, east, and west, but I could find nothing, no way of escape*" (36, 193). The memory of these words prompts Abby to defiance: "'Don't kill me,' she said," as her hand gropes the ground beneath her pinned body and finds Malin's gun (239). She shoots him with it and effectively ends the killing rampage. As the Indian song predicts, Abby and Cole's peregrinations "north, south, east, and west" have failed to provide an "escape" from the hauntings of American history. The answers are in the bloody ground always already beneath the Indian wherever he or she moves; and so are the weapons. At precisely this moment, the ghost of Venancio Asisara appears, apparently conjured by Cole's voice. "'It was a brave thing saying his name like that,'" Onatima tells Cole later; Cole responds, "'No. It was what he wanted all the time'" (243).

Ultimately, the power to speak and name, to narrate and identify, is what liberates these lost souls imprisoned in the ether of American colonial history. This, finally, is Cole's grave "responsibility" at the end of a crime thriller that would otherwise seem of little interest to literary scholars. The murders solved and Abby safe, the family leaves the haunted coast and retreats to New Mexico. Cole and Abby implore the southerners to stay with them; "'We'll be lost without you'" Abby insists (243). But Onatima reassures them that they needn't be geographically bound in order to feel connected and safe:

> "We have to go home, Grandson, we've been gone far too long . . .
>
> When so many were removed, we stayed behind. So how could we leave now? Who would talk to them out there at night if I never went home? And how would I find the path so far away? Who would tell them of their granddaughter in these strange, lightning-struck mountains?" She shook her head again. "Luther and I have our tasks back there . . . So the crux of the matter is that we have to go home." (242–43)

Their "task" is, like Cole's, to "tell" the stories that "talk" across the miles to those homeless wanderers "out there at night" in the darkness of exile. As long as these resistant southerners remain at home, and as long as they are bound by talk and story, Cole and his family will never be lost.

Awiakta's Gift

Such communication becomes possible even while rooted to a stultifying southern context. While Owens transports his fictional southerners across miles and generations, replacing geographical fixity with cultural persistence, Marilou Awiakta's approach is more like Onatima's. That is, her stories function as stubborn telegraphs from the Appalachian mountains in an effort to give voice to those who managed quietly to retain their southern homelands. In her collection of poetry, *Abiding Appalachia: Where Mountain and Atom Meet* and, later, her multigeneric work *Selu: Seeking the Corn-Mother's Wisdom*, Awiakta establishes herself firmly on southern terrain. *Abiding Appalachia* harmoniously reconciles the Agrarian South's age-old resistance to modernity and science. Having grown up on the atomic frontier in Oak Ridge, Tennessee's branch of the Manhattan Project that developed the first atomic bomb, Awiakta recounts her lifelong project of negotiating the rift between nature and technology, writing as an Appalachian southerner as much as a Cherokee. The opening of *Selu* gives another, more playful account of her composite southern-Indian, creative and cultural orientation: "'Write a straightforward introduction,' my editor says . . . I smile. 'Up in Appalachia where I'm from, we never do that when a story's afoot. And this one about Selu is long and winding'" (xiv). From the beginning and consistently throughout her works, Awiakta marks her voice as *both* rural Appalachian and Cherokee; in fact, she grounds herself first in a recognizably southern region and dialect ("a story's afoot"), and only secondly specifies her subject, the story of the Corn Mother Selu, an indigenous parable that appears in different forms across most Native cultures. This staking of territory is important because it signifies a quiet refusal to be separated from the land and the identity that have shaped her identity and her voice, along with an enduring connection to those other Indians "out there in the night."

One section of *Selu* in particular conveys more concretely just how staunchly Awiakta pitches her southern voice in the battle to protect Native culture from literal erasure by the cold, amnesiac mechanisms of American policy. She documents the Tellico Dam controversy that consumed and divided much of Tennessee, the U.S. government, and the eastern band of Cherokee in the closing years of the 1970s. The Tennessee Valley Authority had initiated a project to flood the Tellico region in an effort to generate twenty-three megawatts of energy—a comparatively small boon to the massive TVA power grid and one that promised to cost more money than it would ultimately produce (Awiakta, *Selu* 48). But there were far more grave drawbacks to the project: first, the certain elimination of the endangered snail darter fish, and second, the literal erasure of "the historical and spiritual heartland of the Cherokee nation" with its sacred places and burial mounds (47). Nonetheless, the plan marched forward. Awiakta painstakingly details the catastrophe because it represents, for her, the Trail of Tears all over again, "an old pattern" of expropriation repeating itself on southern soil (44). Worse, the contemporary invisibility of Cherokee community in the South dulls and obscures the public's sense of outrage, muting any protests to an inaudible murmur. "How could such a momentous issue go unnoticed by the national media?" Awiakta asks in disbelief; how could it remain untouched by "even the Memphis media?" (43). When the news stories did begin to circulate, they tended to be "uninterested" reports of the Cherokee as "just one more voice shouting against the dam" (47); brief pieces eventually appeared in local papers, but "with a marked lack of crusading passion" (49). Awiakta's disbelief is answered by a disturbing recognition: this most recent removal fails to touch or move the general public because it is perceived as unreal. "'Indians moved off 200 years ago,'" the mayor of nearby Tellico Plains proclaimed publicly. "'Live Americans—be they black, white or red—are more important than the remains of dead Indians'" (qtd. in Awiakta, *Selu* 58). Despite the rich, vibrant signs of cultural survival in the region, Indians' continued presence as indigenous peoples—for whom the remains of ancestors continue to play a vital role in their culture—had gone unnoticed by even their neighbors. Stunned members of the press wondered, "'Why didn't we know about the Cherokee cause before now?'" and a famous cartoonist whose drawings actively satirized the "dam-versus-fish" controversy admitted to having no idea that the "Cherokee issue" was even an issue in the debate (58). Yet how can we blame such individuals and institutions for failing to know what every public and political proclamation seems to contradict or disregard? The Tellico travesty confirms the persistence of what removal and Manifest Destiny set in motion: whoever gets in the way of American progress will be literally blotted out by those in power.

The force of Awiakta's questions and revelations derives from her inclusive purview; she is concerned not just about Native invisibility but about the miscarriages of American democracy more broadly and with the survival of the earth for all its inhabitants. "If the watchdog of the people can be blind for so long to a domestic issue such as this," Awiakta asks in strikingly prescient tones, "how can we be sure what really is happening abroad, in places like Afghanistan and Iran?" (59). In the Tellico resurgence, Awiakta feels "America heading West, the direction of death and destruction: the Darkening Land" (54). It becomes easier now to see why the western landscape offers Owens such a fitting extension of and perspective on the darkening land of his southern memories. While his lens moves west to isolate the postcolonial Native condition in all its expansive horror, Awiakta's response is to heed the advice of her parents to "'Have faith.' In short, 'Head East'" (63). In the face of continued metaphorical Removal, the motion of hope and renewal lies in a counterthrust back home, back east. The role of the South's silenced Indians in this process is crucial. Awiakta holds firmly to her roots and uses them to trumpet her message across American landscapes more vastly. She introduces *Selu* with a "FAX" to the reader, a form meant to emulate the forward-moving technology of contemporary life, reaching out "To: The Reader / Fax No.: Wherever you are / From: Awiakta / Fax No.: East Tennessee mountains" (xv). Into the space of diaspora and migration, Awiakta sends her message from a very specific, grounded location in the "East." From there, she can begin to do the cultural work her writing represents; indeed, the FAX specifies that the "Content" of the book will be the Corn Mother's "survival wisdoms," employed to mitigate crises like Tellico (xv): "family business, homeland business" (43).

Indeed, Awiakta's writing shows voice and communication in any form to be the key to such survival. In the face of the Tellico debacle, she wonders "what could I do?" Her answer, repeated in myriad ways throughout *Selu*, is simple: "'All I can do is write,' I said. 'I'm not well known. I don't have any clout. Who will publish it? And even if somebody did, what good is it to sling a poem at a dam?' 'Do it'" her Tennessee friend implores (43). Awiakta's gestures come in the form of public appeals, letters to editors, opinion articles in newspapers and journals, interviews; selections from many of these pieces appear in *Selu*, often transformed into prose poems or short verses. The all-encompassing nature of Awiakta's writing, which spans genres and subjects with seamless energy, evokes an urgency simply to keep speaking, writing, and documenting something, anything. But what she intones often cuts to the very heart of colonial silencing: "In plain terms," she warns, "when others want what you have, they make up distorted stories about you" (166). What Malin and the white conquerors represent in *Bone Game*, and what the marvelous fictions of the white South bequeath insidiously to its future generations, Awiakta wards off here by urging the circulation of new stories. The tale of Selu in particular offers wisdom for all people, with its principles of nourishment and balance and even gender equity; her vision is collaborative and inclusive: "if we plant together, we can do much," she encourages (166).

Indeed, Awiakta offers her words and companionship directly to the reader; she repeats verbatim a poem called "I Offer You a Gift" twice in *Selu*, once at the beginning and again near the end (8, 207). The "gift" she imagines and prioritizes so emphatically is, again, the story of Selu the Corn Mother herself. Corn was the Wampanoag's first gift to the Pilgrims, the key to British survival in the alien, cold New World. Awiakta knows well the meaning of this Indian gift, which is yet another ironic inversion of the Corn Mother parable: even "schoolchildren learn that corn was 'a gift from the Indians' and that early settlers would have starved without it.[9] But the recipients of the gift have always written the official history of America" (20). Everywhere in the world she sees other signs of Mother Earth giving and her inhabitants failing to reciprocate, much as America's victors continue to take, to "write" history and silence the givers. The choice to circulate the Corn Mother's story as a metaphor for encouraging "the law of giving back" is heavily symbolic, the kernel of corn not only a reminder of hardiness and hybridity but a veritable "seed-thought for survival" that will bear fruit in time, an "investment" operating on the "natural principle of deferred returns" (20, 37). Awiakta thus revises the terms of the Indian giver dynamic, exemplifying the confidence that the principle of generosity will eventually result in the best kind of returns. Yet her views are neither escapist nor reactionary; rather she envisions a contemporary, progressive America of "truer democracy," and she invites all readers to journey with her to that destination. Indeed, she draws them into a truly conjunctural, collaborative process: "Although this book contains my seed-thoughts about survival and the Corn-Mother, as you gather them up, please add your own. . . . Make this *our* book" (38). At the end of every public speaking or reading engagement, Awiakta routinely invites the audience to come forward to receive a seed of corn that she places reverently in the palm of each hand as a reminder of our common human bond and task. "'This thing they call corn is I,'" she writes. "The kernel is deep red, like a drop of the Corn-Mother's blood. Or like a drop of our own, where genes bring the seeds of memory into the present, so we can have a future. 'We are the stories.' We have to remember that. We are the stories. We are creating them now" (214).

Awiakta designs her own "poetic version" of Selu's story to appeal to a general audience, those readers "wherever" they may be; but the power of her voice comes, like Onatima's wisdom, from its anchor in a specifically southern space and voice—a clear, triumphant message of endurance and survival. "There is . . . one phrase," she says, "that carries special intensity in the South (and perhaps elsewhere): 'Sick and tired.' It means that you've been pushed to the limit of endurance. Something's got to give. And you'll consult the highest power to see that it does. I think the animals in [Selu's] story had reached that point" (24). In the story, the animals are saved from Kanati the hunter's relentless pursuit when Corn Mother is sent to be his wife and to help nourish the earth's inhabitants. No more would the animals be consumed and erased from the earth at the whim of one greedy hunter. The analogy to Indian existence under Anglo American domination is chilling, but the hope encoded in the corn parable is, in Awiakta's capable voice, just as strong. The southern sense of being "Sick and tired" emerges achingly throughout *Selu*'s multifaceted historical, social, and personal reflections, as does a very literal translation of the idiom that, in the face of so much exhaustion and depletion, "something's got to give." Ironically, it is the Indian who "gives" yet again. Stories will heal, Awiakta knows; perhaps words will not stop a dam, but their gathering strength and sense can eventually alter the world. This process would be unimaginable for Awiakta away from her Tennessee homeland: "One way to heal the deep slashes that sever us from relationship and hope," she suggests, "is to go back to our home ground—our primal space—and find within it the deepest human root. In Appalachia, as elsewhere in America, that root is American Indians. They were the first to call the mountains home, as most Appalachians of every ethnic background continue to do" (170).

"Home" can be vibrantly multiethnic and communal, a place of gathering and conjunction rather than separation and silence. Awiakta's inclusive sentiments seem to stem from knowing too acutely and literally the danger of mathematical and scientific division. The 1936 Tennessee world she was born into was nothing if not riven, marked by Depression, World War II, the atomic project, and heightening racial mobility and strife. Most of all, her experiences among technological and economic crises seem to serve as parables for the social catastrophes roiling about the midcentury South. She was raised, as she puts it, on dual frontiers: one ecological (her east Tennessee mountains), the other scientific (the Oak Ridge settlement where her father worked). She learns finally to bridge the two in her *Abiding Appalachia: Where Mountain and Atom Meet* by embracing the principle of environmental balance. What most "traditional" southerners so far have been unable to grasp and critique objectively Awiakta attempts not only to articulate but to subvert. She understands the atom, in a sense, as an all-encompassing trope for race relations, ethnic diversity, and basic human interaction; with its inherent divisiveness and explosive potential, the atom is nonetheless "part of me, too" (*Selu* 31). By abusing it, she warns, "our world will become a charred and steaming heap. Burned flesh. Silence" (71). But by assimilating the atom and its horrific capacity for disaster, one also learns to embody and harmonize difference. The Oak Ridge scientists "emphasized the peaceful potential of the atom and the importance of personal commitment in using it. Essentially, their message was the same as my mother's" (68). Awiakta's own message is both traditional and explosive—it unites past teachings and contemporary progress in a revolutionary way. She repeatedly uses the word *mystery* to describe the advances surrounding the atomic project, which of course culminated in the development of the nuclear bomb. Somehow, Awiakta knows she must inevitably make peace with not just this but with all of the world's engimatic energies and individuals, trusting they can be harnessed for good rather than destruction; she wears around her neck as a constant reminder an emblem uniting her native energies with these scientific laws: Little Deer leaping through the atom, caught in a moment of permanent equilibrium.

But the atom remains troubling: the abuse of Native lands and people for uranium mining, testing, and disposal has been decried by Indian activists like Leslie Marmon Silko as an extreme manifestation of environmental racism.[10] While white writers also lived under and alluded to the shadow of the nuclear bomb at midcentury—most famously Faulkner in his famous Nobel Prize speech query, "when will I be blown up?"—Native Americans seem particularly attuned to who will go first, and who has already suffered, in such catastrophes. As Helen Jaskoski has noted,

> American Indian authors are acutely sensitive to the poisoning of many Indian mine workers and families in the vicinity of uranium mines of the Southwest, to the racism in the choice of the first (and so far only) targets of nuclear weapons, to the misuse of

natural resources and destruction of the environment involved in the production of nuclear weapons, and to the removal of so much of the GNP from support for human needs in favor of weapons. (481)

Without dismissing these concerns, Awiakta decides that her only option is to understand, control, and assimilate the mechanics of the power that can—and has—utterly destroyed her people's history and culture: in Pueblo uranium mines, in the federal government's legislation of economic injustice and human rights abuses, and in the South's explosive racial and ethnic incubators.

The lesson is ultimately about power: about seizing something unfathomably small and giving it the force, through the separation of its parts, to destroy the entire world—and then to hold it still. Cole McCurtain's dreams tell him that he is "everything and everyone at the same time," all the murderers and the murdered throughout time and space (95). The end to violence involves a merging of these perspectives rather than further antagonisms. The atom's lesson deepens: "in the mid-1970s," Awiakta recounts, "the [linear] path ended in an infinitesimal circle: the quark. A particle so small that even with the help of huge machines, humans can see only its trace. . . . It is a mystery that no conceivable research is likely to dispel, the life force in process—nurturing, enabling, enduring, fierce. I call it the atom's mother heart" (68). The linear rules of science and mathematics that teach humans to divide and destroy with such precision become circular. It is an approximation of the "life force," the heart of all things, and perhaps a space of new beginning.

It would seem no accident that Awiakta ends *Selu* with a brief section called "The Ciphers." In mathematics, a *cipher* refers to zero, which was originally a placeholder; as such, it has a secondary meaning of "mystery" or "secret code." Awiakta draws on both implications when she promises to transport the reader imaginatively to the nation's own heart, Washington, D.C., "to see and decode the secret ciphers, the guiding messages for the twenty-first century. . . . They are in plain view. But most people probably pass them every day without recognizing what they really are" (326). The ciphers are, of course, Indians, and Awiakta knows that the future prosperity of not just the South but the entire nation lies in seeing what so many Americans shield from view every day: the walking symbols of a disastrous, colonized past, still in "plain view" but rendered insignificant, "ciphers" and zeroes. Awiakta ends her book here, with the trailing phrase, "the Creator offers us a gift . . ." (326). The hoped-for exchange would take place, importantly, in the nation's capital: there, federal Indian policies have institutionalized blood quantum ratios and employed scientific equations of identity to either bestow or withhold all that the Certificate of Degree of Indian Blood card grants and signifies. The gift of the cipher is figured as a strategic recalibration of the zero status that federal policy labors subtly to insure in Indian affairs nationwide. Awiakta counters this obliteration by urging the public to see Indians for what they "really are"; that in itself is a gift, a "guiding message for the twenty-first century."

The best work on southern literature now acknowledges such diversity and multiplicity within traditionally segregated or reductively biracial spaces; and Awiakta seeks to include herself within that panorama rather than withdraw from it or suffer in silent obscurity any longer. For many tribal communities that seek to retreat from American "progress" and assimilation, this integrationist vision might be less than ideal. But Awiakta embraces without bitterness or reluctance the revolutionary potential of a thoroughly hybrid, "cross-pollinated" race of contemporary Americans. Ultimately, both Owens and Awiakta remind us that the true Indian gift is not about territory or space or possessions but rather human community, relationships, and the survival of nature. Both writers seek in different ways to take back, inhabit, and reterritorialize the U.S. South as a primal space of reconstitution for American Indians, playing out the role of Indian giver in marvelously metaphorical and subversive ways. The gifts they offer are not directed toward any specific tribes or persons, nor are they concrete objects or goods; rather, they are metaphors, shadows of thought, seeds of ideas, sprinkled and disseminated across not just the South but the entire land, planted and tended with the utmost hope that a razed landscape may someday yield a harvest.

Bridging Worlds: Immigrants Re-membering Home

While acknowledging the endurance of Native perspectives on and in the South crucially disrupts its prevailing biracial narratives, additional critiques ought to move not backward and inward but forward and outward. While nontraditional, immigrant southerners have long been a part of the South's fabric, they have only recently begun to be acknowledged not just as southerners but as relevant to discussions of a South and the southern experience. As Raymond A. Mohl avers, the influx of Hispanic immigrants challenges the notion that the South is primarily a black-white phenomenon, as "ubiquitously visible" immigrants have created a "multicultural and multiethnic rather than biracial . . . society in many southern places" (70). While Hispanics comprise the largest percentage of the South's immigrant population, David M. Reimers suggests that Asian settlers are a rapidly growing contingent, particularly in urban communities. Interestingly, Reimers reports that some of the first Chinese to arrive in the South were actively recruited by "post–Civil War planters who wanted to replace newly freed slaves" (103); even the *Vicksburg Times* declared, "'Our prosperity depends entirely upon the recovery of lost ground, and we therefore say let the [Chinese] Coolies come, and we will take the chance of Christianizing them'" (qtd. in Reimers 103). Like the African American and Native American slaves before them, inferior, pagan outsiders are judged by the value they may bring to a South banking on the return of "prosperity" and the "recovery of lost ground." When these figures no longer serve their needs or fail to play their roles of subservience, they become peripheral.

However, these outside influences nonetheless contribute crucial methods for apprehending the self-interestedness of an enduringly potent economic and racial order; moreover, they expose the plantation South's place within a larger panorama of imperial cruelty and violence. Such voices do not necessarily escape or defuse the calculating discourses of separation, hierarchy, and devaluation so much as they suggest the need to understand such imperatives in a context that lays bare the plight of the colonized on a global scale. C. Vann Woodward argued over fifty years ago what recent scholars of the South like James Cobb and William Stueck are only now beginning to acknowledge and explore: "when viewed against a broader global backdrop, the South's experience seems far less distinctive" than historians and Americans have long presumed, for a variety of usually self-serving reasons (xi). The South was, in fact, initially founded by early forces of globalization "that had created a worldwide demand for semitropical products like tobacco and rice and pulled together a remarkable mixture of peoples from around the Atlantic basin" (Peacock, Watson, and Matthews 2).[11] Poised at the nexus of another wave of globalization, the contemporary South continues to utilize the international infusions of capital and populace that fundamentally underwrote the operations of the calculating South as we have come to know it. This is not just an exercise in comparativism or in rendering the South less exceptional than so many have wanted it to be for diverse motives; rather, these analogous outside/inside perspectives seem to offer hopeful strategies for permanently disabling the rhetoric and weapons of mass exploitation and erasure.

As Maureen Ryan's discussion of Vietnamese immigrants to the U.S. South suggests, contemporary outsiders "offer both a challenge to and a reinforcement of traditional southern perceptions of place, history, and family" (240); Richard Gray notes that Lan Cao's *Monkey Bridge* in particular "both reflects and refracts common Southern themes and tropes" ("Some Notes" 21). *Monkey Bridge* opens, significantly, with the Vietnamese narrator Mai remembering her work in a Saigon military hospital where she "acted as a scribe, writing down battlefield memories and dying declarations from those war-wounded who were too weak to write letters" (12). But the action of the novel is far removed from wartime Vietnam, set instead in Arlington, Virginia, in 1978, where Mai's traumatic memories of home resurface as a critical context for her negotiation of her place as an immigrant in the South. The lost homeland constitutes a kind of phantom limb for such refugees, whom Mai sees as "not much unlike the physically wounded. They had continued to hang onto their Vietnam lives, caressing the shape of a country that was no longer there, in a way not much different from amputees who continue to feel the silhouette of their absent limbs. Years later, they continued to deny the fact that some tender and unexpendable part of them had been exiled into a space that could not be reached, and so they would continue to live their lives, like my mother, in a long wail of denial" (256). In echoes of southern nostalgia, the kind of somatic memories that Mai and her mother retain uncannily merge Vietnamese and U.S. southern frameworks. The notion of the phantom limb as a lost origin captures the immigrant's anonymity within the black-white South; but it also suggests the disturbing fact that such absence and erasure is what initiates these outsiders most distinctly *as* southerners.

Much like Owens's grisly postcolonial panorama, the world of Lan Cao's *Monkey Bridge* is littered with shattered bodies and tangled histories that import Vietnam's most grisly scenes into an American southern context. From the start, Mai is as geographically and historically disoriented as Cole McCurtain: walking into Arlington Hospital to visit her mother who has just suffered a stroke, she believes she smells the blood and hears the gunshots around the Saigon military hospital, feeling that "everything was unfurling, everything, and I knew I was back there again" (1). The U.S. flag snapping in the breeze reorients her, and she remembers that she is "not in Saigon" and that "it was not 1968 but 1978"; but in the next moment she pivots back again to Vietnam: "I knew, I knew what I would see next. His face, not the face before the explosion, but the face after, motionless in a liquefied red that poured from a tangle of delicate veins" (2). Inexorably, she finds battlefield imagery and danger wherever she looks; the same is true for her mother, whom Mai blames for what she calls her "flawed eye. . . . Through that eye I could see nothing but danger in the phantom landscape" (20). The "phantom landscape" is simultaneously Virginia and Vietnam, the latter a longed-for but brutally marked absence and the former simply a blank without personal history, a template upon which to project these memories of peril. But if it is her mother's eye that Mai sees through, it is also her mother whom she is looking at; that is, these signs of danger are all associated with her mother, relic of the old world and Mai's primary obstacle to realizing a new American existence. Mai's mother complicates Mai's disorientation by weaving a lifelong fabric of half-truths about her origins. Her mother's face is mutilated and scarred like the Saigon soldier's—not by the stroke that landed her in the hospital bed but by a long-ago accident. She lies about the precise cause of the scars, telling Mai that her disfigurement resulted from a kitchen fire; in reality, she was struck with napalm dropped by a plane in a free-fire zone in Vietnam (250–51). Mai looks at her mother in America and sees the past trying to "thrash its way through her flesh" so violently that she "could practically hear the sound of old memories ripping their way through her face" (5, 9). Mai strains to learn the truth of these memories but cannot break through her mother's wall of protective denial and erasure, her very body rendered "a battlefield, she a war wound fastened to a bed in a suburban hospital," as out of place in Virginia as Mai's haunting flashbacks (7).

While these memories introduce a vision of immigrant experience that is painful and fragmented, they suggest further that being "other" in the American South in particular amounts to a new brand of annihilation and vanishing. Immigrants are uncannily like America's own veterans: "as long as America hated its own soldiers, we would never be welcome in this country. . . . Our fate, [Mrs. Bay] believed, was linked cross-eyed with the fate of the GIs themselves" (65). Significantly, newcomers find themselves relegated to the margins of society reserved for figures of weakness, inferiority, and loss; that their fellow pariahs are reminders of an American imperial mission gone disastrously wrong is telling: to preserve national order and health, symbols of such audacity and failure must be repressed. Their ostracism simply makes these new Americans desire inclusion that much more intensely; while Mai finds herself condemned to her mother's memories, she also begins to differentiate herself in a fashion that Cao describes tellingly as "a war" between Asian and European modes of thought (61). Mai sees her mother as the one who cannot adjust and who lacks substance and integrity in an American context: "Both Mrs. Bay and my mother had seemed unreal since the first day they arrived together in this country. . . . In many ways, they continued to live in a geography of thoughts defined by the map of a country that no longer existed in terms I could understand" (66).

Significantly, Mai's "terms" of orientation in this new geography are mathematical and scientific. She knows that the English language itself represents "power" and "authority"; her "temptation to invent" rather than interpret things for her mother illustrates the control she has over the language and thus over her mother (37, 38). Her position as an "outsider with inside information" means that "seeing both sides to everything" she "belonged to neither" (41, 212, 88). Occupying an in-between space is a classically postcolonial condition, one with empowering potential but something Mai feels compelled to master and escape in a typically American southern way—by appealing to the order of logic and positivism. She develops a mania for truth and certainty: "it was the clear-cut, not the complex, that I longed for" (88). She is controlled by "deadlines, sequences that have to be followed," prefers "itemized" lists of information, and finds the "physical sciences . . . a safe, predictable arena"; she sees herself "as implacable and exact as the sciences my father had taught me" (62, 87, 129, 163). Equipped with these tools, she believes she has the power to offer her mother "reality" in

America, but her mother, "imperfect and unable to adjust, died in my mind" (70). What Mai doesn't realize is that the mechanisms she uses to understand her American reality are part of the operations that work to obliterate people like herself and her mother, and that she becomes complicit in this process by mentally erasing her mother's disruptive existence.

The economic world from which such formulas and precision derive is an imperial one: "in effect," Mai knows, "an American trade embargo . . . could make an entire country vanish like an electronic blip from the living pulses of the world's radar screen" (196). In defeat, the United States retaliates with economic sanctions that have the effect of literally blotting out entire populations, not just conceptually but often physically.[12] As Viet Thanh Nguyen and Tina Chen reflect, global capitalism itself is responsible for creating "the conditions of migrancy and re-settlement for many postcolonial Asian populations," bringing Mai's mother and Mrs. Bay to the dubious refuge of American shores, where even Mai's mother is, after all, "seduced into the American Dream" (5,144). She and Mrs. Bay begin to plan a business, envisioning a "courtly, entrepreneurial future for themselves in the here and now of America"; what orients them in their new environment is "the solidity . . . the precision of numbers, the estimate of supply and demand . . . the projected costs and profits, which appeared to be distinctly plausible and remarkably realistic" (166, 167). Significantly, the women can be seen "going over the numbers" at the precise moment when Mai becomes most curious and hungry for information about the past that will unlock the mystery of her mother's person and history; so when she asks these "unanswerable questions," her mother is distracted from them by tinkering with the problems and solutions of her new country: profit margins and account balances (166).

Even if Mai's mother is attempting valiantly to achieve the American Dream, she does not arrive at its calculations and plans entirely cold. That is, what Mai doesn't realize until late in *Monkey Bridge* is that her mother's language of truth and accounting is not so different from the American southern version after all. The mystery that preoccupies Mai and her mother (who becomes a narrator as well in her journal entries) throughout much of the novel is the question: "What had happened to my grandfather? What sort of sorrow is my mother living with?" (166). Baba Quan was supposed to follow them to America but didn't; "'a farmer who loved his land,'" perhaps he had not wanted to leave it, Mai's mother guesses (162). But this is not the real story, and she knows it: the actual circumstances of his absence reveal a history strikingly reminiscent of a southern neoplantation story, a mystery Mai begins to unfurl only by surreptitiously reading her mother's journal. In Vietnam's feudal society, Mai's mother had belonged to a poor tenant family working the land of "*the most powerful landlord in the delta, Uncle Khan,*" a man "*with a relentless passion for raw, hard numbers*" (232, all original italics).¹³ He treats his tenants as quotients in his account book, quick to evict and erase those who do not produce to his satisfaction: *"Mrs. Bay's parents had been among the very first group evicted. All had been crossed off by a line of red ink drawn ruler-straight across the page. In the columns set next to their names were multidigit numbers recording debts still outstanding and finally, in the last column of the same line, the verdict: eviction"* (232–33). Coldly expunged with one stroke of the pen, these poor laborers find themselves utterly bereft and unviable, evicted from the social order and means of production that is essential to their survival. Mai's grandparents enjoy the opposite fate: they *"ceased being mere tenants with rows of black digits by their names"* when Uncle Khan's wife fails to bear children and asks to adopt Mai's mother; the family experiences a *"sudden shift in status, an unexplainable promotion"* in the planter's accounts (174, 233).

At this point Mai's mother's story becomes an immigrant's version of Ike McCaslin's ledger book revelations in Faulkner's *Go Down, Moses*: she discovers that this simple fairy tale of *"unexplainable promotion"* has, like all plantation operations, a very specific and material explanation, one much darker and more tragic than the polite family legend; and like Ike, Mai's mother learns the secret of her family's elevation and her own position of quasi-privilege by sneaking into Uncle Khan's wine cellar and reading his ledger (much as Mai repeats this subterfuge in reading her mother's diary): *"There, in the book of debts . . . I discovered the truth about my life"* (232). What Mai's mother learns is that her parents, desperate to escape *"another year of slaving on other people's rubber and coffee plantations,"* had agreed that her own mother would sleep with Uncle Khan, with the objective of producing something of great value: Mai's mother, the child that Khan's wife cannot bear (234). Mai's grandmother submits to being a concubine out of desperation and hunger, while her grandfather, Baba Quan, is driven instead by a passion for *"possession"* (234). The modest social elevation satisfies, but in the years following the birth of Mai's mother, Baba Quan becomes consumed with *"the thought of reclaiming what had been wrongfully wrested from him [which] began to sough through every fevered fiber of his being"*; he manages for a time to conceal this rage *"behind the cold, calculating doctrine of class warfare between landlord and peasant"* (234). In this world of calculation and antagonism, there is a typically aristocratic desire for *"sweeping, generational wealth"* and the illusion of *"coveting but never owning,"* another classically elite subterfuge to conceal beneath the veneer of natural prosperity the true facts of possession and its human costs. In this context, *"Baba Quan's desires were wholly personal ones, and the world, for him, narrowed and converged into one dark shaft of revenge"* (234). Like Sutpen, his entire existence morphs into an exercise in retribution, one that drives him eventually to become a Vietcong and to plunge a knife into the landlord's throat. Mai's mother witnesses one father murder the other, and all at once *"realized the raw, untamed anguish of a man who had lived his life like a clenched fist, a man who had dreamed of turning a cool hatred into a tormented howl of revenge—against a landlord who had turned his wife into a concubine and taken from him a child who should be rightly his. I understood it clearly as I stood by the river's edge . . . as nothing more than a pristine lesson in class warfare*" (250). The revenge, of course, does not go unpunished; such a "*deeply personal passion . . . always curls back into the reflection of its own anger*" (251). The cruel, cyclical narcissistic lessons in possession are what ultimately destroy Baba Quan, himself murdered too, a victim of the very plantation scheme that utterly dispossesses him from the start and leaves his daughter, Mai's mother, undone as well: "*A part of me died forever by that river's edge, and I have never been able to touch it since*" (250).

But this is a story Mai's mother will never tell her willingly; instead, she writes to her daughter in the secret pages of her journal, confessing by night the awful truths beneath the "*fictional reimaginings*" she invents by day; "*In the lives I constructed for you,*" she confesses, "*Baba Quan was a devoted husband, a father dedicated to an uncomplicated life among the green terraced fields and fresh plowed earth of Ba Xuyen, a farmer who tilled the land with patience and dignity*" (229). In his grown daughter's imaginative longings, Baba Quan becomes a veritable Agrarian rather than a villain forced by poverty and circumstance to the nadir of immorality. Mai only learns the reality of her mother's past and parentage by reading the journal slyly; in the novel, then, the American diary parallels the Vietnamese ledger in uncanny repetition, as both are the fateful books within which two generations of women learn the truth about their convoluted, storied ancestries. The mother's version of truth is no less harmful, then, than Uncle Khan's book of debts with its monster mask on the cover. Even evacuated from the feudal strife that obliterates her past, Mai's mother knows that these stories yet have the power to tear and erase, that history repeats itself quietly and irrevocably, ripping through the body like a cancer: "*Years later, in a room far away from Ba Xuyen, I can sit in my bed, close my eyes, and still hear the wail of ghosts and the cries of demons submerged in the flesh and blood of my body*" (252). In this context, and in light of the actual disfigurement of her napalmed face, the scenes where Mai sees her mother's memories trying to rip through the flesh are haunting; Mai stares at her in wonder, "yearning for a direct connection" (192). Eventually, she receives it: "*Karma is exactly like this, a continuing presence that is as ongoing as Baba Quan's obsession, as indivisible as our notion of time itself. Our reality, you see, is a simultaneous past, present, and future. . . . And that is what I fear. I fear our family history of sin, revenge, and murder and the imprint it creates in our children's lives as it rips through one generation and tears apart the next*" (252). In a world where truth is "*as stark and irreducible as the numbers*" in a ledger book, the journal of revelations bears the terrible weight of a karmic history that still "*divides and subdivides like a renegade cell in the malignant darkness of our lives*" (229).

The ledger bears and discloses the terrible truth of individuals driven to desperation and death by their place within an embattled social and economic order. Ultimately, these books of revelation bring neither peace nor understanding nor certainty, but simply more mystery and alienation for subsequent generations to inherit and hold in their unquiet bodies. The language Mai and her mother share is unwritten and deeply somatic; while Mai's mother thinks she is protecting her daughter by stifling the words and facts of their history, her physical being continues to speak its ravaged truths—not in clear, precise answers but in physical strokes of pain and loneliness and silence. Mai's mother sleeps "in a tight fetal position like a question mark" (194), her refusal to provide answers to the past embodied in her curled, interrogative form as well as her cocoon of unborn newness rather than the annihilations of the old. In a sense, Mai learns nothing more from reading her mother's diary than she already knew: the paradoxical grace of logic and precision and order to combat profound spiritual loneliness and despair. "You need a precise question if you want to elicit a precise answer," the indomitably scientific new American says shortly after seeing her mother's question-mark body (194); it is the pretext for plunging in to ask her mother directly about Baba Quan, a discussion that leads only to more lies. Yet neither the fabrications nor the truths will be the "precise answer" she wants from her mother's mysterious body; neither the past nor the frailties of human memory and survival can be the stark, irreducible truth she covets. In the pages of her diary, Mai's mother asks a question of her own, "*What do you know about your mother, Mai, about the emptiness that has occupied my heart like a persistent squatter hovering in the brooding silence of our lives?*" (229). Everything, Mai might say: that is, despite her best efforts to break free from her mother's karmic fatalism, she knows that she has inherited the "emptiness" her mother suffered, unconnected by history or intimacy to a tangible past or to any person: "would I fail to make an essential human connection that would truly sustain?" Mai wonders (226).

As in so many of the southern narratives *Disturbing Calculations* has reviewed so far, hidden and reconstructed histories haunt the stunted psyches of those lonely souls who labor to go on and begin anew. The immigrant story offers an appropriate parable for the notion of exorcising historical trauma and starting on fresh accounts. But Mai's mother's body is too heavy, her "pores are full" (211), and in the end she turns viciously on the body whose weight she cannot bear; she takes an overdose of sleeping pills and dies with vomit seeping from nose and mouth, the pathetic overflow of all that she had held in tenaciously throughout her life. Mai's reaction tells us that she will neither break away from this past nor eliminate the destructive rage to order that keeps her own body under tight, mathematical control. "Don't look, keep it in, keep it in," she commands herself in bed, denying her own outpouring of grief over her mother's death; "There is always order to tend to, chaos to push swiftly away," she reasons (258, 259). And like Alice Walker's *Meridian*, her final instinct is to feel even her most rebellious self "make a sudden turn in reverse to rush backward into the folds of my mother's womb" (259).

Yet the end of *Monkey Bridge* finds Mai going forward, off to college and "the openness of an unexplored future" (260); nonetheless, she clings still to an order and a past that offers her nothing but loneliness and division. Her American future is, importantly, the most dangerous context within which to plant her family's memories: there, flimsy narratives of order and opportunity find the most hospitable, contaminated ground in which to flourish. And it is a perilous ascent: "all it took was one slip, one step backward across the boundary, and the entire apparatus of American normality could fall right out of sync. The luxury of seamless, unsuperstitious order, after all, did not come without a price" (212). The "price" that Baba Quan, Mai's mother, and Mai herself pay for the "luxury" of their own deliverance from violence and dispossession returns here in the unscrupulous logic of American advancement. What seems to function as a sign of hope in the novel's closing image thus reads more like a chilling harbinger of the depletion to come, the terrible diminishing fate of the immigrant southerner heavy with the burden of multiple histories. Acceptance letter from Mount Holyoke in hand like a "starlight of reassurance," Mai steps outside to see "a faint sliver of what only two weeks ago had been a full moon dangled like a sea horse from the sky" (260). Suspended in plain view at the close of the text and on the threshold of Mai's bright future is an image of rapid deterioration, much like her mother's quick devolution after her stroke, or the way Saigon "collapsed into itself" (100). What is left is the slender curve of a sea horse, a duplicate of the image of Mai's mother curled in bed like a question mark, retreating toward the fetal stage and eventually into death, to a future where the haunting questions and answers of contemporary America's fate hang exhausted but intrepid in the sky, urging its children on despite the fear of total obliteration.

Things Not Seen: The Atlanta Child Murders and the Politics of Erasure

While the faint optimism in Owens's, Awiakta's, and Cao's visions are in part irrepressibly cultural, it takes heroic feats of will and buoyancy to revise centuries of genocide and erasure. Yet these crippled, invisible southerners attempt indomitably to write themselves into a new and healing present, to re-member a history that reconstitutes a whole, regenerative body situated fully in the present moment and in the South. It remains to be seen whether such models and lessons will be heard, and whether or not all of the South's exploited and erased inhabitants will be similarly able to recuperate a sense of integrity and autonomy, to move forward in the face of unbearable trauma and loss. I end this book by turning back purposefully to African American writers facing the continued crippling of their communities in the closing decades of the twentieth century. The Atlanta child murders terrorizing Atlanta's black community in the late 1970s and early 1980s prompted a real and disabling crisis. Much like the fictional serial killings that compel Owens's Cole McCurtain to quest for historical truth and healing, African Americans were forced to dwell imaginatively on the cultural politics not just of the murders themselves, but of the administration's and the community's injurious response to these tragedies—reaction and treatment that, like the murders themselves, seemed to perpetuate their systemic institutional oversight and erasure.[14] James Baldwin's *The Evidence of Things Not Seen* presents a scathing commentary on black oppression in 1980s America brought into sharpened focus by the recent Atlanta child murder case. In the preface Baldwin reveals that

> what I remembered—or imagined myself to remember—of my life in America (before I left home!) was terror. And what I am trying to suggest by what *one imagines oneself to be able to remember* is that terror cannot be remembered. One blots it out. The organism—the human being—blots it out. One invents, or creates, a personality or a *persona*. Beneath this accumulation (rock of ages!) sleeps or hopes to sleep, that terror which memory repudiates.
>
> Yet, it never sleeps—that terror, which is not the terror of death (which cannot be imagined) but the terror of being destroyed.
>
> *Sometimes I think*, one child in Atlanta said to me, *that I'll be coming home from* (baseball or football) *practice and somebody's car will come behind me and I'll be thrown into the trunk of the car and it will be dark and he'll drive the car away and I'll never be found again.*
>
> *Never be found again*: that terror is far more vivid than the fear of death . . . that child *was* myself. (xii)[15]

Baldwin's perception of the trauma of growing up black in America merges imperceptibly with the experience of the Atlanta child murders plaguing urban Atlanta between September 1979 and June 1981, a period during which at least twenty-nine black children and young adults (mostly males) went missing, their raped and beaten bodies later found in area rivers and woods. Like other writers who attempt to document these horrific years in both nonfiction and narrative form, Baldwin describes the Atlanta child's "terror of being destroyed" as not particular but pervasive, an endemic experience within twentieth-century

America's black communities. In the terrorized child of Atlanta's late 1970s and early 1980s, Baldwin sees his own younger self coming of age, poverty-stricken, fifty years earlier in Harlem. In recounting his own acculturation Baldwin asks, "what has this to do with the murdered, missing children of Atlanta?" He answers with controlled rage and grace:

> It has something to do with the fact that no one wishes to be plunged, head down, into the torrent of what he does not remember and does not wish to remember. It has something to do with the fact that we all came here as candidates for the slaughter of the innocents. It has something to do with the fact that all survivors, however they accommodate or fail to remember it, bear the inexorable guilt of the survivor. It has something to do, in my own case, with having once been a Black child in a White country.
> My memory stammers, but my soul is a witness. (xiii)

In the narratives of the Atlanta child murders, America's black writers bear witness not just to a horrific instance of brutality in the contemporary South but to a protracted "slaughter of the innocents" stretching back to the Middle Passage, conjoining on the American continent with the genocide of the resident Natives, and mirrored in the imperial crimes the United States continues to execute in international reigns of terror. Yet how does one "re-member" such comprehensive and disabling trauma when, as Baldwin claims, such "terror cannot be remembered"? How does one unearth memories of mutilation and begin to heal an entire community riven by continued violence and fear?

The idea of re-assembling bodies, construed as a metaphor for postcolonial remembering elsewhere in this chapter, takes on an amplified horror when applied to the literal circumstances of these murders. As Baldwin apologizes, "No degree of imagination or disciplined power of rehearsal can prepare anyone for the unspeakable; and there can be nothing more unspeakable—nor, alas, very probably, more common—than the violence inflicted on children" (49). That this violence is so "common" and so "unspeakable" at the same time makes it chilling: one of Tayari Jones's young protagonists in *Leaving Atlanta* finds herself eventually not "scared anymore. She could eat an entire plate of spaghetti while the newscaster talked about the Missing and Murdered Children" (41). Underlying this numbness is a buried sense of complicity, much like the ambient, perverse guilt that haunts Richard Wright's characters: another young narrator in Jones's novel lies awake in bed pondering "the state of not being . . . because this is certainly where people go when they leave their bodies in the woods for the police to find" (113). In the telling innocence of youth, the active verbs attributed to the murdered child ("*they* leave their bodies in the woods") are haunting. Such complacency, especially among the youngest members of a race expected to bear these endless reels of tragedy, makes urgent works of witness like those by Baldwin, Jones, and Toni Cade Bambara.

The power of these narratives comes paradoxically in their revelations of historical continuity, in the re-membering of a traumatic past much longer and deeper than Atlanta's relatively momentary crisis. In *Those Bones Are Not My Child*, Bambara's protagonist Zala conducts research with other activists who hope to track down the killer themselves; they turn up numerous sources that point steadily backward in time, linking the string of disappearances to the racist crimes so commonplace in the Jim Crow South: "A white woman had written to Missing Persons, among other divisions, to say that her father and his Klan buddies were killing the Atlanta children just as they'd killed numerous Black children in their hometown in North Carolina while she was growing up there" (363). Theories of Klan implication in the Atlanta murders were widely held but never proven despite substantial and explicit evidence, which Bambara sifts through painstakingly in this massive novel. Not only was such proof obscured, but often the reality of the crimes was denied altogether, made to seem an "accident" in the way that blacks in the South might meet a mysterious fate and no one would seem to know what happened. Jones's novel observes this oversight scathingly when her young protagonist's father bitterly repeats the standard explanation: "'An accident like at Birmingham,' Daddy spat. 'Nothing has changed. When they found that little light-skinned boy, the one was just down here visiting from Ohio, all I could think about was Emmett Till'" (76). In fact, Baldwin makes this same connection in his polemic: "it was the thirteenth murder—that of Clifford Jones—that precipitated the (official) hue and cry. Jones, like Emmett Till, in 1955—a comparison I wish neither to force nor avoid—was an out-of-state visitor from what we still call, quaintly, the North. Had he been a 'Mississippi boy,' his bones might yet be irrecoverable at the bottom of the river, or nourishing the earth of various and celebrated Mississippi plantations, to speak only of Mississippi, and saying nothing of subsidies, and without insisting on the official and lethal power of the Southern states in the august and marble halls of Washington" (40). In Baldwin's critique as well as Bambara's and Jones's narratives, southern blacks' value is still figured as waste, manure for plantations, their bones otherwise invisible and "irrecoverable"; moreover, "what we still call, quaintly, the North" is a separate space that is in no practical sense indicative of a different character or deserving of a different appellation than the South. While Atlanta may seem to be the South's most progressive, metropolitan, least "southern" city—indeed, "The City Too Busy to Hate"—its roots are firmly immured in both the history and the reality of slavery and Jim Crow's most outrageous abuses.

The reality of black and especially southern black impoverishment and suppression sketched by Baldwin weighs heavily on Bambara's and Jones's narratives as well. Significantly, the mechanisms for controlling and dispossessing the African American community are economic and mathematical; in one of the many film reels combed through as potential evidence by Zala and the other activists throughout *Those Bones*, a white woman leans against a Rolls Royce as she announces her participation in a task force to research "troublesome groups" in order to make "those groups become less troublesome" (409). One hears the "Negro problem" resonating in her manicured paternalism; and not surprisingly, the research employed to combat this "problem" group includes statistics, tables, graphs—all in the service of "helping" the black community become less of a "burden" on the American welfare system (410–11). What masquerades as assistance is ultimately an orchestrated use of white surveillance and scientism to deprive black families of support in the guise of rehabilitating them. The white woman summates that "Blacks are an emotional people. They do not respond to facts or care about who's conducting research and compiling statistics. They do, however, respond to charges of low morals and poor family life" (410). In an effort to use these perceived values against them, the researchers compile statistics on teen pregnancies, illegitimacy, and "other perniciousness" with the end result being "that those babies should be separated from those young people who cannot care for even themselves" (411).[16] What may otherwise be seen as a throwaway scene in the midst of a 669-page novel gathers disturbing resonance in the context of this study: in effect, the woman admits to using biased statistical evidence to justify and engineer both material impoverishment and kidnapping. In a narrative about child murders and the politics of economic and racial erasure, the connection is chilling.

While such organizations were strategically devoting a self-interested kind of attention and resources to the African American community, Atlanta's local administration was disconcertingly tentative in its reaction to the murder rampage. Puzzling to many was the fact that the administration itself was largely African American. When in 1973 Maynard Jackson became the first black mayor of Atlanta—indeed, of any major southern city—he "ushered in, as folks were prone to say, the Second Reconstruction" (Bambara 16). Yet his administration's and the police response to the terror-stricken community and parents betrayed an ongoing, deeply ingrained sense that economic prosperity would invariably trump all else, even a potential race war. At the time Atlanta was becoming the South's mecca of commerce and "the country's third-busiest convention center" (Bambara 16). Indeed, the city "too busy to hate" was also too busy to stop and jeopardize its substantial financial operations; these priorities resulted in mystified equations of power, "fact sheets" and bodies of evidence riddled with "factual errors" and "discrepancies" (Bambara 16). The suspected killer was arrested and hustled through a trial, and quickly this light-skinned black man named Wayne Williams was convicted of two seemingly unrelated murders; the judicial system and the public assumed him to be responsible for the rest. The crisis was declared over. But many people remained unconvinced of Williams's guilt for the apparently unconnected murders, never mind for the child killings. Bambara describes the uneasy aftermath: "officialdom had erased the terror of months before by planting the 'no more listed' equals 'no more killed' equation in the public mind. . . . Memory was being rubbed out by the official erasure as gray settled in all over the city" (Bambara 573). Yet the reality of "fresh kills" continued even after the murderer was "officially" caught, signifying a deep mistrust in the simple, elegant, obliterating algebra of authority. In a brutally realistic vein, Williams was portrayed as a black-hating narcissist who would appear to have performed the actions that James Weldon Johnson's ex-coloured narrator fantasizes about: to exterminate the black underclass by "shooting and burning them off." In this sense, it matters little whether or not Williams actually committed the crimes, but it does matter that so many people in Atlanta's administration and the U.S. public needed to believe that he had.[17]

Near the end of Bambara's novel, Zala and Spence miraculously find their missing son. At first he is so traumatized that he will not reveal what has happened to him, but ultimately he confesses that he "had been sold to a slave gang of boys and forced to work on a plantation that outsiders thought was a state-run reform school. This last part seemed a tacked-on improvisation in answer to Kofi [his younger brother]'s question how come the mailman or the meter readers of the neighbors didn't think it was weird that two white men had a bunch of Black boys living with them" (528). No one noticed because the situation, horrifyingly anachronistic as it is, apparently seemed so natural that it didn't raise alarm bells at all. His abduction is obviously not related to the killing spree dominating the headlines, but like Louis Owens's compounded murder mystery, Sonny's experience functions as a parallel epidemic extending the current trauma to astonishing proportions and relating it to an ongoing legacy of plantation trauma. The children detained with Sonny are not just from Atlanta but, as he explains, from "all over. Was some people there spoke only Spanish. And some that spoke only island French" (601). Wrapped here into the experience of racial subjugation are representatives from a broader panorama of global southern colonialism, a composite postplantation society still driven by white progress and prosperity and operated by individuals stolen and lost to their own communities, their subjection and captivity unseen by oblivious outsiders. Throughout *Those Bones*, Bambara calls out for recognition and identification of the bones not just of Atlanta's lost youths but of all the forgotten children of postemancipation, postdesegregation U.S. history. When the protagonist recovers her son, "she looked at him squarely, to show that she could, to show that whatever he'd been through he was seeable"

(518). In this boy aptly named Sonny to conjure all of the missing sons, Bambara not only makes visible but attempts to resurrect the exploited and forgotten children who never will come home.

As in Owens's *The Sharpest Sight* and Lan Cao's immigrant perspective, Vietnam emerges in Bambara's work as a parallel and revealing instance of the fatal tendency of the United States to pursue imperial conflicts, its international iterations rendering its domestic crimes even more bleak and sobering. Throughout his engagement with the murder investigation, Spence, a Vietnam vet, is plagued by memories of combat; in a section dated "Tuesday, February 10, 1981" he is haunted by an issue of *Newsweek* from the previous month, in which "testimony from brothers who'd been in the Charlie Company hadn't been quite on the mark. Edited with a heavy hand, Spence supposed," the "stories and pictures . . . both sickening and protective," leaving him desperate to undo the "click that had ghosted the bones, that had captured the smile" (349, 353). In much the same way that the children prove disposable, the black veterans are "edited" unfairly, misrepresented and erased. At local political events, "the TV cameras worked around to blot us out"—not just the black vets, but "other Black men, Black women, and youngsters" (442). Their survival is a grim triumph over the poverty of choice, the persistent lack of opportunity that drives men like Spence to enlist in a suicidal cause: "In '69," he remembers, "the benches at the induction center had been lined with brothers. His platoon was three quarters Black. The casualty list was four-fifths Black. Not one officer of color on the set. Always Bloods on points, Bloods on the front line" (351). The mathematics of despair, disregard, and waste here are abundantly clear; it is also evident that the power of editing the equations and the ghosting of bones resides somewhere beyond the agency of these black soldiers.

Spence can't help but see Vietnam in Atlanta; the southern city becomes a palimpsest of mutilation and destruction: "for a long time he could never be sure what he was looking at from moment to moment . . . Bodies hung on wire. . . . White phosphorous figures dropping pongi sticks and running down the road of Quang Ngai, flesh flapping like old wallpaper. . . . But there were no spongy gobs of lung on the dashboard, no gray spatter on his sleeve. He was still breathing" (354–55). Yet under the circumstances that breath seems tenuous; he knows that his life back home is as endangered as it was on the road of Quang Ngai, as perilous as Sonny's existence hanging in the balance. He can't help connecting the grisly memories of combat with his worst fears about his son's disappearance; he even thinks he sees "Sonny ducking under a tree and disappearing into a black hole that looked like a doorway in 'Nam about to receive a fragged lob" (646). The possibility of annihilation haunts, enveloping Spence's worries for his son: "thinking about Sonny, thinking about POW training—had he told his son that the best time to escape was in the first few hours of capture?—and thinking about his buddy, who'd say, 'Yeah, sometimes I think I died over there too.' Spence had sat in the limo surrounded by woods and wept over his dead self" (350). It seems no coincidence that entire groups of black vets band together to join in the grassroots attempts to find the child killer, their efforts contributing both to the community and to their own sense of survival and agency. They know what it is like to be lost, abducted by white American authority, "reported missing by their families . . . tracked down not by Missing Persons but by other vets who knew what to look for" (77). Their alliance with the missing children's parents is a natural one, but the larger panorama of erasure into which it fits is disturbing—one where the "official" narrative always attempts to obscure and erase the true version, the one filled with nightmares and hallucinations and mangled bodies. As one of Spence's fellow vets and activists says, "we're both trying to outrun the ghosts who want to make us ghosts" (384).

In a novel about "ghosting the bones" of African Americans on a number of levels, the activists and Bambara alike steadily resist this erasure by continuing to hunt, to fight, and to speak. By having her protagonists find their son, Bambara resurrects the erased children who never will come home; she reverses the history of all the Atlanta mothers who would call "Missing Persons" and be told "to call Homicide" instead. Hearing this recording, Zala "could not even move to write down the number; her thermometer stuck at zero" (61). So Bambara takes the pen and writes for her, pushing past zero and into the sweat of physical agency and the rising barometer of the living. And then she offers the pen to the reader: the anonymous mother in her prologue, identified only (and purposefully) as "you," keeps a journal of "overheards and ruminations about men, women, and children mysteriously vanishing from the community . . . in between entries about books, movies, jobs, meetings, and your dreams" (15). As the number of murders increases, the journal is overtaken by "entries on the case," recorded in a wine-colored spiral notebook that "your" daughter repeatedly mistakes for her math notebook; "you" open the notebook and wonder how your daughter "fared in fifth-period math with your Missing and Murdered notes" (15). As one woman's writing overtakes the systemic equations of authority and overwrites the "official" facts and narratives of erasure, Bambara extends the invitation to all who will read her novel and record the truth and the survival of the black community.

Perhaps, in the end, that is the most hopeful directive these narratives impart: not to erase the histories of calculation, commodification, and erasure, but to take them to school and learn from them; not to wipe the ledger pages clean, but to write over them; not to forget the South's brutal crimes and its terrible revisitations upon generation after generation thereafter, but to remember—and re-member—those silenced, exploited, lost, and obliterated within its meticulously ruled pages.

Conclusion

Disturbing the Calculation

She did not care for money. She wanted to disturb.
OLYMPIA VERNON, *LOGIC*

As we have seen, the crisis of transition to market capitalism and industrial progress in the twentieth-century South prompted intense regional reflection on the catalog of dispossessions the region had incurred during emancipation, Reconstruction, the Great Depression, and finally desegregation. In this accumulation of losses, southerners register a profound sense of foreclosure at the same time that they hunger and strive for restitution and recompense. Throughout *Disturbing Calculations* we have witnessed various examples of narcissistic, fetishized calculations in the service of allaying this sense of regional, spiritual, and personal destitution; but faced with the inequities of colonialism, capitalism, and racism perpetuated by the national market, the quest for solvency becomes a bitter exercise in futility by the end of the twentieth century. Even the most hopeful gestures toward communal remembering in chapter 5 have practical limits: they can mend only textually the bodies, spirits, and psyches fractured and exploited in persistently literal ways. Eventually, the pain of division and calculation becomes the only measure of certainty, of one's "place" in a prescribed social order and often of one's mere humanity.

This is not solely a southern plight or an American one. I have focused on the South here simply because the South has focused on the South for so long, and in doing so has institutionalized the peculiarities of its history; in the same way but for different needs, the North too continues to preserve its own version of the South's exceptionalism—a portrait that helps to characterize and elevate the North over its abject national Other, a phenomenon that C. Vann Woodward, among others, explains in *American Counterpoint*. Such prejudices affect literary reception as well: as Thadious Davis notes in "Sashaying through the South," American readers still maintain "a desire to have the South fixed and frozen in imagination, aesthetics, and race" (61).[1] Such desires create stories, and these narratives (literary and otherwise) in turn influence the very character and identity of the region. Yet now more than ever, that identity seems indistinguishable from the character and values of the nation at large. In his substantial investigation of southern history and distinctiveness, David Goldfield issues a prediction: "What we will become as a nation in this century will depend very much on what happens in the South" (*Still Fighting* 13). Goldfield finds this prospect "both encouraging and frightening"—the former because the region has demonstrated "a great capacity to initiate and experience great change," yet frightening because "at the same time, there is a darkness in the southern soul," an unreconstructed, back-looking idealism that refuses to disappear (13). I share Goldfield's pessimism, but the difference—and perhaps the hope—in my view lies in seeing this doom not as a southern pathology but as a symptom of a national and increasingly global illness. The South's agonized and ambivalent transition to capitalism teaches us more about the dangers of the new order than the perversions of the old.

Few northerners would want to admit that Malcolm X was right when he claimed that "Mississippi was anywhere in the United States south of the Canadian border," but the best work on regional studies is acknowledging that the power of region is increasingly irrelevant and impotent in a world of global capitalism and injustice.[2] The North, it turns out, harbors its own, similarly discriminatory logic and practices, as Jesse Jackson implied in his critique of an economically and racially segregated Boston during a visit to the 2004 Democratic National Convention, an assessment that angered self-congratulatory liberal Yankees.[3] Yet few can dispute that such inequities exist simply because we would rather not see them. The persistence of categorical, fractional, and divisional thinking in contemporary America more broadly makes studies like this one necessary and urgent. The scope of such an analysis might well be expanded to include deeper examinations of the effects of the U.S. market and imperialism, and of other nations crippled by histories and legacies of slavery, colonialism, and capitalism.

It is difficult to deny the imbalances that persist in America's free market, where the Horatio Alger myth crumbles beneath the reality of ingrained racism and sexism. *The Pursuit of Happyness*, the 2006 film version of Christopher Gardner's rags-to-riches autobiography of the same name, is so affecting precisely because its narrative is so extraordinary: a homeless African American man breaks into Wall Street by sheer force of determination and will. Significantly, the Hollywood version of this story evades entirely any reflection whatsoever on Gardner's race, yet it is an unspoken assumption that the same story told about a poor white would not be nearly so exceptional and moving. Such tacit complicities saturate our increasingly self-interested culture, where outrage is stirred only when our own wallets suffer from skyrocketing gas prices or taxes. Yet the wealthier Americans become, Thomas Shapiro argues in *The Hidden Cost of Being African American*, the more radically unequal is the distribution of that wealth. As long as we live lives of relative comfort, we can afford not to see through the fetish of accumulation that makes us believe we have it all, and that those who have less simply matter less. Perhaps it will take a devastating economic blow to shatter the pervasive narcissism of prosperity that continues to haunt and drive American culture.

Such fatalism would hardly seem to allow for hope. The answer, so far as I can tell, is not to eschew the crass materialism of American capitalism in a facile way, as many modern southerners clung to their bygone antebellum virtues by denying an interest in money; while this impulse may be sincere, it is hardly pragmatic. The country must face the culture and the economy that controls it, much as the South had to do in the twentieth century. And just as the South thus gained a clearer, if darker, perspective on what it had been and what it was becoming, so too might Americans better understand the terms and figures of our embroilment and our potential for change. But if our discourse remains attached to a system that evacuates humanity of all substance and hope, can our words ever be subversive? Does number have the potential to disrupt authority, or does it always necessarily serve it? If capitalism and mathematics are a language that require our faith as citizens, can we simply choose not believe in them? As Elizabeth Alexander hopes, "sometimes we encounter truths in culture not necessarily verifiable against census records or voting rolls" (x). It may take a massive force of will, but perhaps "truth" in the twenty-first century can indeed be unhitched from scientific and mathematical and economic measures and united instead with the humanitarian principles that Americans (and especially southerners) have always prized but have not always prioritized.

Perhaps the unexamined logic of American capitalism and its mathematical transparency constitute an elaborate fiction that can be denied and overwritten, just as the South's own dark narratives have been steadily, if at times reluctantly, supplanted. As Bhabha notes, the nation derives its strength from unity and memory; but this force may be disrupted by the colonial subject who "forgets to remember" the region's past and who threatens to undo the homogeneous nation with "the danger of numbers" (161). In the same way that the dominant class diminishes its perceived others, the marginalized might cultivate among themselves a calculated, collective "will to forget" which would rend a hole, a "minus-in-origin," in the national narrative, denying and erasing the coercive stories and justifications on which homogeneous unity rests. Instead of being damaging, this "minus" has subversive potential to "disturb the calculation of power and knowledge" (163). Literature may not be the most potent of weapons, but in this case its power is primary. Just as narratives about southern exceptionalism and American innocence have had such transformative power over our lived realities, so too might the opposite effect be possible. We may not be able to undo the material inequities that inspire the disturbing calculations of our selves, but perhaps we can transform the narratives that make them so vital to our perceptions of character, place, and fundamental human value. In this way, the literature of the modern South teaches us all we may ever need to know about both the peril and the promise of change.

Notes

Introduction: The Fetish of Number

1. For a comprehensive overview of the emergence of the concept of fetish, see Pietz's excellent three-part account of fetishism in these "primitive" societies and religions; Budge, *From Fetish to God in Ancient Egypt*; Milligan, *Fetish Folk of West Africa*; Ellis, *Land of Fetish*; and Anne McClintock, "Psychoanalysis, Race, and Female Fetishism," in *Imperial Leather* 181–203.

2. For Marx's idea of commodity fetishism, see Marx, *Kapital*, vol. 1, ch. 1, sec. 4.

3. Freud specifically roots his theory of the fetish in the concept of female castration, wherein the woman's supposed horror over the lack of a penis compels the compensation or substitution of that lack with a fetish object that conceals the difference that we know to be true but need for some reason to deny and correct. See Freud's "Fetishism" in *Standard Edition* 21:152–58, and his "Unsuitable Subjects for the Sexual Object—Fetishism," in *Three Essays on the Theory of Sexuality*, in *Standard Edition* 7:125–245.

4. Lacan later revises Freud's account of fetishism by emphasizing its symbolic or linguistic significance (versus its specifically physical or visual nature), thus elevating the notion of the symbolic phallus over the actual penis. Both Freud and Lacan tend to agree that sexual fetishism is primarily a male phenomenon; recent works by Emily Apter and William Pietz and by Lorraine Gamman and Merja Makinen have taken issue with this assumption, suggesting the abundant relevance of fetishism to female psychology. Also, as Anne McClintock suggests in *Imperial Leather*, "the denial of female fetishism . . . is less an accurate description than a theoretical necessity that serves to disavow the existence of female sexual agency except on terms prescribed by men" (183).

5. For a full explanation of Bhabha's definition of the colonial fetish, including its origins in the theories of Edward Said and Frantz Fanon, see Bhabha, "The Other Question: Stereotype, Discrimination and the Discourse of Colonialism," in *Location of Culture* 66–84.

6. In his own extensive work on narcissism, Heinz Kohut went much further than Freud in his attempt to show that narcissism was not pathological but rather a common condition that simply needed to be understood and integrated into proper behavior and personality patterns. As Allen M. Siegel notes, "It has been said that Kohut did for narcissism what Dickens did for poverty: he legitimized it" (60).

7. Lasch sees the American narcissist as hampered by a "pervasive despair of understanding the course of modern history or of subjecting it to rational direction" (xiii). While he contends that modern American narcissists have no use for the past, a sure sign of cultural "bankruptcy," he seems not to have factored the obsessively back-looking southerner into his equation (xviii). But the southerner, in a way, fits the model nonetheless: while he does continue to invest his psychic energies in the past, he seems to have only a dawning awareness of the "course of modern history" or the "rational direction" guiding one system of capital fluidly and nightmarishly into the next. The world of consumer emptiness and despair that he attempts to keep at bay is, effectively, the same lost order that he seeks so desperately to retreat to.

8. There is a long tradition of using the concept of narcissism to examine the U.S. South after emancipation. Perhaps most well known is W. J. Cash, who in his *Mind of the South* famously described the white southerner as a kind of Narcissus who "hated [the South] with the exasperated hate of a lover who cannot persuade the object of his affections to his desire. Or, perhaps more accurately, as Narcissus, growing at length analytical, might have suddenly begun to hate his image reflected in the pool" (387). Just as Quentin's profession that "I don't hate the South!" is, as countless critics have understood, riddled with ambivalence and a tortured attachment to the perverse shaping power of his childhood home, Cash also recognizes the ambivalence with which southerners apprehended the loss of status, prosperity, and racial clarity that went along with integration into a national state. As Cash seems acutely aware, the South's particular brand of narcissism was entrenched in an ideology of dispossession, desire, and fantasies of recuperation, engendering a frustrated desire for a potential and unrequited ideal. This entailed, in many ways, a yearning not just for the restoration of a plantation economy but for an equal share in the wealth that the North had and wielded over the debased South. In their narcissistic fantasies of recompense and accumulation, however, these southerners betray stubborn attachments to the plantation and chattel system.

There have been more recent critical uses of narcissism to critique modern southern community and literature. As Jonathan Smith has persuasively argued, southern efforts to invent a hierarchical and fantastical "community," history, and regional distinctiveness in the twentieth century utilize patently narcissistic methods of mirroring and projection. Smith also argues that southern culture asserts itself regularly in moments of fetishism and object-cathexis. His thesis is at least partially indebted, as is mine, to Julius Rowan Raper's earlier argument that southern guilt, fragmentation, and "narcissistic rage" seek remedies in modern southern literature; however, I disagree with his assessment that the region's "extraordinary sense of place" accomplishes this feat (9).

9. In *Dark Continents*, a recent attempt to draw together psychoanalysis and postcolonialism—indeed, to redefine psychoanalysis as a "colonial discipline" (ix)—Ranjana

Khanna notes that postcolonial theory has "frequently rejected psychoanalysis, objecting with some justification that it imposed a uniform notion of self onto the world," and that its infrequent attempts to engage psychoanalytic theory have generally been Lacanian (xii). Though Khanna does not mention Bhabha in this context, it would seem that Bhabha's frequent use and revision of Freud would be a notable exception.

10. See Bhabha 61, 76–77, and Fanon.

11. The coincidence of narcissism and fetishism does not begin with postcolonial theory but in fact has its roots in Freud, Lacan, and E. E. Pritchard. For a full explanation of these precedents and the clinical role of fetish in narcissism, see Béla Grunberger, "On Fetishism," in *New Essays on Narcissism* 139–66.

12. Ovid's original myth in fact includes Narcissus's Echo/other counterpart as an inextricable, marginalized double in an endless power play of articulation and repetition: Echo, who can be summoned to represent the voice of the oppressed, cannot originate but can only replicate language; she can manipulate Narcissus's words slightly, exercising some small degree of agency, but she is bound to the only text at her disposal. Still, a chiasmic relationship between the two reveals how intimately Narcissus is bound to Echo as well, how deeply she undermines his own fantasy of holism: he willfully represses the reality that this spurned "other" is, in fact, a reflection of himself at least as important as his beloved watery image. Importantly, language emblematizes this struggle: Echo cannot summon a voice to express her desire for Narcissus, and Narcissus fails to recognize his own words emanating from Echo's body: Narcissus speaks first, supplying the words that Echo literally cannot, and Echo responds by repeating and reversing his phrase: "*dixerat 'ecquis adest?' et 'adest' responderat Echo*" (Ovid, *Metamorphoses*, Book 3, l.380).

13. Anne Goodwyn Jones is optimistic when she suggests that the marginalized resort to narcissism "'not as exaggerated self-esteem but as a refusal to judge the self by alien, objective means, a willed inability to allow the world to play its customary role in the business of self-evaluation'" (291). But while attempts at self-possession are inherently laudable triumphs, minorities often find themselves locked into a discourse whose terms are neither inviolate nor innocuous. Lured by the promise of wholeness and value, emancipated and liberated others are unable to divorce themselves from either needing or desiring the dominant indices of American status and inclusion: money, class, culture, and advancement.

14. At its core, the plea for anticommercial humanism and land stewardship, divorced from its racial implications, continues to have lasting appeal; but contemporary readers and critics are well aware that the Old South's mores and its materiality cannot be disentangled. As Persky reminds us, "to restore the South's 'humanism' necessarily meant to deal with the region's material conditions" (118). Indeed, the manifesto was so explicitly racist and regressive that it troubled many readers, even some conservative southerners (Persky 125).

15. As Leigh Anne Duck notes, W. Béran Wolfe once judged that the Great Depression incited "a sweeping identity crisis" whose "effect 'on the average American man and woman has been almost identical with the collapse of a romantic notion in the life plan of a blustering, overly aggressive adolescent'" (50). For this "collapse" to have been so

dramatic and the "identity crisis" so totalizing, one must assume that Americans had long identified and measured their very selves in terms of cash, privilege, and prosperity. Wolfe's remark in particular points out the aggressively "romantic," immature, narcissistic character of the American attachment to money. Southerners were emphatic in their claims that their own identity was, on the contrary, refined and community oriented rather than cash driven. Yet, as John Temple Graves notes, the 1930s represented a decade "at the end of which . . . the South was more aware of itself as a region than it had been since 1861," and "a good part of that awareness turned on [its] economic plight" (qtd. in Tindall 20). Dependent on the North in a relationship similar to that of a colony, the already struggling South suffered doubly from the further privation of a national depression. Forced to participate in a national economy that it perceived as inimical to southern values, the South viewed its penurious state as a matter of principle rather than inferiority.

16. A pioneering study in the economic methodology now known as "cliometrics," Fogel and Engerman's exposé offended many who assumed they were effectively arguing in favor of slavery as a profitable institution. Fogel responded with a three-volume work called *Without Consent or Contract* that defends and clarifies his earlier position while arguing that slavery was inherently immoral.

17. Mark M. Smith's *Debating Slavery* provides a thorough overview of how various historians have understood and debated the economic character of antebellum slavery.

18. The legacies of a business-minded agrarianism could be seen well into the twentieth century and beyond the South as well; as Maureen Flanagan reports, "American farmers were . . . 'ambitious, individualistic, and desirous of acquiring means and property.' American farmers were capitalists at heart. They could not envision actually moving outside the system into one of true social democracy" (149).

19. Stephen Hahn examines the transition to capitalism after abolition in his "Emancipation and Development of Capitalist Agriculture." He notes that "while the abolition of slavery and servile labor ended up accelerating the development of capitalist agriculture most everywhere abolition took place, it propelled the South most quickly and fully down that road" (74).

20. For more on the South's post-Reconstruction economic colonialism, see G. Wright, *Old South, New South Revolutions in the Southern Economy Since the Civil War*; Woodward, "The Colonial Economy" in *Origins of the New South*; M. Rothstein, "New South and the International Economy."

21. See Bryant, *Twentieth-Century Southern Literature* 4–5.

22. On the South's post–World War I state, see Cash, *Mind of the South*.

23. Vance, *Human Geography of the South*.

24. One such observation about the colonial economy was Howard Odum, in his 1936 sociological study, *Southern Regions of the United States*, calling the South "essentially colonial in its economy." A separate body of literature arose that viewed the colonial state of North-South relations as a situation of deliberate manipulation and advantage taking; see, for example, Webb, *Divided We Stand*; in 1964 Tindall reports, "Clarence H. Danhof criticized the concept of the colonial economy as touched with paranoia" (220)—that this comment seemed timely in the 1960s is an instructive example of the persistence

of this thinking, and perhaps also the aftereffects of its conditioning. Roosevelt's letter is reprinted at the start of the United States Emergency Council's *Report on Economic Conditions of the South*.

25. According to Krips, fetishism may indeed announce "a form of regression—not to a return to childish innocence, but rather a resurfacing of knowledge repressed in the transition to adulthood" (23). In a southern context, such resurfacings often indicate a repressed knowledge of a perverse past always already colonized by the priorities of the plantation ledger.

26. For a fuller explanation of Frederickson's position, as well as a distillation of the main figures and arguments in this debate, see *Arrogance of Race*, esp. 154–60.

27. See C. Harris, "Whiteness as Property."

28. In the passage I've quoted at length below from *Life and Labor in the Old South*, Phillips professes to use the "figures" and "records" of antebellum history not to "generalize" or stereotype, but to portray "the personal equation" recorded in slavery's logs. Yet as C. Vann Woodward notes, "the 'stereotypes' he attacked were those that pictured the old regime as one of unmitigated cruelty, baseness, and inhumanity" (intro. to Philips iv). Phillips relies on the records simply to return to the moral "truth" of slavery and to justify its paternalism. The following passage from Phillips is additionally interesting because he uses the language of mathematics and accounting so frequently: "A cartographer 'generalizes' a river course if its meanders are not known in detail or if they are too small to be shown in his reduction. A merchant generalizes his customers when he prints an advertisement, and a physician, when classing his patients. . . . The practice is not merely convenient but necessary. . . . The past, however, may remind us on occasion that its people were not lay figures but men, women, and children of flesh and blood, thought and feeling, habits and eccentricities, in the grip of circumstance and struggling more or less to break it. Traditions are simple, conditions were complex; and to get into the records is to get away from the stereotypes. It is from the records and with a sense of the personal equation that I have sought to speak" (vii–viii).

29. Philips was not alone: as Eugene Genovese documents, since the 1850s skilled and learned southern thinkers, legislators, and theologians had attempted to place slavery within a comparative world history that defended the institution on moral and scriptural grounds while demonizing its wage-labor alternative as merely "a morally obnoxious form of white slavery and a doomed historical aberration" ("South in the History" 8). Perhaps the most vociferous of these advocates was the outspoken proslavery figure George Fitzhugh whose 1854 manifesto *Sociology for the South; or, The Failure of Free Society* and 1857 follow-up *Cannibals All!; Or Slaves Without Masters* attacked the foundations of modern liberalism and capitalism in Europe and America.

30. *The Mathematical Manuscripts of Karl Marx*, written in 1881 but published in English translation a century later, in 1983, show Marx working through his own understanding of mathematics and how it might be used to better understand and depict the workings of modern capitalism.

31. See Swetz, *Capitalism and Arithmetic*.

32. See Baudrillard, *Mirror of Production*.

33. See Samuelson, *Foundations of Economic Analysis*.

34. For a comprehensive overview of the history of mathematics, see the classic *History of Mathematics* by Florian Cajori or the more recent *History of Mathematics* by David M. Burton.

35. Gottfried Wilhem Leibniz, a seventeenth-century German philosopher, in particular adapted his foundational knowledge of differential calculus to a mode of logic that would stand up to scientific proof. For more on Leibniz's mathematical logic, see *G. W. Leibniz: Philosophical Essays*, ed. Ariew and Garber; *G. W. Leibniz: De Summa Rerum: Metaphysical Papers*, ed. Parkinson; Russell, *A Critical Exposition of the Philosophy of Leibniz*; and Ishiguro, *Leibniz's Philosophy of Logic and Language*.

36. Antonio Benítez-Rojo describes a resistance to master calculations in Caribbean contexts. In *The Repeating Island* he argues that postcolonial spaces like the Caribbean develop a culture that is performative, a patchworked multicultural resistance to postindustrial science and technology; such a subversive character can be usefully extrapolated to describe other American colonial spaces as well. The rebellious hybridity of both race and culture in a colonial society make it inimical to classification and quantification; yet, as we have seen, such strategies were endemic to plantation culture and did not disappear easily.

37. Mathematics as a discipline has long seemed incapable of such destructive ends, appearing universal and "culture-free": "After all," Alan J. Bishop recalls in "Western Mathematics," "the popular argument went, two twos are four . . . and all triangles have angles which add up to 180 degrees. These are true statements the world over" (51). But Bishop finds, as do Faulkner and Wolfe, that "two twos" might indeed be five, might in fact be countless things other than four—that is, that despite colonial schools' efforts to perpetuate a system of mathematics with clear Western, imperial, Euclidean origins, there remains the possibility that "alternative mathematical systems" might exist in response to different cultural conceptions of space, perspective, and logic (52). Math in the abstract loses its neutrality and becomes instead "one of the most powerful weapons" in colonial pedagogy (51); when used as a metaphorical tool to alter, quantify, and homogenize human worth and impose hierarchical boundaries, its implications can be devastating. Mary Poovey's work on mathematics, particularly that used in accounting systems, offers useful paradigms for considering such figures as repositories of human knowledge and the ability to measure and quantify the world about us. Such equations become vitally important in the South, particularly when the differences between races and classes become difficult to see and quantify; when the other becomes incalculable, so too does the self. For more, see her *History of the Modern Fact*.

38. For more on maps as colonial tools, see Boelhower, *Through a Glass Darkly*, and Huggan, *Territorial Disputes*.

39. In "Indians and Blacks in White America," Charles Crowe quotes Jefferson: "nothing will reduce those wretched so soon as pushing the war into the heart of their country. But I would not stop there. I would never cease pursuing them while one of them remained on this side of the Mississippi. . . . [They] are a useless, expensive, and ungovernable ally" (156). Note the language of use value and reduction that Jefferson employs here. As Arthur H. DeRosier Jr. reports, in the late eighteenth century Thomas Jefferson

instructed the government to begin selling goods to Indians on credit and to take their lands as payment (85). In this way, the Indians were initiated into a calculus of economic exchange that was out of keeping with their cultural practice and distinctly against their interests; but to give it the more palatable guise of fair trade, the illusion of mathematical and economic precision was implemented: "to facilitate debt [Jefferson] offered unlimited credit" (86). Later attempts to dispossess and divide Indian land, specifically the Dawes Act of 1887, also operated on the premise of equality and goodwill: they signified attempts to endow Native Americans with the "white" privilege of land ownership. These gestures, like slavery, were justified by a sense of moral superiority and advanced civility, a calculus of reason supported by these economic factors as well; as Vine Deloria recounts in *Custer Died for Your Sins*, this "white world of abstract symbols became a nightmare for Indian people" (16).

40. Postcolonial theory has already been of tremendous use in helping us to view American slavery, segregation, and the internal colonization of indigenous tribes as chilling reminders of the United States' brutal settlement chronicles and lastingly imperial character, producing provocative works by Arnold Krupat, Anne McClintock, Malini Johar Schueller, Edward Watts, Houston A. Baker Jr., and recently, John Cullen Gruesser.

41. In August 2005, Hurricane Katrina devastated much of southeastern Louisiana and coastal Mississippi, flooding many towns along the Gulf Coast and over 80 percent of New Orleans, and killing almost two thousand individuals. As Jed Horne argues in *Breach of Faith*, the storm revealed the glaring gaps between rich and poor and black and white in twentieth- and twenty-first-century America: "Rich people died along with the indigent. . . . [But] that did not make Katrina an 'equal opportunity destroyer,' as some hastened to call it. Poor blacks did disproportionately more of the dying. And as the engines of recovery creaked into gear, people of mean enjoyed advantages that had been theirs all along" (xv).

42. I find this conviction appealing because I write from the hopeful perspective that identifying and deconstructing the tools facilitating the consent and marginalization of disenfranchised others within the structures of contemporary global capitalism can have profound consciousness-altering effects.

43. Midterm elections in November 2006 shifted the balance of power in U.S. Congress by the slimmest margin from a twelve-year Republican majority; Democrats were able to gain back seats in the South, and Tennessee's moderate, Democratic, and African American candidate Harold Ford surprised the American public by running a fierce and nearly successful campaign against the white businessman and former mayor Bob Corker. As a posting on the weblog *Facing South* declared, "Two pictures emerge from this and other data. One is that the Republican Party is increasingly the party not of 'the South' in general, as some pundits claim, but *older, wealthy and white Southern voters*" (Kromm, original emphasis).

44. Patricia Cohen's article commented on Jason Sokol's *There Goes My Everything*, Matthew Lassiter's *The Silent Majority*, and Kevin M. Kruse's *White Flight*.

45. In addition to the important comparative and postcolonial works offered by Smith, Cohn, Handley, Ladd, and others, a critical anthology called *South to a New Place* (ed.

Jones and Monteith) replaces outdated notions of regionalism with more flexible ideas about geographical place and global reach. The collection expands the category of southernness to include multicultural voices and international influence, deconstructing the monolith of the region from Native American, (contemporary) Agrarian, British, Latin American, cultural studies, postsouthern, and queer perspectives.

46. Philip Joseph's *American Literary Regionalism in a Global Age* examines the place of regionalist literature in an increasingly globalized world.

47. Postcolonialism has routinely failed to acknowledge the Marxist influences underlying its development and often has been explicitly critical of Marxism's failure to apprehend the totality of colonial suffering; likewise, Marxist critics and others have attacked postcolonialism for its perceived inability to engage issues of class, economics, and materiality. Aijaz Ahmad perhaps most strenuously advocates that "we should speak not so much of colonialism or postcolonialism but of capitalist modernity, which takes the colonial form in particular places and at particular times" (7). There is a solution to the ethics of examining material culture, however, that does not necessitate jettisoning the postcolonial approach, as Spivak's work has demonstrated with particular effectiveness. As Crystal Bartolovich argues in her introduction to *Marxism, Modernity, and Postcolonial Studies* (coedited with Lazarus), contemporary critics need to resuscitate the previously marginalized or "disavowed" strands of Marxism that were always attuned to how structures of production intersect with matters of nationalism, imperialism, and racism.

48. See for instance McDowell, "Republican Candidate Admits Supporting Eugenics." McDowell reports on James L. Hart, a Republican congressional candidate then running unopposed in his Tennessee district: "Much of Mr Hart's platform revolves around eugenics, which developed before the Second World War as a pseudoscientific movement to solve social problems by preventing the 'unfit' from having children. It inspired 33 US states to pass laws that allowed the sterilization of some 65,000 people, and Nazi Germany used the US examples to justify programs that sterilized and killed millions."

49. See Armacost, foreword vii.

50. In his *Negro President*, Gary Wills argues that the three-fifths compromise in fact had a permanent, pivotal effect on certain historical events, particularly the 1800 election of Thomas Jefferson, who had used the counting of slaves to his advantage in the determination of electoral college votes; Wills contends that if the South had not counted its slaves, it would not have controlled enough of the Congress to elect Jefferson.

51. See Farley, "Racial Identities in 2000" 33. Stephan Thernstrom reflects on the irony of recent lobbies (mainly by "those on the left, who are pleased to call themselves liberals") to preserve unitary racial categories on the census in order to protect the civil rights programs, such as affirmative action, that rely on such census counts for the widespread administration of their policies.

52. When Benedict Anderson revised his well-known *Imagined Communities*, he included a section on censuses that details their role in the maintenance of nationalism.

53. For more on the one-drop rule and the mania over racial classification, see Guterl, *Color of Race in America*.

54. When in 1920 H. L. Mencken wrote his "Sahara of the Bozart" essay chastising the South as a cultural and literary wasteland, many southerners were forced to agree uncomfortably. Michael Kreyling argues as much in "Faulkner in the Twenty-first Century," where he suggests that the Fugitive poets countered Mencken's characterization of their "'paralyzed cerebrums'" by writing deliberately high modernist poetry and "high-brow" literary criticism; further, he argues that Mencken's essay "played a dynamic part in persuading the early Faulkner . . . to picture himself in non-Southern ways" (16). For a black writer's engagement with Mencken's influence, see Richard Wright, *Black Boy* 267–77.

55. Richard H. King quickly came under fire for failing to include in his study black or women writers (with the exception of Lillian Smith), whose particular struggles King acknowledges but finds ultimately irrelevant to his themes because they simply dismiss them out of hand rather than treat them as problematic. In relegating these figures to the outskirts of a world and institution that implicated and conditioned them, he repeats the oversight that rendered such figures marginal to the tradition from the start.

56. Nell Irvin Painter also incorporates psychoanalytic theory in her own race analyses, but justifies her approach differently: in *Southern History Across the Color Line*, while acknowledging the tenuous "applicability of a field invented in turn-of-the-twentieth-century Vienna by an upper-middle-class Jew to poor southerners" and the serious question as to "whether 'white' psychology works on 'black' people," she nonetheless asserts that at bottom all individuals are variously influenced and shaped by their respective family structures, regardless of their economic or racial origins; further, southern families of "oppressed" subjects often form not just detrimental influences but also serve as "a haven to the physically afflicted, a bulwark against psychological assault." Her ultimate qualification of this controversial application is, I think, important and useful to apply to my findings as well: "From psychoanalysis, psychology, and other tools I borrow from the social sciences, I draw questions, not answers" (5).

57. There are important exceptions: see, for instance, E. G. Anderson, "Native American Literature," and Trefzer, "Tracing the Natchez Trace." There has been considerable attention paid to Faulkner's depictions of Indian histories and figures: for a historical approach, see Don H. Doyle, *Faulkner's County*; for a literary examination, see Dabney, *Indians of Yoknapatawpha* and the special "Faulkner's Indians" issue (ed. G. M. Moore). In the fields of anthropology and history, there has been much work done on prehistoric and preremoval southern tribes, especially by Michael Green and Theda Purdue; studies focusing on contemporary southeastern Indians are less common, but include Paredes, *Indians of the Southeastern United States*. Still, the editors of *Look Away!* acknowledge in a footnote to their introduction the continuing tendency in Southern and New World studies to "privilege the perspectives of those of European and African descent in the hemisphere" as a way of explaining the lack of Native American inclusion in their own volume (16); they do include one essay by Jane Landers ("Slave Resistance in the Southeastern Frontier") that deals in part with the presence of Indians in the early Southeast.

58. Bhabha focuses not just on traditionally recognized postcolonial cultures but considers Toni Morrison's *Beloved* as a central text in the iterations of postcolonial experience.

Chapter One. The Fetish of Surplus Value

1. Margaret Mitchell's *Gone with the Wind* reaches nostalgically back to the Civil War to depict a slaveholding family's ruin, as does Stark Young's *So Red the Rose*, written just two years before. Though further removed from the cataclysmic moment of the Civil War, other novels depicting impoverished families demonstrate the wreckage left behind in the South's slow transition from agrarian to industrial capitalism, which often forced individuals into sharecropping situations that left them in virtually permanent debt. Illustrative examples include Erskine Caldwell's *God's Little Acre* and *Tobacco Road*, Elizabeth Madox Roberts's *The Time of Man*, and Edith Summers Kelley's *Weeds*.

2. Jon Smith argues similarly in "Postcolonial, Black, and Nobody's Margin."

3. See, for instance, Edward Ayers's claim that "the first wave of segregation law is explained ... by the growing ambition, attainments, and assertiveness of blacks, by the striking expansion and importance of the railroad system in the 1880s. . . . Like everything else in the New South, segregation grew out of concrete situations, out of technological, demographic, economic, and political changes that had unforeseen and often unintended consequences" (*Promise* 145).

4. Scott Romine also claims that William Alexander Percy eschews the economic features of aristocratic life in favor of a strictly aesthetic worldview. See *Narrative Forms of Southern Community*.

5. The term *white trash* was first used in the United States in the antebellum South and referred exclusively to "the poor white population in the Southern States of America" (OED). Early usages show, and a plethora of southern literature corroborates, that the white trash southerners were often grouped with the region's blacks. In some instances, as Fanny Kemble notes in her 1835 journal, "the slaves themselves entertain the very highest contempt for white servants, whom they designate as 'poor white trash'" (OED). Antagonism between these two groups seems due to a heightened sense of competition in the free labor market that replaced slavery.

6. Jehlen's monograph continues to be pivotal in turning Faulkner criticism toward issues of class as "the underlying organizing principle in [Yoknapatawpha's] social structure ... more precisely the division between two classes of white society, the planters and the 'rednecks'" (9). The deep sympathy between the two, I argue, also gives way to defensive competitiveness. Ted Atkinson's *Faulkner and the Great Depression* situates Faulkner within the context of the Great Depression and interrogates more precisely his ambivalent perch between agrarian planter and landless poor.

7. See Towner, *Faulkner on the Color Line*.

8. According to Williamson, "Faulkner was reared among an imperialized people, a people much reduced in power from what had been the case within living memory. In writing about their plight, he met the plight of the imperialized people of the world, the people whose land had been raped and labor taken to supply raw materials from the factories of the industrial powers" (363).

9. Godden and Polk suggest that Ike in fact manufactures the evidence he is invested in locating and disavowing in order to justify a rejection of a birthright he judges to be

corrupt. Their reading attempts to evaluate the ledgers "on their own terms, rather than on Isaac's" (359).

10. For a thorough examination of the history of double-entry accounting and its profound influence on modern forms of knowledge, see Poovey, *History of the Modern Fact*.

11. John T. Matthews makes a similar point; asserting Faulkner's "studied conviction that economic exploitation and racial oppression composed a double coil around the modern South," Matthews proposes the need for "a kind of double reading that demonstrates their mutual constitution" ("Touching Race" 25).

12. See Matthews, "Recalling the West Indies"; Handley, *Postslavery Literatures in the Americas*; and Cohn, *History and Memory in the New South*. Also, a collection edited by Deborah Cohn and Jon Smith provides a broader look at the U.S. South and New World studies, and includes essays on Faulkner by Matthews, Wendy B. Faris, Philip Weinstein, Dane Johnson, Helen Oakley, and Earl Fitz.

13. The term *postcolonial* began circulating in 1936 (OED), which coincides with the date of publication for *Absalom, Absalom!*

14. This phrase is a play on the subtitle of John Matthews's "Recalling the West Indies: From Yoknapatawpha to Haiti and Back," in which he suggests that these global connections constitute the South's "fetishized knowledge" of its implication in a vast colonial order that white southerners hold in plain view but overlook in failures of recognition that signify something more than mere repression (239).

15. For a useful comparison of the Snopes and Sutpen families, see Corinne Dale, "*Absalom, Absalom!* and the Snopes Trilogy."

16. Common folk trying to work their way up are a type Faulkner represents most fully and satirically in the upwardly mobile Snopes clan, who ascend from shack to mansion in the course of three novels and countless unscrupulous exploits. A character like Flem Snopes constitutes for Faulkner an object of both fascination and derision, high satire and brutal wit; *Absalom, Absalom!* gives us a similar social trajectory but in radically different, more tragic terms. Such rises were not uncommon in Tidewater Virginia, where Sutpen is born; in the 1830s, George Handley notes, this was "a region of considerable economic opportunity, where many poor white farmers were able to move slowly up the class ladder" (133).

17. As Erik Dussere indicates, Sutpen "goes about making himself a gentleman planter according to his strictly quantitative system"—much like a ledger (50).

18. Indeed, Sutpen finds his Haitian wife not "adjunctive or incremental" to his design because she fails to compensate for what Sutpen himself lacks in natural aristocracy. Sutpen embodies the "minus-in-origin" that Homi Bhabha assigns to the subjugated; the subtraction factor in his imaginative books drives him compulsively to overcompensate, to find adjuncts and increments that will render him solvent.

19. While the state of being "solvent" refers to one's ability to pay one's debts, it also connotes "dissolving" or "laxative" properties, promoting the expulsion of undesirable elements or influences (OED). That this process takes place within Sutpen's body is significant, as it indicates his attempts at forging balance nonetheless exacerbate his depletion as well.

20. A different example of this phenomenon occurs near the end of *Nineteen Eighty-four*, George Orwell's classic dystopia of oppressive totalitarian government. Having captured the dissident Winston, the Ministry of Love has begun the laborious process of torturing and "reprogramming" him, which involves revising the fundamental "truth" of mathematics by his tormentor insisting that "two plus two" makes not four but five "if the Party says" so.

21. The moment at the planter's door instantiates for Sutpen a virtual balance sheet of duty and revenge: because the servant never gave him a chance to state his business, he reasons, the master "*wont know [what it was] and whatever it is wont get done and he wont know it aint done until too late so he will get paid back that much for what he set that nigger to do*" (191–92). With labor incomplete (because of the "nigger's" failure, which is also Sutpen's failure) will the master suffer, "get paid back" in proportion to the slave's lack of industry? In this case, all things are credits and debits, and the master will only profit when the slave puts forth the appropriate energy. But, after all, the master is fundamentally detached from the work ("*he wont know it aint done*") that he reaps the benefits from. In yet another reading, though, the "*he*" getting "paid back" becomes slippery: it could be the master, getting "paid back" in the form of revenge by Sutpen, who will rise to usurp the man who "set that nigger" to occupy a white house and turn away a white boy. Or the "he" may be Sutpen himself, who will himself get "paid back"—will pay himself back—for the indignity and debasement caused by his exclusion from the Big House.

Minus-in-origin is a term used by Homi Bhabha in *Location of Culture* (160 and elsewhere) to describe the subaltern's predetermined status in the national narrative, always already figured as the negation of the colonizer.

22. In a connection that Matthews has recently invigorated ("Recalling"), Mr. Coldfield reluctantly makes an investment in Sutpen's slave-trading enterprise, his abolitionist sentiments defeated by the allure of profit.

23. Faulkner was facing a particularly acute financial crisis at the time he was writing *Go Down, Moses*. Richard J. Gray reports in *Life of William Faulkner* that in 1940 Faulkner frequently wrote his editor to request very specific, large amounts of money, a crisis that Gray suggests may have contributed to the "openly economic bias of the first novel in the Snopes trilogy" published that year (271). Linda Wagner-Martin also suggests that "the novel may have originated from Faulkner's financial straits" during this period, due in part to the purchase of both Rowan Oak and Greenfield Farm in the previous decade (1). In his biography, Joseph Blotner reports Faulkner's intimations (as explained in a letter to Random House, his publisher) that "If he could sell some stories and get through until mid-November, when he could begin to collect on his cotton and tenant crops, he could make it" (421). Helping out in the commissary store, he was known to "neatly itemize" customer purchases "in a small ledger," a frequent activity that Blotner suggests must have made him think "that he had been doing the same thing with Random House" (417); and, in fact, Faulkner did keep an intricate ledgerlike record of his short-story submissions. Such scenes underscore the kind of empathy Faulkner might have felt for Ike in his conflicted relationship to the family accounts and ledgers, lending additional support to

Eric Sundquist's claim that *Go Down, Moses* was "Faulkner's most honest and personally revealing novel" (qtd. by Wagner-Martin 14).

24. Most prominently, Ike's father, Buck, and his Uncle Buddy.

25. See R. King, "Working Through."

26. Dussere suggests similarly that Ike, in his attempt "to even things up and clear the ledger, the book which holds the record of injustice and the unrealized possibility for remuneration," discovers "that this is ultimately a false hope" (338).

27. As Charles Seife reports in his history *Zero*, "zero was so important to the new set of numbers [in Western mathematics] that people started calling all numbers ciphers, which gave the French their term *chiffre*, digit"; the word gained its secondary meaning of "secret code" when Italian merchants used ciphers (for their ease of falsification and disguise) to send encrypted messages via counting boards and other instruments (73, 80–81).

28. This sense of *ciphering* also uncannily resembles the bifurcated idea of solvency that Sutpen desires even as it threatens to dissolve him entirely.

29. This "white trash" stereotype has proven difficult to dismantle even lately. See, for example, Billings, Norman, and Ledford, *Confronting Appalachian Stereotypes*, for a discussion of the ways in which southerners (and rural Appalachians in particular) comprise one of the only American groups that we feel are generally acceptable to stereotype today.

30. Pierre Bourdieu's notion of "cultural capital," in which the benefits of education and knowledge confer status and power, is relevant here.

31. Wolfe's ambivalent attitude toward the Agrarians—and their almost univocal dislike for him—are detailed further in Underwood, "Autobiography and Ideology in the South." In his biography of Wolfe, David Herbert Donald relates that Wolfe was at first intrigued and attracted by some of the Agrarians, as thinkers and as people, but their eventual distaste for him and his work in turn repelled Wolfe, who came to ridicule and denigrate the Twelve Southerners thereafter, seemingly out of spite (359–62). Donald reports that Wolfe wavered much on political matters and grew fairly adept at alienating parties from both sides of the political divide.

32. Wolfe's introduction to *Look Homeward, Angel* admits as much in its claim that "the author has written an experience which is now far and lost, but which was once part of the fabric of his life. . . . It seems to him that all serious work in fiction is autobiographical" (xv). Indeed, many of Wolfe's critics dismissed his work principally because of its relentlessly autobiographical nature; for a synthesis and discussion of these critical views, see C. Hugh Holman, "Thomas Wolfe and the Stigma of Autobiography." In addition to the biographies of Wolfe by Donald, Nowell, and Kennedy, see also Phillip A. Snyder, "*Look Homeward, Angel* as Autobiography and Artist Novel."

33. Donald tells us that Wolfe "could never master" algebra and "even developed a positive hatred for Hortense Pattison," the woman who taught it (24).

34. It is crucial that Faulkner comes back to define this idea of displacement as a northern, specifically New England, antiplantation phenomenon: in *Go Down, Moses*, Ike rumi-

nates on "the New England mechanics who didn't even own land and measured all things by the weight of water and the cost of turning wheels" (274).

Chapter Two. Stealing Themselves Out of Slavery

1. For more on wage-labor-based sharecropping in the twentieth century see Woodward, *Origins*, especially "The Unredeemed Farmer"; Woodman, "Reconstruction of the Cotton Plantation"; Kirby, *Rural Worlds Lost* 26; Daniel, *Shadow of Slavery*; and R. Ransom and Sutch, *One Kind of Freedom*.

2. Cobb's reflections on his experiences as a sharecropper, prisoner, and activist are collected in Theodore Rosengarten's *All God's Dangers*.

3. *Learn to Count*
Naught's a naught
Five's a figger.
All fer de white man.
None fer de Nigger.

Ten's a ten
But it's mighty funny;
When you cain't count good,
You hain't got no money.
(*Negro Folk Rhymes*, 1922)

4. As Benjamin Quarles notes, the South declined to invest equally in the education of the black citizen "on the grounds that he paid few taxes and that there was little point in giving him any training beyond the basic elements of reading and writing" (164). The growth of educational opportunity in the twentieth century was due mainly to church-sponsored or privately funded philanthropic efforts, such as Andrew Carnegie's gift of $600,000 to the Tuskegee Institute in 1903 (Quarles 166).

5. In the context of sharecropping, the Mosses' large output is actually unusual, or perhaps was exaggerated by the jackleg in order to emphasize to them their plight; as Pete Daniel suggests, sharecroppers were more often left "watching the planter or merchant consult ledger books and pronounce the verdict, seldom more than a few dollars' credit or debit" (5).

6. The full interview of George Briggs by Caldwell Sims is of interest and can be found at Project Gutenberg, http://www.gutenberg.org/files/18912/18912-h/18912-h.htm, accessed August 2007.

7. Indeed, Margaret Walker notes in her biography of Richard Wright that this story, along with several others in *Eight Men*, is "patently autobiographical" (331).

8. Historically, interracial union activity was occasionally successful, but the rigid racial antagonisms in the South generally precluded such solidarity. For an excellent account of interracial union efforts among farmers in the Depression-era South, see Donald Grubbs, *Cry from the Cotton*.

9. The notion of "petty larceny" (*n.* "theft of personal property having a value less than a legally specified amount") is specific to "many U.S. states and Great Britain" (OED).

10. What was eventually published in *Eight Men* represents only half of the original full-length text Wright wrote, suggesting that Wright had a substantial commitment to the story's themes. The work's affinities to *Native Son* are clear and have been noted by Wright's critics.

11. Other examples are numerous: he gains inexplicable comfort in a remote sense of blackness: his mother's "great dark eyes" inspire an enduring sense of "purity and safety" (462). He is drawn sensually to other images of darkness as well. Even the strikingly dark "Shiny" "strongly attracted [his] attention from the first day [he] saw him" (465). Yet, the various other boys "of all sizes and kinds . . . seemed . . . like savages" (463). To the undifferentiated narrator, the "other" is simultaneously multiple and metaphorically dark ("savage"); neither hybridity nor blackness are consistent objects of identification for the narrator, but they are distinct sites of desire and revulsion respectively.

12. This observation has become commonplace in literary theory. For a full account of this history, see Henry Louis Gates Jr., *Figures in Black* and *The Signifying Monkey*. Mason Stokes, *The Color of Sex*, examines the issue from the combined perspective of African American and queer theory.

13. Claudia Tate, for example, alludes to the complicating presence of white patronage in the development of black agency and identity through artistic production (11). *Black Writers, White Publishers*, a full-length study by John K. Young, explores further the compromising relationship between African American writers and white publishers from Nella Larsen to Toni Morrison.

14. The kind of "economic solvency" within African American communities that Baker cites is still, of course, far from a condition of prevalence; Henry Louis Gates Jr. marks a contemporary "divergence between poor blacks and prosperous ones" that has been increasing over time, and goes further to assert that as economic differences among blacks increase, the pressure to nationalize and essentialize the race becomes more insistent (*Future of the Race* 19, 37).

15. My approach thus depends implicitly on the Lacanian assumption that personal subjectivity is ordered within and by language, and is deepened by Jürgen Habermas's labor-centered notion that the self is produced within one's own discourse.

16. There is a long history exploring the connections between music and mathematics. Comprehensive contributions include Leon Harkleroad, *The Math Behind the Music*; John Fauvel, Raymond Flood, and Robin Wilson, eds., *Music and Mathematics*; and Edward Rothstein, *Emblems of the Mind*.

17. For an explication of this term see, for example, Ibrahim K. Sundiata, *From Slaving to Neoslavery*.

18. Primarily during the Harlem Renaissance, primitivism in art and culture (often displayed in African American expressions of folk culture and its African roots) became fashionable among white Americans, who clamored to own primitive art and frequent the jazz clubs and nightspots of Harlem.

19. For an expansive study of the negotiation between white and black art (music in particular), high and low culture, and capitalism and communism, see Bernard Gendron, *Between Montmartre and the Mudd Club*.

20. Teaching largely at northern colleges and universities, I have noticed repeatedly that my students generally view racism as irrelevant or anachronistic, a liberal misconception that frees them to make potentially slighting comments like this one rather fearlessly.

21. A common complaint against black bourgeoisie is that they in effect "sell out" and simply mimic white culture. Whereas this condition is posed in such (nonsouthern) African American works as Nella Larsen's, Jessie Fauset's, and Toni Morrison's, in Johnson the predicament encompasses identity entirely, forcing a choice to be made that irrevocably alters one's self-perception as a raced being. Implicit here is Booker T. Washington's proponing of bourgeois capitalism as the black's key to economic and social uplift, a plan castigated by DuBois and others for its strategies of "whitewashing" and mimicry. As Gates Jr. comments in the introduction to Johnson's novella, "The alienation that DuBois had worried over in his critique of Booker T. Washington's advocacy of bourgeois capitalism as the ultimate liberating mechanism for the black proletariat comes to fruition in Johnson's characterization of his protagonist" (xx).

22. He earns his racial freedom at a terrible price, and what he earns from his peers is the chilling title of "professor" (115)—ostensibly for his musical mastery, but implicitly too for the successful orchestration of his racial identity into silence.

23. See "*chink, n.2*" and "*Chink, n.5*," OED.

Chapter Three. The Measures of Love

1. Addie's notion that she "would be I" would seem to indicate a harnessing of selfhood and agency; as Monique Wittig has pronounced, "when one says *I* and, in doing so, reappropriates language as a whole, proceeding from oneself alone, with the tremendous power to use all language, it is then and there, according to linguists and philosophers, that there occurs the supreme act of subjectivity, the advent of subjectivity into consciousness" (6). Of course, Addie's use of language here, like that of the other women under consideration in this chapter, does not "proceed from oneself alone" but from a rigidly prescribed set of cultural norms and needs; her language bears mathematical overtones that weigh down and delineate the "I" expected to replicate the kind of subjectivity necessary for the functioning and health of the community, and specifically its men.

2. The criticism lauding the female writers under examination here is plentiful. Charlotte H. Beck, for example, avers that Katherine Anne Porter "consistently told her stories from a feminist perspective" (174). Anne Firor Scott praises *The Hard-Boiled Virgin* for its "pervasive and corrosive feminism" (xvi) and "narrow but trenchant and persistent social criticism" (xix). Anita Loos's *Gentlemen Prefer Blondes* is almost always read as a sly feminist triumph depicting a sexually liberated, financially independent, subversive character (see Ankum, "Material Girls," and Cella, "Narrative 'Confidence Games'"). While I don't disagree that these writers' feminist sympathies inspire their critical depictions of modern southern society, I am cautious about the extent to which this perspective actively shapes their characters' worldviews, and am especially attuned to moments when "feminism" masks troubling signs of psychological damage. When Beck suggests that Porter "used her personal and professional relationships with men to her

advantage, all the while carefully retaining her autonomy and independence" (174), I disagree fundamentally that women of this period in the South were able to gain "advantage" without sacrificing, in some measure, their "autonomy and independence."

3. This is, of course, not a hard-and-fast distinction. Certainly many female writers of the modern period turned nostalgically to the Lost Cause (for instance, Margaret Mitchell and Caroline Gordon), and certain white male writers were engaged in more clear-eyed progressive efforts (Thomas Wolfe and William Faulkner, in some ways, and Erskine Caldwell). Brantley contends that even the Agrarians "were not without a number of liberal impulses" (8). Perhaps the most complete examination of southern liberalism remains Gunnar Myrdal's *American Dilemma*.

4. I am grateful to Jon Smith for pointing out the relevance of Žižek's observation in this context.

5. See A. G. Jones, *Tomorrow Is Another Day* 22 and her note at 66 for a full explanation and catalog of such strategies.

6. Excellent studies of the "belle" psychology have been advanced by Kathryn Lee Seidel, *The Southern Belle in the American Novel*; Catherine Clinton, *The Plantation Mistress*; and Giselle Roberts, *The Confederate Belle*. Additionally, Entzminger provides a full-length historical and literary survey of southern women's negotiation with and resistance to the belle archetype. A work like Patricia Yaeger's influential *Dirt and Desire* demonstrates in a rich and sweeping examination that the concerns of southern women (both black and white) were not limited to the same tired themes that have long occupied southern critics; she set the standard for new approaches to women's literature from the region by introducing fresh categories of analysis, "figures and ideas that astonish" with their strangeness and power (ix). I wish to follow Yaeger's lead, in this sense, by identifying discursive preoccupations within women's writing that have not yet been acknowledged or explored, although Yaeger might disapprove of my aim to yoke these textual symptoms back to the same tired sources: the plantation codes and myths that spawned the fanatical need for social order. Where Yaeger finds her women exercising a "flagrant desire to abuse a form of cultural capital not traditionally their own" (2), I find these women struggling fiercely to own anything at all: their words, their works, their forms of cultural capital, and least of all themselves.

7. Entzminger explores what she calls the "belle gone bad" phenomenon in southern women's writing, which she identifies as first occurring in the nineteenth century and then recurring in the twentieth century as an expressive "response to the rigid preoccupations of their culture" and a mode of rhetorical resistance (6). A. G. Jones describes the extreme opposite: "some women have determined to shape themselves entirely into the ideal. . . . At the extreme, such women blanked out their perceptions and repressed their feelings until they lost, almost entirely, a sense of self" (23).

8. Indeed, while the image of the footloose, unconventional flapper tends to dominate our perceptions of the New Woman in 1920s America, the southern version of this spirit was somewhat more subdued; women's clubs and organizations often rallied around not the feminist cause but the Lost Cause, and worked to resurrect a regional tradition based on plantation values. See, for instance, J. Johnson, *Southern Ladies, New Women*, who

examines South Carolina clubwomen in particular as "reluctant reformers" dedicated to honoring southern tradition and "white supremacy" and thus "significantly shaped the culture of the newly segregated South" (145, 205, 3).

9. A simple statistic uncannily illustrates this now-familiar phenomenon: Loos's serialized stories about Lorelei Lee (which would eventually become the novel *Gentlemen Prefer Blondes*) garnered for *Harper's Bazaar* its first substantially male readership, causing its subscription sales to triple and its pages to be filled with advertisements for men's clothing, sporting goods, and other products. Loos reports this in "Biography of a Book," her introduction to the novel; while this seems to be a point of pride for the author, I suggest that this fact signals her character's function as a desired, consumable object to the male consumer.

10. A niece of Newman's, Margaret Patterson, wrote a small biography of her aunt that Newman apparently read and enjoyed, as Baugh reports in his introduction to *Frances Newman's Letters*, published shortly after her death in 1928; this excerpt is taken from that study (3). No full-length biography of Newman exists at the time of this writing, although Barbara Anne Wade's *Frances Newman: Southern Satirist and Literary Rebel* offers a study of Newman's work through a biographical lens. Several short sketches also appear. In the same volume of collected letters, a brief portrait of Newman is provided in a preface by James Branch Cabell (v–xi), with whom she was quite close. For an excellent scholarly discussion of Newman's background, drawn from the few available sources, see A. G. Jones, *Tomorrow Is Another Day*; Anne Firor Scott's foreword to Newman's *The Hard-Boiled Virgin* also provides excellent context.

11. I provide more biographical information for the women in this chapter because they have been largely ignored by readers and critics and may be unfamiliar even to southern specialists. Newman's critical neglect has been especially marked. She has been the subject of chapters or articles by A. G. Jones, by Seidel in *Southern Belle in the American Novel*, by Shillingsburg, and by a few others. To date, however, Wade's *Frances Newman* is the only full-length literary biography.

12. Newman herself articulated a similar sentiment: "Like Katharine Faraday, I am only interested in my own ideas and my own emotions, and the people who stimulate both. Of course, I like clothes, and if I ever have a lot of money, I shall doubtless spend most of it for frocks and hats" (*Letters* 274–75). The admission is a near duplicate of her character's modus operandi: Katharine's persistent, calculated self-interest is characterized as an even more haunting desire to embody the perspective of an outsider, shaping and "stimulating" her. The euphemism here is not inadvertent: Katharine's odyssey through Atlanta society, in search of making a proper and successful marriage, is marked and hampered not just by her self-scrutiny but also by the futile narcissistic *desire* that suffuses it.

13. A careful reading of *Hard-Boiled Virgin* reveals that few pages do not contain multiple references to numbers, calculations, or arithmetic.

14. The concept of pedagogy is crucial to much postcolonial theory, particularly that of Homi Bhabha, and I use it here to draw consciously on the way social codes and methods for behavior and quantifying worth become part of the region's cultural indoctrination, written directly into the fabric of its social conditioning; when writers choose pedagogical settings—schoolrooms, for example—to showcase a moment of social or racial learning,

the tremendous homogenizing power of national pedagogy seems to be at least obliquely referenced.

15. On the imitation and internalization stage, see Showalter 13.

16. A. G. Jones remarks that Katharine's "life is increasingly structured by the plots and narratives she imposes on it, like Emma Bovary, from her readings . . . her social world is a plot in itself, an elaborate artifice that keeps its women ignorant and in their places" (xiii–xiv).

17. As Scott notes in her foreword to *The Hard-Boiled Virgin*, Newman reported to a correspondent that "a woman can't write a book without a father anymore than she could have a baby" (x).

18. H. L. Mencken published this essay berating the South as a literary wasteland in his 1920 *Prejudices*; he made a rare exception, however, when in "Violets of the Sahara" he cited Newman as among the very few southern writers of any promise. Mencken and Newman had a fairly close friendship and correspondence, as the number and warmth of their letters make clear (see *Letters*); indeed Joseph M. Flora remarks that Newman's "career illustrates the support the gifted writer often received from Mencken" (281).

19. Newman's critics are few, but most read this moment as one of liberation. Newman was indeed progressive in her bold flouting of southern feminine restrictions, candidly rejecting what Miriam J. Shillingsburg catalogs as "family and deference, virginity and marriage, childbirth and menstruation, and the cult of beauty and propriety" (354). But when critics like Shillingsburg claim that Newman's "feminism is her boldest trait" (356), it seems an inordinately laudatory assessment that Newman's own writing (both fictive and personal) discourages. See also Wade, *Frances Newman*.

20. In her introduction to *Gentlemen Prefer Blondes* Candace Bushnell attests that the "gold digger" archetype survives as a byproduct of American consumer culture well into the twentieth century and beyond. Bushnell recalls meeting her "first genuine gold digger," a woman named Nicole (who eventually befriends Bushnell) whose expensive clothes and travels were financed by wealthy media moguls and industrial titans of the 1980s. Despite Loos's claim that Lorelei Lee was a "'period piece'" exemplifying a particular economic moment, Bushnell claims that Loos in fact hit upon "a new female archetype, one that not only survives today, but thrives" in figures like Nicole (xiv). In fact, Bushnell describes the gold digger type as a "purely American phenomenon" (xiv). The fact that Bushnell's friend Nicole ends up "in a straitjacket" (xiv) is a chilling approximation of the ends to which such digging leads. Yet Bushnell celebrates Lorelei for her hard-working, wily, Horatio Alger–like determination to launch herself into high society by her boot (or high heel) straps by any means necessary, an evaluation I resist in this chapter.

21. In making this connection, I depart from Susan Hegeman's claim that "'education' is a code word for sex" in Lorelei's narrative (540). While Hegeman sees Lorelei's obscured sexual license as a necessary step along the path to gaining the material riches she desires, I am more inclined to read the economic valence of Lorelei's education as primary, even to the exclusion of interest in matters sexual or physical.

22. Perhaps Loos ultimately resents the pretension of the middle-class woman who scrambles to assume the position normally reserved for white women of privileged birth. Since Loos herself was of middle-class origins, this vitriol seems ambivalent, directed in

part at the South's grubby social climbers but also at her own position of deference to the demands of men around her.

23. Loos converts not only sexual desire but also intellect into the language of use value: the first instance of Lorelei's "contact/contract" slip comes in the book's opening pages when Lorelei relates her gentleman friend's claim that "when he comes into contract with brains he always notices it" (4). The moment seems as much a reflection of the man's priorities as the woman's inculcated desire to live up to them.

24. In fact, Newman subtly demonstrated that she didn't see much difference between a "woman" and a "wife," as revealed in a comment to a friend about "women—it was really wives that I meant, and since the English language affords the distinction, I should have been more explicit" (*Letters* 49).

25. Newman echoes this language to describe Isabel's first (and long-awaited) sexual encounter with Charlton (255), emphasizing the correlation between these two women in their attitudes of subjection to one man's desires and whims.

26. As A. G. Jones brilliantly observes, Newman matches this objectification in her prose: "[Evelyn] sees her body as an object. Indeed, Evelyn is the object of her own sentences; Charlton is the subject" (xviii). This claim implicitly draws a close parallel between Evelyn's character and Katharine Faraday, who wants (but fails) to be "the subject of any verb" rather than "its passive object" (155).

27. See in particular Darlene Unrue's introduction to her 2005 biography of Porter.

28. Jane Krause DeMouy suggests also that the purse represents "her own other self" as a young woman (61).

29. The moment strikingly resembles an episode in Porter's life that she relayed in the form of a monologue by her father: "'Don't ever let me hear you talking any of that nonsense about the slavery of women,' said her father, 'I wish all you women who talk about slavery had to be turned into men for just one day. . . . Then you'd know the meaning of slavery.' He wrapped his ragged old bathrobe around him and started down the hall. 'Just look at me with my elbows out trying to keep a houseful of women in fine underclothes. Where are you going this time of day, anyhow?'" (Unrue, *Katherine Anne Porter* 35–36). As biographer Unrue reports, "Katherine Anne became committed to the cause of women's rights and later claimed to have published her first essay on the subject that year" (36).

30. In "Reading the Endings in Katherine Anne Porter's 'Old Mortality,'" Suzanne W. Jones also expresses cautious skepticism about reading the story too optimistically as a feminist text.

Chapter Four. Contemporary Crises of Value

1. In "Rise of the Sunbelt" David R. Goldfield provides a thorough summation of the "relatively new historiography" of the Sunbelt.

2. Mathematically, we know that balance depends paradoxically on nothingness—a zero equilibrium. That is, positive and negative numbers effectively cancel one another out: in the equation $-5 + 5 = 0$, the integers are statistically equivalent because they balance each other effectively out of existence (as a composite "0"). In economics, a zero-sum

budget represents the ideal of balance; in an account ledger, as Robert Kaplan describes it, you "tote up your debits and credits on the same page ... in parallel columns. If the difference between them is zero, your books are balanced" (110). The texts I examine in this chapter depict the postmodern horror of this empty balance, but repeatedly try to insert themselves into either side of the equation, choosing inclusion (even as a negative quantity) rather than relegation to anonymity or nothingness.

3. See, for instance, Bartley, *Rise of Massive Resistance*; Neil McMillen, *The Citizen's Council*; and I. A. Newby, *Challenge to the Court*.

4. As J. Smith and Cohn observe in *Look Away!* the Agrarians "compared the plight of white southern culture (highly pastoralized and sanitized) to that of equally romanticized Native American civilizations: peaceful, art-loving cultures wiped out by Yankee materialism" (6). Despite a number of implicit and explicit references to Native Americans as kindred to southerners in their harmonious relationship with nature (J. Ransom 20; Fletcher 99–100; Nixon 183), the Agrarians' essays in *I'll Take My Stand* nonetheless glorify and sanitize the mythology of hardy New World settlement (J. Ransom 8; Owsley 71) by referring to themselves (without irony) as "natives" and northern carpetbaggers as "invaders" (see, for example, J. Ransom 23; Nixon 193). Nixon's nonchalant reference to the time before "Indians departed" (183) strengthens the fiction that the South's succession was natural and ordained.

5. The writers represented here are just a small sampling of southern authors who use Indian characters or elements strategically in their work. Most comprehensive is Annette Trefzer's *Disturbing Indians*, which examines Native American themes in works by Andrew Lytle, Caroline Gordon, Eudora Welty, and Faulkner. For a discussion of Barry Hannah's use of Native American figures to serve a white southern nativist agenda, see Benson. A full-length study by Lewis M. Dabney uncovers the "neglected" Indians throughout Faulkner's corpus, but ultimately he decides that Faulkner took "imaginative" liberties with his Indian characters due to the relative lack of precise historical information (10). I agree with scholars who conclude that Faulkner's Indian presences are marginal and stereotypical at best (see, for example, Trefzer, "Postcolonial Displacements in Faulkner's Indian Stories of the 1930s") and further suggest that this results from the repressive ideological apparatus of the society that worked to keep Indians at less than "zero." For more views on Faulkner's Indians see the special issue of the *Faulkner Journal* edited by Gene M. Moore. On southern-Indian connections more broadly see the 2007 special issue of the *Mississippi Quarterly* edited by Ellen Arnold. The nativism marking nearly every phase of American settlement, liberation, and "progress" repeatedly posits "white Americans" in the place of "native Americans." For examples of whites who attempt to inhabit Indian identity in an attempt to establish authenticity as Americans, see Philip Deloria's *Playing Indian* and Alan Trachtenberg's *Shades of Hiawatha*. White southerners have their own history of nativism, usually employed to separate the South from the rest of the nation.

6. Dussere discusses the southern gentlemanly notion of a "debt of honor," which he suggests Faulkner's characters employ as a way to "preserve the form of honor as an act of resistance to the 'Northern' capitalist ideology that privileges money and business" (12). Percy's use of this term seems in a sense to appeal to his uncle's aristocratic manners.

7. Michael Kobre discusses Percy's conflicted relationship to southern tradition through an examination of his Bakhtinian, dialogic style; John F. Desmond explores the importance of Percy's Christianity (*Walker Percy's Search for Community*); Mary Deems Howland cannot escape matters of race in her study of Percy's intersubjectivity in *The Gift of the Other*, yet her focus is primarily on Percy's indebtedness to the existential philosopher Gabriel Marcel.

8. Interview by Kathleen Wilkinson, "Dorothy Allison: The Value of Redemption" in *Curve* magazine, online, <http://www.curvemag.com/Detailed/5.html>, accessed August 2007.

9. By presenting Percy as essentially a back-looking, nostalgic writer perhaps uncannily desirous of the old order over the new, I am in disagreement with Percy scholars who find in his work a transcendent faith and optimism for a new age, a sentiment often inspired by the fact of Percy's devout Catholicism. Mary K. Sweeney, for example, argues in *Walker Percy and the Postmodern World* that Percy's characters watch the old world dissolve and anxiously await the emergence of the new day, full of hope, love, and salvation. These categories have, I believe, been marked and disabled by their participation in a southern tradition; love, for example, reveals itself in this text as an unequal narcissistic relationship without which the self cannot sustain itself or have value. The romantic implications of such hyperbole are deeply compromised by the tradition in which such orientations occur, such as I've laid out here.

10. In his postcolonial reading of Walker Percy's confrontation with southern whiteness, Costello does advance such an argument briefly, but only in relation to Uncle Will Percy, suggesting that "his ability to know himself rests largely on his ability to know the Other according to strictly defined terms. Therefore, the elder Percy thought it of supreme importance that no individual violate these terms or take on characteristics of the Other, lest this system of identity lose its defining power"; but Costello goes on to suggest that "Will Percy certainly realizes that the old colonialist system has begun to lose its validity as a means of interacting with the world" and that Walker was better able to assimilate such a realization.

11. Robert Rudnicki examines the fugue state so often exhibited by Percy's characters by deferring to philosophy, religion, and semiosis rather than substantially historical, psychoanalytic and contextual analysis.

12. The OED dates the first usage of the phrase "ground zero" to July 7, 1946, in the *New York Times*, where it was used to reference a blast that then ignited fires 3,500 feet away from its "ground zero" or blast point.

13. Percy's own father committed suicide in 1929 when Walker was just thirteen years old. Critics have not failed to read Will Barrett's father as a combination of Percy's own father and his uncle Will, who suffered his own sense of historical "belatedness." The fact that Will Barrett seems to have been named after Uncle Will deepens our sense of the affiliation between Will the dislocated new southerner and the old guard that he can't stop emulating, hoping to find some identity and location there. In his review of William Rodney Allen's *Walker Percy: A Southern Wayfarer*, James H. Justus notes that "LeRoy Percy's suicide in 1929 (the most significant in a clutch of acts that made suicide a grim

Percy tradition) became the source of his son's life-long struggle to resist what Allen terms 'an inordinate number of fathers'" (127).

14. For more on the connection between Oedipal family relations and tragedy, see Deleuze and Guattari, esp. 296–322. For more on the ubiquity and primacy of Oedipal narratives in southern literature and culture, see R. King, *Southern Renaissance*.

15. Alan J. Bishop points out in *Mathematical Enculturation* that "it is no accident that we often use the phrase 'an elegant proof,'" as the Pythagorean love for "beauty and symmetry" endowed mathematics with an aesthetic character, "where 'fuzziness' and imprecision are replaced by clarity and certainty, where greyness and shadowy half-truths are illuminated by the bright light of reason" (64).

16. Freud's essay "A Child Is Being Beaten" is relevant here.

17. See also Philip Deloria, *Playing Indian*.

18. See Michael Paul Rogin, *Fathers and Children*, for the prototype of the white father as savior to the dark native.

19. Alice Walker's inclusion in a "multicultural" but largely Native literary anthology is a step in the useful direction of assimilating this heritage; her "The Universe Responds: or, How I learned We Can Have Peace on Earth" appears in Barnhill, *At Home on the Earth*.

Chapter Five. Re-membering the Missing

1. Exceptions to southern nativists writing as if Indians were extinct include the excellent aforementioned work on southeastern Indians past and present by Gidley and Gidley, Eric Gary Anderson, Annette Trefzer, Michael Green, Theda Perdue, Tom Mould, and Joel Martin.

2. Jon Smith and Deborah Cohn, the editors of *Look Away!* explain the omission of Native American issues in their volume by critiquing the persistent tendency in southern and New World studies to "privilege the perspectives of those of European and African descent in the hemisphere" (16). While they apologize for seeming to perpetuate this critical aporia, they do point toward forthcoming works on the topic by Annette Trefzer and myself, among many others, that promise to fill the gap; and they do include one essay by Jane Landers that deals in part with Indians of the early Southeast.

3. For criticism on Glancy, see especially Karsten Fitz and Amy J. Elias. Awiakta receives a brief mention in Perry and Weaks, *History of Southern Women's Literature*. Excellent essays on Awiakta by Daniel Heath Justice and Susan Berry Brill de Ramírez appear in Rader and Gould, *Speak to Me Words*; see also Thomas Rain Crowe, "Marilou Awiakta"; and Grace Toney Edwards, "Marilou Awiakta." Justice's *Our Fire Survives the Storm* discusses works by both Glancy and Awiakta as twentieth-century expressions of traditional Cherokee nationhood. Noteworthy full-length studies on Owens by Jacqueline Kilpatrick (*Louis Owens: Literary Reflections on His Life and Work*) and Christopher A. LaLonde (*Grave Concerns, Trickster Turns: The Novels of Louis Owens*) have also appeared.

4. Chippewa author Louise Erdrich voices a similar sentiment through her character Lipsha Morrissey: "the straight-edged shape is not a Chippewa preference. . . .

Only human-made things tend toward cubes and squares" (96). In Erdrich's story, the "squares" are represented symbolically by the orderly grid on a bingo card, which Lipsha disastrously sets his hopes on. The means of "winning" such games rests with the culture who invented the shapes of hope and the illusion of fortune for the deprived. As Michael Dorris asserts, "it is only a matter of time until the cards win" (47). Yet the prize still tantalizes: in Ralph Ellison's "King of the Bingo Game," a black protagonist is similarly unable to relinquish his hold on (and thus control over) a bingo wheel, knowing that he can't possibly "win" in any material and meaningful sense; when he does win, it is by landing the wheel on the target of "double zero" (136), which underscores the notion that for a black man in white America, winning is only an illusion.

5. As an example of Native avoidance of binary identity systems, Algonquian grammar accounts for four different subject positions and, as Michael Booth has subsequently argued, has "at least the possibility of a different intersubjective geometry" (355).

6. The idea of an "Indian gift" was recognized around 1765 in a somewhat neutral description "signifying a present for which an equivalent return is expected"; but the expression did not apply to a specific, negative form of personal behavior (an "Indian giver") with its modern connotations until 1860: "When an Indian gives any thing, he expects to receive an equivalent, or to have his gift returned" (OED). The negative iterations of the phrase increase in later, common usage: a 1904 article refers to an individual who "took the position of the 'Indian giver' and wanted the money back."

7. In one personal example of the extraordinary barriers and delays to tribal recognition and access to federal programs, a branch of the tribe from which I am descended—the Mashpee Wampanoag Indians—was only recently granted recognition by the federal government after nearly thirty years of repeated applications and legislation. The irony of this protracted struggle is perhaps best captured by its historicity, discussed later in this chapter: the Wampanoag Indians were the indigenous allies who helped the Pilgrims survive their first winter in New England.

8. Paul Kantner is revealed as the other murderer and the one who may be responsible for "raping and cutting people up," a *modus* that Malin professes "revolting, disgusting, incredibly sick . . . I never wanted to hurt anyone." Malin's credibility is undercut, however, by the fact that he utters this on the verge of raping and murdering Cole's daughter Abby (238).

9. I am grateful to William Joseph Thomas for his observation about the gift of corn and the Corn Mother parable.

10. For more on the testing of nuclear weapons on western lands and Native American reservations, see Carol Gallagher and Keith Schneider, *American Ground Zero*.

11. See also Peter A. Coclanis, "Globalization before Globalization: The South and the World to 1950," in Cobb and Stueck, eds., *Globalization and the American South*.

12. One need only to think about the effect that U.S. economic sanctions have had on countries like Iraq and Iran, where ill-fated programs like Oil for Food caused what the UN warned would be "dire humanitarian consequences" with tremendous human suffering that was "foreseeable (and foreseen)" (Morran et al.).

13. The portions of Lan Cao's *Monkey Bridge* representing Mai's mother's journal entries appear in italics in the novel.

14. Two full-length studies examine the evidence and racial dynamics of the case: Chet Dettlinger, *The List* (Atlanta: Philmay Enterprises, 1983) and Bernard Headley, *Atlanta Youth Murders and the Politics of Race* (Carbondale: Southern Illinois University Press, 1998). I am greatly indebted especially to Headley's exhaustive analyses of the racial and political implications of the murders and the legal trial.

15. Baldwin channels an unmistakably Faulknerian sense of imperfectly buried and relentlessly recycled terror in phrasing such as "sleeps or hopes to sleep, that terror which memory repudiates."

16. The study echoes the infamous work by white Democratic David Patrick Moynihan in 1965 released as *The Negro Family: The Case for National Action*, known popularly and derisively as "The Moynihan Report." While Moynihan's central objective was at bottom a well-intentioned attempt to connect black economic impoverishment to the decline and crises within the African American family, his findings were greeted by civil rights groups with defensiveness, hostility, and charges of racism—views that have been tempered over time as sociologists have admitted to the usefulness of Moynihan's central findings. For more on this, begin with Godfrey Hodgson's biography, *The Gentleman from New York: Daniel Patrick Moynihan*.

17. Wayne Williams was convicted in 1982 of only two of the twenty-nine kidnappings and deaths that occurred during these years. In response to widespread belief that Williams was not responsible for the child murders, DeKalb County Police Chief Louis Graham reopened the case in 2005 only to close it again a year later due to lack of new evidence. Reactions to the resurrected case were mixed and reflected the ongoing emotionalism over the racial issues swirling about the investigation and trial. In an editorial in the *Atlanta Journal-Constitution* Jim Wooten claims that "rational people" recognize Williams as the killer and know "there's no doubt about Williams' guilt, nor any question that good cops were honest and thorough in putting the right killer in jail"; believing otherwise "plays to the cheap seats and to the black helicopter crowd" (A18). On the next page, an opposing op-ed piece argues that "closing these cases is about money, politics and racism. Poor Americans, white, black, Hispanic or other have never mattered as much or been valued as much as the more fortunate. Never forget Hurricane Katrina" (Ski A19).

Conclusion. Disturbing the Calculation

1. Southerners obviously would be the first to decry the loss of their regional distinctiveness; but keeping the South in its traditional, bastardized position within the larger United States served a purpose for other Americans as well. For more on the Sunbelt's intensification of North-South rivalry, see Bruce J. Schulman, "Sunbelt South." In *From Cotton Belt to Sunbelt*, Schulman suggests that federal policies aimed at the South were not as generous as many northerners believed, but that their support was strategic and limited; he suggests that "much of the sunbelt South shivers still in the dark cold of poverty was

no oversight" but instead represents the more or less intentional result of federal plans and policies (viii).

2. Houston A. Baker Jr. relates the sentiment articulated by Malcolm X as a way to urge revisionary work in "geography, economics, race relations [and] demographics" in order to reinvigorate both southern studies and American cultural studies (10).

3. Adrian Walker notes that Boston has long struggled with its "racist rap," which intensified the defensive response to Jackson's "innocuous" remarks.

Bibliography

Ahmad, Aijaz. "The Politics of Literary Postcoloniality." *Race and Class* 36.3 (1995): 1–20.

Alexander, Elizabeth. *The Black Interior.* Saint Paul: Graywolf Press, 2004.

Allen, William Rodney. *Walker Percy: A Southern Wayfarer.* Jackson: University Press of Mississippi, 1986.

Allison, Dorothy. *Bastard Out of Carolina.* New York: Penguin, 1992.

Anderson, Benedict. *Imagined Communities: Reflections on the Origin and Spread of Nationalism.* London: Verso, 1983.

Anderson, Eric Gary. "Native American Literature, Ecocriticism, and the South." In Jones and Monteith, *South to a New Place*, 165–83.

Ankum, Katharina Von. "Material Girls: Consumer Culture and the 'New Woman' in Anita Loos' *Gentlemen Prefer Blondes* and Irmgard Keun's *Das kunstseidene Mädchen*," *Colloquia Germanica* 27.2 (1994) 159–72.

Appadurai, Arjun. "Number in the Colonial Imagination." *Modernity at Large: Cultural Dimensions of Globalization.* Minneapolis: University of Minnesota Press, 1996.

Apter, Emily, and William Pietz, eds. *Fetishism as Cultural Discourse.* Ithaca: Cornell University Press, 1993.

Ariew, Roger, and Daniel Garber, eds. *G. W. Leibniz: Philosophical Essays.* Indianapolis: Hackett, 1989.

Armacost, Michael H. Foreword to *Counting on the Census?: Race, Group Identity, and the Evasion of Politics*, by Peter Skerry. Washington, D.C.: Brookings Institution, 2000.

Ashcroft, Bill, et al. *The Empire Writes Back.* New York: Routledge, 1989.

———, Gareth Griffiths, and Helen Tiffin, eds. *The Post-Colonial Studies Reader.* New York: Routledge, 1995.

Atkinson, Ted. *Faulkner and the Great Depression: Aesthetics, Ideology, and Cultural Politics.* Athens: University of Georgia Press, 2005.

Attaway, William. *Blood on the Forge.* 1941. New York: New York Review of Books, 2005.

Awiakta, Marilou. *Abiding Appalachia: Where Mountain and Atom Meet.* Memphis: St. Luke's Press, 1978.

———. *Selu: Seeking the Corn-Mother's Wisdom*. Golden, Colo.: Fulcrum, 1993.

Ayers, Edward L. "The Inevitable Future of the South." In Hobson, *South to the Future*, 87–105.

———. *The Promise of the New South: Life After Reconstruction*. New York: Oxford University Press, 1992.

Baker, Houston A., Jr., *Turning South Again: Re-thinking Modernism/Re-reading Booker T.* Durham: Duke University Press, 2001.

Baldwin, James. *The Evidence of Things Not Seen*. New York: Holt, Rinehart, and Winston, 1985.

Bambara, Toni Cade. *Those Bones Are Not My Child*. New York: Pantheon, 1999.

Barnhill, David Landis. *At Home on the Earth: Becoming Native to Our Place: A Multicultural Anthology*. Berkeley: University of California Press, 1999.

Bartley, Numan. *The New South, 1945–1980*. Baton Rouge: Louisiana State University Press, 1995.

———. *The Rise of Massive Resistance: Race and Politics in the South During the 1950s*. Baton Rouge: Louisiana State University Press, 1969.

Bartolovich, Crystal, and Neil Lazarus, eds. *Marxism, Modernity, and Postcolonial Studies*. New York: Cambridge University Press, 2002.

Baudrillard, Jean. *The Mirror of Production*. Trans. Mark Poster. St. Louis: Telos Press, 1975.

———. *Simulacra and Simulation*. Trans. Sheila Faria Glaser. Ann Arbor: University of Michigan Press, 1994.

———. *Symbolic Exchange and Death*. Trans. Iain Hamilton Grant. London: Sage Publications, 1993.

Baugh, Hansell, ed. *Frances Newman's Letters*. New York: Liveright, 1929.

Beck, Charlotte. *The Fugitive Legacy: A Critical History*. Baton Rouge: Louisiana State University Press, 2001.

Beeby, James, and Donald G. Nieman. "The Rise of Jim Crow, 1880–1920." In Boles, *Companion to the American South*, 336–47.

Benítez-Rojo, Antonio. *The Repeating Island: The Caribbean and the Postmodern Perspective*. Durham: Duke University Press, 1992.

Benson, Melanie. "Southern and Western Native Americans in Barry Hannah's Fiction." In *New Perspectives on Barry Hannah*. Ed. Martyn Bone. Oxford: University Press of Mississippi, 2006.

Bergland, Renée. *The National Uncanny: Indian Ghosts and American Subjects*. Hanover: University Press of New England, 2000.

Betts, Doris. "Beasts of the Southern Wild." In Perry and Weaks, *Southern Women's Writing*, 305–17.

Bhabha, Homi. *The Location of Culture*. New York: Routledge, 1994.

Billings, Dwight B., Gurney Norman, and Katherine Ledford, eds. *Confronting Appalachian Stereotypes: Back Talk from an American Region*. Lexington: University Press of Kentucky, 1999.

Bishop, Alan J. *Mathematical Enculturation: A Cultural Perspective on Mathematics Education.* Boston: Kluwer, 1988.

———. "Western Mathematics: The Secret Weapon of Cultural Imperialism." *Race and Class* 32 (1990): 51–65.

Blotner, Joseph. *Faulkner: A Biography.* New York: Vintage, 1974.

Boelhower, William. *Through a Glass Darkly: Ethnic Semiosis in American Literature.* New York: Oxford University Press, 1987.

Boles, John B., ed. *A Companion to the American South.* Malden, U.K.: Blackwell, 2001.

Booth, Michael. "Thomas Harriot's Translations." *Yale Journal of Criticism* 16.2 (2003): 345–61.

Boyd, Valerie. *Wrapped in Rainbows: The Life of Zora Neale Hurston.* New York: Scribner's, 2003.

Brace, Marianne. Interview. "Valerie Martin: Good Girls, Bad Girls, Sex, and Power." Independent.co.uk, July 4, 2004 <http://www.independent.co.uk>, accessed August 2007.

Bragg, Rick. *All Over But the Shoutin'.* New York: Vintage, 1987.

Brantley, Will. *Feminine Sense in Southern Memoir: Smith, Glasgow, Welty, Hellman, Porter, and Hurston.* Jackson: University Press of Mississippi, 1993.

Brill de Ramírez, Susan Berry. "The Power and Presence of Native Oral Storytelling Traditions in the Poetry of Marilou Awiakta, Kimberly Blaeser, and Marilyn Dumont." In Rader and Gould, *Speak to Me Words,* 82–102.

Bryant, J. A., Jr. *Twentieth-Century Southern Literature.* Lexington: University Press of Kentucky, 1997.

Budge, E. A. Wallis, Sir. *From Fetish to God in Ancient Egypt.* London: Oxford University Press, 1934.

Burton, David M. *The History of Mathematics: An Introduction.* New York: McGraw Hill, 1997.

Bushnell, Amy Turner. "The First Southerners: Indians of the Early South." In Boles, *Companion to the American South,* 3–23.

Cajori, Florian. *A History of Mathematics.* New York: MacMillan, 1919.

Caldwell, Erskine. *God's Little Acre.* New York: Grosset and Dunlap, 1933.

———. *Tobacco Road.* New York: Grosset and Dunlap, 1932.

Cao, Lan. *Monkey Bridge.* New York: Penguin, 1997.

Carey, Gary. *Anita Loos: A Biography.* New York: Knopf, 1988.

Cash, W. J. *The Mind of the South.* New York: Vintage, 1941.

Cella, Laurie J. C. "Narrative 'Confidence Games': Framing the Blonde Spectacle in *Gentlemen Prefer Blondes* (1925) and *Nights at the Circus* (1984)." *Frontiers* 25.3 (2004): 47–62.

Césaire, Aimé. *Discourse on Colonialism.* 1950. Trans. Joan Pinkham. New York: Monthly Review Press, 2000.

Clawson, Calvin. *The Mathematical Traveler: Exploring the Grand History of Numbers.* Cambridge: Perseus, 1994.

Clinton, Catherine. *The Plantation Mistress: Women's World in the Old South.* New York: Pantheon, 1982.

Cobb, James C., and William Stueck, eds. *Globalization and the American South.* Athens: University of Georgia Press, 2005.

Cohen, Patricia. "Interpreting Some Overlooked Stories from the South." *New York Times*, May 1, 2007.

Cohn, Deborah N. *History and Memory in the Two Souths: Recent Southern and Spanish American Fiction.* Nashville: Vanderbilt University Press, 1999.

Conkin, Paul K. *The Southern Agrarians.* Knoxville: University of Tennessee Press, 1988.

Costello, Brannon. "Hybridity and Racial Identity in Walker Percy's *The Last Gentleman*," *Mississippi Quarterly* 55.1 (winter 2001/02): 3–41.

Crowe, Charles. "Indians and Blacks in White America." In Hudson, *Four Centuries of Southern Indians*, 148–69.

Crowe, Thomas Rain. "Marilou Awiakta: Reweaving the Future." *Appalachian Journal* 18.1 (fall 1990): 40–54.

Dabney, Lewis M. *The Indians of Yoknapatawpha.* Baton Rouge: Louisiana State University Press, 1974.

Dale, Corinne. "*Absalom, Absalom!* and the Snopes Trilogy: Southern Patriarchy in Revision." *Mississippi Quarterly* 45.3 (summer 1992): 321–37.

Daniel, Pete. *Lost Revolutions: The South in the 1950s.* Chapel Hill: University of North Carolina Press, 2000.

———. *The Shadow of Slavery: Peonage in the South, 1901–1969.* New York: Oxford University Press, 1972.

———. *Standing at the Crossroads: Southern Life in the Twentieth Century.* Baltimore: Johns Hopkins University Press, 1996.

Dash, Michael. "In Search of the Lost Body: Redefining the Subject in Caribbean Literature." *Kunapipi* 11.1 (1989).

Davis, Thadious. "Alice Walker's Celebration of Self in Southern Generations." *Southern Quarterly* 21.4 (1983): 39–53.

———. "Sashaying Through the South." *South to the Future.* Athens: University of Georgia Press, 2002.

Deleuze, Gilles, and Félix Guattari. *The Anti-Oedipus: Capitalism and Schizophrenia.* Minneapolis: University of Minnesota Press, 1983.

Deloria, Philip. *Playing Indian.* New Haven: Yale University Press, 1998.

Deloria, Vine, Jr. *Custer Died for Your Sins: An Indian Manifesto.* New York: Avon, 1970.

DeMouy, Jane Krause. *Katherine Anne Porter's Women: The Eye of Her Fiction.* Austin: University of Texas Press, 1983.

DeRosier, Arthur H., Jr. "Myths and Realities in Indian Westward Removal: The Choctaw Example." In Hudson, *Four Centuries of Southern Indians*.

Desmond, John F. *Walker Percy's Search for Community.* Athens: University of Georgia Press, 2004.

Dettlinger, Chet. *The List.* With Jeff Prugh. Atlanta: Philmay Enterprises, 1983.

Dictionary.com. <http://dictionary.reference.com/> accessed August 2007.
Dictionary of Philosophy. New York: International, 1984.
Dimond, E. Grey, and Herman Hattaway, eds. *Letters from Forest Place: A Plantation Family's Correspondence 1846–1881.* Jackson: University Press of Mississippi, 1993.
Donald, David Herbert. *Look Homeward: A Life of Thomas Wolfe.* New York: Fawcett Columbine, 1987.
Dorris, Michael. "Queen of Diamonds." In Lesley, *Talking Leaves,* 46–60.
Doyle, Don H. *Faulkner's County: The Historical Roots of Yoknapatawpha.* Chapel Hill: University of North Carolina Press, 2001.
Doyle, Laura. "The Body Against Itself in Faulkner's Phenomenology of Race." *American Literature* 73.2 (2001): 339–64.
DuBois, W. E. B. *The Souls of Black Folk: Writings.* New York: Library of America, 1986.
Duck, Leigh Anne. *The Nation's Region: Southern Modernism, Segregation, and U.S. Nationalism.* Athens: University of Georgia Press, 2006.
Dussere, Erik. *Balancing the Books: Faulkner, Morrison, and the Economies of Slavery.* New York: Routledge, 2003.
Early, James. *The Making of Go Down, Moses.* Dallas: Southern Methodist University Press, 1972.
Edwards, Grace Toney. "Marilou Awiakta: Poet for the People." In *Her Words: Diverse Voices in Contemporary Appalachian Women's Poetry,* 17–34. Ed. Felicia Mitchell. Knoxville: University of Tennessee Press, 2002.
Elias, Amy J. "Fragments that Run Up the Shores: *Pushing the Bear,* Coyote Aesthetics, and Recovered History." *Modern Fiction Studies* 45.1 (spring 1999): 185–211.
Ellis, A. B. *The Land of Fetish.* Westport, Conn.: Negro University Press, 1970.
Ellison, Ralph. "King of the Bingo Game." In *Flying Home,* 123–36. New York: Vintage, 1996.
Entzminger, Betina. *The Belle Gone Bad: White Southern Women Writers and the Dark Seductress.* Baton Rouge: Louisiana State University Press, 2002.
Erdrich, Louise. "The Bingo Van." In Lesley, *Talking Leaves,* 82–99.
Fanon, Frantz. *Black Skin, White Masks.* Trans. Charles Lam Markmann. New York: Grove, 1967.
———. *The Wretched of the Earth.* Trans. Constance Farrington. New York: Grove, 1968.
Farley, Reynolds. "Racial Identities in 2000: The Response to the Multiple-Race Question." In *The New Race Question: How the Census Counts Multiracial Individuals,* 33–61. Eds. Joel Perlmann and Mary C. Waters. New York: Russell Sage Foundation, 2002.
Faulkner, William. *Absalom, Absalom!* 1936. New York: Vintage, 1990.
———. *As I Lay Dying.* 1930. New York: Vintage, 1957.
———. *Go Down, Moses.* 1942. New York: Vintage, 1990.
———. *The Hamlet.* New York: Random House, 1940.
———. *Intruder in the Dust.* 1948. New York: Vintage, 1991.

———. *Light in August*. 1932. New York: Vintage, 1990.

———. *The Mansion*. New York: Random House, 1959.

———. *The Sound and the Fury*. 1929. New York: Vintage, 1990.

———. *The Town*. New York: Random House, 1957.

Fauvel, John, Raymond Flood, and Robin Wilson, eds., *Music and Mathematics: From Pythagoras to Fractals*. New York: Oxford University Press, 2004.

Fitz, Karsten. "Native and Christian: Religion and Spirituality as Transcultural Negotiation in American Indian Novels of the 1990s." *American Indian Culture and Research Journal* 26.2 (2002): 1–15.

Fitzhugh, George. *Cannibals All!; or, Slaves Without Masters*. Richmond: A. Morris, 1857.

———. *Sociology for the South; or, The Failure of Free Society*. Richmond: A. Morris, 1854.

Flanagan, Maureen. *America Reformed: Progressives and Progressivism, 1890s–1920s*. New York: Oxford University Press, 2007.

Fletcher, John Gould. "Education, Past and Present." In *I'll Take My Stand*, 92–121.

Flora, Joseph M. "The Fiction of the 1920s: Some New Voices." In Rubin, *History of Southern Literature*, 279–90.

Fogel, Robert William. *Without Consent or Contract*. Vol. 1, *The Rise and Fall of American Slavery*. New York: W. W. Norton, 1989.

Fogel, Robert William, and Stanley L. Engerman. *Time on the Cross: The Economics of American Negro Slavery*. 1974. New York: W. W. Norton, 1995.

Foucault, Michel. "George Canguilhem: Philosopher of Error." *Ideology and Consciousness* 7 (1980):53–54.

Frederickson, George M. *The Arrogance of Race: Historical Perspectives on Slavery, Racism, and Social Inequality*. Middletown: Wesleyan University Press, 1988.

Freud, Sigmund. "A Child Is Being Beaten." 1919. *Penguin Freud Library*, Vol. 10, *On Psychopathology*, 159–94. Ed. Angela Richards. London: Penguin, 1993.

———. *The Standard Edition of the Complete Psychological Works of Sigmund Freud*. Ed. James Strachey. 24 vols. London: Hogarth, 1953–74.

Gallagher, Carol, and Keith Schneider. *American Ground Zero: The Secret Nuclear War*. Cambridge: MIT Press, 1993.

Gamman, Lorraine, and Merja Makinen. *Female Fetishism*. New York: New York University Press, 1994.

Gandhi, Leela. *Postcolonial Theory: A Critical Introduction*. New York: Columbia University Press, 1998.

Gardner, Christopher. *The Pursuit of Happyness*. With Quincy Troupe and Mim Eichler Rivas. New York: Amistad, 2006.

Garner, Marcus K. "Books: I grew up [during the] . . . child murders. That affected me." Interview with Karin Slaughter. Main Edition. *Atlanta Journal-Constitution*, Aug 18, 2006, K6.

Gates, Henry Louis, Jr. *Figures in Black*. New York: Oxford University Press, 1987.

———. *Future of the Race*. New York: Alfred A. Knopf, 1996.

———. "Introduction: Zora Neale Hurston: Establishing the Canon." *The Complete Stories*, ix–xxiii. New York: Harper Perennial, 2006.

———. "Introduction to the Vintage Edition." In *The Autobiography of an Ex-Coloured Man*, by James Weldon Johnson (1927). New York: Vintage, 1989.

———. *The Signifying Monkey: A Theory of African-American Literary Criticism*. New York: Oxford University Press, 1988.

Gendron, Bernard. *Between Montmartre and the Mudd Club: Popular Music and the Avant Garde*. Chicago: University of Chicago Press, 2002.

Genovese, Eugene D. *In Red and Black: Marxian Explorations in Southern and Afro-American History*. Knoxville: University of Tennessee Press, 1984.

———. *The Political Economy of Slavery: Studies in the Economy and Society of the Slave South*. New York: Pantheon, 1965.

———. *Roll, Jordan, Roll*. New York: Pantheon, 1972.

Gidley, Mick, and Ben Gidley. "The Native-American South." In *A Companion to the Literature and Culture of the American South*, 166–84. Ed. Richard Gray and Owen Robinson. Malden, U.K.: Blackwell, 2004.

Gispen, Kees, ed. *What Made the South Different? Essays and Comments*. Porter L. Fortune Chancellor's Symposium on Southern History Series (1989). Jackson: University Press of Mississippi, 1990.

Glymph, Thavolia, ed. *Essays on the Postbellum Southern Economy*. College Station: Texas A&M University Press, 1985.

———. "The South in the History of the Transatlantic World." In Gispen, *What Made the South Different?*, 3–18.

Godden, Richard. *Fictions of Labor: William Faulkner and the South's Long Revolution*. New York: Cambridge University Press, 1997.

Godden, Richard, and Noel Polk. "Reading the Ledgers." *Mississippi Quarterly* 55.3 (summer 2002): 301–59.

Goldfield, David R. "The Rise of the Sunbelt: Urbanization and Industrialization." In Boles, *Companion to the American South*, 474–93.

———. *Still Fighting the Civil War: The American South and Southern History*. Baton Rouge: Louisiana State University Press, 2002.

Gray, Richard J. *The Life of William Faulkner*. Cambridge, U.K.: Blackwell Press, 1994.

———. "'Maybe Nothing Ever Happens Once and Is Finished': Some Notes on Recent Southern Fiction and Social Change." Eccles Centre for American Studies, Plenary Lecture, British American Studies Association Annual Conference, 2004.

Grubbs, Donald. *Cry from the Cotton: The Southern Tenant Farmers' Union and the New Deal*. Chapel Hill: University of North Carolina Press, 1971.

Gruesser, John Cullen. *Confluences: Postcolonialism, African American Literary Studies, and the Black Atlantic*. Athens: University of Georgia Press, 2005.

Grunberger, Béla. *New Essays on Narcissism*. Ed. and trans. David Macey. London: Free Association Books, 1989.

Guterl, Matthew Press. *The Color of Race in America, 1900–1940*. Cambridge: Harvard University Press, 2004.

Hahn, Steven. "Emancipation and the Development of Capitalist Agriculture: The South in Comparative Perspective." In Gispen, *What Made the South Different?*, 71–88.

———. *A Nation Under Our Feet: Black Political Struggles in the Rural South from Slavery to Migration*. Cambridge: Harvard University Press, 2003.

Hale, Grace Elizabeth. *Making Whiteness: The Culture of Segregation in the South, 1890–1940*. New York: Vintage, 1999.

Hamblin, Robert W., and Ann Abadie, eds. *Faulkner in the Twenty-First Century*. Jackson: University Press of Mississippi, 2003.

Handley, George B. *Postslavery Literatures in the Americas: Family Portraits in Black and White*. Charlottesville: University Press of Virginia, 2000.

Harjo, Joy. "We Must Call a Meeting." In *In Mad Love and War*, 9–10. Hanover, N.H.: Wesleyan University Press, 1990.

Harkleroad, Leon. *The Math Behind the Music*. New York: Cambridge University Press, 2006.

Harris, Cheryl. "Whiteness as Property." *Harvard Law Review* 106 (June 1993): 1709–91.

Harris, Wilson. "History, Fable, and Myth in the Caribbean and the Guianas." *Explorations: A Selection of Talks and Articles 1966–81*. Mundlestrup, Australia: Dangaroo, 1981.

Harwell, David Horace. *Walker Percy Remembered: A Portrait in the Words of Those Who Knew Him*. Chapel Hill: University of North Carolina Press, 2006.

Headley, Bernard. *The Atlanta Youth Murders and the Politics of Race*. Carbondale: Southern Illinois University Press, 1998.

Hegeman, Susan. "Taking Blondes Seriously." *American Literary History* 7.3 (fall 1995): 535–54.

Hobson, Fred, ed. *South to the Future: An American Region in the Twenty-first Century*. Athens: University of Georgia Press, 2002.

Hodgson, Godfrey. *The Gentleman from New York: Daniel Patrick Moynihan*. New York: Houghton Mifflin, 2000.

Hoeller, Hildegard. "Racial Currency: Zora Neale Hurston's "The Gilded Six-Bits and the Gold Standard Debate." *American Literature* 77.4 (Dec. 2005): 761–85.

Holland, Eugene W. "*The Anti-Oedipus*: Postmodernism in Theory; Or, the Post-Lacanian Historical Contextualization of Psychoanalysis." *Boundary 2* 14.1/2 (autumn 1985–winter 1986): 291–307.

Holman, C. Hugh. "Thomas Wolfe and the Stigma of Autobiography." *Virginia Quarterly Review* 40.4 (autumn 1964): 614–25.

Horne, Jed. *Breach of Faith: Hurricane Katrina and the Near Death of a Great American City*. New York: Random House, 2006.

Howland, Mary Deems. *The Gift of the Other: Gabriel Marcel's Concept of Intersubjectivity in Walker Percy's Novels*. Pittsburgh: Duquesne University Press, 1990.

Hudson, Charles M., ed. *Four Centuries of Southern Indians*. Athens: University of Georgia Press, 1975.

Huggan, Graham. *Territorial Disputes: Maps and Mapping Strategies in Contemporary Canadian and Australian Fiction*. Toronto: University of Toronto Press, 1994.

Hurston, Zora Neale. "The Gilded Six-Bits." In *The Complete Stories*, 86–98. New York: Harper Perennial, 2006.

I'll Take My Stand: The South and the Agrarian Tradition. Twelve Southerners. 1930. Baton Rouge: Louisiana State University Press, 1977.

Ishiguro, Hide. *Leibniz's Philosophy of Logic and Language.* New York: Cambridge University Press, 1990.

JanMohamed, Abdul R. "The Economy of Manichean Allegory." In Ashcroft et al., *Postcolonial Studies Reader*, 18–23.

Jaskoski, Helen. "Two Comments on 'Teaching in a Nuclear Age.'" *College English* 49.4 (Apr. 1987): 480–82.

Jehlen, Myra. *Class and Character in Faulkner's South.* Secaucus: Citadel, 1978.

Johnson, James Weldon. *Along This Way.* New York: Viking Press, 1933.

———. *The Autobiography of an Ex-Coloured Man.* 1927. New York: Vintage, 1989.

Johnson, Joan Marie. *Southern Ladies, New Women: Race, Region, and Clubwomen in South Carolina, 1890–1930.* Gainesville: University Press of Florida, 2004.

Johnson, Walter. *Soul By Soul: Life Inside the Antebellum Slave Market.* Cambridge: Harvard University Press, 1999.

Jones, Anne Goodwyn. *Tomorrow Is Another Day: The Woman Writer in the South, 1859–1936.* Baton Rouge: Louisiana State University Press, 1981.

Jones, Gayl. "Breaking Out of the Conventions of Dialect." In Wall, *Sweat*, 153–68.

Jones, Suzanne W. "Reading the Endings in Katherine Anne Porter's 'Old Mortality.'" *Southern Quarterly* 31 (spring 1993): 29–44.

Jones, Suzanne W., and Sharon Monteith, eds. *South to a New Place: Region, Literature, Culture.* Baton Rouge: Louisiana State University Press, 2002.

Jones, Tayari. *Leaving Atlanta.* New York: Warner, 2002.

Joseph, Philip. *American Literary Regionalism in a Global Age.* Baton Rouge: Louisiana State University Press, 2006.

Justice, Daniel Heath. "Beloved Woman Returns: The Doubleweaving of Homeland and Identity in the Poetry of Marilou Awiakta." In Rader and Gould, *Speak to Me Words*, 71–81.

———. *Our Fire Survives the Storm: A Cherokee Literary History.* Minneapolis: University of Minnesota Press, 2006.

Justus, James H. Review of *Walker Percy: A Southern Wayfarer*, by William Rodney Allen. *American Literature* 61 (1989): 127–28.

Kaplan, Robert. *The Nothing That Is.* New York: Oxford University Press, 1999.

Kawash, Samira. "*The Autobiography of an Ex-Coloured Man*: (Passing for) Black Passing for White." In *Passing and the Fictions of Identity*, 59–74. Ed. Elaine K. Ginsberg. Durham: Duke University Press, 1996.

Kelley, Edith Summers. *Weeds.* New York: Feminist Press, 1923.

Kennedy, Richard S. *The Window of Memory: The Literary Career of Thomas Wolfe.* Chapel Hill: University of North Carolina Press, 1962.

Kertzer, David I., and Dominique Arel. *Census and Identity.* New York: Cambridge University Press, 2002.

Khanna, Ranjana. *Dark Continents: Psychoanalysis and Colonialism*. Durham: Duke University Press, 2003.

Kidwell, Clara Sue. *Choctaws and Missionaries in Mississippi, 1818–1918*. Norman: University of Oklahoma Press, 1995.

Kilpatrick, Jacqueline. *Louis Owens: Literary Reflections on His Life and Work*. Norman: University of Oklahoma Press, 2004.

Kincaid, Jamaica. *The Autobiography of My Mother*. New York: Plume, 1997.

King, C. Richard. *Postcolonial America*. Urbana: University of Illinois Press, 2000.

King, Richard H. *A Southern Renaissance: The Cultural Awakening of the American South, 1930–1955*. New York: Oxford University Press, 1980.

———. "Working Through: Faulkner's *Go Down, Moses*." In *Modern Critical Views: William Faulkner*, 193–205. Ed. Harold Bloom. New York: Chelsea House, 1986.

Kirby, Jack Temple. *Rural Worlds Lost: The American South, 1920–1960*. Baton Rouge: Louisiana State University Press, 1987.

Kobre, Michael. *Walker Percy's Voices*. Athens: University of Georgia Press, 2000.

Kreyling, Michael. "Faulkner in the Twenty-first Century: Boundaries of Meaning, Boundaries of Mississippi." In Hamblin and Abadie, *Faulkner in the Twenty-first Century*, 14–30.

Krips, Henry. *Fetish: An Erotics of Culture*. Ithaca: Cornell University Press, 1999.

Kromm, Chris. "Election Lesson: Democrats, DON'T write off the South." *Facing South*, Nov. 15, 2006, <http://southernstudies.org/facingsouth/2006/11/election-lesson-democrats-dont-write.asp>, accessed August 2007.

Krupat, Arnold. *Ethnocriticism: Ethnography, History, Literature*. Berkeley: University of California Press, 1992.

———. *The Turn to the Native: Studies in Criticism and Culture*. Lincoln: University of Nebraska Press, 1996.

Kruse, Kevin M. *White Flight: Atlanta and the Making of Modern Conservatism*. Princeton: Princeton University Press, 2005.

Lacan, Jacques. *Écrits*. Trans. Alan Sheridan. New York: Tavistock, 1977.

Ladd, Barbara. *Nationalism and the Color Line in George W. Cable, Mark Twain, and William Faulkner*. Baton Rouge: Louisiana State University Press, 1996.

LaLonde, Christopher A. *Grave Concerns, Trickster Turns: The Novels of Louis Owens*. Norman: University of Oklahoma Press, 2002.

Landers, Jane. "Slave Resistance in the Southeastern Frontier: Fugitives, Maroons, and Banditti in the Age of Revolution." In Smith and Cohn, *Look Away!* 80–93.

Lasch, Christopher. *The Culture of Narcissism: American Life in an Age of Diminishing Expectations*. New York: W. W. Norton, 1978.

Lassiter, Matthew. *The Silent Majority: Suburban Politics in the Sunbelt South*. Princeton: Princeton University Press, 2005.

Lawson, Lewis A. *Still Following Percy*. Jackson: University Press of Mississippi, 1996.

Leibniz, G. W. *G. W. Leibniz: De Summa Rerum: Metaphysical Papers, 1675–76*. Ed. G. H. R. Parkinson. New Haven: Yale University Press, 1992.

———. *G. W. Leibniz: Philosophical Essays.* Edited by Roger Ariew and Daniel Garber. Indianapolis: Hackett, 1989.

Lesley, Craig, ed. *Talking Leaves.* New York: Laurel, 1991.

Letwin, Daniel. "Labor Relations in the Industrializing South." In Boles, *Companion to the American South,* 424–43.

Limon, Jose. *American Encounters: Greater Mexico, the United States, and the Erotics of Culture.* Boston: Beacon Press, 1998.

Lipsitz, George. *The Possessive Investment in Whiteness: How White People Profit from Identity Politics.* Philadelphia: Temple University Press, 2006.

Loos, Anita. *Gentlemen Prefer Blondes: The Illuminating Diary of a Professional Lady.* Introduction by Candace Bushnell. New York: Liveright, 1998.

———. *Gentlemen Prefer Blondes* and *But Gentlemen Marry Brunettes.* New York: Penguin, 1989.

Lowe, John. "From 'Jump at the Sun': Zora Neale Hurston's Cosmic Comedy." In Wall, *Sweat,* 183–92.

Mackethun, Gesa. "America's Troubled Post-coloniality: Some Reflections from Abroad." *Discourse* 22.3 (fall 2000): 34–45.

Madsen, Deborah L. *Beyond the Borders: American Literature and Post-colonial Theory.* Sterling: Pluto, 2003.

Magi, Aldo P., and Richard Walser, eds. *Thomas Wolfe Interviewed, 1929–1938.* Baton Rouge: Louisiana State University Press, 1985.

Makowsky, Veronica. "Walker Percy and Southern Literature." *The Walker Percy Project.* 1996. <http://www.ibiblio.org/wpercy/makowsky.html>, accessed August 2007.

Martin, Biddy, and Chandra Talpande Mohanty. "Feminist Politics: What's Home Got to Do With It?" In *Feminist Studies/Critical Studies,* 191–212. Ed. Teresa de Lauretis. Bloomington: Indiana University Press, 1986.

Martin, Joel W. "'My Grandmother Was a Cherokee Princess': Representations of Indians in Southern History." In *Dressing in Feathers: The Construction of the Indian in American Popular Culture,* 129–47. Ed. S. Elizabeth Bird. Boulder: Westview Press, 1996.

Martin, Valerie. *Mary Reilly.* New York: Doubleday, 1990.

———. *Property.* New York: Vintage, 2003.

Marx, Karl. *Kapital.* Chicago: C. H. Kerr and Co, 1906.

Matthews, John T. "Recalling the West Indies: From Yoknapatawpha to Haiti and Back." *American Literary History* 16.2 (2004): 238–62.

———. "Touching Race in *Go Down, Moses.*" In Wagner-Martin, *New Essays on "Go Down, Moses,"* 21–47.

McClintock, Anne. "The Angel of Progress: Pitfalls of the Term 'Post-colonialism.'" *Social Text* (1992): 1–15.

———. *Imperial Leather: Race, Gender, and Sexuality in the Colonial Contest.* New York: Routledge, 1995.

———, Aamir Mufti, and Ella Shohat, eds. *Dangerous Liaisons: Gender, Nation, and Postcolonial Perspectives.* Minnesota: University of Minnesota Press, 1997.

McDowell, Amber. "Republican Candidate Admits Supporting Eugenics." *Independent / UK*, Aug. 4, 2004. Viewed online at CommonDreams.org News Center, <http://www.commondreams.org/headlines04/0804-01.htm>, accessed August 2007.

McLaughlin, Glenn E., and Stefan Robock. *Why Industry Moves South: A Study of the Factors Influencing the Recent Location of Manufacturing Plants in the South*. Kingsport, Tenn.: Kingsport Press, 1949.

McMillen, Neil. *The Citizen's Council: Organized Resistance to the Second Reconstruction, 1954–1964*. Urbana: University of Illinois Press, 1971.

Mencken, H. L. "Sahara of the Bozart." In *Prejudices: Second Series*. New York: Knopf, 1920.

Meyer, Carter Jones, and Diana Royer, eds. *Selling the Indian: Commercializing and Appropriating American Indian Cultures*. Tucson: University of Arizona Press, 2001.

Michaelsen, Scott. *The Limits of Multiculturalism: Interrogating the Origins of American Anthropology*. Minneapolis: University of Minnesota Press, 1999.

Milligan, Robert. *The Fetish Folk of West Africa*. New York: AMS Press, 1970.

Minh-ha, Trinh T. *Woman, Native, Other*. Bloomington: Indiana University Press, 1989.

Mitchell, Margaret. *Gone with the Wind*. New York: Macmillan, 1936.

Mohl, Raymond A. "Globalization, Latinization, and the *Nuevo* New South." In Cobb and Stueck, *Globalization and the American South*, 66–99.

Moore, Gene M., ed. "Faulkner's Indians—Special Issue." *Faulkner Journal*. 18.1/2 (fall 2002 / spring 2003).

Moore, MariJo. *Feeding the Ancient Fires: A Collection of Writings by N.C. American Indians*. Greensboro: Crossroads Press, 1999.

———. *Genocide of the Mind: New Native American Writing*. New York: Nation Books, 2003.

Morran, Richard, et al. "Iraq Sanctions: Humanitarian Implications and Options for the Future." Global Policy Forum, Aug. 6, 2002, <http://www.globalpolicy.org/security/sanction/iraq1/2002/paper.htm#3>, accessed August 2007.

Morrison, Toni. *The Bluest Eye*. New York: Holt, Rinehart, and Winston, 1970.

———. *Playing in the Dark: Whiteness and the Literary Imagination*. New York: Vintage, 1993.

Mould, Tom. *Choctaw Prophecy: A Legacy of the Future*. Tuscaloosa: University of Alabama Press, 2003.

Mulvey, Laura. "*Xala*, Ousmane Sembene 1976: The Carapace That Failed." In *Colonial Discourse and Post-Colonial Theory: A Reader*, 517–34. Ed. Patrick Williams and Laura Chrisman. New York: Columbia University Press, 1994.

Myrdal, Gunnar. *An American Dilemma: The Negro Problem and Modern Democracy*. New York: Harper and Row, 1944.

Newby, I. A. *Challenge to the Court: Social Scientists and the Defense of Segregation, 1954–1966*. Baton Rouge: Louisiana State University Press, 1967.

Newman, Frances. *Dead Lovers Are Faithful Lovers*. 1928. Athens: University of Georgia Press, 1994.

———. *Frances Newman's Letters.* Edited by Hansell Baugh, with a prefatory note by James Branch Cabell. New York: Liveright, 1929.

———. *The Hard-Boiled Virgin.* 1926. Athens: University of Georgia Press, 1980. Foreword by Anne Firor Scott.

Nguyen, Viet Thanh, and Tina Chen, eds. "Postcolonial Asian America." Special issue, *Jouvert* 4.3 (spring/summer 2000).

Nixon, Herman Clarence. "Whither Southern Economy?" In *I'll Take My Stand*, 176–200.

Nowell, Elizabeth. *Thomas Wolfe, A Biography.* Garden City, N.Y.: Doubleday, 1960.

Odum, Howard. *Southern Regions of the United States.* Chapel Hill: University of North Carolina Press, 1936.

Orwell, George. *Nineteen Eighty-four.* New York: Signet, 1949.

Ovid, *Metamorphoses, Books 1–5.* Edited by William S. Anderson. Norman: University of Oklahoma, 1997.

Owens, Louis. "As If an Indian Were Really an Indian: Native American Voices and Postcolonial Theory." In *Native American Representations: First Encounters, Distorted Images, and Literary Appropriations*, 11–24. Ed. Gretchen M. Bataille. Lincoln: University of Nebraska Press, 2001.

———. *Bone Game.* Norman: University of Oklahoma Press, 1993.

———. "Finding Gene." *Weber Studies* 16.2 (winter 1999), at <http://weberstudies.weber.edu/archive/archive%20C%20Vol.%2016.2–18.1/Vol.%2016.2/louisowens.html>, accessed July 19, 2006.

———. *Mixedblood Messages.* Norman: University of Oklahoma Press, 1998.

———. *The Sharpest Sight.* Norman: University of Oklahoma Press, 1992.

———. "'The Song Is Very Short': Native American Literature and Literary Theory." *Weber Studies* 12.3 (fall 1995): 51–62.

———. "The Syllogistic Mixedblood: How Roland Barthes Saved Me from the *indians*." In *Mixing Race, Mixing Culture: Inter-American Literary Dialogues*, 227–39. Ed. Monika Kaup and Debra K. Rosenthal. Austin: University of Texas Press, 2002.

Owsley, Frank Lawrence. "The Irrepressible Conflict." In *I'll Take My Stand*, 61–91.

Oxford English Dictionary. 2nd ed. New York: Oxford University Press, 1989. OED Online. <http://dictionary.oed.com>, accessed Jan.–Nov. 2006.

Painter, Nell Irvin. *Southern History across the Color Line.* Chapel Hill: University of North Carolina Press, 2002.

Paredes, J. Anthony, ed. *Indians of the Southeastern United States in the Late Twentieth Century.* Tuscaloosa: University of Alabama Press, 1992.

Parkinson, G. H. R., ed. *G. W. Leibniz: De Summa Rerum: Metaphysical Papers, 1675–76.* New Haven: Yale University Press, 1992.

Peacock, James L., Harry L. Watson, and Carrie R. Matthews, eds. *The American South in a Global World.* Chapel Hill: University of North Carolina Press, 2005.

Percy, Walker. *The Last Gentleman.* New York: Picador, 1966.

Percy, William Alexander. *Lanterns on the Levee: Reflections of a Planter's Son.* 1941. Baton Rouge: Louisiana State University Press, 1973.

Perry, Carolyn, and Mary Louise Weaks, eds. *The History of Southern Women's Literature*. Baton Rouge: Louisiana State University Press, 2002.

Persky, Joseph J. *The Burden of Dependency: Colonial Themes in Southern Economic Thought*. Baltimore: Johns Hopkins University Press, 1992.

Peterson, Carla L. "Capitalism, Black (Under)Development, and the Production of the African-American Novel in the 1850s." In Singh and Schmidt, *Postcolonial Theory and the United States*, 176–95.

Peterson, John H., Jr. Introduction, part 1, "Setting the Stage: The Original Mississippians." In *Ethnic Heritage in Mississippi*. Ed. Barbara Carpenter. Jackson: Mississippi Humanities Council, 1992.

Phillips, Ulrich B. *Life and Labor in the Old South*. Boston: Little, Brown, 1929.

Pietz, William. "The Problem of the Fetish." Parts 1–3. *RES: Journal of Anthropology and Aesthetics* 9 (1985): 5–17; 13 (1987): 23–45; 16 (1988): 105–23.

Pifer, Lynn. "Coming to Voice in Alice Walker's *Meridian*: Speaking Out for the Revolution." *African American Review* 26.1 (spring 1992): 77–88.

Pioch, Nicolas. "Degas, (Hilaire-Germain-) Edgar," WebMuseum, Paris entry, Aug. 19, 2002, at <http://www.ibiblio.org/wm/paint/auth/degas/>, accessed August 2007.

Poovey, Mary. *History of the Modern Fact: Problems of Knowledge in the Sciences of Wealth and Society*. Chicago: University of Chicago, 1998.

Porter, Katherine Anne. *Flowering Judas and Other Stories*. 1930. New York: Signet, 1970.

———. *Pale Horse, Pale Rider*. New York: Signet, 1939.

Posnock, Ross. *Color and Culture: Black Writers and the Making of the Modern Intellectual*. Cambridge: Harvard University Press, 1998.

Purdue, Theda, and Michael D. Green. *The Columbia Guide to American Indians of the Southeast*. New York: Columbia University Press, 2001.

Purdy, John. "A Conversation with Louis Owens." *Studies in American Indian Literatures* Series 2, 10.2 (summer 1998): 6–22.

Quarles, Benjamin. *The Negro in the Making of America*. New York: Collier-MacMillan, 1970.

Rader, Dean, and Janice Gould, eds. *Speak to Me Words: Essays on Contemporary American Indian Poetry*. Tucson: University of Arizona Press, 2003.

Railey, Kevin. *Natural Aristocracy: History, Ideology, and the Production of William Faulkner*. Tuscaloosa: University of Alabama Press, 1999.

Ransom, John Crowe. "Reconstructed but Unregenerate." In *I'll Take My Stand*, 1–27.

Ransom, Roger L., and Richard Sutch. *One Kind of Freedom: The Economic Consequences of Emancipation*. New York: Cambridge University Press, 1977.

Raper, Julius Rowan. "Inventing Modern Southern Fiction: A Postmodern View." *Southern Literary Journal* 22.2 (1990): 3–18.

Reimers, David M. "Asian Immigrants in the South." In Cobb and Stueck, *Globalization and the American South*, 100–134.

Rivkin, Julie, and Michael Ryan, eds. *Literary Theory: An Anthology.* Malden, U.K.: Blackwell, 1998.

Roberts, Elizabeth Madox. *The Time of Man.* New York: Viking, 1926.

Roberts, Giselle. *The Confederate Belle.* Columbia: University of Missouri Press, 2003.

Roediger, David R. *The Wages of Whiteness: Race and the Making of the American Working Class.* New York: Verso, 1999.

Rogin, Michael. *Fathers and Children: Andrew Jackson and the Subjugation of the American Indian.* New York: Knopf, 1975.

Romine, Scott. *The Narrative Forms of Southern Community.* Baton Rouge: Lousiana State University Press, 1999.

Rosengarten, Theodore. *All God's Dangers: The Life of Nate Shaw.* New York: Knopf, 1974.

Rothstein, Edward. *Emblems of the Mind: The Inner World of Music and Mathematics.* New York: Random House, 1995.

Rothstein, Morton. "The New South and the International Economy." *Agricultural History* 57 (Oct. 1983): 385–402.

Rowley, Hazel. *Richard Wright: The Life and Times.* New York: Henry Holt, 2001.

Rozek, Barbara. *Come to Texas: Attracting Immigrants, 1865–1915.* College Station: Texas A&M University Press, 2003.

Rubin, Louis D., Jr., et al., eds. *The History of Southern Literature.* Baton Rouge: Louisiana State University Press, 1985.

Rudnicki, Robert. *Percyscapes: The Fugue State in Twentieth-Century Southern Fiction.* Baton Rouge: Louisiana State University Press, 1999.

Russell, Bertrand. *A Critical Exposition of the Philosophy of Leibniz.* London: George Allen and Unwin, 1967.

Ryan, Maureen. "Outsiders with Inside Information: The Vietnamese in the Fiction of the Contemporary South." In Jones and Monteith, *South to a New Place*, 235–52.

Saldívar, Ramón. "Looking for a Master Plan: Faulkner, Paredes, and the Colonial and Postcolonial Subject." In *The Cambridge Companion to William Faulkner*, 96–120. Ed. Philip M. Weinstein. New York: Cambridge University Press, 1995.

Samuelson, Paul. *Foundations of Economic Analysis.* 1947. Enlarged ed. Cambridge: Harvard University Press, 1983.

Schomburg, Connie R. "Southern Women Writers in a Changing Landscape." In Perry and Weaks, *History of Southern Women's Literature*, 478–90.

Schueller, Malini Johar. *U.S. Orientalisms: Race, Nation, and Gender in Literature, 1790–1890.* Ann Arbor: University of Michigan Press, 1998.

Schueller, Malini Johar, and Edward Watts, eds. *Messy Beginnings: Postcoloniality and Early American Studies.* New Brunswick: Rutgers University Press, 2003.

Schulman, Bruce J. *From Cotton Belt to Sunbelt: Federal Policy, Economic Development, and the Transformation of the South, 1938–80.* New York: Oxford University Press, 1991.

———. "The Sunbelt South: Old Times Forgotten." *Reviews in American History* 21.2 (June 1993): 340–45.

Schulz, Jennifer Lea. "Restaging the Racial Contract: James Weldon Johnson's Signatory Strategies." *American Literature* 74.1 (2002): 31–58.

Seidel, Kathryn Lee. *The Southern Belle in the American Novel*. Tampa: University of South Florida Press, 1985.

Seife, Charles. *Zero: The Biography of a Dangerous Idea*. New York: Penguin, 2000.

Shapiro, Thomas M. *The Hidden Cost of Being African American: How Wealth Perpetuates Inequality*. New York: Oxford University Press, 2004.

Shillingsburg, Miriam. "Frances Newman." In Perry and Weaks, *History of Southern Women's Literature*, 354–58.

Showalter, Elaine. *A Literature of Their Own: British Women Novelists from Brontë to Lessing*. Princeton: Princeton University Press, 1977.

Siegel, Allen M. *Heinz Kohut and the Psychology of the Self*. New York: Routledge, 1996.

Simmons, Christina. "Women's Power in Sex: Radical Challenges to Marriage in the Early-Twentieth-Century United States." *Feminist Studies* 29.1 (spring 2003): 168–99.

Simpson, Lewis P. *The Dispossessed Garden: Pastoral and History in Southern Literature*. 1975. Baton Rouge: Louisiana State University Press, 1983.

Singh, Amritjit, and Peter Schmidt, eds. *Postcolonial Theory and the United States: Race, Ethnicity, and Literature*. Jackson: University Press of Mississippi, 2000.

Ski, Frank. "Young Victims Overlooked." *Atlanta Journal-Constitution*, June 22, 2006, A19.

Smith, Jon[athan]. "Postcolonial, Black, and Nobody's Margin: The U.S. South in New World Studies." *American Literary History* 16.1 (2004): 144–61.

———. "Southern Culture on the Skids: Punk, Retro, Narcissism, and the Burden of Southern History." In Jones and Monteith, *South to a New Place*, 76–95.

Smith, Jon[athan], and Deborah Cohn, eds. *Look Away! The U.S. South in New World Studies*. Durham: Duke University Press, 2004.

Smith, Lillian. *Killers of the Dream*. New York: W. W. Norton, 1949.

Smith, Mark M. *Debating Slavery: Economy and Society in the Antebellum American South*. New York: Cambridge University Press, 1998.

Snyder, Phillip A. "*Look Homeward, Angel* as Autobiography and Artist Novel." *Thomas Wolfe Review* 19.1 (spring 1995): 44–53.

Sokol, Jason. *There Goes My Everything: White Southerners in the Age of Civil Rights, 1945–1975*. New York: Knopf, 2006.

Sollors, Werner. *Neither White Nor Black Yet Both: Thematic Explorations of Interracial Literature*. New York: Oxford University Press, 1997.

Spillers, Hortense J. *Black, White, and in Color: Essays on American Literature and Culture*. Chicago: University of Chicago Press, 2003.

Squires, Radcliffe. *Allen Tate: A Literary Biography*. New York: Pegasus, 1971.

Stanton, William. *The Leopard's Spots: Scientific Attitudes Toward Race in America, 1815–59*. Chicago: University of Chicago Press, 1960.

Stein, Karen. "*Meridian*: Alice Walker's Critique of Revolution." *Black American Literature Forum* 20 (1986): 129–41.

Stephenson, Wendell Holmes. "A Quarter-Century of a Mississippi Plantation: Eli J. Capell of 'Pleasant Hill.'" *Mississippi Historical Review* 23.3 (Dec. 1936): 355–74.

Stokes, Mason. *The Color of Sex: Whiteness, Heterosexuality, and the Fictions of White Supremacy.* Durham: Duke University Press, 2001.

Sundiata, Ibrahim K. *From Slaving to Neoslavery.* Madison: University of Wisconsin, 1996.

Sundquist, Eric. *Faulkner, the House Divided.* Baltimore: Johns Hopkins University Press, 1983.

Sweeney, Mary K. *Walker Percy and the Postmodern World.* Chicago: Loyola University Press, 1987.

Swetz, Frank. *Capitalism and Arithmetic: The New Math of the Fifteenth Century.* La Salle, Ill.: Open Court, 1987.

Talley, Thomas W., ed. *Negro Folk Rhymes.* New York: MacMillan, 1922.

Tate, Allen. *The Fathers.* 1938. Athens: Swallow Press, 1984.

Tate, Claudia. *Psychoanalysis and Black Novels: Desire and the Protocols of Race.* New York: Oxford University Press, 1998.

Terry, Jennifer, and Jacqueline Urla, eds. *Deviant Bodies: Critical Perspectives on Difference in Science and Popular Culture.* Bloomington: Indiana University Press, 1995.

Thernstrom, Stephan. "New Life for the 'One Drop' Rule." *National Review*, Apr. 29, 2000, at TYSK <http://www.tysknews.com/Depts/Constitution_Issues/one_drop_rule.htm>, accessed August 2007.

Tindall, George Brown. *The Ethnic Southerners.* Baton Rouge: Louisiana State University Press, 1976.

Towner, Theresa. *Faulkner on the Color Line: The Later Novels.* Jackson: University Press of Mississippi, 2000.

Trachtenberg, Alan. *Shades of Hiawatha: Staging Indians, Making Americans, 1880–1930.* New York: Farrar, Straus and Giroux, 2004.

Trefzer, Annette. *Disturbing Indians: The Archaeology of Southern Fiction.* Tuscaloosa: University of Alabama Press, 2006.

———. "Postcolonial Displacements in Faulkner's Indian Stories of the 1930s." In Hamblin and Abadie, *Faulkner in the Twenty-first Century*, 68–88.

———. "Tracing the Natchez Trace: Native Americans and National Anxieties in Eudora Welty's 'First Love.'" *Mississippi Quarterly* 55.3 (summer 2002): 419–40.

Turner, Elizabeth Hayes. "Women in the Post-Civil War South." In Boles, *Companion to the American South*, 348–68.

Twain, Mark. *The Adventures of Huckleberry Finn.* 1885. New York: Dell, 1960.

2003 Prize Winning Author Interview (with Valerie Martin), *Orange Prize for Fiction*, at <http://www.orangeprize.co.uk/2003prize/winner/marint.shtml>, accessed July 2004.

Underwood, Thomas A. *Allen Tate: Orphan of the South.* Princeton: Princeton University Press, 2000.

———. "Autobiography and Ideology in the South: Thomas Wolfe and the Vanderbilt Agrarians." *American Literature* 61.1 (March 1989): 31–45.

United States Emergency Council. *Report on Economic Conditions of the South*. 1938. New York: DaCapo Press, 1972.
Unrue, Darlene Harbour. *Katherine Anne Porter: The Life of an Artist*. Jackson: University Press of Mississippi, 2005.
———. "Katherine Anne Porter, Politics, and Another Reading of 'Theft.'" *Studies in Short Fiction* 30.2 (spring 1993): 119–26.
Vance, Rupert B. *Human Geography of the South: A Study in Regional Resources and Human Adequacy*. 1935. New York: Russell and Russell, 1968.
Vernon, Olympia. *Logic*. New York: Grove Press, 2004.
Wade, Barbara Anne. *Frances Newman: Southern Satirist and Literary Rebel*. Tuscaloosa: University of Alabama Press, 1998.
Wagner-Martin, Linda, ed. *New Essays on "Go Down, Moses."* New York: Cambridge University Press, 1996.
Walcott, Derek. "The Muse of History." In *Is Massa Day Dead?*, 1–28. Ed. Orde Coombs. Garden City, N.Y.: Doubleday, 1974.
Walker, Adrian. "Thin Skin Hard to Heal." *Boston Globe*, Aug. 2, 2004.
Walker, Alice. *In Search of Our Mothers' Gardens*. New York: Harcourt Brace and Jovanovich, 1983.
———. *Meridian*. New York: Washington Square, 1976.
———. "The Universe Responds: or, How I learned We Can Have Peace on Earth." In *At Home on the Earth: Becoming Native to Our Place: A Multicultural Anthology*. Ed. David Landis Barnhill. Berkeley: University of California Press, 1999.
———. *The Way Forward Is with a Broken Heart*. New York: Random, 2000.
Walker, Margaret. *Richard Wright: Daemonic Genius*. New York: Amistad, 1988.
Wall, Cheryl A., ed. *Sweat: Texts and Contexts*. New Brunswick: Rutgers University Press, 1997.
Warren, Robert Penn. "The Briar Patch." In *I'll Take My Stand*, 246–64.
Warrior, Robert. *Tribal Secrets: Recovering American Indian Intellectual Traditions*. Minneapolis: University of Minnesota Press, 1994.
Watts, Edward. *Writing and Postcolonialism in the Early Republic*. Charlottesville: University Press of Virginia, 1998.
Webb, Walter Prescott. *Divided We Stand: The Crisis of a Frontierless Democracy*. New York: Farrar and Rinehart, 1937.
Weber, Max. *The Protestant Ethic and the Spirit of Capitalism*. Trans. Talcott Parsons. London: George Allen and Unwin, 1930.
Weinstein, Philip M. *Faulkner's Subject: A Cosmos No One Owns*. New York: Cambridge University Press, 1992.
Westling, Louise. *Sacred Groves and Ravaged Gardens: The Fiction of Eudora Welty, Carson McCullers, and Flannery O'Connor*. Athens: University of Georgia Press, 1985.
White, Walter. *The Fire in the Flint*. 1924. Athens: University of Georgia Press, 1996.
Williams, Linda Faye. *Constraint of Race: Legacies of White Skin Privilege in America*. University Park: Penn State University Press, 2004.

Williamson, Joel. *William Faulkner and Southern History.* New York: Oxford University Press, 1993.
Wills, Gary. *Negro President: Jefferson and the Slave Power.* New York: Houghton Mifflin, 2003.
Winchell, Mark Royden. *Reinventing the South: Versions of a Literary Region.* Columbia: University of Missouri Press, 2006.
Wittig, Monique. "The Mark of Gender." *Feminist Issues* 5.2 (1985): 3–12.
Wolfe, Thomas. *Look Homeward, Angel.* 1929. New York: Scribner, 1957.
Womack, Craig. *Red on Red: Native American Literary Separatism.* Minneapolis: University of Minnesota Press, 1999.
Woodman, Harold D. "Reconstruction of the Cotton Plantation." In Glymph, *Essays on the Postbellum Southern Economy,* 95–119.
Woodward, C. Vann. *American Counterpoint: Slavery and Racism in the North-South Dialogue.* 1971. New York: Oxford University Press, 1983.
———. *Origins of the New South, 1877–1913.* Baton Rouge: Louisiana State University Press, 1971.
Wooten, Jim. "Our Opinions: Child Murders Given Ample Inquiry." *Atlanta Journal-Constitution,* June 22, 2006, A18.
Wright, Gavin. *Old South, New South Revolutions in the Southern Economy Since the Civil War.* New York: Basic, 1986.
Wright, Richard. *Black Boy.* 1937. New York: Signet, 1963.
———. *Eight Men.* 1961. New York: Pyramid, 1970.
———. *Native Son.* 1940. New York: Harper Perennial, 1998.
———. *Uncle Tom's Children.* 1940. New York: Harper and Row, 1989.
Yaeger, Patricia. *Dirt and Desire: Reconstructing Southern Women's Writing, 1930–1990.* Chicago: University of Chicago Press, 2000.
———. "Ghosts and Shattered Bodies, or What Does it Mean To Still Be Haunted by Southern Literature?" *South Central Review* 22.1 (spring 2005): 87–108.
Yezzi, David. "The Violence of Allen Tate." *New Criterion* 20.1 (Sept. 2001), at <http://www.newcriterion.com/archive/20/sept01/tate.htm>, accessed August 2007.
Young, Cristobal. "The Politics, Mathematics, and Morality of Economics: A Review Essay on Robert Nelson's *Economics as Religion.*" *Socio Economic Review* 3.1 (Jan. 2005): 161–75.
Young, John K. *Black Writers, White Publishers: Marketplace Politics in Twentieth-Century African American Literature.* Jackson: University Press of Mississippi, 2006.
Young, Stark. *So Red the Rose.* New York: Scribner's, 1934.
Žižek, Slavoj. *How to Read Lacan.* New York: W. W. Norton, 2007.
———. "The Sublime Object of Ideology." In Rivkin and Ryan, *Literary Theory,* 312–25.

Index

Abiding Appalachia: Where Mountain and Atom Meet (Awiakta), 179–80, 184
abjection, 2, 62, 69, 74, 86, 131, 163, 203
Absalom, Absalom! (Faulkner), 40–43, 44, 51, 53, 212n37, 217n13, 217n15–16
account book, 10, 38, 42, 46, 118; balance and, 38, 40, 56, 148, 166, 190, 227n2; sharecropping and, 65, 71, 191; tax collector's book and, 50. *See also* ledger
accounting, 15, 32, 42, 56, 165, 211n28; double-entry, 15, 40, 217n10; human, 148, 191; mathematics and, 10, 15, 32, 211n28, 212n37; as a metaphor, 14, 88, 148; new (commercial), 32, 38, 42, 46; personal, 38, 51, 102; slavery and, 10, 14, 32, 34, 40, 88, 118; truth and, 40, 190. *See also* arithmetic; calculation; ledger; mathematics; quantification
accounts, bookkeeping, 10, 32, 38, 44–46, 47, 50, 191; African American, 46, 55–56; historical, 39, 100, 108, 161; personal, 41, 52, 53, 193. *See also* ledger
Afghanistan, 16, 181
African Americans: activism among, 63–64, 139, 143, 161–62; art and, 25, 62, 82–85, 221n13, 221n18, 222n21; capitalism and, 22–23, 53, 95, 135, 198, 203–4, 221n14, 231n16; Native Americans and, 161–63, 177, 187; "passing" and, 63, 79–89; socialism and, 63–64; southern, modern, 22, 25, 47, 53, 60, 63, 66, 164–65, 213n43; unionization and, 63–64, 70–71, 72. *See also* Atlanta child murders, slavery
After Virtue (MacIntyre), 15
Agrarianism, 28, 30, 48, 178, 210n18; aristocracy and, 100; capitalism and, 216n1. *See also* Agrarians; Nashville Agrarians
Agrarians: agriculture and, 44, 130; contemporary, 214; industrialism and, 6, 28, 48, 180; influence of, on southern writing, 27–28, 52; liberalism and, 223n3; as literary group, 29, 49, 134, 219n31; Native American experience and, 134, 227n4; nobility and, 39, 49, 192; nostalgia and, 48–49. *See also* Nashville Agrarians
Alabama, 160
algebra: authority and, 199; class and, 50–51, 52; racial identity and, 20; social order and, 24, 134, 142, 157; Thomas Wolfe and, 219n33. *See also* calculation
Allison, Dorothy, 24, 132, 228n8; *Bastard Out of Carolina*, 131, 135–36, 137, 138, 140–42, 144, 146–47, 148, 149–50, 152–53, 156–59, 162
American Dilemma, An (Myrdal), 60, 223n3
American Dream, 33, 110, 190
American South in a Global World (Peacock, Watson, and Matthews, eds.), 18
amnesia: elite, 24, 142, 147; fugue and, 138; Native Americans and, 170, 180; New South and, 139, 142, 144, 148, 150, 154; postcolonial, 138; repression and, 76
amnesiac, 147, 148
Anderson, Benedict, 20, 214n52
Anderson, Eric Gary, 167, 168, 215n57, 229n1
"Angel of Progress" (McClintock), 16
antebellum era, 40; black writers of, 62; as idyll, 6, 9, 27; myth of, 27, 48; priorities of, 28; slavery in, 7, 21, 34, 61, 210n17, 211n18; South during, 2, 4, 7, 43, 216n5; virtues of, 204. *See also* slavery
Anti-Oedipus (Deleuze and Guattari), 13, 229n14
Apache, 159
Appadurai, Arjun, 19, 131

253

Appalachia, 40, 48, 49, 167, 169, 170, 179–80, 183–84; stereotypes of, 219
aristocracy: African Americans and, 86–88; agrarianism and, 48; capitalism and, 30, 31, 32–33, 34, 49; devolution and, 35–37; Europe and, 112; labor and, 42, 111; lineage and, 126; morality and, 115, 118, 142; natural, 21, 27, 31, 33, 39, 43; nostalgia of, 30; poor whites and, 38, 123; racism and, 60, 135; women and, 96, 101. *See also* elite, white; neoaristocracy
arithmetic, 218n20, 224n13; capitalism and, 211n31; mental, 102, 121; morality and, 14. *See also* accounting; calculation; fetish of number; mathematics; quantification
Arkansas, 110, 111, 112, 113, 114
As I Lay Dying (Faulkner), 94–95, 120, 128, 152, 222n1
"As If an Indian Were Really an Indian" (Owens), 168
Ashcroft, Bill, 18
assimilation, 17, 168, 169, 186
Atlanta, 96, 100, 130, 150, 224n12, 231n14, 231n17
Atlanta child murders, 25, 165, 194–201
atom bomb, 179–80, 184–85; Native American reservations and, 185, 230n10
Attaway, William, 22, 83; *Blood on the Forge*, 64–67, 68–71, 89–90
Autobiography of an Ex-Coloured Man, The (Johnson), 22, 63, 79–89, 91, 199, 222n21–22
Awiakta, Marilou, 25, 165, 167, 168–69, 170–71, 194, 229n3
—works of: *Abiding Appalachia: Where Mountain and Atom Meet*, 179–80, 184; *Selu: Seeking the Corn Mother's Wisdom*, 179–86
Ayers, Edward L., 164

Baker, Houston A., Jr., 213n40; *Turning South Again*, 60, 82, 84, 221n14, 232n2
Balancing the Books (Dussere), 13–14
Baldwin, James, 165; *The Evidence of Things Not Seen*, 195–96, 197, 198, 231n15
Bambara, Toni Cade, 165; *Those Bones Are Not My Child*, 197–201
Bartley, Numan, 130, 132, 227n3
Bastard Out of Carolina (Allison), 135–36, 137, 138, 140–42, 144, 146–47, 148, 149–50, 152–53, 156–59, 162
Baudrillard, Jean, 13, 24, 57, 58; *Mirror of Production*, 130–31, 211n32; *Simulacra and Simulation*, 131; *Symbolic Exchange and Death*, 137, 167
"Bear, The" (Faulkner), 45–46
"Beasts of the Southern Wild" (Betts), 1, 21
Beloved (Morrison), 215n58
Betts, Doris, 1, 21
Bhabha, Homi, 18; colonial calculations, 19, 20, 25–26, 42, 204; desire for Other, 80; fetish, 4, 207n5; hybridity, 19, 84, 168; *Location of Culture*, 25, 207n5, 218n21; mimicry, 38, 62–63, 84; minus-in-origin, 217n18, 218n21; narcissism of mastery, 5; pedagogy and, 224n14; psychoanalysis and, 209n9; remembering, 166, 177, 204
biracial antagonisms, 159; in Communist movement, 64; and economy, 25, 133, 165, 168; narratives of, 164, 186; in the South, 133, 162–63, 186; as subjects, 24, 133
Bishop, Alan J., 15, 212n37, 229n15
Bishop, John Peal, 33
Black Boy (R. Wright), 1, 63, 72–73, 77, 143, 215n54
Black Skin, White Masks (Fanon), 5, 63, 126, 207, 209
Blood on the Forge (Attaway), 64–67, 68–71, 89–90
Blotner, Joseph, 218n23
Bluest Eye, The (Morrison), 147
Bone, Martyn, 18
Bone Game (Owens), 173–79, 181, 188, 195, 199
bookkeeping, 38, 41, 50, 52. *See also* accounting
Boyd, Valerie, 91
Bragg, Rick, 36
Brantley, Will, 96–97, 106
Brown v. Board of Education, 132
Bryant, J. A., Jr., 61, 210n21
Bushnell, Candace, 108, 225n20
But Gentlemen Marry Brunettes (Loos), 99, 116–19

calculation, 2, 5, 21, 31, 40; capitalism and, 9, 11, 21; compensation and, 8; Homi Bhabha and, 25–26, 42; human, 6, 165; ledger and, 42; mastery and, 15, 21, 23, 26, 40, 41; narcissism and, 23; obsessed with, 2, 10; slavery and, 2, 9; as textual fetish, 3, 4, 5, 10. *See also* accounting; algebra; arithmetic; fetish of number; mathematics; quantification
calculus, 212n35; of capital, 13, 32, 35, 58, 213n39; of reason, 14, 15, 213n39; of slavery, 2, 19, 29, 31. *See also* accounting;

254 Index

arithmetic; calculation; mathematics; quantification
Caldwell, Erskine, 75, 216n1, 223n3
California, 110, 117, 173, 174, 176, 177
Cao, Lan, 200; *Monkey Bridge*, 25, 165, 187–94, 231n13
capitalism, 2, 11; Agrarians and, 28, 210n18; anti-, 6, 7, 9, 27, 34; ascent and, 99, 108, 110, 115, 222n21; Baudrillard and, 24; census and, 20; colonial, 166; desperation and, 71, 92; global, 14, 19, 56, 137, 190, 203, 211n29–30; inequities of, 4, 29, 85; labor and, 33; liberalism and, 211n29; Marx and, 3, 211n30; mathematics and, 10, 11–14, 50, 204, 211n31; narcissism and, 5, 12, 23, 72, 87; in New South, 6, 21, 28, 32, 100, 202; northern, 5, 6, 7, 27, 35, 138, 227n6; opportunity and, 2, 35, 36–37, 61; paternalism and, 31; perversion and, 30, 54; plantation, 6, 7, 24, 28, 29, 61; planter, 96; postcolonialism and, 214n47; pre-, 35; proto-, 7, 9, 10; psychoanalysis and, 13; psychology and, 2; sharecropping and, 62, 216n1; slavery and, 6, 9, 10, 21, 53, 62, 128, 167; socialism/communism and, 70, 124, 221n19; theology/religion of, 12, 204. *See also* economics
Capitalism and Slavery (E. Williams), 9
Carey, Gary, 109, 115
Caribbean, 18, 41, 44, 167, 212n36. *See also* Haiti; West Indies
cartography, 15–16, 212n38; maps and, 131, 147, 157, 162–63, 189
Cartwright, Samuel A., 19
Cash, W. J., 208n8, 210n22
census, 20, 204, 214n51–52
Césaire, Aimé, 60, 86
Cherokee: as characters, 174; stereotypes of, 158–59, 164, 169; Tellico controversy and, 181; tribe, 166; writers, 25, 163, 167–69, 180, 229n3
Choctaw, 25, 166, 167, 171, 172, 174, 177, 178
cipher, 45, 144, 185–86, 219n27–28. *See also* zero
civil rights, 23, 135, 161, 214n51, 231n16; movement, 129, 132, 133, 139, 145
Civil War: after the war, 101, 186; battlefields, 138, 142, 210n20; emancipation and, 28, 170; nostalgia and, 27, 150, 161; slavery and, 19; in southern literature, 27, 30, 32–33, 150, 161, 216n1
Cobb, James, 18, 187, 230n11

Cohn, Deborah, 18, 24, 39, 213n45, 217n12, 227n4, 229n2
colonialism, 2, 11, 15, 174, 202, 203, 207n5; American, 173; anti-, 18; body and, 177; calculability and, 20; and cartography, 212n38; character and, 16; contact and, 19; contexts/societies and, 4, 11, 18, 43, 60, 212n36, 217n14; critique and, 16; cultures and, 3, 39; discourse of, 4, 169; domination and, 5; economy/capitalism and, 7–9, 26, 166; and European power, 15; expansion and, 174; fetish and, 207n5; histories and, 25, 134, 170, 176, 179; hypocrisy and, 170; inequity and, 17; master and, 59; and mathematics, 212n37; New World, 44, 56; pathology and, 131; pre-, 24; projects and, 16, 18, 165; silencing and, 182; southern, 112, 199, 228n10; subjects of, 59, 204; trauma of, 4, 40, 45, 166, 174, 177, 214n47; violence and, 175, 177. *See also* economic colonialism; imperialism; postcolonialism
commodification, 2, 10, 21, 201
commodity, 62, 63, 81–82; fetishism, 3, 207n12; sexual, 99, 114, 117
Conkin, Paul, 129–30
Conrad, Joseph, 111–12
Costello, Brannon, 135, 228n10
Culture of Narcissism, The (Lasch), 5, 12, 208n7
Custer Died for Your Sins (V. Deloria), 175, 213n39

Daniel, Pete, 28, 66, 129, 220n1, 220n5
Dead Lovers Are Faithful Lovers (Newman), 99–100, 119–23, 226n25–26
Degas, Edgar, 101
Deleuze, Gilles, 13, 229n14
Deloria, Philip, 227n5, 229n17
Deloria, Vine, Jr., 175, 213n39
Delta, 35, 36, 55
Derrida, Jacques, 15
Descartes, René, 15
desegregation, 97, 132, 154, 199, 202. *See also* Jim Crow; segregation
Deviant Bodies (Urla and Terry), 19
diaspora, 17, 171, 177, 181
Discourse on Colonialism (Césaire), 60, 86
Dostoevsky, Fyodor, 73
Doyle, Don H., 37–38, 40, 215n57
Doyle, Laura, 165
DuBois, W. E. B., 17, 83, 133, 145, 222n21
Duck, Leigh Anne, 75, 82, 209n15

Index 255

Dussere, Erik, 13–14, 53, 88, 217n17, 219n26, 227n6

economic colonialism, 7–9, 27–29, 210n20, 210n24

economics, 31, 54, 34; Keynesian, 13; literature and, 14, 19; market, 6, 7; mathematics and, 10–11; postcolonial theory and, 214n47; race and, 39, 47, 60, 85; slavery and, 6, 10, 14; theology of, 12. *See also* capitalism

Economics as Religion (Nelson), 12

Eight Men (R. Wright), 67, 73

elite, "black," 83

elite, white: amnesia, 24; anticapitalism and, 2, 22, 31, 34, 191; dispossessed, 5, 21, 29, 53, 131; economics and, 34, 47, 53, 64, 130, 137; education and, 50; ethical superiority and, 39, 43, 52, 59; narcissism of mastery and, 5, 63; nostalgia and, 49; plantation and, 2, 28, 48, 52; racism and, 4, 9, 11, 36, 37, 63; women and, 95; writers, 9, 29, 49, 132, 138. *See also* aristocracy

emancipation: capitalism and, 2, 32, 33, 61, 210n19; dispossession and, 202, 208n8; as literary trope, 76; post-, 199; racism and, 19; sexual, 99, 100, 108, 128; of slaves, 161; social flux and, 19, 35, 161

Emerson, John, 109

Engerman, Stanley, 7, 210n16

Enlightenment, 14–16, 21

Entzminger, Bettina, 99, 105, 223n6–7

essentialism, racial, 17, 20, 79, 163

eugenics, 19, 214n48

Evidence of Things Not Seen, The (Baldwin), 195–96, 197, 198, 231n15

exceptionalism: American, 16, 17, 24, 41, 166; black, 163, 204; southern, 2, 17, 24, 39, 165, 187, 202, 205

Fanon, Frantz, 17, 207n5; *Black Skin, White Masks*, 5, 63, 126, 207, 209n10

Faulkner, William, 1; class and, 29, 37–38, 53, 216n6, 217n16; colonialism and, 44, 57–58, 216n8; economics and, 53, 217n11–12, 218n23, 219–20n34, 227n6; female characters and, 94–95, 128, 152; global/transnational contexts and, 37–39, 217n12; ledger and, 10, 14, 38–39, 40, 43, 191, 218n23; liberalism and, 223n3; mathematics and, 40, 212n37; Mencken and, 215n54; Native American characters and, 46, 173, 215n57, 227n5; natural aristocracy and, 39; Nobel Prize speech and, 184; race and, 47, 48, 55–56, 216n7, 217n11; white male subjectivity and, 21

—works of: *Absalom, Absalom!* 40–43, 44, 51, 53, 212n37, 217n13, 217n15–16; *As I Lay Dying*, 94–95, 120, 128, 152, 222n1; "The Bear," 45–46; *Go Down, Moses*, 38, 39, 43–47, 53, 191, 218–19n23, 219n26, 219–20n34; *The Hamlet*, 38, 217n15–16; *If I Forget Thee, Jerusalem (The Wild Palms)*, 128; *Intruder in the Dust*, 55–56; *Light in August*, 40, 47–48, 55; *The Mansion*, 37, 217n15–16; *The Sound and the Fury*, 38, 40, 56–58; *The Town*, 37, 217n15–16

Faulkner's County (D. Doyle), 37–38, 40, 215n57

feminism: criticism and, 95; economics and, 99; marriage and, 98, 126; slavery and, 97; in the South, 96, 132–33, 223–24n8; southern writers and, 23, 95–96, 101, 123, 222n2, 225n19, 226n30

fetish: commodity, 3, 24, 63, 207n2; economy and, 97, 112–13, 130, 166, 204; narcissism and, 4–5, 98, 130, 134, 202, 208n8, 209n11; object, 10, 130, 208n8; in psychoanalysis, 3–4, 207n3–4, 211n25; racial/colonial, 4, 21, 59, 63, 86, 207n5, 217n14; religious, 3, 207n1; sexual, 3, 99, 103, 207n3–4; of surplus value, 21, 27–58, 60, 130; textual, 10, 99

fetish of number: African Americans and, 23; capitalism and, 2, 12, 23, 29, 49; narcissism and, 4–5, 130; postcolonialism and, 19; southern, 3; women and, 99

"Finding Gene" (Owens), 172–73

"Fire and Cloud" (R. Wright), 63–64

Flood of 1927, 34–35

Florida, 86, 167

Flowering Judas and Other Stories (Porter), 123

Fogel, Robert, 7, 210n16

Foucault, Michel, 15

Foundations of Economic Analysis (Samuelson), 13

Frederickson, George, 9–10, 211n26

Freud, Sigmund, 3, 4, 96, 207n3–4, 207n6, 209n9, 209n11, 229n16

Friedman, Milton, 11

Gandhi, Mahatma, 5–6

Gates, Henry Louis, Jr., 81, 82, 87, 91, 92, 221n12, 221n14, 222n21

genocide, 24, 44, 175, 194, 196
Genovese, Eugene, 7, 211n29; *Political Economy of Slavery*, 32; *Roll, Jordan, Roll*, 62
Gentlemen Prefer Blondes (Loos), 96, 99–100, 108–16, 119, 222n2, 224n9, 225n20–21, 226n23
Gidley, Ben, 134, 229n1
Gidley, Mick, 134, 229n1
Gilbert, Sandra, 105
"Gilded Six-Bits, The" (Hurston), 23, 89, 90–93, 95, 124
Gispen, Kees, 6
global South, 17, 18, 165, 199, 214n45, 217n14
globalization, 18, 40, 45, 56, 131, 187, 203, 214n46, 230n11; capitalism and, 14, 19, 39, 137, 190, 203, 213n42
Globalization and the American South (Cobb and Stueck, eds.), 18
Go Down, Moses (Faulkner), 38, 39, 43–47, 53, 191, 218–19n23, 219n26, 219–20n34
Godden, Richard, 35, 38, 39, 216n9
Gold Fish Bowl, The (Newman), 100
gold teeth, 89–91
Gone with the Wind (Mitchell), 27
Grady, Henry, 7
Grantham, Dewey, 9
Great Depression: African Americans and, 75, 89; Faulkner and, 216n6; GE / Welfare economists project and, 11; psychology and, 209–10n15; South during, 103, 129, 184, 202, 210n15; unionization during, 220n8
Great Migration, 22, 61, 69–70
Guattari, Felix, 13, 229n14
Gubar, Susan, 105

Haiti, 40, 41, 42–45, 46, 217n14, 217n18. *See also* Caribbean; West Indies
Hale, Grace Elizabeth, 79, 133
Hamlet, The (Faulkner), 38, 217n15–16
Handley, George, 39; *Postslavery Literatures in the Americas*, 18, 213n45, 217n12, 217n16
Hard-Boiled Virgin, The (Newman), 99–108, 114, 141, 224n10, 224n12–13, 224n16–17
Harlem Renaissance, 82, 221n18
Harris, Cheryl, 10, 211n27
Harris, Wilson, 167
Hegel, Georg Wilhelm Friedrich, 14, 82
Hegeman, Susan, 98–99, 114, 115, 225n21
hegemony, 15, 26, 32, 83, 169
"Hind Tit, The" (Lytle), 28
Hispanic. *See* Latin American (Hispanic)

History and Memory in the Two Souths (Cohn), 18, 217n12
History of Southern Literature (Rubin, et al.), 8, 9
Hobson, Fred, 18
Hoeller, Hildegard, 92
Hogan, Linda, 167
Holland, Eugene W., 13
Huck Finn (Twain), 62, 173
Hurricane Katrina, 17, 213n41, 231n17
Hurston, Zora Neale, 23; "The Gilded Six-Bits" 89, 90–93, 95, 124
hybrid: America as a, 186; South as a, 17, 133, 168; southerners as a, 131, 132, 165
hybridity, 19, 84, 133, 169; colonialism and, 19, 169, 212n36; cultural, 83–84; ethnic, 168–69, 182; racial, 55, 80, 86, 89, 221n11

If I Forget Thee, Jerusalem (The Wild Palms) (Faulkner), 128
I'll Take My Stand: The South and the Agrarian Tradition (Twelve Southerners), 6, 28, 29, 37, 134, 227n4
Imperial Leather (McClintock), 3, 23, 207n1, 207n4
imperialism: American, 8, 16, 163, 166, 203; authority and, 18; calculation and, 26; capitalism and, 21, 166, 190; global, 40, 165, 187; male, 23; Marxism and, 214n47; Native Americans under, 56, 169, 173, 174, 175, 196, 213n40; natural aristocracy and, 43; neo–, 39; pedagogy and, 41, 56; South under, 38, 216n8; Vietnam War and, 173, 189, 200; Western, 11, 15, 166, 212n37. *See also* colonialism
In Search of Our Mothers' Gardens (A. Walker), 135
India, 4, 15
Indian giver, 169, 182, 230n6
Intruder in the Dust (Faulkner), 55–56
Iraq, 16, 230n12

JanMohamed, Abdul, 59
Jefferson, Thomas, 15–16
Jehlen, Myra, 37, 216n6
Jim Crow: cars, 54; laws, 29, 72; migration and, 69, 71, 73; one-drop rule and, 20; South, 9, 80; violence and, 197; whiteness and, 133. *See also* desegregation; segregation
Johnson, James Weldon, 22, 63, 79–89, 91, 199, 222n21–22

Johnson, Walter, 10, 29, 60–61, 82, 88
Jones, Anne Goodwyn, 97, 98, 105, 209n13, 223n5, 223n7, 224n10–11, 225n16, 226n26
Jones, Gayl, 91
Jones, Suzanne, 18, 213–14n45, 226n30
Jones, Tayari, 165; *Leaving Atlanta*, 196–97, 198

Kant, Immanuel, 14, 82
Kidwell, Clara Sue, 172
Killers of the Dream (L. Smith), 58
Kincaid, Jamaica, 59
King, Richard H., 22, 30–31, 44, 215n55, 219n25, 229n14
Kirby, Jack Temple, 9, 29, 37, 61–62, 220n1
Kobre, Michael, 139, 142, 148, 228n7
Krips, Henry, 3, 211n25
Kruse, Kevin, 17, 213n44

Lacan, Jacques, 3, 97, 130, 207n4, 209n9, 209n11, 221n15
Ladd, Barbara, 8, 213n45
Lanterns on the Levee (W. A. Percy), 34–37, 42, 51–52, 134
Lasch, Christopher, 5, 12, 208n7
Lassiter, Matthew, 17, 213n44
Last Gentleman, The (W. Percy), 136–37, 138–40, 141, 142–43, 144–46, 147–48, 150–51, 153–55, 156, 157, 159–61
Latin American (Hispanic), 18, 186, 214n45, 231n17
Lawson, Lewis, 142
Leaving Atlanta (T. Jones), 196–97
ledger: as anachronism, 43; arithmetic/mathematics and, 10, 53, 55, 102; balance and, 38, 40, 56, 227n2; in Cao, *Monkey Bridge*, 190–93; capitalism and, 39, 43, 50, 53, 62; double-entry, 40; facts/truth and, 37, 38, 40, 192, 193; in Faulkner, *Go Down, Moses*, 38, 39–40, 43–46, 191, 218n23; as fetish object, 10, 39; history of, 39, 61–62; mentality, 40–41, 55, 57, 102, 139; plantation/slave, 10, 20, 28–29, 38, 42, 50, 51, 53, 61–62; sharecropping and, 65–66, 67, 71, 191; trope, 10, 14, 39–40, 43, 53, 58, 62, 201. *See also* account book; accounting
Leibniz, Gottfried, 14, 212n35
Levertov, Denise, 106
Light in August (Faulkner), 40, 47–48, 55
Limon, Jose, 18
Lipsitz, George, 79

Location of Culture (Bhabha), 25, 207n5, 218n21
Look Away! (Cohn and Smith, eds.), 18, 24, 215n57, 227n4, 229n2
Look Homeward, Angel (Wolfe), 1, 48–51, 142, 212, 219n32
Loos, Anita: biography of, 108–10, 115, 118, 225–26n22; critique by, of South; 110, 117, 123; as feminist, 23, 96, 119, 122, 132; fictional proxies for, 115–18; films and, 113
—works of: *But Gentlemen Marry Brunettes*, 99, 116–19; *Gentlemen Prefer Blondes*, 96, 99–100, 108–16, 119, 222n2, 224n9, 225n20–21, 226n23
Lost Cause, 13, 21, 223n3, 223n8
Louisiana, 19, 97, 101, 135, 213n41
Lowe, John, 91
lynching, 60, 75, 86, 88
Lytle, Andrew Nelson, 28, 227n5

MacIntyre, Alasdair, 15
MacPherson, C. B., 12
Madsen, Deborah L., 17
Makowsky, Veronica, 135
"Man Who Lived Underground, The" (R. Wright), 73–79, 82–83, 89, 120, 149, 177, 196, 220n7, 221n10
"Man Who Was Almost a Man, The" (R. Wright), 67–68, 69
Mansfield, Katherine, 106
Mansion, The (Faulkner), 37, 217n15–16
maps. *See* cartography
Marx, Karl: colonialism and, 15; commodity fetish and, 3, 207n2; ideology and, 57; mathematics and, 11, 211n30
Marxism, 2, 4, 7, 13; postcolonialism and, 214n47
masochism, 24, 107, 121–22, 131, 141–47, 148–50
mathematics, 1, 24, 40, 219n27, 226n2, 229n15; capitalism and, 11–14, 35, 75, 112–13, 204, 211n30–31; class and, 50–51, 142–43; as colonial tool, 10, 14–16, 19–21, 25, 66, 131, 163, 198, 212n37; as fetish, 4, 13, 87–88, 132, 138, 142–43, 147–57; history of, 14–16, 212n34–35; as language, 10, 12–14, 19, 85, 112–13, 147–50, 204, 211n28, 222n1; of ledger, 65–66; music and, 221n16; plantation, 10, 36, 66; racism and, 19–22, 25, 36, 65–66, 75, 85, 87–88, 198; science and, 14–16, 19,

85, 143, 184–85, 189; sexism and, 93, 94–95, 95–96, 98, 102, 114, 115–16, 118. *See also* accounting; arithmetic; calculation; fetish of number; quantification
Matthews, John T., 39, 40, 43, 45, 55, 217n11–12, 217n14, 218n22
McClintock, Anne, 3–4, 16, 23, 207n1, 207n4, 213n40
Mencken, H. L., 106, 109–10, 215n54, 225n18
Meridian (A. Walker), 131, 136, 137–38, 139–40, 141, 143–44, 145–46, 148–49, 151–52, 153, 155–56, 161–63, 194
Middle Passage, 69, 196
mimicry, 4, 22, 62–63, 82–84, 222n21
Minh-ha, Trinh T., 106
minus-in-origin, 25–26, 42, 205, 217n18, 218n21
minusness, 4, 87
Mirror of Production, The (Baudrillard), 130–31, 211n32
Mississippi, 203; African Americans in, 197; Choctaw, 166–67, 171–72, 176–77; colonial trauma in, 174; Hurricane Katrina and, 213n41; land development in, 43; Native American removal from, 163, 212n39; plantation parable from, 46; planter, 61
Mississippi River, 56, 212n39
Mitchell, Margaret, 27
Mixedblood Messages (Owens), 171, 173–74, 177
Moby-Dick (Melville), 173
Mohl, Raymond A., 186
Monkey Bridge (Cao), 25, 165, 187–94, 231n13
Monteith, Sharon, 18, 213–14n45
Morrison, Toni, 14, 88, 177, 221n13, 222n21; *Beloved*, 215n58; *The Bluest Eye*, 147; *Playing in the Dark*, 84–85
Mulvey, Laura, 3
Myrdal, Gunnar, 60, 223n3

narcissism, classical (mirror), 24, 58, 80, 102, 120, 153, 208n8, 209n12; calculations and, 23; compensation and, 51–52, 79, 134, 209n13; delirium and, 12; as desire for Other, 13, 19, 80; desperation and, 22; and economic desire, 5, 13, 79, 81, 112, 130, 134, 204; fetishism and, 4–5, 13, 98, 130, 134, 202, 208n8, 209n11; Freud and, 4–5, 208n6, 209n11; Heinz Kohut and, 208n6; knowledge and, 15; masochism and, 107; of mastery, 5; as pathology, 24; postcolonial trauma and, 4, 80; primary, 4; racism and, 25, 53, 54, 112,

130, 134, 175; self-love and, 4–5; sexism and, 102, 120; U.S. South and, 208n8
Nashville Agrarians (Twelve Southerners), 6, 29, 48, 49, 52, 134, 219n31, 223n3, 227n4
nationalism, 3, 16, 175, 214n47, 214n52
Native American Indians, 16, 17, 159–60, 165, 169, 171, 187, 213n39, 230n7; African Americans and, 161–63, 177; in Faulkner, 44, 46, 56; nuclear testing and, 184–85, 230n10; of the Southeast, 24–25, 133–34, 158–86, 214n45, 215n57, 227n4–5, 229n2; stereotypes and, 175. *See also* Indian giver
Native Son (R. Wright), 67, 71–72
nativism, 24, 134, 158, 162, 166, 227n5
natural aristocracy, 21, 27, 31, 33, 39, 43, 217n18
Navajo, 160, 174, 177
Nazi Germany, 19, 214n48
Nelson, Robert, 12
neoaristocracy: capitalism and, 30, 34; hierarchy and, 53; in the New South, 12, 24, 35; plantation and, 29, 52; poor whites and, 37; privilege and, 12; women and, 101, 108, 137
New Criticism, 52–53
New Deal, 8, 66, 129; Agricultural Adjustment Act and, 8; WPA and, 66
New South, 3, 9, 40, 134, 138, 153, 157; African Americans in, 64, 216n3; Faulkner's, 39, 40; global economy and, 39, 210n20; materialism and, 35, 38, 51, 100, 136; New Woman and, 95, 98, 99, 100; problem of, 33; reactionary, 43, 52, 100
New Southern studies, 24, 167
New Southerners, 2, 9, 39, 150, 228n13; farmers, 7; women, 99, 100
New Woman, 95, 98, 99, 114, 223n8
New World: American settlement in, 182, 227n4; amnesia, 138; colonial trauma in, 40, 44; narrative, 24; plantation and, 43; studies, 17, 215n57, 217n12, 229n2; U.S. South and, 18, 39, 44–45
Newman, Frances: autobiographical protagonists and, 101, 119; biography of, 100–101, 224n10–13; criticism of 225n16–19; as feminist writer, 23, 96, 99–100, 132, 226n24
—works of: *Dead Lovers Are Faithful Lovers*, 99–100, 119–23, 226n25–26; *The Gold Fish Bowl*, 100; *The Hard-Boiled Virgin*, 99–108, 114, 141, 224n10, 224n12–13, 224n16–17; *The Short Story's Mutations*, 100

North Carolina, 167, 197
number. *See* arithmetic; calculation; fetish of number; mathematics; quantification
numerical fetish. *See* fetish of number

"Ode to the Confederate Dead" (Tate), 30
Ohlone, 174–79
"Old Mortality" (Porter), 126, 127, 226n30
Old South, 7, 10, 27, 29, 61, 69, 131, 132, 209n14
Orientalism (Said), 15, 18
Owens, Louis, 25, 165, 167, 170–79, 186, 194, 229n3
—works of: "As If an Indian Were Really an Indian," 168; *Bone Game*, 173–79, 181, 188, 195, 199; "Finding Gene," 172–73; *Mixedblood Messages*, 171, 173–74, 177; *The Sharpest Sight*, 171–73, 174, 177, 200; "The Song Is Very Short," 169; "The Syllogistic Mixedblood," 168

Painter, Nell Irvin, 19, 215n56
"Pale Horse, Pale Rider" (Porter), 126–28
Pareto, Vilfredo, 11
passing, racial, 79–89
Patterson, Orlando, 88
pedagogy, colonial/imperial, 19, 41, 49–51, 85, 102, 154, 212n37, 224–25n14
Pennsylvania, 69, 70
Percy, Walker, 24, 132, 134–36; criticism of, 228n7, 228n9–11, 228–29n13; *The Last Gentleman*, 131, 136–37, 138–40, 141, 142–43, 144–46, 147–48, 150–51, 153–55, 156, 157, 159–61, 177
Percy, William Alexander, 21, 29, 134–35, 228n10, 228–29n13; *Lanterns on the Levee*, 34–37, 42, 51–52, 134
Peterson, Carla L., 62
phantom limb, 167, 188
Phillips, Ulrich Bonnell, 10, 211n28
Pifer, Lynn, 145
plantation, 6, 13, 165; capitalism, 7; economy, 17; ledger, 10, 20; order, 21; as protocapitalist, 9. *See also* slavery
Playing in the Dark (Morrison), 84–85
Political Economy of Slavery (Genovese), 32
Polk, Noel, 38–39, 216–17n9
poor whites: education and, 50; labor and, 75, 136–37; "on the make," 35–38, 42, 111–12, 217n16; racing of, 47, 48, 53, 56–57; racism among, 159; unionization among, 72; women as, 94. *See also* "white trash"
Poovey, Mary, 15, 40, 212n37, 217n10
Porter, Katherine Anne, 23, 96, 98, 100, 123–28, 132, 149, 222n2, 226n27–30; *Flowering Judas and Other Stories*, 123; "Old Mortality," 126, 127, 226n30; "Pale Horse, Pale Rider," 126–28; "Theft," 123–26, 127, 149, 226n28–29
Posnock, Ross, 84
possessive individualism, 12
"Postcolonial, Black, and Nobody's Margin: The U.S. South in New World Studies" (Smith), 17, 216n2
Postcolonial Theory and the United States (Schmidt and Singh, eds.), 17
postcolonialism: fetish in, 4, 39, 131, 209n11; immigrant, Asian, 17, 188–90; Marxism and, 4, 214n47; narcissism and, 4–5, 209n11; Native Americans and, 17, 134, 173–74, 177, 181, 227n5; origins of term, 217n13; pedagogy and, 224–25n14; performativity and, 212n36; postregionalism and, 171; psychoanalysis and, 4–5, 23, 208–9n9, 209n11; race relations and, 17, 79–80, 83, 135, 167, 228n10; re-membering and, 196; subject and, 25, 126, 131; as theory, 2, 4–5, 16–23, 25, 131, 177, 213n40; United States and, 16–17, 213n40, 213–14n45, 215n58; and U.S. South, 2, 17–18, 23, 134. *See also* colonialism
Postslavery Literatures in the Americas (Handley), 18, 213n45, 217n12, 217n16
Postsouthern Sense of Place, The (Bone), 18
Power (Hogan), 167
Pratt, Mary Louise, 169
Protestant Ethic and the Spirit of Capitalism (Weber), 6
psychoanalysis, 215n56; capitalism and, 13; fetish and, 3–4, 207n1; postcolonialism and, 4–5, 23, 208–9n9, 209n11. *See also* fetish; Freud; narcissism, classical (mirror)
Pursuit of Happyness (Gardner), 203–4

quantification: capitalism and, 35, 70, 87–88, 112–13; as colonial tool, 11, 131, 212n36–37; human, 2, 57, 130; language of, 9, 40, 102; pedagogy and, 224n14; slavery and, 20, 28; of women, 93, 96, 98, 114, 115, 120, 121.

See also accounting; arithmetic; calculation; fetish of number; mathematics

Railey, Kevin, 39
Reconstruction, 2, 5, 7, 160, 202; economic colonialism and, 5, 7–8, 28, 210n20; post-, 70, 210n20; Second, 198; sharecropping and, 61, 220n1
register, 45, 54, 55, 118. *See also* account book; ledger
Reimers, David M., 186–87
re-membering, 25, 165–66, 177, 186, 194–95, 196–97, 201, 202
Report on Economic Conditions of the South (United States Emergency Council), 8
Roediger, David, 79
Roll, Jordan, Roll (Genovese), 62
Romine, Scott, 34, 35, 36, 48, 216n4
Roosevelt, Theodore, 8, 211n24
Rural Worlds Lost (Kirby), 9, 29, 37, 61–62, 220n1
Rushdie, Salman, 18
Ryan, Maureen, 187

"Sahara of the Bozart" (Mencken), 106, 110, 215n54, 225n18
Said, Edward, 15, 17, 18, 207n5
Saldívar, Ramón, 43
Samuelson, Paul, 13, 212n33
Schmidt, Peter, 17
Schulman, Bruce, 9, 231n1
Schulz, Jennifer Lea, 87
segregation: effect of, on African Americans, 78, 92; Jim Crow and, 29; laws, 17, 162, 216n3; in North, 203; postcolonialism and, 213n40; progressive liberalism versus, 96; white supremacy and, 132, 133. *See also* desegregation; Jim Crow
Selu: Seeking the Corn Mother's Wisdom (Awiakta), 179–86
sharecropping: in Attaway, 65, 70, 89; debt and, 216n1, 220n5; in Faulkner, 46; neoplantation and, 29, 61; racial tension under, 37, 62; southern, 216n1, 220n1–2; Tuskegee Syphilis Experiment and, 19; in Wright, 67; in Vietnam, 190–91
Sharpest Sight, The (Owens), 171–73, 174, 177, 200
Short Story's Mutations, The (Newman), 100
Showalter, Elaine, 105, 225n15

Simmons, Christina, 96
Simulacra and Simulation (Baudrillard), 131
Singh, Amritjit, 17
slavery: accounting and, 10, 14, 39, 43, 53, 88, 118; African American music (modern) and, 84–85; African American sharecropping after, 23, 37, 61–62; biracial society and, 133, 167; calculus of, 2, 19; capitalist character of, 2, 6, 10, 19, 31–34, 39, 60, 210n17; in Conrad, 112; defenses of, 19, 211n29, 213n39; families separated by, 155; global, 203; hauntings of, 14, 21, 76–78, 82, 196; hierarchy during, 38; human commodification during, 21, 62; humanism and, 32, 34, 39, 60, 211n28–29; in Loos, 111–12; market economy after, 2, 4, 7–9, 53, 62, 136, 210n19, 216n5; as metaphor for sexism, 118–19, 128, 226n29; narcissism of mastery and, 5, 6–7, 53–54; Native Americans displaced by, 163, 166–67; neoslavery, 83, 221n17; nostalgia for, 29, 56; opportunity after, 23, 86–87, 95; postcolonialism and, 17, 213n40; profitability of, 7, 61, 210n16; racial classification and, 10, 19–20; racial debasement after, 60, 73; racial debasement during, 9–10, 35, 143–44; repetitions of, 21, 56, 62; Thirteenth Amendment and, 20
Smith, Adam, 11
Smith, Jon, 213n45, 223n4; *Look Away!* 18, 24, 217n12, 227n4, 229n2; "Postcolonial, Black, and Nobody's Margin," 17, 216n2; "Southern Culture on the Skids," 208n8
Smith, Lillian, 58, 215n55
Smith, Mark M., 7, 37, 61, 210n17
Sollors, Werner, 20–21
"Song Is Very Short, The" (Owens), 169
Soul by Soul (W. Johnson), 10, 29, 60–61, 82, 88
Sound and the Fury, The (Faulkner), 38, 40, 56–58
South Carolina, 137, 224n8
South to a New Place (Jones and Monteith, eds.), 18, 167
South to the Future (Hobson, ed.), 18
Southern History across the Color Line (Painter), 19
Southern Renaissance, 22
Southern Renaissance, A (King), 22, 31, 229n14
southern studies, 6; new, 17–18, 24, 167, 232n2
Spanish-American War of 1898, 8
Spillers, Hortense J., 22–23

Index 261

Spivak, Gayatri Chakravorty, 18, 55, 214n47
Stein, Karen, 145
Stueck, William, 187
subaltern, 25–26, 218n21
suicide, 22, 47, 58, 88, 135, 142, 153–54, 228–29n13
Suleri, Sara, 18
Sun Belt South, 23, 129, 130, 136–37
Swetz, Frank, 11, 211n31
"Syllogistic Mixedblood, The" (Owens), 168
Symbolic Exchange and Death (Baudrillard), 137, 167

Tate, Allen, 10, 21, 29–34, 52; *The Fathers*, 30–34, 35, 50; "Ode to the Confederate Dead," 30
Tate, Claudia, 22, 221n13
Tellico Dam, 180–82
tenant farming. *See* sharecropping
Tennessee, 167, 170, 180, 181, 182, 183, 184, 213n43, 214n48
Tennessee Valley Authority, 180
Terry, Jennifer, 19
theft, 15, 22, 62, 72–73, 75–76, 77–78, 91, 123–26, 220n9
"Theft" (Porter), 123–26, 127, 149, 226n28–29
Thirteenth Amendment, 20. *See also* emancipation
Those Bones Are Not My Child (Bambara), 197–201
Three-fifths Compromise, 20, 60, 214n50
Time on the Cross (Fogel and Engerman), 7
Town, The (Faulkner), 37, 40, 217n15–16
Trachtenberg, Alan, 175, 227n5
transnational South, 17, 18, 165; in southern studies, 24, 39. *See also* global South
Turning South Again (Baker), 60, 82, 84, 221n14, 232n2
Tuskegee Syphilis Experiment, 19
Twain, Mark, 7, 173

uncanny, 5, 21, 120; nativism and, 133, 134; reflection and, 24, 25, 43, 137, 149; repetition and, 6, 21, 192
Uncle Tom's Children (R. Wright), 63, 64, 67
unionization, 64, 68, 70–71, 72, 220n8
Unrue, Darlene Harbour, 123, 124, 126
Urla, Jacqueline, 19

Van Evrie, John H., 19
Vance, Rupert, 8, 210n23

Vietnam, 172–73, 187–94; war, 172–73, 187, 200–201
Vietnamese Americans, 25, 187–94
Virginia, 30, 33, 142, 187, 188, 189, 217n16

Wade, Barbara Anne, 100, 224n10–11, 225n19
Walcott, Derek, 138
Walker, Alice, 24, 132, 135–36
—works of: *Meridian*, 131, 136, 137–38, 139–40, 141, 143–44, 145–46, 148–49, 151–52, 153, 155–56, 161–63, 194; *In Search of Our Mothers' Gardens*, 135; *The Way Forward Is with a Broken Heart*, 163
Walker, Margaret, 68, 220n7
Walras, Leon, 11
Warren, Robert Penn, 37
Way Forward Is with a Broken Heart, The (A. Walker), 163
Weber, Max, 6, 15, 32
West Indies, 40–41, 44, 217n12, 217n14. *See also* Caribbean; Haiti
Westling, Louise, 105
What Made the South Different? (Gispen, ed.), 6
white mastery, 4, 28, 29, 32, 34, 35, 38, 41, 43; mimicry and, 5, 22, 62, 71–73, 80, 82, 87, 111; narcissism of, 5, 38. *See also* aristocracy; elite, white
"white trash," 36–38, 47, 132, 137, 140–41, 149, 159, 216n5, 219n29. *See also* poor whites
Williams, Eric, 9
Williams, Linda Faye, 79
Williams, Wayne, 198–99, 231n17
Williamson, Joel, 38, 216n8
Without Consent or Contract (Fogel), 210n16
Wolfe, Thomas, 21, 29, 52, 86, 219n31–33, 223n3; *Look Homeward, Angel*, 1, 48–51, 142, 212, 219n32
Woodward, C. Vann, 7–8, 9, 110, 187, 203, 210n20, 211n28, 220n1
World War I, 8, 96, 127, 210
World War II, 23, 61, 129, 184, 214
Wright, Gavin, 8, 210n20
Wright, Richard, 22, 63–64, 71–79, 91
—works of: *Black Boy*, 1, 63, 72–73, 77, 143, 215n54; *Eight Men*, 67, 73; "Fire and Cloud," 63–64; "The Man Who Lived Underground," 73–79, 82–83, 89, 120, 149, 177, 196, 220n7, 221n10; "The Man Who Was Almost a Man," 67–68, 69; *Native Son*, 67, 71–72; *Uncle Tom's Children*, 63, 64, 67
Wyatt-Brown, Bertram, 6

Yaeger, Patricia, 97–98, 223n6
Yezzi, David, 30
Young, Cristobal, 11, 12
Young, Stark, 216n1
Young, Thomas Daniel, 8

zero, 28, 45, 144, 201, 226–27n2, 230n4; "ground," 141, 228n12, 230n10; history of, 219n27; Native Americans as, 25, 134, 143, 163, 167–68, 185–86, 227n5; women as, 94–95
Žižek, Slavoj, 57, 97

THE NEW SOUTHERN STUDIES

The Nation's Region: Southern Modernism, Segregation, and U.S. Nationalism
by Leigh Anne Duck

Black Masculinity and the U.S. South: From Uncle Tom to Gangsta
by Riché Richardson

Grounded Globalism: How the U.S. South Embraces the World
by James L. Peacock

Disturbing Calculations: The Economics of Identity in Postcolonial Southern Literature, 1912–2002
by Melanie R. Benson